Ritual Worship of the Great Goddess

McGill Studies in the History of Religions,
A Series Devoted to International Scholarship
Katherine K. Young, editor

Ritual Worship of the Great Goddess

THE LITURGY OF THE DURGĀ PŪJĀ
WITH INTERPRETATIONS

Hillary Peter Rodrigues

STATE UNIVERSITY OF NEW YORK PRESS

Published by
State University of New York Press, Albany

Printed in the United States of America

For information, address State University of New York Press,
90 State Street, Suite 700, Albany, NY 12207

Production by Diane Ganeles
Marketing by Fran Keneston

Library of Congress Cataloging-in-Publication Data

Rodrigues, Hillary, 1953–
Ritual worship of the great goddess : the liturgy of the Durgā Pūjā with interpretations / Hillary Peter Rodrigues.
p. cm. — (McGill studies in the history of religions)
Includes index.
ISBN 0-7914-5399-5 (alk. paper) — ISBN 0-7914-5400-2 (pbk. : alk. paper)
1. Durgā (Hindu deity)—Cult. 2. Durgā-pūjā (Hindu festival) I. Title. II. Series.

BL1225.D82 R63 2002
294.5'38—dc21 2001049444

10 9 8 7 6 5 4 3 2 1

To my mother

Contents

Part II: Description of the Durgā Pūjā

Part III: Interpretations

Illustrations

Acknowledgments

First and foremost, I wish to thank David Kinsley for his inspiration, encouragement, and support through every stage of the research for this project. He not only sparked my interest in Hindu goddesses, but provided sustained guidance whenever it was needed. In our final conversation before his death he pressed me with characteristic humor to publish my research. Among my many regrets with his passing is my inability to show him that I did indeed bring this work to completion. I am particularly grateful to Pandit Hemendra Nath Chakravarty, without whose knowledge, patience, and constant helpfulness this study could not have been accomplished. I owe a debt of gratitude to my language instructors, who include Rosalind Lefeber, Phyllis Granoff, Pandit Vagish Shastri, and Virendra Singh. Om Prakash Sharma and his delightful family assisted me in numberless ways during my fieldwork in Banāras.

This book has benefited from my conversations with dozens of friends and colleagues. Among these are Christopher Justice, Patricia Dold, Mark Dyczkowski, Mariana Caixero, Bruce Graham, Roxanne Gupta, Oscar Pujol, Lynn Teskey Denton, Anne Pearson, and Ruth Rickard (some of whose photos are included in this book). I am also grateful to Sudarshan Chowdhury for his friendship and help in my research. I was truly fortunate to have been invited by Manindra Mohan Lahiri to study the Durgā Pūjā in his home, where I was received with graciousness and generosity of spirit by all his family members. Satyabrata and Anjana Moitra, in particular, provided me with extremely useful interviews. Paramita Sanyal recounted useful stories, and Somok Moitra rendered invaluable assistance and information on details of the *pūjā* in the years immediately preceding the completion of this book.

Generous funding for the initial research was provided by the Social Sciences and Humanities Research Council of Canada and the School of Graduate Studies at McMaster University. Subsequent funding for additional fieldwork came via grants from the University of Lethbridge. A stipend from the Religious Studies Interfaith Fund at the University of Lethbridge partially alleviated the burden of production costs entailed in bringing this manuscript to print. I must also thank Bill Rodman and Ellen Badone for having taught me about anthropology and my colleagues at the University of Lethbridge who continue to teach me about it. Clifford Geertz inspired me and provided helpful comments when my research was in its incipient stages. I would also like to thank Arvind Sharma and Katherine Young for the interest they showed in the study as it matured. I must extend my gratitude to four anonymous reviewers for SUNY Press, whose able eyes and discerning comments led to improvements in both content and structure. My gratitude also extends to my research assistant Jordan Orthalek. It most especially extends to Ralph Pollock, whose keen attention to detail has substantially reduced the number of errors in this text, and whose efforts are evident in this study's comprehensive index.

A debt of thanks for enduring me during trying periods of the writing must go to my family, all goddesses, and especially to Joanne, for her patience and understanding.

Abbreviations

AV	*Atharva Veda*
ArS	*Āraṇya Saṃhitā*
Beng	*Bengali term*
DBP	*Devī Bhāgavata Purāṇa*
DSS	*Durgā Saptaśatī*
H	*Hindi term*
RV	*Ṛg Veda*
ŚB	*Śatapatha Brāhmaṇa*
Skt	Sanskrit term
SV	*Sāma Veda*
TA	*Taittirīya Āraṇyaka*
VS	*Vājasaneyi Saṃhitā*
YV	*Yajur Veda*

A Note on Transliteration and Pronunciation

The vast majority of foreign words that appear in this text are in Sanskrit. For Sanskrit words, I have mostly followed the system of transliteration conventionally accepted by scholars. Alternate spellings, often without diacritic marks, appear in extracts that replicate the form used in their sources. Hindi or Bengali words are often reproduced phonetically, rather than in accord with any particular system of transliteration. Proper names are mostly reproduced without any diacritics, although there are some exceptions, such as Banāras and Durgā Kuṇḍ temple. Since there is an extensive presentation of Sanskrit verses in this text, the following abbreviated pronunciation guide may prove useful.

a	like the *u*	in h*u*t	*ā*	like the *a*	in f*a*ther
i	like the *i*	in t*i*n	*ī*	like the *ee*	in b*ee*t
u	like the *u*	in p*u*t	*ū*	like the *oo*	in l*oo*t
ṛ	like the *ri*	in *ri*ff			
e	like the *ay*	in pl*ay*	*ai*	like the *i*	in sm*i*le
o	like the *o*	in h*o*me	*au*	like the *ow*	in t*ow*n

Consonants are pronounced mostly as in English. A *g* is hard as in *g*et. A *c* is pronounced as the *ch* in *ch*ip. An *ṅ* is like the *ng* in ru*ng*. The *ñ* is pronounced like the *ny* in ca*ny*on or as the *ñ* in the Spanish se*ñ*or. The sibilant *s* is pronounced as the *s* in English (e.g., *s*it), but the other two sibilants *ś* and *ṣ* both sound similar to the *sh* in *sh*arp. Actually letters with diacritic dots beneath them (*ṛ, ḷ, ṭ, ṭh, ḍ, ḍh, ṇ*, and *ṣ*) are retroflex. They are pronounced like their corresponding nonretroflex counterparts, but with the tip of the tongue placed at the roof of the mouth. Consonants written with a following *h* (*kh, gh, ch, jh, th, dh, ṭh, ḍh, ph, bh*) are aspirated. For example, the pronunciation difference between *t* and *th* is as between the sound of the *t* in ho*t* and the *t-h* in ho*t-h*ouse. The *ph* is pronounced as the *p-h* in cu*p-h*andle.

Syllables containing long vowels (e.g., *ā*, *ī*, *ū*) or diphthongs (*e*, *o*, *ai*, *au*) are stressed. An *ṃ* nasalizes the previous vowel with a sound somewhere between an *m* and an *ng*. The *ḥ* is pronounced with a rough exhalation of breath and causes the preceding vowel to echo.

Note: Technically, words ending in *m* are rendered with an *anusvāra* (*ṃ*) if followed by a word beginning with a consonant or semi-vowel. This rule has not been applied consistently in the transliteration provided.

CHAPTER 1

Introduction

Traditions of goddess worship on the Indian subcontinent have deep historical roots. However, our knowledge of the nature of the goddesses and the ways they were worshipped in the earliest times in India is limited. We can, for instance, discern traces of goddess worship in the Indus Valley Civilization, an ancient South Asian culture that flourished in the second millennium B.C.E.[1] But we cannot say with certainty that the origins of contemporary Hindu worship rituals belong to the Indus Valley or any such ancient civilization. Nevertheless, modern Hindu goddess worship clearly derives many elements of practice from a culturally varied and remote past. Symbolic, verbal, and gestural components from ancient rites were utilized, rearranged, supplemented with newer elements, and syncretized into ritual mosaics that prove meaningful to worshippers today. A detailed study of any contemporary goddess-centered ritual would therefore provide us with a rich array of information grounded in an equally rich and ancient cultural soil.

During the Indian lunar month of Āśvina, on the first nine nights of the waxing new moon, Hindus celebrate the autumn worship of the Great Goddess or Mahādevī.[2] The Great Goddess is most often identified with Durgā, an irresistibly beautiful female who rides a lion. Durgā embodies the powers of all the gods and symbolically wields all of their weapons (See Figure 1.1). She is regarded as the mother of all creation and the power that sustains the entire cosmos. During the nine-day autumn festival, throughout the subcontinent, communities buzz with excitement as worship activities reach a fever pitch in homes and temples. Festival activities actually begin months earlier, as communities organize themselves, collect money, purchase votive materials, and commission artisans and priests to prepare images and perform the rituals. And then, over the course of those nine autumn nights, the preparations culminate in a remarkable blend of revelry, visual pageantry, emotional catharsis, and high ritual in the votive rites to the Great Goddess.

Figure 1.1. Commercial lithograph of the Great Goddess Durgā slaying the Buffalo Demon, Mahiṣa

This book is primarily a description of the Durgā Pūjā, an elaborate ritual of worship (*pūjā*), which for many Hindus constitutes the climax of their varied devotional rites to the Great Goddess.[3] The Durgā Pūjā begins on the sixth day of the nine-night festival and continues for approximately five days. The *pūjā* peaks on the cusp of the eighth and ninth lunar day, but actually concludes on the day following the nine-day festival. Of the hundreds of religious festivals celebrated annually in Hindu India, few can match the Durgā Pūjā in its combination of widespread popularity, visual splendour, community participation, and ritual complexity. Furthermore, popular interest in this *pūjā* is increasing among Hindu communities in India and abroad. A detailed examination of the Durgā Pūjā reveals an abundance of information on the practice and meaning of Hindu *pūjā*, and on the perceived nature of the Great Goddess herself. Although my main intent is to provide a comprehensive description of the ritual (constituting Part II), Part I, comments throughout Part II, and Part III do contain interpretive material on such themes as the nature of *pūjā*, the Great Goddess, the function of the Durgā Pūjā, and even religious ritual in general, but these are supplemental and not exhaustive.

Genesis of this Study

My interest in this ritual developed from my intention to conduct a study on the Great Goddess Durgā for my doctoral dissertation. I decided to base myself at a renowned centre of Durgā worship and so selected the Durgā Kuṇḍ temple in Banāras, perhaps the best-known temple to the Great Goddess, under the epithet of Durgā, in all of India.[4] I was aware that during the autumn nine-night (Navarātra) festival to the Goddess, a large number of temporarily constructed shrines would mushroom throughout the city. Although the Durgā Kuṇḍ and other permanent goddess temples thronged with imposing numbers of devotees during this period, worship at the temporary shrines was an equally striking phenomenon. Some community shrines attracted tens of thousands of visitors. Furthermore, instead of the temples, certain of these temporary shrines, particularly those in homes and religious institutions, served as *the* primary locus of Goddess worship for many people. I was particularly intrigued that the ritual being performed by the priests at these temporary shrines differed from the worship at the large Durgā Kuṇḍ temple. This was the Durgā Pūjā, a ritual deemed unnecessary by the permanent temples housing the Goddess, for the rite involves the awakening and installation of the Great Goddess into an impermanent abode, where she is worshipped and eventually dismissed. By a stroke of extremely good fortune, I had been invited to attend the Durgā Pūjā celebrations at the home of the late Manindra Mohan Lahiri, a Bengali brahmin (*brāhmaṇa*) gentleman, who had retired to Banāras.[5] The Lahiris' home *pūjā* is one of the few elaborate Bengali-styled domestic *pūjā*s to survive in the city. During that first Navarātra, I spent my time frantically racing between the *pūjā* celebrations at the Lahiri home and worship rituals at the Durgā Kuṇḍ and other temples and temporary shrines in the city to conduct observations.

When the Navarātra had ended, I found myself intrigued by what I had seen at the Lahiris' home. Previous readings on the Durgā Pūjā and conversations with the Lahiris had provided a fair understanding of the events of those five days, but I was puzzled by certain observations. For instance, a cluster of plants appeared to be venerated as the Goddess, but was referred

Figure 1.2. Pandit Hemendra Nath Chakravarty, scholar and ritualist. (All unacknowledged photos are by the author).

to by votaries as the wife of Gaṇeśa. My training in Sanskrit piqued my curiosity about the content of the prayers being uttered by the priest, during what appeared to be countless offerings and anointments. Could the ritual acts and prayers perhaps tell me more about the nature of the Great Goddess Durgā, whom I had set about to study? The Lahiris' ritualist, Pandit Nitai Bhattacharya Bharadvaja, whose facility with English was limited, directed me to Pandit Hemendra Nath Chakravarty (see Figure 1.2), who graciously offered to help and became my main source of information on the book that follows.

During my early studies of Hinduism a couple of decades ago, I endured a certain insecurity about the mechanics of Hindu *pūjā*. This is because many presentations within the scholarly literature on *pūjā* either left me overwhelmed with the form, detail, and expectations of background knowledge, or underwhelmed with the lack of detail.[6] Documentary films and even firsthand observations of *pūjā* at temples and in home shrines would leave me with the nagging feeling that I had only experienced a small portion of what was actually occurring. A rite before a lithograph with a duration of thirty seconds and a ritual spanning several days were both referred to as *pūjā* and often analyzed in the same way. What were the priests or votaries doing and saying? Anthropological accounts of *pūjā* were similarly unsatisfactory because they only referred to the general nature of the worship ritual and provided an abbreviated account of the items offered.[7] "The priest offers flowers and utters prayers of homage to Durgā," struck me as woefully inadequate. What prayers? What does he actually say and do? Purāṇic texts were not always much more helpful.[8] They sometimes provided general advice on specific *pūjās*, with injunctions that assumed an esoteric knowledge of the exact ritual action on the part of the reader.[9]

I had not originally intended to compile an exhaustive description of the Bengali Durgā Pūjā. A Bengali city would have been the more obvious site for such an undertaking. The focal point of my doctoral dissertation research, as previously mentioned, was to construct a portrait of the Great Goddess Durgā, grounded in temple worship in Banāras.[10] However, I could not ignore the significant impact the Durgā Pūjā celebrations had on city life and on people's perception of the Devī. Goaded by my previous insecurities and a determination to "understand *pūjā*," I seized each opportunity to watch closely and tried to comprehend what was going on as best I could. While the daily *pūjās* to Durgā in temples, conducted by priests and votaries, were not particularly enigmatic, I was deeply impressed by the complexity of the Durgā Pūjā, and of the two main types of the Durgā Pūjā (i.e., the Bengali and non-Bengali) that I had discerned, found myself progressively immersed in a study of the so-called Bengali style. Since it is an annual ritual, I realized that I would have only one opportunity to view it again before my dissertation fieldwork was completed. I wanted to have a much deeper appreciation of the rite before the next autumn celebrations.

I merely began by asking Pandit Chakravarty questions in order to satisfy my curiosity about details I was sure I had missed. The review of his comments from one meeting, however, in which he would mention consecrating baths or the use of imprintments (*nyāsa*) would inevitably lead me to further questions at our next session. "What are the nine kinds of water in which the plant form of the Devī is bathed?" Or, "What exactly is done in a *nyāsa*?" I would ask. "Oh, you want to know about that?!" he would reply and proceed to give me more details. In our meetings over the first month or two, in response to questions about the prayers uttered by the priest, Pandit Chakravarty was casual. He might respond by saying, "The priest says a quick, 'Obeisance to Gaṇeśa' and a prayer," or as he recognized my familiarity with Sanskrit, would simply say, "*Om gaṇeśāya namaḥ.*" As my requests for details increased, and the complexity of the prayers swelled correspondingly, he would often recite the prayers from memory, and I would endeavour to scribble them down. Here I overreached the limit of my abilities with oral Sanskrit comprehension, a capacity further inhibited by my inability to distinguish between his pronunciations of the three Sanskrit sibilants, as well as "v" and "b."

So it was in an accordion fashion, with certain compressed and incomplete sections expanding over the months and years, that the details of the Durgā Pūjā description that follows came about. It initially derived from my questions based on close observations of the Lahiris' home *pūjā*. These were followed by details of ritual act and Sanskrit prayers derived from Pandit Chakravarty's memory of his own extensive experience performing the *pūjā*. The translation of the Sanskrit was sometimes his and sometimes mine. When I had reached the limits of my ability to record the oral Sanskrit accurately and translate it quickly enough, Pandit Chakravarty took to providing me with both the Sanskrit prayers and their English translations. These I sometimes modified slightly in phrasing, but tried not to deviate far from the form he provided. It was by this time clear to both of us that I was interested in a thorough description of the rite. When he was no longer able to remember exact details of the ritual (such as comprehensive lists of substances offered and their corresponding prayers), Pandit Chakravarty consulted the *Purohita Darpaṇa*, an exhaustively detailed manual that contains information on most rituals. At several stages, he reread most of the manuscript of the *pūjā* description we had produced, correcting sections and validating the accuracy of its content. I thus clearly cannot assign particular verse translations to either him or me, since the effort was collaborative. Nevertheless, Pandit Chakravarty's memory was the source of the bulk of the Sanskrit verses, and as such they may contain minor deviations from printed versions of the prayers. For a majority of these prayers, he provided both a preliminary English translation, and later, an approved version of any modifications that I had made. He ought to be credited for what is commendable and grammatically sound within the translations.

My methodological approach, from the start, leaned toward an anthropologically grounded study of a ritual, to provide me with an understanding of *pūjā* and the nature of the Great Goddess. It was not aimed at creating a work of textual scholarship on the Durgā Pūjā grounded in translation. Had this been my intent, I would have maintained scrupulous records of the origins of elements of the liturgy, as well as the sources of the translation. However, since I had amassed such a detailed description of the rite, I was encouraged by colleagues and mentors to publish this useful resource and hope that it is received in the spirit in which it was conceived and realized. In order to bring the manuscript to completion, I did not then start again from scratch, but instead worked to complete the missing sections of the *pūjā* description. Rather than provide the reader with the bare bones of a description, I have added what I hope are useful interpretive chapters.

As a result of the process through which this description emerged, some of the translations of the simpler Sanskrit prayers are entirely mine, and I had subjected many which were not mine to slight modifications in wording (e.g., adding or removing articles) and phrasing. However, since I was particularly interested in how a ritualist understood the *mantra*s, I generally deferred to Pandit Chakravarty's choice of terms and syntax. Those who have facility with the language and can translate the Sanskrit for themselves, may thus note how the Sanskrit *mantra*s are understood by an actual practitioner of the *pūjā*. I hope that what follows is a most comprehensive description of the Durgā Pūjā, which simultaneously conveys, through the translation of the litany, not a Western scholar's erudition, but much of an actual ritualist's sentiments and understandings.

The Durgā Pūjā

The nine-night (Navarātra) festival of the Great Goddess (Devī or Mahādevī) attracts worshippers even from the Śaiva and Vaiṣṇava sectarian traditions centered on the male deities Śiva and Viṣṇu, respectively.[11] However, the most elaborate forms of worship are conducted by those belonging to the Śākta branch of Hinduism. Śāktas identify Śakti, the Feminine Power that governs creation, as the supreme form of divinity.[12] Śāktas worship the Devī in numerous ways within their own homes. These domestic celebrations vary in their ritual complexity. In certain homes, prayers of homage are uttered daily, and a votive lamp may be lit and kept burning before the Devī's image for the entire nine days of Navarātra. It is common for votaries, both male and female, to engage in some sort of vowed ascetic observance (*vrata*), involving forms of fasting or night-long vigils, for a few if not all the days of Navarātra.[13] In other homes, a pot/jar (*kalaśa*) embodying the Devī may be

Figure 1.3. A traditional Bengali clay image complex. Durgā, her lion, and the demon, as well as the attendant deities, are grouped in a single arrangement topped with a painted arch.

Figure 1.4. Large clay images installed in a community (*sārvajanīna*) group's temporary shrine (*paṇḍal*).

established, and the *Durgā Saptaśatī*, an influential scripture that glorifies the Goddess, is recited daily (see Figures 4.2.1 and 6.1).[14] But of all the domestic forms of Devī worship, the Durgā Pūjā that originated in the state of Bengal is the most elaborate and includes most of the rites performed in non-Bengali Devī *pūjā*s.[15]

The domestic celebration of Durgā Pūjā differs from the highly visible public *pūjā*s (*sārvajanīna pūjā*), in that the latter are performed for a community with funds gathered by that community. Home *pūjā*s, by contrast, are staged by families using their own financial resources.[16] One major expense in the Durgā Pūjā is the purchase of the brightly colored, eye-catching clay images (*mūrti*) of Durgā and her lion-mount portrayed in one of her best-known mythic exploits, the act of slaying the buffalo demon Mahiṣa. This dramatic triad of figures, together with certain other attending deities, forms a large, polychrome, image-array that is usually installed in a temporary shrine (*paṇḍal*) erected especially for the ritual. The attending deities most commonly present in the clay image-array are the goddesses, Lakṣmī and Sarasvatī, and the gods, Gaṇeśa and Kārtikeya (See Figures 1.3 and 1.4). At the end of the *pūjā*, these images are delivered into a venerated body of water, such as the river Gaṅgā, and the shrine, which in communal celebrations may be several stories high, is dismantled.[17] Due to the escalating costs of staging such a *pūjā*, domestic celebrations are only commissioned by wealthy votaries who set aside a spacious part of their homes as the place of worship. By contrast, public (*sārvajanīna*) *pūjā*s are only limited by the enthusiasm and economic circumstances of the community that stages them. As a result, the proportion of the images, the shrines, and the overall costs continue to escalate as local clubs and communities compete with each other through the scale of their public celebrations (See Figure 1.4).

As the costs grow prohibitively expensive for families to stage such a ritual, the elaborate Bengali-style home *pūjā* is disappearing.[18] In Banāras, a city renowned as a centre of Hindu culture, certain organizations, such as the Ānandamayī Mā Āśram, Bhārat Sevāśram Saṅgha, and the Rāmakṛṣṇa Mission perform Durgā Pūjā in the elaborate domestic style with their own funds.[19] Thus they continue to keep this ritual tradition alive, although within the confines of a spiritual community center. The Bengali style of domestic *pūjā* has strongly influenced the growing phenomenon of public Durgā Pūjās even among non-Bengali communities in Banāras. The public worship among the oldest community clubs (which incidentally are Bengali) is certainly derived directly from the elaborate Bengali style of domestic worship. The community *pūjā*s, however, tend to streamline their rituals making them less suited for the most thorough examination.

Although the size of the clay image complex in a home *pūjā* may be smaller than those used in the community celebrations, the domestic *pūjā*s are often more attentive to the rituals of worship. These are closely observed by the patron and his family members and may incorporate elements drawn from the family's own worship traditions. The domestic *pūjā*s also enjoy a mood of intimacy, evoking a devotional fervor altogether different in character from the atmosphere generated by the large surging crowds at the public celebrations.

The casual observer might be inclined to think that the clay effigy (*mūrti*) is the only image of the Goddess worshipped during the Durgā Pūjā, when in fact, in the very same ritual, the Devī is actually worshipped under a plethora of other forms and names.[20] Although closer observation of the ritual reveals several explicit images of the Goddess, such as an earthen jar and a cluster of plants, there are numerous other names and forms of the Devī not perceived by most votaries. This is because most devotees are unaware of deeper layers of symbolic meaning inherent in the ritual items and in the activities of the priest (*purohita*) who performs the *pūjā*.[21] For instance, most votaries do not understand the Sanskrit litany that the *purohita* recites during the liturgy. Sanskrit is a classical Indian language mainly known by scholars and religious specialists. Although most Hindu ritualists recite Sanskrit prayers, many of them, too, do not know the language or even the meanings of these prayers. When I asked people (devotees, ritualists, and Sanskrit-speaking/reading pandits) for a rough estimate of what fraction of the ritualist (*purohita*) class who performed the Durgā Pūjā actually understood the Sanskrit prayers, I received responses ranging from "very few" up to "perhaps 25 percent." The litany of the Durgā Pūjā actually refers to the Goddess through a wide assortment of epithets and, on occasion, even offers explanations of the meaning of symbols and symbolic acts. Thus, a detailed description of the ritual acts of the Durgā Pūjā, including its litany, evidently has a vital role in furthering our understanding of the Great Goddess in the Hindu tradition. Such a description, which constitutes the backbone of this study, is also intended to provide reference material toward a deeper understanding of the ritual of *pūjā*, the preeminent act of Hindu devotional worship. For instance, the Durgā Pūjā reveals that *pūjā* is a series of acts that impels deities and votaries toward each other, bringing about and intensifying the desired encounter known as *darśana*.

Many of the Devī's astonishing array of epithets and forms revealed in the course of the Durgā Pūjā clearly originate from earlier, related, cult worship of the Goddess. These conceptual and manifest images, conjoined with the ritual process of the Durgā Pūjā, testify to my proposal that the Durgā Pūjā is a yearly ritual of cosmic renewal. Throughout the book I advance evidence that the Durgā Pūjā is designed to elicit the manifestation of the Great Goddess into a ritually reconstructed cosmos. This manifestation, however, is not a movement by the Goddess from a transcendent abode to an immanent presence within the creation. Rather, it is perceived as an awakening of the Devī from her latent presence within the constituent elements (e.g., earth, water, and life) of Nature into active and expansive, yet accessible manifestations. The *Kālikā Purāṇa* 60.78 is explicit in this regard, stating that the Goddess "being awakened (*bodhita*)" is conceptually identical with her "being manifest (*prādurbhūta*)."[22] This awakening of divine feminine energy in forms that are personal and approachable as well as comprehensive, encompassing nothing less than the fullness of the manifest cosmos, brings about a rejuvenation of the entire creation.

Without ignoring several of the *pūjā's* diverse functions, many of which involve empowerment at personal and communal levels, I dwell at some length on the effect the yearly rite has on women in the household. I suggest that an important function of the *pūjā* is to orchestrate the movement of creative energy within the household by influencing the "human feminine." Women in particular states of development (e.g., pre-menarche girl, mother) are venerated, while other states of womanhood (e.g., post-menarche unmarried girls) are tacitly slighted. The ritual aims at releasing the creative potential within the feminine, but also controlling that energy through marriage, motherhood, or religious dedication. The Durgā Pūjā is thus an attempt to orchestrate the movement of creative feminine energy, at both the cosmic and human levels, from dormancy to activity, and to regulate that power in ways that are manageable and construed as traditionally desirable.

I conclude by offering a general definition of religious ritual. I use the Durgā Pūjā to illustrate the definition and the definition to provide further commentary on the ritual. Although such a cursory presentation cannot possibly address the countless minute and thorny theoretical issues that arise in the contemplation of ritual, I hope my contributions will add to our understanding of this pervasive human activity. Since gender assumptions by readers about the author's voice definitely affect the readings of texts, especially one such as this, which concerns the Goddess, I ought also to state at the outset and by way of introduction that despite the feminine gender evoked by my name, I, Hillary Peter Rodrigues, am male.

PART I

Context and Overview

CHAPTER 2

The Setting

WHICH NAVARĀTRA?

According to several Śākta sources, the three hundred and sixty-day annual cycle is divided into forty nine-night periods, known as Navarātras.[1] Of these, four Navarātras equidistantly placed around the calendar are prominent for Goddess worship.[2] For instance, the Navarātra that falls in the rainy season month of Śrāvaṇa (July/August) corresponds with a ten-day festival at the Nainā Devī and Cintpūrṇī Devī temples in Himachal Pradesh.[3] However, it is the spring and autumn Navarātras that are traditionally the most popular for the worship of the Goddess.[4] The spring or Vasanta Navarātra, celebrated in the lunar month of Caitra (March/April), is characterized by smaller scale worship rituals and appears to be the older of the two.[5] Villagers may make modest pilgrimages to visit larger, often urban, temples sites, and a jar form of the Devī is established and worshipped. The jar form of the Devī is rich in earthen and agricultural symbolism, suggestive of concerns with fertility (vegetative and human) among the rural classes. The autumn or Śāradiya Navarātra, celebrated in the month of Āśvina with great visual pomp in urban centers, addresses a broader range of needs. The Durgā Pūjā, in particular, which is held during the Āśvina Navarātra, elaborates upon the fertility rites found in the spring celebration, to which it then adds substantial martial and metaphysical elements. It strongly suggests that the Āśvina Navarātra, and the Durgā Pūjā in particular, are evident examples of the Sanskritization of Devī worship.[6] Sanskritization is the term coined for a variety of processes in which certain practices of the non-*brāhmaṇa* classes are accepted by *brāhmaṇas*. One method by which such practices attain legitimacy for the upper classes is by being prescribed in Sanskritic scriptural literature. Sanskrit, and the acceptance by *brāhmaṇas*, confers an enviable status on the reconfigured practice, which in turn filters back to the lower classes. The spring worship rituals to the Goddess that originated among the rural agricultural classes percolated upwards to the warrior (*kṣatriya*) and priestly (*brāhmaṇa*) classes. In its urban setting, where large sums of money are spent by communities, the autumn celebration also affects the merchant (*vaiśya*) classes of Hindu society.[7] Thus all the classes of Hindu India are actively involved in the enterprise of Devī worship during the autumn Navarātra.

A cycle of myths in wide oral circulation supports the aforementioned analysis. They tell how the north Indian prince, Rāma, invoked the Devī in the autumn for help on the eve of his battle with the demon Rāvaṇa, ruler of the southern kingdom of Laṅka. Rāma's invocation was untimely (*akāla*), since the Devī was thought to be asleep in the autumn and was generally worshipped in the spring.[8] The myth affirms the greater antiquity of the spring celebrations and the martial intent of the autumn celebration.[9] Certain variants of the myth tell how Rāma, the warrior patron of the ritual, commissioned as the priest the demon Rāvaṇa himself, a *brāhmaṇa*, to perform the rite which would lead to his own demise.[10] Since Rāma, regarded as an incarnation of the Vedic deity Viṣṇu, eventually slays Rāvaṇa, who is regarded as a devotee of the non-Vedic god Śiva, the myth highlights a number of tensions. The southern, non-Vedic, Śaivite, and *brāhmaṇa* elements are subordinated to the northern, Vedic, Vaiṣṇavite, and *kṣatriya* elements. And yet both Rāma and Rāvaṇa participate in the Devī *pūjā*, forging a union between north and south, Vedic and non-Vedic, Vaiṣṇava and Śaiva worship practices with *kṣatriya* objectives and *brāhmaṇa* ritual forms.[11] Diverse classes, regions, and sects were united by common participation in the ritual of Goddess worship.

Which Goddess?

During both Navarātras, devotees crowd into virtually every goddess temple for *darśana*, profound perceptual interaction with the Divine. Visits to major goddess temples are commonplace, but devotees also worship at smaller shrines, at sacred water tanks, at rivers, and at numerous goddess effigies constructed and established specifically at these times of the year. The goddesses in this vast array of locales are addressed by an assortment of names.[12] Furthermore, even in a single *pūjā*, as the description of the Durgā Pūjā that follows clearly demonstrates, devotion may be addressed to goddesses in different forms and names. This profusion of images, epithets, and places of worship makes one wonder if only one or several *devīs* are the objects of devotion. Observation, inquiry, and a study of scripture and the litany of rituals provide the answer. During the Navarātras, devotion is offered to the divine in its supreme aspect. Furthermore this sovereign form of divinity is regarded as feminine. I thus refer to the Navarātras as times of worship of the Great Goddess rather than any goddess in particular. This worship is conducted through the medium of any of an astonishing assortment of chosen goddess images, epithets, or image clusters.[13]

When asked whom they worship during the Navarātras, devotees refer to the Goddess simply as Devī, or on occasion, as Mahādevī (Great Goddess).[14] Mā (mother), Durgā (She who is Formidable), Caṇḍī (She who is Fierce), or Mā Durgā are the names they use most frequently to address the Great Goddess.[15] These epithets again reiterate the motifs of fertility and martial success. The Great Goddess is regarded as the Cosmic Mother, creatrix, nourisher, and nurturer of the world, or as the regal warrior-goddess Durgā, whose many arms wield a host of weapons.[16] The epithet Durgā is difficult to translate, primarily since it carries various shades of meaning. In the masculine, the term *durga* may denote worldly adversity (e.g., dangerous passages) or an unassailable fortification. The Devī thus aids one in overcoming difficulties and traversing hardships, or is herself an impenetrable mystery and difficult to overcome.[17] I have opted for the term "formidable" since it best conveys many of the diverse meanings of her epithet. Payne (1997 [1933]:6) suggests that Durgā "may be an aboriginal word, though it is generally taken to mean 'inaccessible,' either as a description of the goddess herself or because she is pictured as the slayer of a demon [Durga] whom it was difficult to get at." Durgā is often portrayed astride her mount, a great lion, or engaged in slaying the Buffalo demon, Mahiṣa (See Figure 1.1). Although certain devotees may identify the Mahādevī with some other renowned goddess such as Kālī, Lakṣmī, or Sarasvatī, the *pūjā*s of these goddesses take place at other times in the year. Only the Durgā Pūjā occurs during the autumn Navarātra, a feature that even leads many worshippers to use the terms Durgā Pūjā and Āśvina Navarātra synonymously.[18] My use of the term Durgā Pūjā is restricted to the celebrations, both domestic and communal, which occur mainly during the last days of the autumn Navarātra.[19]

Which Durgā Pūjā?

There are enormous variations in any given set of worship practices in the Hindu tradition. The Durgā Pūjā is no exception. I have observed numerous types of *pūjā* to Durgā celebrated within a stone's throw of each other in homes, temples, and temporarily erected shrines (*paṇḍal*) in Banāras alone. Two main types of Durgā Pūjā were most evident in Banāras, and I refer to these as the Bengali and non-Bengali.[20] It is not my intention to compare these types of Durgā Pūjās. Instead, I have decided to focus on the Bengali style of domestic Durgā Pūjā since, as explained earlier, circumstances led me to study it. Furthermore, it appeared to me to be the most elaborate of the Durgā Pūjās that I had witnessed and encompasses most of the ritual elements found in non-Bengali types of celebration. The Bengali style of domestic Durgā Pūjā is similar to the public (*sārvajanīna*) Durgā Pūjās celebrated by Bengali communities throughout India and has exercised a considerable influence on non-Bengali public Durgā Pūjās across the subcontinent. The presence of large, flamboyant, clay images, the most salient feature of the public non-Bengali Durgā Pūjās, is the most obvious element that has been derived from the smaller, traditional image cluster used in most Bengali Durgā Pūjās. The Bengali style of Durgā Pūjā draws on Vedic, Purāṇic, and Tantric elements. However, the Tantric nature of the *pūjā* is the prime feature distinguishing it from the non-Bengali Durgā Pūjā. The non-Bengali Durgā Pūjā is essentially an orthodox (*smārta*) *brāhmaṇa*s' Devī *pūjā*, also known as Vedic/Vaidik *pūjā*.[21] Although Tantrism often appears in forms that contradict, and even outrightly reject, many of Vedic-Brāhmaṇism's normative features (such as caste and gender obligations), the Durgā Pūjā is an example of Vaidik Tantric ritual. It is clearly grounded in Tantric practices (e.g., purifications [*bhūta śuddhi*], imprintments [*nyāsa*]) and offers many Tantric variants to Vedic procedures (e.g., establishment of the jar, sacrificial offering). However, since it makes abundant use of Vedic *mantra*s and ritual procedures whose performance is traditionally restricted to male *brāhmaṇa*s, it requires that the ritualist be adept at conducting both Vedic and Tantric rites.

Durgā Pūjā in Bengal

The exact origins of the revival of the autumn celebrations of Durgā Pūjā are unclear. Ray (n.d.:141) claims that one Calcutta family's *pūjā* dates to 1411 C.E., but the image of their Devī (called Caṇḍī), who is depicted atop a lion slaying the demon, is not accompanied by her children and thus does not exhibit the entire array of deities we have come to associate with the Durgā Pūjā.[22] In her exploration of the *pūjā's* origins in Bengal, McDermott (1995) encountered a number of contradictory explanations. Certain sources attributed the origin to Kamsanarayan, a landlord (*zamīndār*) of the Tahebpur region of Rajshahi, in present-day Bangladesh. Upon assuming control of the *zamīndārī* in 1583, he is said to have held the *pūjā* as a substitute for an *aśvamedha*, the great Vedic horse-sacrifice.

One detailed account of the *pūjā's* revival in Bengal is provided by R. Roy (1990).[23] He claims that it was revived in the early seventeenth century by Lakshmi Kant, one of Bengal's earliest known *zamīndār*s. Lakshmi Kant was the descendent of a certain Panchananda Shakti Kant, of the Sabarni lineage (*gotra*).[24] Panchananda Shakti Kant, who had gained a title due to his bravery, fathered seven children. The seventh child, Shambhupatti, had a son by the name of Jio (Jiv). Jio's daughter died on the feast day of Lakṣmī Pūrṇimā in 1570 after delivering a son who was named Lakshmi Kant, after the goddess.[25] Lakshmi Kant's grandfather, Jio, unable to care for the child, left him in the care of Brahmananda Giri and Atmaram Giri, two spiritual preceptors at the Kālīghāṭ temple in Calcutta.[26] Jio left for Banāras to become a world-renouncer (*saṃnyāsin*) and eventually became famous under the name of Kamadeva Brahmachari. Meanwhile Lakshmi Kant, through dint of his efforts, educated himself and rose in prominence until he was the right-hand man of Pratapaditya, the king of Jessore, a small state in Bengal. According to the historian S. Roy (1991), Lakshmi Kant was adopted by Rānī Kamalā, the younger wife of Rāja Basanta Rai (builder of Kālīghaṭ temple), and was brought up in their family home of Sursoona with a traditional education and military training (1991:198). He thus grew to consider Rāja Basanta Rai as his "uncle."

Lakshmi Kant's "uncle," Rāja Basanta Rai, ruled the state of Raigarh in which was located the village of Barisha (Behala). Lakshmi Kant had established a court (*H: kacaṛi baṛi*) there and had also built a place of worship called Āt Cala, after the distinctive eight pairs of pillars in its construction. It was at Āt Cala in Barisha in 1610 that Lakshmi Kant and Rāja Basanta Rai celebrated the first autumn Durgā Pūjā. According to S. Roy (1991:198), the first celebration actually took place there in 1585, with Lakshmi Kant serving as the priest for Rāja Basanta Rai's Durgā Pūjā.[27] Although people normally worshipped the Devī during the spring Navarātra, this celebration apparently set a precedent, and a few families began to follow the newly revived tradition of autumn worship. After 1610 Lakshmi Kant's family, who had now come to be known as the Sabarna Rai Choudarys, continued to celebrate the autumn Durgā Pūjā at Āt Cala. These *pūjā*s used to be open to the general public, and the images were not disposed of after the celebration but reused every year.

R. Roy (1990) claims that the Durgā Pūjā of Lakshmi Kant and Rāja Basanta Rai was a reenactment of the primordial act of invoking and worshipping Durgā out of time (*akāla bodana*) initiated by Rāma for the destruction of Rāvaṇa. Yet it is difficult to know with certainty what motivated the reestablishment of their Durgā Pūjā, and if it was, as is suggested, initiated in resistance to Mughal rule. The *pūjā* may well have been instituted as a demonstration of the burgeoning wealth and power of this particular family, although it is true that Bengali kingdoms of that period were engaged in rebellions against the Mughals.

The kingdom of Jessore eventually fell to the Hindu general of the Mughals, Man Singh, through an unusual turn of events. The Mughal emperor Jehangir had come to power in 1605. Man Singh, his general, on his conquests from Delhi in the direction of Bengal stopped in Banāras and became a student of Kamadeva Brahmachari (i.e., Lakshmi Kant's grandfather, Jio). In gratitude to his mentor (*guru dakṣinā*), and as a means of undermining Pratapaditya's support, Man Singh had given Lakshmi Kant, Kamadeva Brahmachari's grandson, five pieces (*pargana*) of land. These were Khaspur, Magura, Colicatta, Baikant, and Anwarpur. Eventually the *pargana* of Hetelpur was also bestowed on him.[28] Thus Lakshmi Kant became one of the major *zamīndārs* in Bengal. Together with Bhavananda of Nadia and Jayananda of Bhansbedia he became one of Bengal's three tax collectors.[29] Since Lakshmi Kant had grown up in Kālīghāṭ temple, he was familiar with the three villages, Colicatta, Sutanuti, and Govindapur that would later become Calcutta. They were part of his *zamīndārī* and were rather poor and poorly populated at the time. Through his association with Kamadeva Brahmachari, Lakshmi Kant, and others, Man Singh learned much about the geography and other characteristics of Bengal and was thus able to conquer the kingdom of Jessore, which had staged a rebellion. Man Singh's trip to quell Pratapaditya's rebellion in Bengal took place in1612 (S. Roy 1991:8).

On November 10, 1698, the villages of Colicatta, Sutanuti, and Govindapur were sold by the Rai Choudary family to the East India Company, and those historic documents were signed at Āt Cala. These villages constituted the city of Calcutta and became the seat of British power in India.[30] Like their predecessor Pratapaditya, the Bengali *zamīndārs* of the 1700s, such as Rāja Krishnachandra Rai and Rānī Bhavānī, are said to have been well known for their resistance to Mughal rule (A. C. Roy 1968:356). Rāja Krishnachandra, who ruled the *zamīndārī* of Nadia from 1728–1782, and who was a contemporary of Rānī Bhavānī, also "played a glorious role in the evolution of Bengal's society, art, and literature," was "the most important man of the period in the Hindu society of Bengal" (A. C. Roy 1968:361–362).

Maratha invasions of Bengal during the period from 1741–1751, kept the Nawab (Mughal Viceroy) Alivardi Khan occupied with the frontiers of the territory, allowing the British to gain in strength. When he was succeeded by the young and impetuous Siraj-ud-daula, the British found an opportunity to further their position by conspiring against the young Nawab (A. C. Roy 1968:396–397).[31] In 1756 Siraj-ud-daula attacked Calcutta and defeated the British at their outpost there.[32] The British recaptured Calcutta in 1757, marking the beginning of the deterioration of the British relationship with the Mughal empire and the former's rise to power in India (A. C. Roy 1968:398). Although Siraj-ud-daula signed a treaty with the British, they conspired with Rāja Krishnachandra and others to oust Siraj from power (S. Roy 1991:203).[33] At the Battle of Plassey, fought in June of the same year, the British won a decisive victory over the Nawab, and he was subsequently murdered (A. C. Roy 1968:400).

It is significant that later in this very year, 1757, Rāja Krishnachandra of Nadia and Rāja Navakrishna (of the Rai Choudary family) of Shova Bazaar are reputed to have initiated grand scale celebrations of the Āśvina (September/October) Durgā Pūjā. These lavish celebrations obviously marked their own ascendency to power, in alliance with the British, against their Mughal overlords. While it is certain that these Durgā Pūjās did promote both Hindu religion and culture, it is not certain if the *pūjās* were primarily designed to sustain Hindu solidarity while stirring up sentiments against the influence of Islam. These "domestic" Durgā Pūjās were also open to the general public, as were the less grandiose celebrations that had been taking place since the *pūjā* of the Rai Choudarys almost a century and a half earlier. However, it was these *pūjās* in the period of British rule that are remembered as capturing the public imagination and triggering the tradition that now flourishes in Bengal, Banāras, and throughout India.[34]

Durgā Pūjā in Banāras

The grand celebrations of the Durgā Pūjā by the powerful *zamīndār*s in Bengal in the middle of the eighteenth century occurred not long before the construction of the Durgā Kuṇḍ temple in Banāras by Rānī Bhavānī, the wealthy *zamīndār* of Natore, and who, we are told, celebrated Durgā Pūjā with a grandeur commensurate with her status (Ghosh 1986:181). In the actions of Lakshmi Kant's grandfather, Kamadeva Brahmachari, who left for Banāras to pursue the religious life, and in Rānī Bhavānī's extensive patronage of the Banārasi religious community, we note two examples of the close relationship between Bengali culture and the city of Banāras. Both figures' behaviors acknowledge the eminence of Banāras as a religious center. Rānī Bhavānī herself played an instrumental role in the revival of Hindu worship traditions in the city in the wake of Mughal persecution. Bengali benefactors such as Rānī Bhavānī, who were involved in the Hindu revival in Banāras, and other Bengalis, who also went there to retire, brought their characteristic styles of Durgā worship to the city.

While the Sabarna Rai Choudary family is reputed to be the first affluent *brāhmaṇa* family in the area of Calcutta, in time other powerful *brāhmaṇa* and *kāyastha* families settled in the area.[35] In fact, the "most eminent families of eighteenth century Calcutta were non-brahmins" (S. Roy 1991:10). Among the eminent *brāhmaṇa* families were the Tagores, and among the *kāyastha* families were the Mitras.[36] The oldest, and still enduring, domestic celebration of the Durgā Pūjā in Banāras occurs at the home of the Mitra/Basu family in the Chaukhamba municipality. This Bengali family's first performance of the Durgā Pūjā in Banāras took place in 1773 in the same mansion in which it is currently held.[37] That first celebration was a relatively small affair, held by Anandamayi Mitra, son of Govindaram Mitra, known as the Black Zamīndār of Bengal. According to family members in Banāras, Govindapur, which together with Sutanati and Colicatta were the three villages that constituted early Calcutta, was named after Govindaram Mitra. It was he, they claim, who gave the Durgā Pūjā in Bengal its glamour and cultural impetus. Anandamayi Mitra's Durgā Pūjā, which took place at the Chaukhamba home, was the first Durgā Pūjā held outside of Bengal.

When Anandamayi's son, Rajendra, expanded his *zamīndārī* through holdings in present day Bihar and Uttar Pradesh, he reintroduced the grandeur that characterized his grandfather's celebrations. There were fifteen days of festivities with dramas and performances by musicians, singers, and dancing girls who were some of the most renowned artists in India. Members of the British gentry were also invited to attend the celebrations. These festivities took place in the large quadrangle (*nautch ghar*) where the *pūjā* is still held, although nowadays the audience in attendance has dwindled dramatically. The current head of the household, Tarun Kanti Basu, explained that the home passed into the hands of the Basus through his grandfather's mother (a Mitra). Besides being *zamīndārs*, the Mitras and the Basus were intellectuals who expected from the priests (*purohita)* the highest standards of ritual performance and the proper pronunciation of Sanskrit *mantras*. Although they were not *brāhmaṇas*, but *kāyasthas*, they were also great patrons of Hindu philosophy and the arts. Swami Vivekananda was one of the distinguished visitors to the home, and such renowned musicians as Bismillah Khan and Ravi Shankar have performed there. Despite the Basus' ownership of the home and their patronage of the Durgā Pūjā in Chaukhamba for three generations, the celebration is still generally referred to by Banārasis as the Mitra family *pūjā*, due to the Mitra clan's great reputation, and I, too, will refer to it that way in this study.

The Mitra family *pūjā* has certain distinct features, such as the inclusion of Rāma and Śiva in the image complex.[38] Unlike the typical traditional Bengali clay image complex, in which the multiple images of Durgā, her lion mount, the demon, and attending deities are all attached to a single structural frame, the Mitra family images are separate. The deities are each placed within an alcove in a permanent structure referred to as the *śṛngārāsana* (see Figure 2.1). The Lahiri family *pūjā*, too, has distinct features. They establish the jar form of the Devī on the first day of Navarātra, not on the sixth day as is customary. Such variations underscore the diversity even among the so-called Bengali-styled Durgā Pūjās. Not only do performances vary from one setting to another, but the same *pūjā* performed by the same priest may vary from one year to the next due to such factors as time or material constraints.

Figure 2.1 Priests (*purohita*) perform the Durgā Pūjā at the site of the oldest celebration in Banāras, the Mitra family's home in Chaukhamba. (Photo: Ruth Rickard)

The *pūjā* description in this book is comprehensive, but by that very virtue it is likely to deviate from many Durgā Pūjās as they are actually performed.[39]

Durgā Pūjās resembling the style presented in this book are performed in a number of locations within Banāras. These include the public *pūjā*s of the Durgotsav Sammilini, the oldest community celebration in the city (in Bengali Tola), Śaradotsava Sabsang, and Jain Sporting Club, both in Bhelupura.[40] Celebrations in religious centers include those at the Ānandamayī Mā Āśram, Bhārat Sevāśram Saṅgha (whose first performances were in 1928), and the Rāmakṛṣṇa Maṭh.[41] The Mitra family *pūjā* and the one that takes place in the home of Mr. Manindra Mohan Lahiri, where I conducted my most detailed observations, are examples of the ritual in a domestic setting.[42]

Bengali *Brāhmaṇas* in Banāras

The main actor in the Bengali Durgā Pūjā is the *purohita*, a Bengali *brāhmaṇa* male who is initiated into the practice of Devī worship. Most people with whom I conversed estimated that Bengalis constitute about 5 percent of the population in urban Banāras and are primarily settled in the south and southwest of the city.[43] Banāras is a religious center well patronized by Bengalis, and has been generally hospitable to them for many centuries. As previously mentioned, the Durgā Pūjā was first celebrated in Banāras by the Mitra family, wealthy Bengali *zamīndār*s.[44] Also, Rānī Bhavānī, the wealthy Bengali *zamīndār*, renowned for her patronage in the city, retired in Banāras with her own widowed daughter Tārā Sundarī. Such patrons (*yajamāna*) often brought with them Bengali *brāhmaṇas*, their traditional family priests (*purohita*) to perform the Durgā Pūjā on their behalf. For instance, as members of the *kāyastha* caste (*jātī*), the Mitra family in Chaukhamba needs to commission *brāhmaṇa purohita*s to perform the *pūjā* for them. They are also reputed to have brought to Banāras members of the Pals, an artisan caste (*jātī*) that fabricates the clay images of Durgā (and other deities).

The Bengali *brāhmaṇa*s may accordingly be classified into three types: 1. *Purohita*: these occupy themselves with their own rituals and have enough patrons (*yajamāna*) whose commissions keep them fully occupied exclusively with ritual activities throughout the year. This is the main type of *brāhmaṇa* engaged to perform the Durgā Pūjā. They have a strong bond of loyalty to their *yajamāna* that often spans many generations. Only in cases where the *purohita* is sick or ritually impure (e.g., due to the death of parents) will some other *brāhmaṇa* (ritually initiated, of course) be commissioned. 2. *Purohita* with strong knowledge of Sanskrit: members of this group have fewer *yajamāna*s. They do not make a living from rituals alone and generally are involved in other occupations (often of a scholarly nature). 3. Occasional: these *brāhmaṇa*s perform other jobs for a living, but may on occasion function as *purohita*s, since they are qualified to do so.

According to orthodox tradition, Pandit Chakravarty explained, *brāhmaṇa*s have six specific occupations. These are: a) *yajana*: performing rituals for one's own good; b) *yājana*: performing rituals for the good of the patron (*yajamāna*); c) *adhyayana*: studying; d) *adhyāpana*: teaching others; e) *dāna*: offering gifts to others who are socially and morally good; f) *pratigraha*: receiving gifts from those who are socially and morally good. In addition, *brāhmaṇa*s are expected to bestow initiation on disciples. *Brāhmaṇa*s of the first type, who are generally commissioned to perform the Durgā Pūjā, follow *yajana*, *yājana*, and *pratigraha* (and also bestow initiations). Pandit Nitai Bhattacharya, the Lahiris' ritualist for the Durgā Pūjā, is an example of this type. *Brāhmaṇa*s of the second type place greater emphasis on *adhyayana* and *adhyāpana*. Pandit Hemendra Nath Chakravarty, my prime consultant for the details of the *pūjā*, is an example. Members of the third type, if wealthy, may themselves function as *yajamāna*s and thus provide employment for other *brāhmaṇa*s and *dāna* (charitable gifts) to the community at large. The Lahiri family, whose Durgā Pūjā I closely studied, could be regarded as belonging to this category.[45]

From my conversations with these Bengali *brāhmaṇa*s, I further discerned that there are three main classes: Vaidikas, Rāḍhis/Rarhis, and Vārendras/Bārendras.[46] In addition, there are some other mixed classes. There are two sections of the Vaidika class. One group originated in Kanauj, in the east, and is known as the Paścatya Vaidikas (or Kanyakubjikas), while the other came from Orissa in the south (originally from the Deccan further south) and is known as the Dakṣinatya Vaidikas. The Vaidika class enjoys greater status than the other two classes. This is because the Bārendras (from the region of Barend Bhumi in present-day Bangladesh) and Rāḍhi *brāhmaṇa*s (from the Raḍh Bhumi region in West Bengal) had for several centuries lost their knowledge of Vedic traditions due to the influence of Buddhism in Bengal.[47] Nevertheless, *brāhmaṇa*s from any of these classes may perform the Durgā Pūjā provided they have received the appropriate initiation (*dīkṣā*) to conduct a Tantric *pūjā* to the Devī.[48] The sectarian orientation of the vast majority of Bengali *brāhmaṇas* is Śākta, with but a few Vaiṣṇavas, and even fewer Śaivas (Raychauduri 1981:107). While women rarely, if ever, function as *purohita*s, they perform an important role in the preparation of cooked food (*bhog*) offerings to Durgā.[49] Such women must also have the appropriate Tantric initiation, without which cooked food may not be offered in the *pūjā*.

Pandit Nitai Bhattacharya Bharadvaja, who performs the Durgā Pūjā for the Lahiris, is a Paścatya Vaidika *brāhmaṇa* (see Figure 3.1).[50] He has performed the ritual since 1971 and was preceded by his father, the late Paśupati

Bhattacharya. He and his family clearly command an enormous respect as *purohitas* in the Bengali community. They were also chosen to perform the Durgā Pūjā for the Durgostav Sammilini, whose celebrations commenced in 1922, making it the oldest public (*sārvajanīna*) Durgā Pūjā in Banāras.[51] Although the Lahiris have a family priest who performs the worship of the deities in their home temples and shrine room thrice daily, they do not consider him to have the same proficiency as Pandit Nitai.[52]

Pandit Hemendra Nath Chakravarty, my main source of information on the Durgā Pūjā, is a Bārendra *brāhmaṇa* scholar (see Figure 1.2). Pandit Chakravarty came to Banāras to study Sanskrit and became a student of the renowned Bengali Tantric scholar Gopinath Kaviraj. Since he had learned the ritual from his father, uncle, and family teacher, he began performing the Durgā Pūjā while primarily engaged in Sanskrit studies. As a novice, he first served as an apprentice/helper (*tantradhāraka*) and later began to consult the handwritten Durgā Pūjā guidebooks that belonged to the patron (*yajamāna*) families. He had performed the Durgā Pūjā more than forty times in his life, but had given it up for about four years before I consulted with him in 1990. He recently sat again as a *tantradhāraka* in the home of a friend who performed the *pūjā*. Pandit Chakravarty currently works at the Indira Gandhi National Centre for the Arts in Banāras. He is regarded as the teacher (not of *pūjā*) of many respected *brāhmaṇas* in the Bengali community, some of whom are ritualists and scholars. He is frequently consulted by western scholars in Banāras, particularly those who are investigating aspects of Tantric Hinduism.

The late Manindra Mohan Lahiri, at whose home I performed my closest observations of the Durgā Pūjā, was also a Bārendra *brāhmaṇa* (see Figures 4.4.1 and 4.7.3). As the former *zamīndār* of Rangpur, with other estates in East Bengal as well as other parts of India, he enjoyed both prestige and wealth.[53] His grandparents, who had already been engaged in the tradition of performing the Durgā Pūjā for about seventy years at their home in Rangpur, East Bengal, moved the celebrations to Banāras sometime in the 1890s.[54] Following a common tradition, they had retired to Banāras, where, after his grandfather's death, his grandmother had continued to live as a widow.[55] Since that time more than a hundred years ago, the *pūjā* has been held, with no known interruptions, at the Lahiri home in Banāras. Mr. Lahiri's father died (c. 1926/7) when he was a small boy, and so he grew up with his mother who went back to live in Rangpur, but returned annually to the Banāras home for the Durgā Pūjā and eventually for her own retirement. With the partition of India, and Indian independence, Mr. Lahiri's estates in East Bengal (now Bangladesh) and India were appropriated by the governments of those countries, and his family's wealth began to decline. Regardless of where he happened to reside (his eldest daughter was born at his home in Darjeeling), the family always gathered in Banāras for the Durgā Pūjā.

When I conducted my research in Banāras, in 1990 and 1991, Mr. Lahiri and his wife, Anjali, had been living in retirement in Banāras for well over a decade. His four daughters (all of whom hold post-secondary degrees in the Arts & Sciences), their husbands (one scientist, two engineers, and a chartered accountant), and children (some of whom were teenagers), who lived as far away as Calcutta and Durgapur, gathered at the family home on both occasions for the *pūjā*. Since Mr. Lahiri's funds depended entirely on the fixed income of his bank deposits, his wealth decreased with the years. The lavish scale of the *pūjā*, he informed me, had diminished in the last half century, but the traditional religious requirements continued to be more than merely fulfilled. When he was younger, as many as three hundred people would attend the celebration and receive blessed food (*prasāda*). At present that number is closer to fifty. I shall make frequent references to features of the Lahiris' home celebration throughout the book (see Figures 4.8.3 and 6.2).

The public Durgā Pūjās, Mr. Lahiri claimed, began with "good sentiment," and his own uncle, Dr. G. S. Bagchi, was one of their earliest promoters in Banāras. Mr. Lahiri predicted the demise of family Durgā Pūjās like his own very soon. When asked about why he continued to celebrate the *pūjā*, despite its expense, he replied, "We are out and out religious." He later explained that he also continues for fear of the consequences, and his inability to break tradition, adding, "I also do it for my peace of mind. As long as my wife and I live, we will continue to do it." Since Mr. Lahiri's death in December 1993, the family has continued to gather at the Banāras home, where his widow resides, for the *pūjā*. With no male heir to the Banāras home, the future of the *pūjā* after Mrs. Lahiri's death is uncertain.

The Ritual Performer (*Purohita*)

The ritual celebration of Durgā Pūjā is performed by the *purohita* for the benefit of the patron (*yajamāna*) or the community. The celebration of Durgā Pūjā, for the earnest Śākta *purohita*, such as Pandit Nitai Bhattacharya, is the *magnum opus* of ritual performance. It may well be the highest expression of his profession, bringing together most of the forms of his ritual learning. It demands an astounding display of memory, concentration, yogic achievement, dramatic art, and finesse (See Figures 3.1, 4.2.2, 4.2.3, 4.3, 4.4.1, 4.4.2, and 4.7.3). On many occasions through the course of the *pūjā*, he is expected to embody the Goddess herself before transferring that embodiment to the numerous devotional images before him. It is therefore imperative that he perform complex ritual purifications and visualizations in order to become a fit receptacle for the divine. At the same time, through his proficiency, he draws, directs, and heightens the perceptions of the devotees toward the deity. In a successful ritual performance the *purohita* forges a link between the divine and mundane realms, so that the deity, tangibly manifest in material forms, and the votaries, with their senses suitably refined and purified, can meet each other in the most intimate act of perceptual contact. This profound meeting of the senses, gross and subtle, active and passive, outer and inner, with the material embodiment of divinity, is known as *darśana*. More details on the nature of *darśana* and the *purohita*'s actions are presented in subsequent chapters.

The Audience

In public celebrations of the Durgā Pūjā, there is a flurry of activity as members of the organizing committees oversee and aid in the erection of the temporary shrines (*paṇḍal*). In domestic celebrations energy is spent in cleaning and decorating the area that will serve as the place of worship (*pūjālaya*). In both settings there are careful checks performed to insure that all the necessary *pūjā* items (ritual implements and offerings) are present. Everyone gathers for the arrival of the clay image complex. It is often the first view that most family/committee members have of these beautifully constructed images, which will become focal points for their celebrations over the next few days (see Figures 1.3 and 4.3). Homes bustle with excitement as family members arrive to join in the celebrations. Durgā Pūjā is viewed as a time when married daughters, who due to certain Hindu virilocal customs may reside with their husbands' families, return to the home of their parents. They are accompanied by their children and not infrequently by their husbands. "Mother and father give gifts. Fathers give the money and mothers buy the gifts for male and female close relatives," explained one of the grandchildren.[56] These gifts typically include new clothes. In the Lahiri family, these are traditional *sārīs* and *dhotis* that are then worn by family members during the days of the *pūjā*. During the Durgā Pūjā, Mr. Lahiri's four married daughters, their husbands, and children would return to his Banāras home. Mr. Lahiri told me in no uncertain terms that his sense of Durgā's presence in his home was inseparable from the energy and atmosphere generated by the women gathered in the household.

Other than Mr. Lahiri, who oversaw the details of the *pūjā* closely, I noted that others showed little interest in the *purohita*'s activities on the first day, when the Goddess is awakened into a branch of a wood-apple tree. In the Lahiri home a jar form of the Devī had already been established on the first day of Navarātra, although in other Durgā Pūjās it is conventionally done on this day, which is the sixth day of Navarātra. Although there were few discernable cues, several family members would somehow know when to gather the children and equip them with an array of gongs and bells, which they sounded with abandon precisely while the *purohita* performed a flame worship (*ārati*) of the Devī. As the days progressed, and the worship shifted to the clay image complex, the atmosphere within the place of worship intensified. Family members, close relatives, friends, neighbors and other invited guests, and even uninvited guests were progressively drawn to the house and toward the focal point of the *pūjā*: the clay image complex and the *purohita*'s ministrations to it. They lingered longer, socialized less during the ritual, and were most closely attentive during the flame worship and food offerings to the Devī. A similar pattern occurs at the public shrines, with the notable exception that visitors may often perform their own short devotional worship (*pūjā*, *upacāra*) to the image, as they would in a temple setting, when the priest is not present. The public shrines offer devotees easier and local access to the Devī, to whom they may offer devotional service. Such personal devotional service is not permitted in the private home celebrations.

The food offerings are very important components of the rite. The Devī's consumption of the food consecrates it, and the devotees look forward to partaking in the blessed offerings (*prasāda*). In public settings, the prospect of a delicious consecrated meal attracts both sponsoring community members and invited guests. Public celebrations may include a range of other community activities. Devotional singing, plays with religious themes, music performances and so on, often form part of the extraritual events that draw the community to the *pūjā* site.

In the domestic setting, the largest groups gather, and the most intense feelings arise on the third and fourth day of the *pūjā*. This is when Durgā is believed to be fully manifest within the clay image and thus completely accessible to her devotees. The *purohita* has successfully managed to execute this difficult task on the previous day. With the votaries in attendance on the second, third, and fourth days, he performs a systematic and lengthy worship of the Goddess. Besides participating in the flame worship and the consumption of blessed food, there is one other important opportunity for the audience to worship the Devī. This is the *puṣpāñjali*, a flower offering. Devotees, after a ritual cleansing of their hands with water, gather purified flowers from a basket that is circulated among the crowd. They repeat a Sanskrit verse of adoration uttered by the *purohita*, and then, in exuberant unison, shower the Goddess with the flowers.

The *purohita*'s role is unarguably central and indispensable in virtually the entire process of the *pūjā*. He enlivens numerous items with the presence of the Devī and facilitates her worship by the votaries who are present. On the fourth day of the *pūjā*, he conducts a fire oblation with the patron (*yajamāna*), a rite that illustrates the triangular relationship that exists between the *purohita*, *yajamāna*, and Devī, particularly well. The *purohita*, connected to both human (*yajamāna*) and divine (Devī) realms, forges a direct link between them for the duration of the rite.

The third and fourth day of the *pūjā* also see tens of thousands of people choking the streets as they swarm to visit the city's most elaborate public shrines (*paṇḍal*). The jubilant mood of the visitors cannot be described as purely religious. Navarātras in Banāras have long been characterized by the tradition of visiting particular Durgā temples, one on each of the nine festival days. Although this form of worship of the Great Goddess has not waned, the rapidly growing trend toward visiting temporary shrines is a phenomenon of this century. These festivities culminate with elaborate processions on the fifth day, in which the clay image complex is carried with an express fanfare to the river Gaṅgā and delivered into its waters. Since this aspect of the rite is primarily in the hands of the public, it is open to exuberant innovations. Organizations such as the Bhārat Sevāśram Saṅgha stage dramatic enactments of the myths of the *Durgā Saptaśatī*, which is simultaneously recited and broadcast on the river banks prior to the immersion of their organization's image. The Durgā Pūjā, whether celebrated publically or domestically, in the Bengali or Smārta fashion, undoubtedly continues to play a vibrant role in shaping (and transforming) the modes of worship of the Great Goddess in one of Hindu India's most sacred cities.

Ritual Manuals

The rituals pertaining to the Bengali style of Durgā Pūjā are described in a number of texts, such as the *Purohita Darpaṇa* (Mirror for the Priest), which contains the techniques for most other *pūjā*s as well.[57] It is a comprehensive text, written in Bengali script, and highly regarded among the large variety of ritual manuals (*paddhati, prayoga*) accessible to Bengali *purohita*s (priests). As a comprehensive manual on *pūjā*, the *Purohita Darpaṇa* includes three different methods of performing the Durgā Pūjā, derived from prescriptions in the *Kālikā*, *Devī*, and *Bṛhannandikeśvara Purāṇas*.[58]

While useful as a reference text, the *Purohita Darpaṇa* is not practical as a guide while actually performing the ritual. It would require the *purohita* to perform cumbersome navigation through its sections, particularly since certain ritual acts, such as purifications, are routinely performed in most *pūjā*s, but described only once in some other area of the text. References to prayers and sacred utterances (*mantra*) are often abbreviated, leaving the *purohita* to fend for himself from memory. There are scant instructions on the methods of drawing ritual diagrams (*yantra/maṇḍala*) or the forms of ritual gestures (*mudrā*). Thus most *purohita*s who perform the Durgā Pūjā possess some personalized printed version or handwritten manuscript of the entire ritual from beginning to end. These may belong either to the priest or to the family or group that commissions the *pūjā*. The Lahiris, for instance, have a family manual (*paddhati*) which is used by Pandit Nitai. Their family tradition is said to derive from prescriptions in the *Devī* and *Kālikā Purāṇas*. The majority of *purohita*s who perform the *pūjā* at the public temporary shrines (*paṇḍal*) where the public celebrations occur, use commercial editions. Other manuals include the *Durgārcana-paddhati* by Raghunandana, and the *Durgā Pūjā Paddhati*.[59]

English Literature on the Durgā Pūjā

Among English-language treatments, the most comprehensive description of the Durgā Pūjā thus far was provided by Pratāpachandra Ghosha (1871), but his treatment, which is quite dated, has other shortcomings. It is not published as a monograph and lacks the Sanskrit *mantra*s used in the litany. Revealing a trend common in his day, Ghosha's interpretations are reductive. Drawing heavily on the interpretive tradition characterized by Max Müller and many of his contemporaries, Ghosha sees religion as emanating from the deification of powers of nature.[60] He works hard to identify the Devī with the Dawn. The best interpretive account of the Durgā Pūjā is Ákos Östör's (1980), which derives from observations at the temple in Vishnupur, Bengal. Due to its specific location, in a temple setting, where the presence and activities of the king are significant, the analysis is not readily transferable to the type of Durgā Pūjā celebrated in the Bengali fashion elsewhere. Östör's presentation incorporates little in its interpretation from such pertinent aspects as the prayers uttered during the liturgy.[61]

This Description of the Durgā Pūjā

After my first observation of the Durgā Pūjā at the Lahiris' home in 1990, I had several other opportunities to view the ritual. My most detailed observations occurred the following autumn at the Lahiris' home. Needless to say, with the lion's share of the descriptive work conducted with Pandit Chakravarty already complete, what I saw and understood was greatly enhanced. I also observed the Bengali style of the Durgā Pūjā, conducted in the spring at the Ānandamayī Mā Āśram in Banāras. I have observed numerous non-Bengali *pūjā*s performed in Banāras and other parts of India and have even observed the *pūjā* among the Hindu diaspora in Canada. I have maintained my contact and friendship with the Lahiri family to the present and have followed up on changes (such as the role played by Mr. Lahiri's widow) that have occurred in the ritual after the death of Mr. Lahiri in 1993. I have brought this information, along with answers to questions posed to ritualists and worshippers, to bear on both the descriptive and interpretive segments of this study.

I have included the Sanskrit prayers (not just their translations) in this description of the liturgy for several reasons. The most compelling argument is that the mysterious power of the sounds (*śabda*) of the sacred Sanskrit utterances (*mantra*) themselves are considered by practitioners to be crucial to the success of the ritual. It is through the medium of the sacred *mantra*s (not their translations) that the presence of the deity is invoked from the formless, undifferentiated state into particular perceptible manifestations. As Jan Gonda (1963:259) explains, *mantras* are "words believed to be of 'superhuman origin,' received, fashioned and spoken by the 'inspired' seers, poets and reciters in order to evoke divine powers and especially conceived of as creating, conveying, concentrating and realizing intentional and efficient thought, and of coming into touch or identifying oneself with the essence of divinity which is present in the *mantra*." Frits Staal (1979:9) contends that in the Hindu tradition, language is used not merely for naming, but actually to *do something*. André Padoux (1989:301) concurs, pointing out that speech (*vāc*), particularly *mantra*, is energy (*śakti*), the power through which action is accomplished. Thus, in a description of the *pūjā*, one could argue (albeit hyperbolically) that presentation of the Sanskrit *mantra*s alone is adequate, without their corresponding translations.

In support of such a view, Thomas Coburn's (1984b:445) observations are pertinent. He remarks that "the holiness of holy words is not a function of their intelligibility," and at times it even appears as if sanctity is "inversely related to comprehensibility." My inquiries upheld the view that pure, sacred sound takes precedence over the meaning. Bengali votaries told me that they were pleased with Pandit Nitai's ritual performance, because as one put it, he and his family "have good voices, pronunciation, and are strict followers of the rituals." Most seemed unconcerned as to whether or not Pandit Nitai understood Sanskrit. They themselves certainly did not.

Pandit Chakravarty explained that many *purohita*s do understand the gist of the prayers, even though they may not be experts in Sanskrit. There is enough resemblance to vernacular languages to convey meaning, or they have learned what the prayers mean. However, he conceded that this does not generally hold for the Vedic Sanskrit verses, which are far more poorly understood than the non-Vedic ones. The innate mantric power of the sounds of Vedic passages thus enjoys a far greater prestige among ritualists than the non-Vedic prayers. In keeping with that psychological attitude toward the Vedic passages, it would have been most accurate to treat them in the same manner as Tantric seed syllables (*bīja mantra*) such as "Hrīṃ," and leave them completely untranslated. He himself suggested that I do so. However, in the interest of being exhaustive I have included translations, although the fashion in which they appear needs explanation.

Pandit Chakravarty was reluctant to offer translations of Vedic verses, since he did not feel suitably competent with Vedic Sanskrit. When I said that I would like to know the meanings, he suggested that I turn to western translations. Since the process of extracting the details of the *pūjā* spanned several years, the Vedic verses were often the last to emerge. As they arose, I hunted down references using Bloomfield's (1981) *A Vedic Concordance* but was occasionally unable to find published English translations readily in Banāras. I turned to Pandit Chakravarty and after much persuasion had him offer his rendition of their translations. As it stands, virtually all the verses from the *Ṛg Veda* and *Sāma Veda Saṃhitā*s are those of Ralph T. H. Griffith, while most of the others are from Pandit Chakravarty. I have placed variant translations that I have subsequently found in footnotes.

Pandit Chakravarty did hold that when "knowing the meanings and uttering them with devotional sincerity, the utterance of the *mantra* properly creates [the] right vibration which becomes fruitful."[62] He, himself, when performing rituals such as the Durgā Pūjā, has this capacity. However, he held in equal regard that *mantras* become effective even if meanings are not known, provided there is "adequate attention and right pronunciation."

One may assert that the choice of *mantra*s which constitute the litany in rituals such as the Durgā Pūjā is arbitrary, at times merely having been culled from earlier Vedic rites and applied purely because of a remote similarity to some aspect of the later rite. However true this observation might be in numerous instances, sweeping application of such a claim would be an unfortunate generalization, which does not give due regard to the sacred powers held to be contained within the *mantra*s themselves. Ritual, like language, may draw upon an ancient vocabulary but continues to utilize those constituent elements in modified, yet meaningful ways. Although the significance of the *mantra*s is not always apparent or even overtly related to their verbal content, I found that the prayers do, at times, convey meaningful interpretations of the ritual action and can enhance our understanding of the conceptual image of Durgā, the exploration of which was my original objective.

I shall end this section with an amusing story that I heard on several occasions which pertains to the potency of *mantras* in the context of a Durgā Pūjā, and the dangers inherent in distorting them.[63] During Rāma's war with Rāvaṇa, when the demon's fortunes had turned for the worse with the slaying of his giant brother, Kumbhakarna, and his son, Meghanāda, Rāvaṇa thought to propitiate the Goddess himself. He decided to conduct a huge fire oblation to Durgā, known as the Caṇḍī Mahāyajña. By repeating a powerful mantric incantation to the Goddess for a requisite number of times, while making oblations into the fire, Rāvaṇa knew he could secure the Devī's help and attain certain victory over Rāma.

However, Rāma's monkey general, Hanumān, hearing of Rāvaṇa's intentions decided to foil the plan. Disguising himself as a *brāhmaṇa* student, he mixed with the *brāhmaṇa* priests commissioned to prepare the elaborate rite. By impressing them with his knowledge of Sanskrit grammar, his dedication, and loyal service, he was able to persuade them to change a single consonant in the *mantra*. Instead of chanting "*Jai tvam devi Cāmunde, Jai bhūtārti hāriṇi. Jai sarve gate devi, Kālarātri namo'stute!*" they chanted "*kāriṇī*" instead of "*hāriṇī.*" The prayer, which would mean "Victory to you, O Goddess Cāmuṇḍā. Victory, O Remover of affliction. Victory, O Goddess, Refuge of all. Salutations, O Goddess Kālarātrī!" had its second line transformed into "O Causer of affliction!" This change did not merely void the efficacy of Rāvaṇa's ritual, but actually brought misfortune to him and his cause.

CHAPTER 3

Overview of the Durgā Pūjā

"*Pūjā*s bring together the human and the divine worlds at specific times and places by actualizing the presence of a deity in a physical form that in some way "embodies" the reality of that deity. All the events, in turn, rest upon a network of shared beliefs, assumptions, myths, and ritual formulations. Hence *pūjā*, the basic formal means by which Hindus establish relationships with their deity, embodies the very reality that it seeks to adore. Or put another way, *pūjā*s create or invoke their own worlds of meaning" (Courtright 1985b:33).

General Comments on Pūjā

Pūjā is the quintessential form of devotional worship practiced by Hindus today. The practice is first mentioned in the *Gṛhya Sūtras*, Vedic texts that provide rules for domestic rites.[1] There, the term *pūjā* referred to the hospitality prescriptions to honor *brāhmaṇa* priests who were invited to one's home to preside over rituals for departed ancestors. With the rise of popular devotional theism (*bhakti*) centuries later, many of these ritual actions and prayers were modified and applied to the *deva-pūjā*, rituals that honor a deity (*deva*) as one would a welcome guest. Prescriptions on how to perform *deva-pūjā* became common features added to the Purāṇic corpus of literature, which date from the sixth century C.E. onwards. *Pūjā* thus melds Vedic rites with popular devotional elements in its ritual form.

The Durgā Pūjā serves as an ideal example through which to examine *pūjā* to any deity (*deva-pūjā*). It is a complex procedure that includes the installation of the deity into a temporarily sanctified place of worship (*pūjālaya*), as well as the honorific worship that follows the invocation. Furthermore, there are distinctive elements that pertain to the feminine nature of the deity being worshipped. For instance, the Durgā Pūjā includes characteristic offerings such as red lacquer for the Devī's feet, collyrium for her eyes, and a mirror with which to view herself, all of which acknowledge the Devī's femininity. She is also offered a blood sacrifice. Her *pūjā* clearly derives from a combination not only of Vedic and Purāṇic prescriptions, but from Tantric rites as well.

Vedic rituals centered on the worship of deities through oblations into a sacrificial fire. Both vegetable and animal offerings, thought to nourish the gods, were made in these rites, collectively known as *yajña*. Fire, which mediated between the human and heavenly realms, transformed the offerings and carried them up to the gods. In turn, the gods nourished the cosmos, sustaining the cosmic and social order. One of the most enduring themes in the interpretation of Vedic ritual is derived from the *Puruṣa Sukta* of the *Ṛg Veda* (10.90). This influential cosmogonic hymn recounts that the creation itself is the result of the immolation of the deity, Puruṣa. Puruṣa, later identified in the literature of the Brāhmaṅas with the lord of the creation, Prajāpati, is dismembered by the gods in this primordial sacrifice. The sacrifice led to the formation of the manifold cosmos, to the various social classes in human society, and even to the Vedas themselves. Through oblations into the sacred fire, the sacrificer reverses this process of cosmic manifestation, reintegrates the diversified creation which includes himself, and attains to the unmanifest state which precedes each cycle of creation.[2]

In contrast to Vedic *yajña*, where offerings were made to deities through the medium of fire, in *pūjā* deities are induced to assume material form, where they may then be offered reverential worship. Since they are invited from their customary abodes, they are treated like honored guests who have arrived at the place of worship after a long journey. The Great Goddess Durgā, who is regarded as the summation of all goddesses, is perceived as arriving from a variety of places. As Pārvatī, the consort of Śiva, she descends from Mt. Kailāsa. She also descends from the breast of Viṣṇu. Quite significantly, however, she is thought to maintain a constant, although generally latent, presence in the earth itself, in waters, such as the river Gaṅgā, and in vegetation. In the Durgā Pūjā, the place where she is to be worshipped (*pūjālaya*) is meticulously prepared, decorated, and purified, in anticipation of her arrival.

Despite the differences between Vedic sacrificial rituals (*yajña*) and the devotionally (*bhakti*) oriented purpose of *pūjā*, there is a pervasive effort to link the two in form and function. The Durgā Pūjā, for instance, includes a Vedic-styled fire oblation rite (*homa*) within its many structural elements. As Brian Smith (1989: 215-216) observes, "The Vedic sacrifice provides later Hinduism with a kind of standard of worth by which non-Vedic religious practices may be gauged." Simple devotional acts, such as visiting pilgrimage spots, may win the pilgrim "the fruit of the soma sacrifice" or "the fruit of the horse sacrifice." "In this way," Smith continues, "the new and relatively simple religious practices of Hindu worship are said to resume in themselves the power of the most complex Vedic sacrifices. . . . The purpose of shrouding new Hindu practices in sacrificial clothing is not simply to prove the superiority of the new to the old, but first and foremost to present the new *as* the old. Sacrifice has functioned throughout Indian history as a marker for traditionalism and as a means for acceptable innovation."

One of the most elaborate Vedic *yajñas* was the horse-sacrifice (*aśvamedha*), a rite that lasted longer than a year and culminated in a three-day ritual involving the immolation of a horse. The ritual was designed to confer power to the patron monarch and fertility to him and his wives. In a symbolic parallel to the function of the Vedic horse-sacrifice, it is often cited that the "Durgā Pūjā is the horse sacrifice (*aśvamedha*) of the Kali Yuga."[3] During the Kali Yuga, the most degenerate of the four ages *(yuga)* in Hindu cosmic reckoning, currently underway, people are regarded as incapable of performing that great Vedic rite. The Durgā Pūjā, once itself the hallmark of aristocracy, is viewed by some as a surrogate for that elite Vedic ritual, with the similar aims of enhancing power and fertility. As the *pūjā*'s patronage broadens to encompass wider social and class groups, the ritual's function of providing power and fecundity is further democratized, extending to the entire community.

Overview of the Ritual

"Do you have the Maliya cassette? You must purchase the Maliya cassette, with songs to Durgā and recitation of the *Caṇḍī Pāṭh* interspersed. It is a full programme. The one with the recitation by Virendra Krishna Bhadra is the one you want. His recitation is the best. At our *paṇḍal*, some boys and girls stage a *Caṇḍī Pāṭh* program just like that one, on Ṣaṣṭhī [the sixth day of Navarātra]. But his is best. For us, Durgā Pūjā starts with this Maliya *Caṇḍī Pāṭh*. It is known as the Āvāhana—Calling of the Mother."[4]

I can certainly vouch for the engaging quality of Virendra Krishna Bhadra's recitation of sections of the *Durgā Saptaśatī*. The recitation aroused coincident feelings of power and dread in me, enough to produce goose bumps every time I heard it. Bengali devotees clearly experience similarly strong emotional responses. The recitation is broken up with soft-voiced songs to Durgā by women. These are called *āgamani* (arrival), Mahālaya (Supreme Spirit/place of worship), or Mahiṣamardinī (Slayer of Mahiṣa) songs. The mood of the songs contrasts sharply with the recitation and dramatically conveys the ambivalent nature of the Devī who is about to appear. She is soft and maternal, but also powerful and deadly. All-India Radio broadcasts this recording, which is generally heard in Banāras at about five in the morning of Ṣaṣṭhī (the sixth day of Navarātra).

The Durgā Pūjā consists of a series of invocations, in which Durgā and other deities are invited to take up temporary abode in an assortment of forms. The divinities, when manifest in these forms, are subsequently worshipped through a variety of offerings, which include a blood sacrifice. The ritual terminates after five days, when Durgā and the other deities are asked to leave. What follows is an overview of the ritual's structure and major components. It is intended to facilitate the reader's progress through the detailed description of the ritual in Part II. I use this overview as an opportunity to elaborate on the meanings of certain patterns of ritual actions, such as imprintments (*nyāsa*) and purifications (e.g., *bhūta śuddhi*), as well as to comment on the general dynamics of *pūjā*. A more detailed interpretive analysis of the Durgā Pūjā itself and what it tells us about the nature of the Great Goddess is found in Part III, which draws upon material presented here and in Part II.

"This time [1991] Durgā came on a horse and leaves on a *dola* (swing). Traditionally she comes in different ways on each year: a boat, a *palki* (palanquin), etc. An elephant is good: slow, and so on, thus very prosperous. A horse is fast and galloping. [The] swing is not good, very changing. A boat also means floods, etc."[5]

The Preliminary Duties (*Sāmānya Vidhi*)

The preliminary duties purify and prepare the *purohita* for the ritual acts to come. The preliminary duties begin with a ritual sipping of water (*ācamana*) and an offering to the sun (*argha*). The *purohita* then performs a series of purifications. He purifies the water (*jala śuddhi*) to be used for the subsequent rites. He purifies the flowers (*puṣpa śuddhi*) to be used as offerings, his seat (*āsana śuddhi*), and also performs a general purification of the elements (*bhūta śuddhi*) that constitute the cosmos and his body. He "ritually imprints" his hands (*kara nyāsa*) and limbs (*aṅga nyāsa*) with *mantras* and then "restrains the directions" (*dig bandhana*). After ritually dispersing any forces which may act as obstacles (*bhūtāpasāraṇa*) to the ritual, he gives offerings to the *brāhmaṇa*s who are in attendance. He also utters an oath (*saṅkalpa*) expressing his objectives and his commitment to perform the rite. The preliminary duties end with a hymn (*saṅkalpa sūkta*) to the oath.

Bodhana

The Durgā Pūjā begins with the *bodhana* rite to awaken the Goddess from her dormant state. It involves the installation of a jar (*ghaṭasthāpana*) form of the Devī, a rite performed before a wood-apple tree (*bilva vṛkṣa*) or one of its branches. The *purohita* begins the installation by drawing a sacred diagram (*yantra*) on the ground. This *yantra*, a simple triangle or the much more elaborate *sarvatobhadra maṇḍala*, represents the Devī, who is both the source and portal of her own manifestation (See Figure 4.5). Upon this *yantra*, the *purohita* builds a low soil altar. He identifies it as the earth, the supporter of the world, and as Aditi, the mother of the gods. He then sprinkles five types of grain, symbols of nourishment, upon the altar. The *purohita* next sets a narrow-necked, full-bodied jar, filled with clean water, upon it. After placing five leaf-bearing twigs around its wide mouth, he tops the jar with a coconut. He next wraps the coconut-topped jar with a cloth, so that it resembles a woman clad in a *sārī* (the single cloth garment traditionally worn by Indian women). The jar is anointed with a paste of sandalwood, given "steadiness" (*sthirī karaṇa*), and its sacred perimeter demarcated (*kāṇḍā ropaṇam*) (See Figure 4.2.1). The installation takes about half an hour.

The Sanskrit litany reveals that the Devī is not invoked into the jar form. Although certain symbolic acts, such as the drawing of *yantra*s, appear to orchestrate her movement into specific locales, the earthen altar is directly identified as Aditi, and the Earth, divine, manifest forms of the goddess. The jar, too, is thus clearly a manifest form of the Devī. Thus a clear distinction is drawn between abodes in which the Devī resides permanently and forms into which she is invoked. Through the power of the Goddess, the *purohita* performs a series of ritual actions which, although appearing symbolic, are conceived of as actually inducing particular results. Using gestures (*mudrā*) and utterances (*mantra*), he ritually induces sacred female rivers to flow into the water which will be used in the ritual. With this consecrated water, he then purifies himself, the worship materials, and the images. By scattering white mustard seed, he drives away inimical spirits and next begins a process of bodily transformation.

Bhūta Śuddhi

Utilizing the yogic technique of breath control (*prāṅāyāma*), he commences the purification (*śuddhi*) of his constituent elements (*bhūta/tattva*) (See Figure 3.1). He does so by reversing the creative process through which these elements are thought to manifest. Beginning with the grossest elements (*mahābhūta*), he meditatively dissolves these one into the other, then into the subtle elements (*tanmātra*), into the sense organs (*jñānendriya*), into the organs of activity (*karmendriya*), into the inner mental elements of mind (*manas*), ego (*ahaṅkāra*), and intellect (*buddhi*), and finally into sentient primordial matter (*prakṛtī*). This purification is performed through the method of Kuṇḍalinī Yoga. The goddess Kuṇḍalinī, who lies dormant at the base of the *purohita*'s subtle body is awakened and allowed to rise through the central energy channel

Figure 3.1. The Lahiris' ritualist, Pandit Nitai Bhattacharya, performs yogic breath control (*prāṇāyāma*) as part of the *bhūta śuddhi*, an internal purification rite.

(*suṣumnā*) via various energy vortices (*cakra*), until she unites with the supreme reality (*paramaśiva*) in the thousand-petalled lotus (*sahasrāra padma*) vortex located approximately at the top of the head. This union leads to the transformation of the elements of his body from gross to immaculate substance.[6]

This process of bodily transformation and purification is one of many features that distinguishes Tantric *pūjās* from Smārta/Vedic ones, which generally do not include such procedures. Nevertheless, the themes of nourishment and cosmic reintegration characteristic of Vedic *yajña* are still present in the Durgā Pūjā. The *bhūta śuddhi* ritual, performed frequently during the Durgā Pūjā, is one of the most explicit instances of the theme of reintegration, which occurs at the heart of both Tantric and Vedic *pūjās*. In the *bhūta śuddhi*, the priest (*purohita*) first gathers all the constituent elements (*bhūta*) of creation. These are present in his own body, which is regarded a microcosm of the whole of reality. Through the psychophysical practice of Kuṇḍalinī Yoga, he dissolves each of these elements from the grossest to the most subtle, one into the other. Controlled breathing (*prāṇāyāma*), meditative visualizations, and sacred utterances (*mantra*), work together like a snake-charmer's flute to orchestrate Kuṇḍalinī's movement upwards through energy channels, until she unites with the male principle at the top of the subtle body. This union of female and male polarities transforms the *purohita*'s bodily elements, utterly purifying (*śuddhi*) them. By enfolding the elements of creation into each other with the aid of the Kuṇḍalinī energy, the *purohita* has taken himself to the precreative state.

There is a clear relationship between the awakening of the Goddess Durgā in the *bodhana* ritual and the awakening of the goddess Kuṇḍalinī in the *bhūta śuddhi* procedure. The *purohita* serves as the primary human locus into which the awakening Devī's energy flows. This energy manifests as Kuṇḍalinī arising within him. The Devī is thought to have a latent presence in the earth, waters, and vegetative matter. The jar, installed at the beginning of the Durgā Pūjā, incorporates those very elements and constitutes the Goddess's "body cosmos." In the *bodhana* ritual, she is awakened from her dormant state. The first human vehicle through which her energy flows is the body of the spiritual adept, the *purohita*. Through initiation (*dīkṣā*), spiritual training (*śākta sādhana*), and frequent encounters with the Devī's energy through ritual performance, the *purohita* is the ideally suited and necessary channel for the flow of Śakti. As the Devī's energy awakens within him, his body is progressively purified and transformed from base to pristine substance.

Having performed this "journey" to the source of all creation, the *purohita*'s transformed body merges with that of the Devī in a highly sublime state. The Devī's most sublime state is sometimes referred to in Śākta Tantrism as *avyakta śakti*, the unutterable or inconceivable power. Despite my repeated emphasis in this study on the Devī's manifest presence, both latent and active, within the creation, it is equally important to recognize that such manifest presence is not regarded as the totality of her being. The Goddess is simultaneously transcendent and manifest. Certain dualistic religio-philosophical systems, such as the Sāṅkhya school, postulate two transcendent entities. These are Puruṣa, pure consciousness, which comes to be identified with a male principle, and Prakṛti, identified as the female principle, and which, although transcendent, becomes the manifest creation. In contrast to such schemes, Śākta philosophy is ultimately nondualistic, with the Devī as the sole reality. In this respect the philosophy more closely resembles Śaṅkara's nondualistic Vedānta, in which Brahman is the sole reality. Śaṅkara's notion of Brahman in its absolute nature is beyond conception or predication. It is beyond being assigned attributes or qualities (*guṇa*). It is Nirguṇa. The transcendent nature of the Goddess in Śākta philosophy is akin to this Nirguṇa Brahman, and is thus referred to as *avyakta śakti*. It is also known as the unmanifest (*avyākṛtā*).

Schools of Śākta philosophy provide a variety of formulations on how the unmanifest Devī becomes manifest (*vikṛti*) as the material creation, and how she manifests in various eons in particular divine forms (*mūrti*), such as Durgā. For instance, the *Prādhānika Rahasya*, *Vaikṛtika Rahasya*, and the *Mūrti Rahasya*, three appendages (*aṅga*) to the *Durgā Saptaśatī*, expound particular formulations.[7] The Devī's transcendent self (*avyakta śakti*) may also be conceived as expressing itself as the male and female principles, Śiva and Śakti, and it is this secondary Śakti which in turn develops into the manifest creation. Manuals describing the *bhūta śuddhi* rite do not generally provide explicit conceptions of the transcendent reality, thus allowing *purohita*s to perform the rite in accord with their own metaphysical frameworks. Nevertheless, it is from a highly sublime state, ideally an unmanifest one, to which the priest has in theory journeyed, that he will eventually undertake the task of awakening the Devī and invoking her into material manifestations, where she may be honoured by her votaries. To do so he performs a series of psychic imprintments collectively known as *nyāsa*.

Nyāsa

Nyāsa consists of conceptually imprinting the purified body with the syllables of the Sanskrit language (*mātṛkā nyāsa*). The *purohita* also imprints his hands and limbs (*kara* and *aṅga nyāsa*) and the energy vortices of his subtle inner body (*antarmātṛkā nyāsa*). In performing the external imprintment of syllables (*bahya mātṛkā nyāsa*), the *purohita* takes refuge (*āśraye*) in the deity of speech (*vāgdevatā*), whose body is composed of the fifty Sanskrit syllables. Through the preceding imprintments, the *purohita*'s body becomes a vibrational body of creative sound. Through the external imprintment and the subsequent enfolding imprintment (*saṃhāra mātṛkā nyāsa*), the *purohita* effects a unitive identification of his vibrational body with Vāc, the goddess of speech and creation. Speech (*vāc*), through its connection with conceptualization, is identified with the creative process. The manifest differentiated universe is thought to be created from the transcendent and undifferentiated singularity through conceptualization, through naming. Thus speech or sound vibration is that through which creation occurs.

The *purohita* next assigns various abodes of the Goddess to his body parts in the *pīṭha nyāsa* procedure. These abodes of the Goddess, seats or places where she is thought to reside, are conceptual (e.g., the supreme supporting power), locational (e.g., the earth), symbolic (e.g., the jewelled pavilion, the wish-fulfilling tree), and qualitative (e.g., righteousness, dispassion, ignorance). The Devī has now taken up her abode in his body. Through a special imprintment known as the *ṛṣyādi nyāsa,* he secures (*kīlaka*) the union, and with the *vyāpaka nyāsa,* he completes the transformation by making the Devī's presence thoroughly pervasive in him. This entire sequence of *nyāsa*s, which takes about half an hour to perform, is considered preliminary to the awakening of the Goddess externally.

The *purohita* now turns his attention to Gaṇeśa who must be propitiated at the start of any *pūjā*. The priest then worships the other deities and celestial beings and drives away inimical spirits before turning to Durgā. Durgā is first mentally visualized and worshipped. Recharging his limbs and hands with the seed syllable "Hrīṃ," the *purohita* holds a flower in the meditative visualization gesture (*dhyāna mudrā*), to visualize and worship the Goddess mentally. In order to do this he first utters Durgā's *dhyāna śloka*, a verbal description of the image of the Goddess. While uttering these Sanskrit verses, he meditatively visualizes her image so that she takes form within his body, which, as a result of the *nyāsas* is now composed of the sound vibrations of the Sanskrit syllabary. His generic body of Sanskrit sound vibrations, identified with the goddess of creation, Vāc, through the vibratory power of the Sanskrit *mantras* of the *dhyāna śloka* harnessed by his meditative capacities, progressively transforms into the particular vibratory manifestation of the invoked deity, Durgā. One notes that the process of awakening the Devī unequivocally occurs through the *purohita*, who is at the completion of this meditation both the Goddess herself and her abode. The awakening has begun at one of the most subtle levels of manifestation, the vibrations of conceptual thought, which more coarsely manifest as the sounds of speech.

Holding a flower atop his head, he next offers a mental devotional service (*mānasa upacāra*) to Durgā's meditatively visualized form. Then, by placing the same flower on an external material form of his choice, he proceeds to convey the Goddess to that image. The Devī will thus move from her latent presence in the jar, and a wood-apple (*bilva*) tree branch, through the *purohita*, into such forms as a conch shell, a cluster of nine plants (*navapatrikā*), an anthropomorphic clay image, a sacred diagram (*sarvatobhadra maṇḍala*), and a living virgin girl (*kumārī*).

Durgā is next invoked into a conch shell. After worshipping the Devī in this manifestation, the *purohita* invokes her into the *bilva* tree. The prayers suggest that he both awakens her into and asks her to take up her abode in the *bilva* tree, asking that she stay there as long as it pleases her. He makes offerings and says prayers to the Guardians of the Fields (*kṣetrapāla*) and the elemental spirits. Then, invoking the divine *bilva* tree into the local *bilva* tree, he carries a branch of it to the place of worship and explicitly states that it will be worshipped as Durgā. Again the sacred space surrounding the Goddess in the *bilva* tree is cordoned off. The *bilva* branch will later be incorporated into the Cluster of Nine Plants (*navapatrikā*), a vegetative form of the Devī. Quite significantly, the Devī is worshipped as the protector/concealer of the secret of all secrets (*guhyāti guhya goptrī*). This epithet identifies Durgā with Mahāmāyā, the great power of illusion which conceals the divine mystery from being revealed to all but those on whom she chooses to bestow her grace. This constitutes the end of the *bodhana* ritual, which takes about an hour and a half to perform.

Adhivāsanam

The anointing (*adhivāsanam*) ritual, in which various forms where the Devī will manifest during the *pūjā* are ritually anointed, follows *bodhana*. It is generally performed later, within the same lunar day as the *bodhana*, unless the *bodhana* ritual was performed a day earlier due to limitations in the window of auspicious time. Both the *bodhana* and *adhivāsanam* rituals generally take place on the sixth day of the Āśvina Navarātra, which is referred to as Ṣaṣṭhī, the Sixth.

The *purohita* anoints the Devī with a wide assortment of materials, each of which is, in fact, a subtle form of the Goddess herself. He anoints the *ghaṭa* (jar), the conch shell, and the *bilva* tree, by lightly stroking these manifest forms of the Devī with the appropriate material. These materials include sandalwood paste, soil, a small stone, unhusked rice, *dūrvā* grass, flowers, fruit, curd, ghee, the *svāstika* symbol, vermillion, a conch shell, collyrium, cow bile, yellow mustard, gold, silver, copper, a yak's tail, a mirror, and the light of a lamp. These forms of the Devī are then symbolically anointed with all the materials together. Appropriate Sanskrit *mantra*s are uttered with each item. The sword (*khaḍga*) and the mirror (*darpaṇa*), other forms of the Devī, are also anointed. Durgā will later be offered a blood sacrifice with this sword, and she will be symbolically bathed through her reflection in this mirror.

In the *adhivāsa* ritual one recognizes that the materials offered in worship are themselves subtle forms of the Devī. Many of these materials are also commonly offered in virtually all other *pūjās* to deities other than the Goddess. For instance, in *pūjās* to Śiva, the Śiva *liṅga* is routinely bathed with water. While Śiva is not typically identified with water, the Devī is. This type of bathing does evoke the mythic association of the river goddess Gaṅgā with Śiva.[8] Similarly, the Goddess is also regarded as embodied within other standard *pūjā* material offerings, such as flowers, fruit, ghee, milk, and sandalwood paste. However, when votaries make an offering of any such item to male deities, such as Śiva, they probably do not generally conceive of it as a symbolic union of the Devī with Śiva. But it is easy to imagine that Śākta *purohitas*, such as the Bengali *brāhmaṇas* who perform the Durgā Pūjā, are well disposed to make such a connection. After years of ritual worship of the Goddess, who is regularly conceived of as embodied within the material elements of creation, they are decidedly apt to intuit that each material *pūjā* item offered to a male deity, such as Śiva, is a symbolic union between Śiva and the Goddess. Indeed, such a conception is quite consistent with Tantric symbolism in which the entire creation is viewed in terms of a union between male and female principles, such as Śiva and Śakti. In the worship of female deities, such as the Devī, these materials, which are components of her own body, are offered back to her. In such a Śākta Tantric conceptual scheme, *pūjā* may thus be categorized into two types. In the first type, which is directed to male deities, *pūjā* offerings enact a union between the feminine principle's manifest forms and the male principle, while in the second type, *pūjā* offerings enact a reintegration of the various manifest forms of the feminine principle itself.

The Devī in her dormant cosmic body in the form of the *ghaṭa*, awakened through the medium of sound vibration into the conch shell, and invoked to take up take up her abode in the *bilva* tree is now "teased" out of these forms via her numerous material manifestations (i.e., the anointing items) into other loci, such as the sword and the mirror, which will resonate with her presence. Certain devotees, too, who attend this ritual, sometimes experience a sort of "quickening," which expresses itself in trance, gooseflesh, and the uttering of moans. This "quickening" reflects the Devī's growing presence within the worshippers as well.

The *purohita* then anoints the Cluster of Nine Plants (*navapatrikā*), each of which represents an aspect of the Devī. The goddesses who embody these aspects are named Brahmāṇī, Cāmuṇḍā, Kālikā, Durgā, Kārtikī, Sivā, Raktadantikā, Śokarahitā, and Lakṣmī.[9] *Navapatrikā* worship may have been incorporated into the Durgā Pūjā from other goddess-worshipping traditions.

The *navapatrikā* itself appears to be a symbolic amalgamation of cults centering on trees and vegetation as abodes of goddesses and may well have its roots in the extremely ancient worship of tree spirits (*yakṣī*).[10]

The *purohita* now moves from the location of the *bilva* tree or from the shrine where the *bodhana* and *adhivāsa* were performed to the *pūjālaya*, the place where the clay image is to be installed (See Figure 4.3). Using sandalwood paste or colored rice grains, he draws a *yantra* on the floor. He establishes another *ghaṭa* on a small earthen altar which he constructs upon the yantra. He then moves the *ghaṭa* to the front of the altar, leaving room for the clay image which will be installed there (See Figure 4.4.3). He then places the clay image on the altar and performs an *adhivāsa* to all the images in the cluster, including the buffalo demon, Mahiṣāsura. The Devī's presence is thus induced to move from the *ghaṭa* to the clay image complex, and her power (*śakti*) is thought to begin a rudimentary resonance within these images as well. The demon, too, it should be noted, is enlivened with the Devī's power. The priest cordons the sacred space terminating his activities for the day. The *adhivāsanam* rite may also take about an hour and a half to perform.

Mahāsaptamī

On the following day, known as the Great Seventh, Mahāsaptamī, or simply Saptamī, the rituals center on the bathing of Durgā in a variety of forms. The rites begin with the *varaṇa*, an obligatory ritual in which the sacrificer (*yajamāna*) formally selects the *purohita*. This ritual establishes the relationship of reciprocity between the patron of the sacrifice and the *purohita*. The ritual dialogue clearly states that the *yajamāna* pays reverence and obeisance to the *purohita*, who is symbolically identified with the sun. The *purohita* has previously established his intimate connection with the Goddess by tying a thread around her wrist (on the clay image), as a symbol of protection (as in the Hindu ritual of *rakṣa bandhana*) or contractual union (as in the rite of *guru pūjā*).

Anointing and Bathing

After performing the common preliminary purification rituals, the *purohita* cuts a branch from the *bilva* tree (or takes the previously cut branch) and lashes it to the *navapatrikā*. He now proceeds to bathe the *navapatrikā*. The *navapatrikā* Devī is first anointed with a pinch of turmeric and oil. The prayers suggest that although the Devī's place of origin, nature, and purpose are mysterious, her presence is auspicious. This presence is capable of assuming a variety of forms (*nānārūpadhare*), and the smearing of these forms with unguents destroys spiritual impurities (*sarva pāpam vinaśyati*). It is crucial to note that although it is the Devī who is being anointed, the sins of the worshippers are at the same time being cleansed.

The *navapatrikā* is then bathed in the five products of the cow (*pañcagavya*) and the five nectars (*pañcāmṛta*), after these have been purified (See Figure 4.4.2). The *purohita* next bathes the *navapatrikā* in nine types of water, each of which is directed to a particular one of the nine plants. Through the litany we are told that the Goddess abides in the breast of Viṣṇu (*viṣṇuvakṣaḥ sthalāśrāye*) and is Śiva's beloved (*harapriye*). She is the abode of beauty/glory (*śrīniketā*), the giver of life (*prāṇadāyinī*) to all living beings, and she gives fulfillment of desires (*kāmapradā*). She is paid reverence by both gods and demons, removes the sorrow of separation, removes sin and hunger, and bestows all attainments (*sarvasiddhi*). She is the embodiment of victory (*jayarūpā*), the cause of victory (*jayahetu*), and the increaser of victory (*jaya bardhanā*).

This preceding section is a choice, illustrative example of how the Sanskrit litany of the Durgā Pūjā ritual, generally overlooked in most studies, reveals important information about the Goddess. The earlier epithet, made towards the end of the *bodhana* ritual, which accentuated the mystery of her origin, nature, and purpose (*guhyāti guhya goptrī*) contrasts dramatically with the statements made during the ablution. Through the intimate act of bathing the Devī, certain details of her being are revealed to the worshipper (through the *purohita*). The mystery begins to reveal itself. As the Devī is symbolically cleansed, an actual cleansing of the perceptual faculties of the votaries is being enacted, so that they may more clearly discern the Goddess's presence.

The *navapatrikā* Devī is then bathed in eight different waters. She is bathed by different divine beings with each water in an honorific gesture of subservience. The *navapatrikā* is then dried and draped in a *sārī*, so that she resembles, as did the *ghaṭa* which was installed earlier, a woman who has pulled her *sārī* well over her head, modestly concealing most of her face. She is placed next to the image of Gaṇeśa, where many devotees identify her as his wife. It is clear that the *navapatrikā* Devī is none other than Durgā, although in a manifest form that is more primordial than those in which the Devī will later manifest (i.e., the anthropomorphic clay image and a living virgin girl).

The *purohita* next symbolically bathes the clay image of the Devī through bathing its reflection in a mirror (*darpaṇa*) placed on a tripod. The mirror, through the *adhivāsa* ritual, had already been identified as a form of the Goddess. Sometimes the mirror is placed on a triangle formed from twigs, which is placed over an earthen jar (See Figure 4.4.3). The triangle or the tripod reflect the tripartite natures of the Goddess. For instance, in the symbolism of

Sāṅkhya metaphysics, the triad represents the three qualities (*guṇa*) present within all material manifestations, which come to be identified with the feminine principle. These qualities are the *guṇa*s of purity (*sattva*), activity (*rajas*), and dullness (*tamas*). In various Tantric formulations, the triad may represent three forms of *śakti*, such as action (*kriyā*), knowledge (*jñāna*), and will (*icchā*). The *purohita* rubs the mirror with rice powder and explicitly states that he is washing the body of the Goddess in the earthen image and the *bilva* tree. He then bathes the reflected image with the *pañcagavya*. Then, parallelling royal consecration rituals, he bathes Durgā with a special spouted vessel (*bhṛṅgāra*). The litany states that the Goddess is bathed by a host of entities both benevolent and malevolent, divine and mundane, including sacred rivers, gods and goddesses, the Mothers (Mātṛs), planets, sages, sacred places, the divisions of time, and demons. In tandem with the obvious symbolic meaning that the manifold creation pays homage to her, is the sense that this vast diversity is part of the Devī and emanates from her.

Durgā is then bathed with numerous watery infusions or waters obtained from varied sources poured from a conch shell. This conch shell was previously identified as a form of the Devī. Next she is bathed with water that flows through a container pierced with dozens of holes. The numerous streams of water that flow from this millifluent (*sahasradhāra*) symbolize countless rivers. After a bath with eight different types of water, the mirror is dried, smeared with vermillion on which a seed syllable of Durgā is written, wrapped in cloth and placed on the altar. This ends the great bath (*mahāsnāna*). The bathing rites may take anywhere from fifteen minutes to several hours.

Throughout the Durgā Pūjā, the *purohita* is engaged in inducing the Devī to manifest in a variety of the material forms in which she is ever present, but latent. Simultaneously, the worshippers are led, through the refining of their consciousness and perception, to "see" the Devī's manifest presence. The cloudy mirror is an ideal symbol of the devotees' dulled perception and the indistinct view of the Devī reflected within it. As the Devī's reflected image is bathed in the mirror, the mirror of their perception is itself cleansed. Innumerable aspects of the image of the Devī are revealed in the process, and the devotees' perceptions are steadily heightened, dramatically deepening the experience of *darśana*.[11]

These procedures, which both cleanse the Devī and purify the votary, suggest an important nuance to the widespread practice of *darśana*. *Darśana* is the act through which devotee and deity meet each other for an intimate act of perceptual contact. Not only must devotees perform their own purifications to prepare for *darśana*, but this cleansing is furthered by the *purohita*'s actions on their behalf. The *purohita*'s cleansing of the Goddess surely is honorific and symbolic. The bath may be a gesture of welcoming and honoring the Devī, but it is also a method through which the votary is raised to a suitable state of purity for encounter with the Goddess, who herself is not truly in need of purification. This bathing is categorically different from the bathing that takes place during the devotional service (*upacāra*), which occurs later. An abbreviated form of such devotional service, which is performed by priests and votaries before deities in temples and simple shrines, is generally referred to as *pūjā*. *Pūjā*, in the case of the Durgā Pūjā, is obviously a far more encompassing ritual than the condensed forms commonly practiced. Furthermore, the anointing and bathing procedures of the *adhivāsa* and *mahāsnāna* serve a different function from that which occurs during devotional service. They progressively reveal the Devī's ubiquitous and awakening presence to the transforming (cleansed and awakening) eye of the worshipper. This process lends further credence to the interpretation that the Durgā Pūjā is a rite of cosmic rejuvenation. Through the symbolic anointments, bathings, and invocations, it is not merely the material forms in front of the *purohita* that are being fully vitalized with the Devī's presence, but the entire manifest body of the Great Goddess, including the votaries' perceptions of her manifestation, which is nothing less than the cosmos itself.

Installing "Life" into the Image

When the bathing rite is completed, the *purohita* then drives away the inimical spirits and now worships the *navapatrikā* with a ten-part devotional service (*daśopacāra*). While touching the altar of the clay image, he urges Durgā to enter the place of worship (*pūjālaya*). Next he installs another jar (*ghaṭa*) and performs the preliminary procedures of purification of the worship materials, as well as himself. Durgā and the other deities in the clay image cluster are soon to be "brought to life." The *ghaṭa*'s form suggests a cosmic egg (*brahmāṇḍa*) from which the living deity will hatch.

Placing the central jar before the clay images, the *purohita* performs the meditative visualization of Durgā and beckons her and her eight attendant *śaktis* (*aṣṭabhiḥ śaktibhiḥ saha*) into the image with a powerfully charged set of invocations. He invites all the other deities to be present. He asks Durgā to take up her abode in the clay image, in the *bilva* tree, in the plants and herbs, in the twigs and fruit, and to remain as long as she is being worshipped. Anointing her three eyes with collyrium from a *bilva* leaf he performs the ritual of giving eyesight (*cakṣur dāna*) to the image. Touching the heart of the image with a flower, with the use of appropriate seed syllables, he induces life energy (*prāṇa*) into the image. He installs the soul (*jīva*) and activates the sense organs and other vital energies within the now-living image.

The difference between temple *pūjā* and this ritual of worship hinges on the manifest presence of the Goddess. The Durgā Kuṇḍ temple, in Banāras, for instance, enjoys a far-reaching reputation as a seat of power and attainment (*siddha pīṭha*) where the Devī is ever-present and accessible. During the Durgā Pūjā ritual, however, the Goddess is invoked into places where she is not normally available and where she will be worshipped only during the course of the festival. The Devī does not abide in some remote place but is "awakened" at the very locations where she will be worshipped. The notion of her arrival from her abode in the mountains or from the breast of Viṣṇu is a metaphor of this awakening process from dormancy. The bulk of the *purohita*'s actions, entirely absent in temple *pūjā*, is directed towards this process of awakening the Goddess and intensifying her manifest presence. When investing the clay images with eyesight and vital breath, the *purohita* has, in effect, brought what appeared to be an inanimate figure of earth to life. Actually the *ghaṭa*, too, was precisely such a "living" manifestation of the Devī, but the clay image embodies the Goddess in her most dramatic anthropomorphic form.

These two rites, in which the *purohita* first gives the image eyesight (*cakṣur dāna*) and then breathes vital energy (*prāṇa pratiṣṭhā*) into the clay form, are of pivotal importance. They may only be effected by uttering certain *mantra*s conferred through special initiation (*dīkṣā*). Writings as early as the Vedas relate that the wind itself, Vāyu, emanated from the *prāṇa* of the cosmic progenitor, Puruṣa (*Ṛg Veda* 10.90.13). "*Prāṇa* is the primal animating power upon which the self and the cosmos find their mutual support, their *pratiṣṭhā*" (Courtright 1985b:44). The divine guest has finally arrived.

Mythic Connections

The clay image complex is one of the most visible expressions of the Purāṇic heritage of the Durgā Pūjā. It clearly forges a relationship between Purāṇic myth and the ritual. The *Durgā Saptaśatī* (DSS), a scripture glorifying the Great Goddess that circulates independently, but which is also contained within the *Mārkaṇḍeya Purāṇa*, recounts three of the Devī's demon-slaying exploits. Among these is perhaps the earliest account of the well-known myth of the Devī's destruction of the demon Mahiṣa. Versions of this myth are also found in the *Varāha*, *Vāmana*, *Skanda*, *Kālikā* and *Devī Bhāgavata Purāṇas* (DBP).[12] In the myth, whose configuration is no longer solely determined by the account in the *Durgā Saptaśatī*, a buffalo demon named Mahiṣa, who was capable of assuming any shape at will (DSS 3.20-32), attained a special boon from the gods (DBP 5.2.3-7). Although his request for immortality was denied, Mahiṣa settled for the condition that he could only be killed by a woman. He arrogantly thought that this would make him invincible (DBP 5.2.8-14). He indeed succeeded in defeating the gods (DSS 2.1-2). In order to defeat Mahiṣa and regain their heavenly abode, the

Figure 3.2. An artisan ensnares the demon Mahiṣa with Durgā's snake noose in his workshop, as he puts the finishing touches on the clay images prior to their delivery to the *pūjā* sites.

gods pooled their powers. Their energies streamed out of their heads to produce a vast body of light that congealed to produce a woman of irresistible beauty, the Mahādevī, Durgā (DSS 2.8-12). They armed her with each of their weapons, and she was presented with a lion as her mount (DSS 2.19-30). The demon Mahiṣa was soon lured by her charms and attempted to win her hand (DBP 5.16.46-65). She promised she would yield to him only if defeated in deadly combat. Gripped by lust, he forgot his single weakness and eagerly began the battle (DBP 5.16.35-65). At an opportune time, the Devī, intoxicated with nectar, beheaded him (DBP 5.18.54-70, DSS 3.35-39) (See Figure 1.1).

The clay image complex derives its imagery from no single textual source. Although the Bengali images conform quite closely to the meditative verses (*dhyāna śloka*) used in the *pūjā*, the non-Bengali images reveal many creative liberties (such as utilizing multiple demons). Generally, however, at the apex of the clay image complex is the image of Durgā, beautiful and serene (in contrast to her passionate expression in the *Durgā Saptaśatī*), with ten arms, each of which wields a divine weapon.[13] One of her feet is astride Siṃha, her great lion mount. The other is atop the decapitated body of a buffalo. The demon, Mahiṣa, in human form, emerges from the severed neck of the buffalo. He is snared by her serpent noose (*nāgapāśa*) (see Figure 3.2). Durgā is portrayed impaling him with a spear (See Figures 1.3 and 1.4). This most dramatic anthropomorphic form assumed by the Devī in the Durgā Pūjā is as the goddess Mahiṣamardiṇī, Slayer (literally, crusher) of Mahiṣa.

Such myths, which belong to the Purāṇic literary corpus, display dimensions of devotional (*bhakti*) worship. *Bhakti* is a form of worship open to all, not just the upper, twice-born (*dvija*) classes. Strands of Devī worship in particular derive from tribal (*caṇḍāla*) and rural agricultural classes. These groups, which belong to the lowermost strata of the Hindu social order, performed their own rituals of worship, without the aid of *brāhmaṇa* priests. In Indian villages, there are ongoing examples of many such rites of Devī worship today. Even the *Durgā Saptaśatī* 13.5-11 tells how king Suratha (a *kṣatriya*) and the merchant Samādhi (a *vaiśya*) invoke the Devī and worship her on their own, albeit on the advice of the *brāhmaṇa* sage Medhas. Unlike the Durgā Pūjā, these rites involved intense austerities and even included offerings of the votaries' own blood, but they do illustrate the capacity for worship without the mediation of a priest.[14] And yet, although anyone may conduct the rituals to invoke and worship the Devī, members of the twice-born classes (*brāhmaṇa*, *kṣatriya*, and *vaiśya*) customarily commission *brāhmaṇa* specialists to perform the rite. Kṛttivāsa's *Rāmāyaṇa*, a fifteenth century Bengali composition of the celebrated Hindu epic, tells how the prince, Rāma, wished to invoke the aid of the Devī prior to his battle with the demon Rāvaṇa (N. N. Bhattacharyya 1974:149). Although the Devī was traditionally worshipped during the spring (a practice said to have been revived by Rāvaṇa himself [Östör 1980:18]), Rāma's awakening of the Goddess was untimely (*akāla bodhana*). Rāvaṇa, a *brāhmaṇa*, himself served as the *purohita* for the *kṣatriya* prince's Durgā Pūjā. Thus, despite the potential for everyone from *brāhmaṇas* to *caṇḍālas* to conduct the rites of worship of the Devī, the Durgā Pūjā almost always displays a triangular relationship in which the Devī's accessibility to the devotee is mediated by the *brāhmaṇa purohita*.

Devotional Service (*Upacāra*) and *Darśana*

The *purohita* next worships Durgā embodied in this clay image with an elaborate form of what is traditionally referred to as a sixteen-part devotional service (*ṣoḍaśopacāra*), a rite which may take up to an hour. Commencing by offering the Devī a seat (*āsana*), he moves through offerings of water for washing her feet (*pādya*), general food offerings (*naivedya*), and specific ones that include a honeyed mixture (*madhūpārka*), betel nut (*tāmbūla*), and sweet balls (*modaka*). These are normally followed with frequent offerings of water for sipping (*ācamanīya*). Amid these food offerings are the standard offerings of bath water and clothing. A number of feminine accoutrements are also offered such as ornaments (*alaṅkara*), including a conch-shell bangle, vermillion, collyrium, and a mirror. Flowers and flower garlands, fragrant incense, and flame worship (*ārati*) are part of the offerings (See Figure 2.1).

I have already pointed out how the anointings and bathings in such devotional services (*upacāra*) are different in nature from those performed in the earlier rites of the *pūjā*. These are primarily honorific, parallelling the treatment of an honored guest. They are directed at the Devī who is now fully awakened and present within the material forms. Nevertheless, I suggest that even this procedure of devotional service (*upacāra*), which is commonly called *pūjā*, by virtue of its similarity in form and substance to the awakening procedures, intensifies the progress of the process that was begun by the *purohita*'s earlier rites of anointing and bathing. That process, the effective accomplishment of which is the *purohita*'s central task, has as its primary objective a profound encounter between devotee and deity. This is *darśana*.

Devotees have not paid much attention to the activities of the *purohita* thus far. It is mainly during this devotional service stage of the ritual that they gather around the image and begin their participation. Their participation peaks during the flame worship (*ārati*). At the Lahiri household the children in particular were given gongs and bells, which they rang with spirited abandon, while the *purohita* passed the sacred ghee flame before the Devī. As one of the children humorously remarked, "The most important thing is to ring the largest bell during *ārati*. Whoever can capture the largest bell is successful. It isn't the sound which is the key. The commotion is expected in Durgā Pūjā. There is a different mood in Sarasvatī Pūjā, more sober. Durgā Pūjā is everything, all feelings."[15]

The women of the household utter a blood-curdling cry, onomatopoeically called the *ululu*, during the *ārati*. Bengali women utter this cry during all the high points of the Durgā Pūjā ritual. They had also uttered the *ululu* during the *bodhana* and *adhivāsa* rituals. In the words of the women, "the *ululu* is like group meditation. It produces a better feeling when many do it together." The cry mobilizes the entire household, induces goose bumps, and suggests the excitement and dread that accompanies Durgā's arrival and her tangible presence.The *ululu* is a unique practice through which female devotees participate in the adoration of Durgā. In the *Durgā Saptaśatī* (8.22-27) the *śakti* of the goddess Caṇḍikā herself, a gruesome deity known as Śivadūtī (She who makes Śiva a Messenger), appears and yelps like a hundred jackals. Śiva's own *śakti* is closely associated with the jackal, since the Sanskrit term for jackal is *śivā*. The *ululu* uttered by Bengali women is reminiscent of such a blood-curdling, jackal-like yelp. It forges a direct connection, even an identification, between women and the Devī.

One of the highest points of the devotional service in elaborate home *pūjā*s is the offering of cooked food (*anna/bhoga*). It is even important at the public celebrations. In the words of an organizer of one of those celebrations, "If you come from any *paṇḍal*, you will notice that there is a large crowd here. Why? First because Mother is going to eat. She will take *bhog*. She has come to her father's place, where she was born, her original place. She is about to eat. She is the daughter of Himālaya."[16] Although most of the offering materials have been painstakingly gathered by the *yajamāna*'s family, often for months prior to the *pūjā*, the food offerings provide a direct participatory liaison between the female worshippers and the Devī. While the uncooked food may have been prepared somewhat earlier, the cooked food is prepared immediately before the offering. To the chilling reverberations of the *ululu*, the matriarch of the home (if she is initiated, as in the case of Mrs. Lahiri) carries the food from the kitchen to the place of worship (*pūjālaya*) with utmost care while water is sprinkled before her, purifying the ground on which she will tread. The elderly initiated women in the worshipping household are extremely active during the *pūjā* in the preparation of the food. This is not merely festive preparation, for although the food will be eaten by the household and guests, it is *prasāda*, food that was first offered to Durgā and then distributed as blessings from the Goddess.

There are rituals of purity that accompany the food preparation, and as a foreign male ethnographer, I was skillfully sidetracked from the kitchen throughout my observations of the *pūjā*. The household kitchen is very much women's space, possessing its own mysterious aura to males and others who do not enter it. It would not be an exaggeration to suggest that the kitchen functions like another *pūjālaya,* where the miraculous chemistry of cooking is taking place. During the *pūjā*, an initiated postmenopausal woman, in a role not unlike that of the *purohita*, oversees the preparation of the food. Married daughters who have returned to the family household are requested not to lift a hand in the preparations. I was told that this "prohibition" insures that they have a relaxing time and enjoy being treated to the beneficence of the *pūjā* rather than be bothered with their traditional domestic burdens. In a sense they are living embodiments of Durgā/Pārvatī, perceived as the spouse of Śiva, who has returned to her father's home, where she is treated as a royal guest. The restriction also insures that no woman during her menstrual period enters the food preparation area. The devotional service ends with the offering of special cooked foods such as *paramānna* and cakes (*piṣṭaka*), and with obeisance (*vandana*) to the Devī.

While the *pūjā* commenced at least a day earlier for the *purohita*, most votaries explained that they view Mahāsaptamī as the first day because only now can they worship their honored visitor who is fully present. This attitude clarifies their nominal participation during the *bodhana* and *adhivāsa* rites. The rites of Mahāsaptamī, however, in which life is breathed into the Goddess, allows both votary and deity to engage in the crucially significant experience of *darśana*. Through *darśana*, deity and devotee finally come face to face; they not only actually see each other, but engage in a profoundly intimate encounter. Through *pūjā*, devotees are able to pay homage to the deity, not as a remote and inscrutable power, but as a flesh and blood guest in their midst. They honor her with a devotional service (*upacāra*), which includes offerings of water, ornaments and eyeliner, clothes, and food. Food offerings constitute an important part of the veneration process, resonating with the Vedic themes of providing the gods with nourishment. The transactional nature of *pūjā* is most evident here, for while the devotees (through the *purohita*) minister to the needs of Durgā, the Devī graces them with her presence, blessing all items that are offered to her. These blessed offerings are known as *prasāda*, a concrete symbol of divine grace.

This observation does not undermine an argument that I forward in greater detail later in this study, which centers on the notion that the Devī truly has no needs that require ministration. The devotees' service is primarily honorific, and expressive of love, gratitude, respect, and so on. When explaining why they worship the Goddess, some votaries explained, "If you ask your father for five rupees, he will give you two. But if you ask your mother, she would give you ten if she could." Through the devotional service, the votary, like a child in relationship to the benevolent Cosmic Mother, renders back to the Devī only a small portion of the bounty the Goddess herself has provided out of her very being. Votaries do not, for they cannot, give the Devī anything but what she has previously given them, from their material goods to their very lives. The *pūjā* transaction is ultimately not one of genuine material exchange, as in the case of *yajña*, but a gesture of devotion reciprocated by proof of divine presence and acceptance.

The *purohita* next invokes nine goddesses into the *navapatrikā* and worships each of them separately with a ten-part devotional service (*daśopacāra*). He invokes Brahmāṇī into the plantain, Kālikā into the *kacvī*, Durgā into the turmeric, Kārtikī into the *jayantī*, Śivā into the *bilva*, Raktadantikā into the pomegranate, Śokarahitā into the Aśoka, Cāmuṇḍā into the *māna*, and Lakṣmī into the rice paddy. After offerings to the directional guardians (*dikpāla*), the *purohita* invokes Gaṇeśa into the clay image, gives it eyesight and installs its vital energy. He worships Gaṇeśa with an elaborate devotional service. He repeats the procedure for Nārāyaṇa and Śiva, Kārtikeya, Lakṣmī, Sarasvatī, the mounts (*vāhana*) of the deities, the snake (*nāga*), Durgā's lion-mount (*mahāsiṃha*), and the demon Mahiṣāsura. When the entire image cluster is animated and worshipped, the *purohita* turns again to the Goddess and worships her with a repetition of her *mantra* and an elaborate *ārati* in which numerous honorific items, such as a lamp and a yak's tail whisk are passed before her. A hymn of adoration is recited, and the day's rituals end with a communal flower offering (*puṣpāñjali*). For votaries this is an important part of the ritual, since it allows them to move from being merely spectators with interior devotion, to actual participation in the rite of worship. They repeat prayers uttered by the *purohita* and shower the Devī with purified flowers. The entire Saptamī rites may take between two to four hours depending primarily on the duration of the rituals of bathing and devotional service. In the heyday of domestic Durgā Pūjās, the bathing rites were the times allocated for exuberant music and dance performances, and were thus lengthy and elaborate procedures.

The *purohita* has effected the difficult task of enabling the Devī to manifest within various media. Through successive and successful transmuting purifications of the matter around him, of the worshipper, and of himself, he has induced the Goddess to take up her abode in the *navapatrikā* and the earthen image, where her presence is now palpable to all who have participated in the process. The Durgā Pūjā clearly involves significant differences for the votary and the priest. To the devotee, *pūjā* is the procedure through which a deity who is already present is worshipped. Strictly speaking, this procedure is merely *upacāra* (devotional service) for which the term *pūjā* is synecdochic. This type of *pūjā* is frequently performed by devotees themselves in domestic shrines and temples, where the deity is thought to reside constantly. In these *pūjā*s there is no invocation or dismissal. Votaries purify themselves in preparation for the encounter by bathing and donning clean clothes. They may also fast and recite prayers. However, their preparations cannot match those of the *purohita*, who by virtue of his spiritual status, attained through birth, initiation, and regular practice, is the only one suited to perform the ritual. Naturally, to the *purohita* conducting the Durgā Pūjā or any such ritual, the concept of *pūjā* entails much more than it does to the devotee. He himself must first become a suitably pure vessel for the manifestation of the Devī. After numerous rites of purification, awakening, and invocation, he must skillfully bring her to life in forms accessible to the worshipper. After offering her devotional service, he must also conduct the rituals for her departure.

Mahāṣṭamī

The rituals of Mahāṣṭamī, the Great Eighth, are repetitions of those of Mahāsaptamī. The *purohita* purifies the place of worship and the worship materials. He purifies himself through appropriate imprintments and after the meditative visualization of Durgā, repeats the bathing ritual of the clay image using the mirror. He proceeds to worship Gaṇeśa and the other deities, but this time there is no installation of jars. This change reflects the notion that the deities are already present in the earthen images. They have germinated from the cosmic womb or seed that the *ghaṭa* also represents. Similarly, the *purohita* does not perform the installation of vital energy or eye-opening rituals. After the meditative visualization, the *purohita* worships Durgā embodied in the clay image and also worships the *navapatrikā*.

The *Sarvatobhadra Maṇḍala*

He now proceeds to the ritual which is of central importance on this day, the worship of Durgā in the *sarvatobhadra maṇḍala* (Sphere of All Auspiciousness), a diagram that he had drawn on the floor the previous night. The *sarvatobhadra maṇḍala* consists of an eight-petalled lotus in the centre, surrounded by a checkerboard of squares grouped in particular patterns. Colored red, yellow/green, white, and blue/black, the patterns appear to emanate outwards from the center.

Perhaps it is because the Great Goddess is accessible to, and has been traditionally worshipped by, all segments of Hindu society that the Durgā Pūjā includes such a variety of ritual elements. In the establishment of the earthen jar and the worship of the *bilva* tree and the Cluster of Nine Plants, we note that the Devī is associated with fertility, agriculture, and the forest. Elements of the rites pertaining to these forms of the Devī likely derive from pre-Vedic and tribal practices. The *homa* rite that takes place later is clearly Vedic in form, while the Purāṇic heritage is evident in the clay image complex and the devotional nature of the *pūjā*. Tantric components, too, are found throughout the *pūjā*. For instance, *nyāsa*s and Tantric seed syllables (*bīja mantra*), such as uttered in the *bhūta śuddhi* procedure, which itself is a Tantric procedure, may be used when establishing the clay jar or when performing the blood sacrifice. The key rite on Aṣṭamī, which centers on the *sarvatobhadra maṇḍala*, is also an excellent example of the Tantric aspect of the Durgā Pūjā.

The *sarvatobhadra maṇḍala* is a sacred diagram (*yantra*) that is a form of the Devī. It is sometimes drawn at the very inception of the *pūjā* to serve as the base upon which the earthen altar and jar are established. More often the *purohita* draws simpler *yantra*s, such as an inverted triangle inscribed with "Duṃ," the seed syllable of Durgā, which act as substitutes for the *sarvatobhadra maṇḍala*. On Aṣṭamī, Durgā is worshipped as the *sarvatobhadra maṇḍala* in a procedure that reveals that she is the supreme deity who presides over the entire cosmic realm peopled by all gods and goddesses. More correctly, in the form of the *yantra*, she actually *is* the entire cosmos.

The word *yantra*, which means "tool" or "instrument," is equated with the term *maṇḍala*, which means "circle." Although the terms are used synonymously, their original meanings evoke distinct aspects of the nature of these sacred diagrams. *Yantra* evokes the instrumental nature of the diagram, which serves as a tool through which the Devī is configured and conveyed from one location to another. It serves as a portal for her manifestations and a device through which she may be propitiated. *Maṇḍala* evokes the notion of a sphere of influence, the realm over which the deity presides. The Devī sits at the center of her *maṇḍala*, reigning over the entire cosmos, which is not only her creation, but her manifest body itself.[17]

The *purohita* begins the practice of the *maṇḍala* by invoking and worshipping the eight *śakti*s of Durgā into the eight petals of the lotus. Starting with the east and moving in a clockwise direction, he invokes Ugracaṇḍā, Pracaṇḍā, Caṇḍogrā, Caṇḍanayīkā, Caṇḍā, Caṇḍavatī, Caṇḍrūpā, and Aticaṇḍikā respectively. He then invokes and worships the sixty-four *yoginī*s into the center of the sacred instrument. It is noteworthy that he next worships goddesses who "dwell in other regions/countries" (*nānādeśanivāsinī*), universalizing the forms of the Devī in the *maṇḍala*. All goddesses, named or unnamed, are thus accounted for in this ritual. The *purohita* invokes and worships the Mothers (*mātṛ*) Brahmāṇī and Maheśvarī in the northeast corner of the *maṇḍala*, Kaumārī and Vaiṣṇavī in the southeast, Vārāhī and Nārasiṃhī in the southwest, Indrāṇī and Cāmuṇḍā in the northwest, and Kātyāyanī in the center. He worships Caṇḍikā and the Nine Durgās (unnamed) and then Jayantī and other goddesses.

Leaving the *maṇḍala* temporarily, the *purohita* moves to the worship of Durgā's weapons (*āyudha pūjā*). By situating the *āyudha pūjā* within the *maṇḍala* process, the ritual forges a connection between the earthen image and the symbolic diagram. The weapons are symbols of Durgā's powers. Armed with the weapons of all the deities, she is the summation of all their potencies. The deities that have been invoked and that will subsequently be invoked into the *maṇḍala* are, like her weapons, aspects of her power. They are her *śakti*s. The *purohita* worships the trident, sword, discus, sharp arrow, the śakti weapon, the staff, the fully-drawn bow, the goad, bell, axe, and the serpent noose. He also worships the Devī as the bearer of all weapons.

The *purohita* next worships the Devī's ornaments, a ritual which, by being situated within the *maṇḍala* process, again extends the symbolic dimensions of the instrument. The diagram represents not only Durgā's powers but her attributes and adornments. Returning to the *maṇḍala*, the *purohita* worships in the four cardinal directions, the young lads (*baṭuka*), considered to be male offspring of the four desirable states of attainment (*siddha*), knowledge (*jñāna*), friendship (*sahaja*), and togetherness (*samāya*). Between the lotus petals and the filament, the *purohita* worships the Guardians of the Fields (*kṣetrapāla*). The fierce forms of Śiva (*bhairava*) are next invoked into various sections of the *maṇḍala*. The Mahāṣṭamī rituals end with the worship of Durgā as the entire *maṇḍala*. If the *maṇḍala* was drawn earlier, its worship rites take about an hour to perform, and thus all the Aṣṭamī rites may be completed in as few as three hours.

Sandhi Pūjā

"In our Bengali tradition, the Aṣṭamī day is very important for us. The actual time is when Aṣṭamī and Navamī meet (*sandhi khana*) because this is when Mahiṣāsura was killed. For non-Bengalis, Navamī is more important. Śakti is a symbol of power, and it is this power which destroyed the demon. . . . No one is allowed to enter the room when Sandhi Pūjā is done. There is no *bali* offered here, but in some organizations, the blood sacrifice is given."[18]

The Sandhi Pūjā, which takes place during a forty-eight minute period at the juncture of the eight and ninth lunar day, is the high point of the Durgā Pūjā. After quickly performing the necessary purifications, the *purohita* meditatively visualizes a dreadful form of Durgā as Cāmuṇḍā/Kālī. The Goddess is worshipped with a sixteen-part devotional service, but the significant addition is offering of a blood sacrifice. The Devī has been receiving a range of offerings over the course of the Durgā Pūjā. As an honored guest, she was welcomed, offered a seat, bathed, is adorned with ornaments, and nourished with food on Saptamī and Aṣṭamī. The food offerings progressively escalate in scale. They began with uncooked items and culminate in the offering of *bhog*, cooked food, to Durgā. Only women who have the proper initiation and ritual purity are permitted to prepare the *bhog*, and in the Lahiri home, it was the patron's own wife who carried the offering to the Goddess. The sacrificed animal constitutes the most sublime constituent of the cooked food offerings. The animal is generally a dark male goat (*chāga bali*), occasionally a buffalo, and often a surrogate offering such as a white *kuṣmāṇḍa* melon.[19] The sword (*khaḍga*) is worshipped as the body of the Devī, the composite of the major gods and goddesses. The goat's head is then severed with a single stroke. The animal's head with blood and a lamp is offered to Durgā. Baṭuka, the *yoginīs*, the *kṣetrapālas*, and Gaṇeśa all partake in the flesh and blood offerings. The actual beheading may take place at an alternate site, such as the Durgā Kuṇḍ temple.

One hundred and eight ghee lamps are lit by the *yajamāna* and his family, allowing them to participate more intimately in the worship of the Goddess at this most crucial juncture of time. This offering is an *ārati par excellence*, and like the blood sacrifice, takes place within the context of the Sandhi Pūjā's exalted devotional service.

Young girls who have not yet reached puberty are next worshipped in the *kumārī pūjā*. One of the maidens is selected to represent the others. She is placed on a large brass plate and is worshipped as a living embodiment of the Goddess. The *purohita* washes her feet and after performing a meditative visualization of the goddess Kumārī worships the virgin girl with a sixteen-part devotional service. The girls are given sweets and gifts upon departure.[20]

Since the sacrifice may take half an hour to perform, and the *kumārī pūjā* may also take half an hour, modifications are common, since the duration of Sandhi is only forty-eight minutes. The sacrifice may be performed using the Tantric method, and the *kumārī pūjā* is occasionally moved to Navamī, where it may be performed in a more leisurely fashion for an hour or more. The symbolic conjunction of the blood sacrifice (*bali dāna*) and the *kumārī pūjā* reveals crucial truths about the Durgā Pūjā.

Blood Sacrifice and Virgin Worship in the Context of Pūjā

Among its varied functions, the Durgā Pūjā is a ritual of cosmic revitalization and fecundity. As Norman Cutler notes, "The divine image is a microcosm of a special kind. It is not only a concentrated representation of the entire cosmos; the material of which it is made is a part of the cosmos. The image is simultaneously part and whole. Like everything in the world, it is a part of God insofar as everything is an emanation of God's energy (or the energy which is God)" (Waghorne and Cutler 1985:163-4). This observation is especially germane when applied to worship of the Goddess, for she is unequivocally regarded as both the manifest cosmos and the energy that vitalizes it. At the climax of the rite, the Sandhi Pūjā, the *kumārī*, not far from the onset of her menstrual cycle and the power to engender life, incarnates the form of the newly awakened and fully manifest Goddess. Quite significantly, she symbolizes the entire creation. She is immaculate and full of creative potential. In her budding fertility, the sap of life pulses in contained yet creative readiness. In the animal sacrifice, which is juxtaposed with the *kumārī* worship in the Sandhi Pūjā, blood, the creative life essence is induced to flow. Even in the surrogate offering, this symbolism is maintained. The Devī, manifest as the virgin, is offered blood, the sap of life. The offering takes place in a number of symbolic ways. For instance, blood from the sacrificed animal's severed neck falls to the earth, which is the Goddess herself. At the Durgā Kuṇḍ temple, the blood may flow into the water tank (*kuṇḍ*), which itself is an abode of the Goddess. The animal is later cooked and offered as *bhog* to the Devī. Devotees eventually partake of the food offerings after these have been consumed by the Goddess.

In the Sandhi Pūjā, human and divine realms converge, and one notes, particularly in the consumption of the *bhog*, the intermingling of human and divine substance at the heart of *pūjā*. It is here that the devotee and the deity may enjoy a most intimate connection. Just as the word *darśana* conveys the sense of a mutual visual encounter, *pūjā* is a process through which a deep mutual sensory engagement may occur. In fact, the term *darśana* is itself obviously an abbreviation of the process of thorough encounter that is at the heart of *pūjā*. When devotees state that they are going for *darśana* to a temple, they almost always bring some *pūjā* offerings, such as fresh flowers for the deity. For many others, "going for *darśana*" is an abbreviated way of stating that they are going to pay homage to a deity by performing a more elaborate *pūjā*. *Darśana* is a metonym for *pūjā*. Through *pūjā*, the deity, if not already present, may be made to manifest in material form and thus be seen. In *pūjā* a deity and a devotee do not merely exchange glances. Both participate in a profound encounter. They see each other, but also share touch, smell, sound, and taste. The devotee anoints the Goddess with sandalwood paste, burns incense, rings bells, and utters verses of praise. Furthermore, in the prayer of homage and in the gestures of reverence, including prostration, votaries offer their inner psychological selves to the Devī as well. Quite clearly, in *pūjā* devotees offer the entirety of their being to the Goddess. This is particularly evident in the consumption of the *bhog* prepared from the blood sacrifice or surrogate. This, we note, symbolizes life and often represents the votaries themselves. *Pūjā* thus maintains the sacrificial configuration in which the constituent elements of the cosmos, including the votary's life itself, which emanate from the Devī's own being, are offered back to her.

Although there is historical evidence of devotees actually sacrificing themselves to the Goddess, in the Durgā Pūjā the self-sacrifice is symbolic, with the animal sacrifice or fruit, such as a coconut, serving as a surrogate for the votaries' selves. When cracked, the coconut spills its water, in the same manner that blood flows from the severed head of the sacrificed creature. While no votary offered this explicit interpretation, extrapolation of the symbolism would imply that the blood of the sacrificial animal cannot be other than the Devī's own blood. It is offered to her in a symbolic statement of the *pūjā*'s intent. This is to honor and propitiate the Devī with the highest offering possible, namely life. It is life that sustains and nourishes life. By accepting this offering, the Devī figuratively drinks of her own blood. By consuming the consecrated *bhog*, the votaries eat of themselves and the Goddess.

Furthermore, the flowing blood of the animal sacrifice or surrogate offering, consumed by the Devī and devotee, symbolically induces the sap of life, which is the Devī's vivifying energy, to flow into the newly reconstituted cosmos, rejuvenating it. The vitalizing essence flows into the seed grains that sprout in the earthen altar of the installed jar, into the diverse forms of vegetation of the *navapatrikā*, and into the virgin girl, whose budding fertility is a central symbol in the ritual. These embodiments of the Goddess evoke a world of earth and water, seeded with young vegetative and human life, poised to burst forth in creation. The Durgā Pūjā is clearly a rite performed with an intent to stimulate fecundity into this newly awakened, reconstructed, and living cosmos.

Mahānavamī

The Mahānavamī, or Great Ninth, rituals again repeat those performed on Mahāsaptamī. The special variant is the Fire Oblation (*homa*). A fire pit called a *sthaṇḍila,* is constructed according to ritual specifications (See Figure 4.7.2). Various deities and aspects of the Goddess are worshipped in sections of the *sthaṇḍila,* which is itself a cosmic *yantra*. The *purohita* performs a meditative visualization (*dhyāna*) of Vāgīśvarī, the goddess of Speech (i.e., Sarasvatī). He recites a verse and imagines her as entering into playful sexual union with the god of Speech (*vāgīśvarena saṃyuktaṃ krīḍā bhava samānvitam*) (i.e., Brahmā) after her postmenstrual purificatory bath (*ṛtusnātam*). While uttering this verse, the *purohita* collects fire from an ember and kindles tinder, which he lays down into the *sthaṇḍila*. Fire is thus visualized as the playful copulation of male and female creative vibratory principles, personified as the deities of speech (*vāc*). The *purohita* offers obeisance to the fire and other deities.

He then divides a plate of ghee into three sections by placing within it two lengths of *kuśa* grass. Having thus created a microcosm of the subtle body of a person, he selects ghee from the right, left, or central sections of the plate for offering into the fire. These sections correspond, respectively, to the *iḍā*, *piṅgalā*, and *suṣumnā* energy channels of the subtle body. The *purohita* next makes offerings of ghee, using the great mystical utterances (*mahāvyāhṛti*). These are syllables that form part of the Gāyatrī *mantra*. He proceeds to offer twenty-five ladles of ghee into the fire, while reciting the *mūlamantra* (root *mantra*) of Durgā.

The *purohita* then conceives of himself as identical with the fire and with Durgā, firming the identification with appropriate oblations and mantras. The *purohita* now turns to the offering of 108, undamaged, trifoliate *bilva* leaves into the fire with the *mūlamantra* of Durgā. The trifoliate leaves, symbolizing the trident (*triśūla*) of Durgā (and Śiva), represents such triads as the three *guṇa*s and the tripartite aspects of manifest *śakti*, namely the energies of desire (*icchā*), knowledge (*jñāna*), and action (*kriyā*). The *purohita* now offers himself (he is identified with the Devī and the fire) the items that the *yajamāna* has allocated as his payment for performing the ritual. It includes food and money representing gold (*dakṣinam kāñcanamūlyam*). He allays any faults that may have occurred during the procedure and then extinguishes the fire. Ashes from the *homa* are used to mark his body. He also anoints the *yajamāna* and other onlookers with the auspicious ashes. This ends the rituals of the ninth day. The *homa* rite takes about an hour, while the entire Navamī rites may be completed in three to four hours.

Although the *purohita* conducts the *homa* ritual, the *yajamāna* is an essential participant in it (See Figure 4.7.3). The *yajamāna* offers quantities of material into the fire and often recites the *mantra*s in their entirety or merely echoes their terminating utterance, "*svāhā*" with the *purohita*. The *homa* ritual harkens back to the earliest Vedic fire sacrifices (*yajña*) and allows the sacrificer (*yajamāna*) a close communion with the deity in a nonanthropomorphic form. In response to my questions about why fire oblations are still performed, I was often told that certain votaries prefer to worship deities through fire rather than an image because it is more internal, mental, and abstract. The identifications of the *purohita* with the sacred fire and the goddess Durgā imply that the offerings made into the *homa* fire, or offerings made through the *purohita*, go directly to the Goddess. The *yajamāna* may also make special requests at this time. The *homa* also strategically places the *yajamāna* in direct physical relationship with the *purohita*, at the time when the former must reward the latter for his services.

The triangular relationship delineated in Vedic fire oblations (*yajña*), which has the deity, the *purohita*, and the worshipper at the triangle's vertices, is also clearly evident in the Durgā Pūjā. The *purohita* is the mediator between the divine and human realms, linking the devotee with the deity. While Vedic priests made oblations into the fire on behalf of the patron (*yajamāna*) who commissioned the ritual, in *pūjā*, the *purohita* actually brings the deity into direct physical contact with the *yajamāna* and all other devotees present. Vedic elements such as the fire oblation rite (*homa*), which carry the prestige of Vedic rites (e.g., antiquity, brāhmaṇism), nevertheless endure or have been purposefully situated in the Durgā Pūjā. However, the *homa*'s place is not central since it takes place on Navamī, following the Durgā Pūjā's climax. During the climax on Sandhi Pūjā, a 108-lamp flame offering is made, which obviously derives from the sentiments of *bhakti* worship, not Vedic *yajña*.

Vijayā Daśamī

The "Tenth for Victory" technically follows the nine days of Navarātra but clearly is a continuation of the Durgā Pūjā celebrations. The *purohita* visits the place of worship and after the appropriate purifications worships the Devī with a ten-part devotional service (*daśopacāra*). He then prays that the Devī's grace confer fulfillment on any rituals that may have been performed inadequately. Next he dislodges the jar (*ghaṭa*) from its established position and also moves the platform on which the clay images rest. These actions initiate the dismissal procedure, which constitutes the central ritual of this day.

The *purohita* pays obeisance to the Goddess as Nirmālyavāsinī (She who Abides in Purity). He also worships the goddess Ucchiṣṭacāṇḍālinī (She who is the Impure Outcaste).[21] The *purohita* then asks the Devī as Cāmuṇḍā, with her eight *śakti*s, to leave and to return to her highest abode (*paramasthānam*). The litany here is vitally important, since it reveals to us that the Devī is not dismissed in her entirety. She is asked to remain in the water, in the house, and in the earth (*jale tiṣṭha gehe ca bhūtale*). These are precisely the substances from which and the locations from where the Devī will be invoked and awakened in the following year's Durgā Pūjā. The Devī does not abandon the site where she has been invoked, but lingers there permanently. Parallelling the sanctification of the food offerings to the Devī, in which the "polluted" remains, "purified" by the Devī's divine digestion, are returned as blessings (*prasāda*) to her devotees, the "polluted remains" (*ucchiṣṭa/nirmālyam*) of the entire Durgā Pūjā ritual leave in their wake the lingering, "sanctifying," and stainless presence of the Devī even after her dismissal.[22]

The *purohita* immerses the mirror (*darpaṇa*), which is a form of the Devī, in water and touching the altar of the clay image he again dismisses Durgā, as the beloved of Śaṅkara, and in the form of the Nine Durgās, to her abode atop Mt. Kailāsa. He also dismisses all the other deities to their respective places after they have granted their devotees the requested boons. This ritual officially constitutes the immersion and dismissal (*visarjana*) of the Goddess. The visibly dramatic disposal of the clay image in the waters of the Gaṅgā, although generally identified with the *visarjana* ritual, is more an act of "lay" rather than "virtuoso" religious activity. The *purohita* will not be involved in that process, and the responsibility of disposal of the clay image rests with the *yajamāna*.

The *purohita*'s duties are not entirely finished however. Prior to the immersion of the clay images, he performs the worship of the Devī as Aparājitā (She who is Invincible). Resonating with the notions of victory (*vijayā*), this Aparājitā Pūjā is generally performed on the Vijayā Daśamī (The Tenth for Victory). The Goddess as Aparājitā is normally worshipped in the form of a deep purple floral creeper. The *purohita* performs a *dhyāna* of her and worships her with devotional service. A yellow string is used to affix bits of the creeper to the upper arm or wrist of devotees. During immersion, this creeper is also surrendered to the water. However, a flower may be retained and installed into a small container (often silver). This serves as a protective amulet, which is worn around the neck or arm. The Daśamī rites are completed in about an hour.

Also prior to immersion, the ladies of the house feed each other sweets and betel nut in a rite known in Bengali as *varana/barana*. They also smear the mouths of the clay images with sweets and drape them with betel leaves (See Figure 4.8.1). Even the demon Mahiṣa is treated this way. One explanation for this ritual is that since Durgā is returning to her husband's abode atop Mt. Kailāsa, she will experience great hardships during the ensuing year with that austere master *yogi*. The sweets will fatten her up for the year ahead. They also crown the symbolism of the gracious treatment she has received during her stay in her paternal home, the memory of which will hopefully encourage her to return again the next year.

Sax (1991:117-126) and others (e.g., Bennett 1983:167) have explored the traumatic nature of a young Hindu girl's departure upon marriage away from her natal home. Not only is she obliged to leave home, family, and friends, but she must enter into a deeply intimate relationship with her husband who, like the people in her new home environment, is a virtual stranger. The depiction of Sītā's departure in the popular televised serial, the *Rāmāyaṇa*, is an excellent example of the deep emotions conventionally expected to be felt by the bride upon leaving her home, even with a husband as desirable as Rāma. Furthermore, it is not only Sītā who weeps, but her mother, father, and close relatives. It is little wonder that a return to the natal home is a highly desirable event for most young brides, as well as for their loved ones at home. In the Garwahl region of Himachal Pradesh, Sax (1991:97-98) noted that impeding a woman from returning to her home village is thought to be fraught with danger, for she may effectively place a destructive curse on the household that inhibits her movement.

In two well-known myths of the goddesses Satī and Pārvatī, this motif is acted out, once dysfunctionally, and once appropriately. In the first myth

Satī's father, Dakṣa, does not invite her home for a large sacrificial celebration. Her husband Śiva, too, tries to restrict her from going. As a result Satī curses her father's household and ends up immolating herself on his sacrificial fire. Śiva, in his anger, destroys Dakṣa and his home, and spends aeons mourning the loss of his wife. In the parallel myth, Satī's reincarnation, Pārvatī, with whom Durgā is frequently identified, has no such parental problems. Although her mother Menā is distraught at the unconventional appearance of Śiva, both parents accept their daughter's choice of marital partner, and gladly welcome her back.[23] In many parts of India, such invitations and returns to the natal home by daughters occur during major festivals and events. A very important such festival in North India is the Durgā Pūjā, which serves as an institutionalized mechanism for an annual reunification of married daughters in their natal home.[24]

It is clear that the feminine presence of the reunited women creates an atmosphere in the home that is crucial to the mood of the domestic Durgā Pūjā. As is the case in many religious festivals worldwide, it would be misleading to insinuate that the psychological moods and motivations that most participants associate with the Durgā Pūjā are exclusively, or even primarily, religious. The merrymaking dimensions of the *pūjā* are very evident in the community celebrations. But even in the intimate and undoubtedly religious setting of the Lahiris' home, the Durgā Pūjā is as centrally about the reunion of the family's married daughters as it is about the Devī's invocation and veneration. When I asked Mr. Lahiri why he persists in performing the Durgā Pūjā, he said he could not imagine not performing it. It is one of the main focal points of his life. "Throughout the year, this house is quiet. It is just me and my wife. Sometimes some friends come to visit. But look at the house now," he said. "Look at it during this time of the year. It is so full of life. Somehow when Durgā is in the *mandapa*, my house is unlike any other time of year. Mother is smiling. The children are around. My daughters are back, and my grandchildren are here. My house is like this at no other time. No other festival, religious feast, party, gives the house this feeling. There is nothing like it."[25] Thus although she is perceived as a returning daughter, the Devī also presides as the arch matriarch, the symbol and embodiment of womanhood, under whose nurturing and protective wing the family's female lineage may gather. The Devī brings them together, and at the end of the *pūjā*, like the Devī, they too will be depart, leaving only the lingering perfume of their presence until the next year.

After the celebrations are completed, people collect the weapons from the images as souvenirs. While these weapons are now made of metal of disposable quality (e.g., by the tin-working caste), in the earlier celebrations of this ritual the image of Durgā was equipped with items of weaponry that would have been actually used in battle. The *pūjā* would have consecrated those weapons with the Devī's power and durability.[26] With great fanfare, the image cluster is carried to the Gaṅgā, where it is placed on a boat, floated some distance from the bank, and discharged into the water (See Figure 4.8.3). A jar of Gaṅgā water is brought back to the place of worship. The *purohita* sprinkles this water on the heads of devotees. The *pūjā* has ended, but the festive feelings continue at least until Kālī Pūjā (Dīpāvalī, for most Hindus) some weeks later. As one of the Lahiri grandchildren put it, "Aṣṭamī is the climax of the Durgā Pūjā. Actually, Sandhi Pūjā is the climax, but the feeling peaks during Aṣṭamī. I feel truly uplifted at that time. It is a religious feeling. I feel able to get into the *pūjā*. It is like an approaching train, the anticipation changes when it comes, and you can board the train. I'm just getting organized during Saptamī; it peaks at Aṣṭamī, and the momentum carries onto Navamī. Daśamī is less. A kind of feeling lingers till Dīvalī."

While most accounts of Durgā Pūjā end on Vijayā Daśamī, the worship of the Goddess continues to the eleventh (*ekādaśī*) day of the waxing fortnight of Āśvina. On the *ekādaśī*, many Banārasi Śāktas (particularly young men) are likely to visit the temple of Vindhyavāsinī Devī, located about eighty kilometres upriver from Banāras. The working poor often take a holiday on this day and allocate a healthy amount of their savings for the trip. Vindhyavāsinī temple is an extremely renowned abode of the "Goddess who Resides in the [Hills of] Vindhya" and is visited by large numbers of worshippers throughout Navarātra. A sizable percentage of pilgrims will perform a triangular (*yoni*-shaped) pilgrimage circuit to the temples of Mahālakṣmī, Mahākālī, and Mahāsarasvatī in the hills surrounding Vindhyavāsinī temple. This pilgrimage is said to follow the tradition of the Rahasyas, appendages (*aṅga*) to the *Durgā Saptaśatī*.[27] The *Prādhānika Rahasya* (see verses 1, 2, and 4), for instance, speaks of Mahālakṣmī, Mahākālī, and Mahāsarasvatī as the Devī's primary (*pradhāna*) or intrinsic forms (*svarūpa*). The tradition of visiting Vindhyavāsinī temple predates the communal Durgā Pūjā tradition in Banāras. When public celebrations of the Durgā Pūjā in Banāras began, the organizers recommended that ritualists and votaries should offer a *pūjā* to Vindhyavāsinī Devī prior to commencing the Durgā Pūjā celebrations. To facilitate this procedure, community centers for celebrating the *pūjā* were once set up in Vindhyachal town itself. However, the growth of public celebrations of Durgā Pūjā in Banāras, in both scale and number, is likely responsible for the trend towards now visiting Vindhyavāsinī on *ekādaśī*.

Bengali Śāktas celebrate in a unique way on this day. In the words of a member of the Bengali community,

> Watch us on *ekādaśī* where we are seen coming together, doing a musical performance, a show. We meet each other, greet our seniors, touch their feet, get *asirvad* (blessings), and so on. It is sure that visitors are offered

> sweets and pleasantries. This eleventh day celebration is called Vijayā Sammilini. Rāma fought a battle against Rāvaṇa. He performed a *pūjā* to Durgā. He won, and then celebrated this with a great festival of gathering. Non-Bengalis generally don't celebrate it. But those who have been influenced by the Bengali's way, and all Bengali clubs, will celebrate Vijayā Sammilini. On Vijayā Sammilini, Durgā Pūjā ends.[28]

With this preliminary excursus through the significant points of the Durgā Pūjā complete, the reader may now turn to the detailed description that begins in Part II. I shall further develop some interpretations of the Durgā Pūjā's functions and intent, which are obviously diverse, in Part III. The Durgā Pūjā enables individual devotees to approach and address the Devī in the most intimate manner possible. For some it is an opportunity to show reverence; for others it is a chance to give thanks for favors already granted. Many seek access to the Devī's power (*śakti*), thought to be most accessible at this time. Artists may solicit enhancement of their creativity and healers of their healing powers. The Devī is willing to grant boons to every worshipper, and for most devotees this is an opportunity to make requests. There is an amoral aspect to the Devī's power, which is bestowed on anyone who performs her worship sincerely. Like a human mother, the Cosmic Mother does not turn her back on any of her children, and even sorcerers and thieves may propitiate the Goddess for success in their undertakings. The Devī is capable of granting boons of a worldly nature, but can also grant the highest form of spiritual liberation (*mokṣa*) to her devotees. The *Durgā Saptaśatī* narrates that the Devī, albeit as the result of their intensely austere worship, appeared to king Suratha and the merchant Samādhi. To king Suratha she granted boons of temporal power: initially the return of his own kingdom, and later, rebirth as a son of Sūrya, the Sun God, as the eighth Manu, Sāvarṇi, overlord of the cosmic eon known as a Manvantara. To the merchant Samādhi, she granted the knowledge that leads to liberating perfection.

PART II

Description of the Durgā Pūjā

CHAPTER 4

The Durgā Pūjā

4.1: Preliminaries

Categories of *Pūjā*

Every specific or special rite (*viśeṣa vidhi*), such as Durgā Pūjā, for example, is normally preceded by general preliminary rites (*sāmānya vidhi*). Typically, *pūjā*s themselves may be of two types: one performed as the obligatory worship (*nitya pūjā*) of deities daily or at specific times during the year, and the other performed optionally for the obtainment of special desires (*kāmya pūjā*). For example, the worship prescribed for members of the twice-born (*dvija*) classes, to be performed at the confluence periods (*sandhyā*) of the day, namely dawn, noon, and dusk, is regarded as a *nitya pūjā*. Śaiva and Śākta *pūjā*s (if the *purohita* is initiated), performed for the *purohita*'s personal preferred deity (*iṣṭadevatā*) on a regular basis, are also *nitya*. The term *nitya* is actually ambiguous since it can refer to *pūjā*s that are either obligatory or regular. *Nitya pūjā*s may be simple or elaborate. *Kāmya pūjās* are neither regular nor required. Their performance is entirely the choice of patrons who wish to achieve particular goals for themselves or others. The goals may include offspring, longevity, wealth, success in an undertaking, and even bringing harm to one's enemies. Both obligatory and optional *pūjā*s may be further categorized as occasional (*naimittika*), since they are only performed when the occasion (*nimitta*) arises. However, in the case of *nitya pūjā*s the occasion is mandatory, while for *kāmya pūjā*s it is a matter of choice or personal desire.

Within the prayer of intention (*saṅkalpa*) and towards the end of a *kāmya pūjā*, a prayer is usually uttered that indicates the "fruit" of the ritual and to whom it should go. In the spirit of loving devotion (*bhakti*), the patron often offers the fruits of the *pūjā* back to the deity. Such a *pūjā* is then referred to as *niṣkāmya* or "without desire."[1] It must be remembered that all the aforementioned categories are not mutually exclusive and may overlap. The Durgā Pūjā as performed by families such as the Mitras and Lahiris, annually for over a hundred years, could be regarded as regular (*nitya*). However, since the *pūjā* is only celebrated on the occasion of the autumn Navarātra, it could be classified as occasional (*naimittika*). Furthermore, since the *pūjā* is not obligatory, it should be regarded as optional (*kāmya*). And if conducted for no particular reason than to honor the Devī, as is generally the case, especially for community Durgā Pūjās, it will be regarded as *niṣkāmya*.[2]

The *Purohita*'s Own Obligatory Duties (*Nitya Pūjā*)

Before the *purohita* can begin his preliminary duties (*sāmānya vidhi*) for Durgā Pūjā, he must perform his personal obligatory daily rituals (*nitya pūjā*) for these are actually part of the preliminary procedures. For instance, upon awakening, *mantra*s are supposed to be recited before getting up, and the proper foot should be placed on the floor when alighting from the bed. A tooth stick may be collected from a *nīm* tree, more *mantra*s recited before and after brushing, and the stick should then be discarded in the proper direction. He should defecate and perform his other morning ablutions facing the proper direction. Underwater silt may be collected from the riverbank where he has gone to bathe and fashioned into three balls (*piṇḍa*). One is smeared on the lower body, one the upper body, and with the third a sacred diagram (*yantra*) with triangles is drawn on the ground, and the mantric seed syllable (*bīja mantra*) of Durgā inscribed within it. Only if Durgā was his personal preferred deity (*iṣṭadevatā*) or if he was preparing for the Durgā Pūjā ritual, would he likely use such a *yantra*.[3] This procedure enacts a symbolic identification of the *purohita*'s body with the body of Durgā (in the *yantra*). The three balls are said to represent the lower, human, and divine realms (*triloka*). After his bath, donning a clean cloth over his shoulder, he would return to his shrine. He might then smear the shrine door with sandalwood paste and throw purified flowers, water, and other purifying agents, while facing appropriate directions for the various goals of life (e.g., *dharma*, *artha*, *mokṣa*, *bhoga*).

These days, such elaborate procedures are greatly curtailed. The *purohita* normally gets out of bed without any ritual action. He may say "Hail Durgā, Durgā," go to his toilet and bath at home like most people, and then proceed to his shrine. There he sits on a special seat, the *kuśāsana*, a rectangular mat ideally made of *kuśa* grass, covered with a wool blanket for comfort. He now begins the preliminary duties (*sāmānya vidhi*), common or generic rites that are either performed regularly by themselves or before all special (*viśeṣa*) *pūjās*. If he is performing the Durgā Pūjā for someone else, the priest will move to the patron/worshipper's (*yajamāna*) shrine room for the *sāmānya vidhi* and subsequent rituals.

Normally, however, the Śākta *purohita* will at least install a jar (*ghaṭa*) embodying the Goddess in his own home shrine, to be worshipped for the duration of the festival. Pandit Nitai Bhattacharya, the *purohita* who performs the Lahiri family's Durgā Pūjā, as well as the one at the Durgotsav Sammilini, installs a jar form of the Devī in his own home and performs a daily recitation of the *Durgā Saptaśatī* (see Fig. 4.2.1). This is the extent of his personal worship of the Goddess during the Navarātra celebrations. In the Lahiri family tradition, the jar is established on the first day of Navarātra. *Durgā Sapatśatī* recitation begins from that day until Mahānavamī.

Donning special garments of unstitched rough silk or a cotton-blend, Pandit Nitai departs for the Lahiri home. Were he performing the Kālī Pūjā, he might choose red garments, but for the Durgā Pūjā Pandit Nitai wears a white *dhoti* (several metres of fabric draped around the waist and through the legs) and a *chaddar* (a smaller piece of fabric worn on the upper body [Skt. *prāvaraṇa*]). Even his underwear must be of material that has not been stitched. Unlike most *purohita*s, who buy their own clothes, he has received these items from his patrons during a previous ritual and will be provided with a new set on Saptamī. This clothing is set aside specifically for *pūjā* use and may not be used as street clothes.

The Preliminary Duties (*Sāmānya Vidhi*)

The *sāmānya vidhi* described here is followed by a particular group of *purohita*s in Banāras prior to their performance of the Durgā Pūjā. It is a modification of the *sāmānya vidhi* commonly followed for other *pūjā*s. This occurs because the Durgā Pūjā ritual is lengthy, and the time allotted for the ritual may be limited (e.g., the sixth lunar day [Ṣaṣṭhī *tithi*] may only last for a few hours after dawn on the sixth solar day of Navarātra, and the entire Ṣaṣṭhī *pūjā* must be performed during those hours). Furthermore, several elements of the *sāmānya vidhi* are included in each day's Durgā Pūjā ritual itself, and so the *purohita* may omit those repetitive sections from the common (*sāmānya*) observances (*vidhi*).

Ācamana (Sipping of Water)

A *kośā*, a specially shaped copper vessel, is filled with fresh pure water (See Figure 4.4.3). A particularly large version is used for Durgā Pūjā due to the complexity of the ritual and the amounts of water that will be used. The *purohita* scoops water into his palm with the smaller copper *kuśī* and takes three sips while repeating the *mantra* "Om Viṣṇuḥ," thrice. The *kośā* and *kuśī* are likened in appearance to wood-apple (*bilva*) leaves or to the cavity formed by the hands cupped in the gesture of offering (*añjali*). I could not help but note that they also resemble the female reproductive organ (*yoni*). The *purohita* holds the water he sips and then wipes his mouth ritually with the aid of the *gokarna* (cow's ear) *mudrā*. To do so he cups his palm upwards so that it can hold just enough water to immerse completely a small legume. He sips the water from a location at the base of his thumb, known as the *brahmatīrtha*, the site sacred to Brahman. The entire procedure is called *ācamana*.

*Mudrā*s are ritual postures or, more commonly, gestures made with the hands and fingers. They may convey messages (e.g., fear not [*abhaya*]), symbolize processes (e.g., *dhenu mudrā*), or seal a ritual act (e.g., *matsya mudrā*). Just as writing and speech are fashioned from alphabetic characters and primary sounds, the nonverbal language of "signing" is composed of archetypal gestures. *Mudrā*s are especially powerful gestures which, like mantric seed syllables (*bīja*), resonate with meaning. Such sacred gestures form a vital part of Hindu religious ritual activity. While static *mudrā*s are known and identified through iconography and descriptions in literature, the immensely important "litany" of dynamic ritual action is only observable in the ritual process itself. Humphrey and Laidlaw (1994) use the example of Jain *pūjā* to forward a theory of ritual that is grounded in action. They emphasize the action-centered nature of ritual wherein each ritual act need not have a corresponding intentional meaning. Staal (1979), who examined Vedic rites, goes as far as saying that ritual is pure meaningless action. Although one may challenge these ideas, they derive from observations of the overwhelming significance of action in ritual. I concur that it would be difficult to overstate the importance of visualizing the "flow" of the *purohita*'s bodily movements throughout the Durgā Pūjā if one wishes to appreciate more fully the nature (i.e., purpose, effect, etc.) of the ritual. I have, for this reason, included numerous details on the gestural litany.

If, as in this case, the special (*viśeṣa*) *pūjā* to be performed after these preliminary rites (*sāmānya vidhi*) is for Durgā or Kālī, a Tantric style of *ācamana* is performed. Instead of repeating "Om Viṣṇuḥ" three times, the *purohita* says:

Om ātma tattvāya svāhā	Om svāhā to the supreme reality that is Ātma
Om vidyā tattvāya svāhā	Om svāhā to the supreme reality that is Vidyā
Om śiva tattvāya svāhā	Om svāhā to the supreme reality that is Śiva

Om or *Aum* is the universal primordial vibration of all manifestation and is thus generally uttered before all sacred utterances (*mantra*). *Svāhā* is one such sacred utterance offered to all deities. It is generally uttered at the end of a *mantra*, often in conjunction with oblations into the fire. *Ātma* refers to the Supreme Self, identical with the singular underlying reality which is the Absolute Brahman. *Vidyā* means "knowledge," "magical lore," or "science."[4] It is also an epithet of Durgā, the Great Goddess.[5] Here, understood within its Tantric context, it may refer to the Divine Feminine which is synonymous with the Divine Masculine, *Śiva*, and the Supreme Self, *Ātma*. Alternately, *Vidyā* and *Śiva* may also be conceived of as complementary polarities of the Absolute. According to Pandit Chakravarty, the application of such meanings depends on the knowledge and philosophical predilection of the *purohita*. Here, and throughout this study, information on symbols and terms is furnished for the benefit of the reader. I do not wish to imply that all *purohita*s know or adhere to the meanings or interpretations provided.

Then various parts of the body (specifically, the mouth, nostrils, ears, joints of the shoulders, *sahasrāra*, navel, and heart) are touched, and the "Om Viṣṇuḥ" or Tantric *mantra*s are repeated for each body part. The *sahasrāra* is an energy center of the subtle body, visualized as a thousand-petalled lotus approximately located at the top of the head of the physical body. When engaged in this process, the *purohita* thinks:

> By sipping this water, I remember Viṣṇu, the all pervading consciousness, in the highest abode (*sahasrāra*), in the mouth, and so on.

Argha (Offering to the Sun)

Next, the priest purifies flowers, washed rice, *dūrvā* (a common, resilient, green grass), a red flower (e.g., hibiscus), and perhaps *kuśa* grass, and placing these into the small copper *kuśī*, makes this offering (*argha*) to the Sun. The *argha* offerings are sometimes made in more elaborate containers such as conch shells, which are also referred to as jars. Since they contain water, flowers, grass, rice, and sometimes fruit, they are symbolically identified with the Earth and thus constitute another implicit form of the Devī. *Dūrvā* grass (*Cynodon dactylon, Pers*) is said to be the hairs of Viṣṇu rubbed off his body by friction from the serpent Vasuki when the gods churned the milky ocean. The nectar of immortality that was obtained from this act was placed on the grass, consecrating it (Ghosha 1871: xxvi).

The *purohita* then pours the *argha* into a copper plate (*tāmra pātra*). This offering, which is for the Sun, is not made just to the visible sun (*sūrya*) but also to the inner self (*ātman*) and the supreme self (*brahman*). These three are said to constitute the notion of "Sun," and they must be conceptually unified while offering the *argha* to the visible sun. Occasionally, a disc of smeared red sandalwood paste representing the Sun itself is made in the center of the *tāmra pātra*.

Jalaśuddhi (Purification of Water)

Next, the *purohita* draws a *yantra* with a seed (*bīja*) syllable in the center. If he is to be performing the Durgā Pūjā that day he may use a goddess *yantra* and *bīja*. He places the *kośā* on the *yantra* and recites a *mantra* (see below) while stirring the water within. To do so he forms his hand into a fist and then extends his middle finger, in what is known as the *aṅkuśa* (goad) *mudrā*. The goad (*aṅkuśa*), used by elephant trainers, is a symbol of control. The goad, tiny in comparison to the elephant, when properly used steers, directs, and generally compels the large power to follow the trainer's directions. Similarly, the *purohita*'s middle finger compels the waters to enter the *kośā*. Through these *mantra*s and *mudrā*s, he invokes the "Sun" to deliver other sacred waters (*tīrtha*), known for their capacity to carry people to liberation, into the *kośā*'s water. Since everything is thought to be dissolved in the "Sun," it is the source of all *tīrtha*s. Since the Sanskrit word "*kara*" means both a ray of the sun and the hand, and since the chest area of the body is also conceived of as the sun, through his stirring and pointing *mudrā* the *purohita*'s "body sun" delivers the "ray" into the *kośā*. In this way, with the *aṅkuśa* (goad) *mudrā*, the Gaṅgā, Yamunā, Sarasvatī, and other holy rivers are delivered into the *kośā*.

> *Om gaṅge ca yamune caiva godāvarī sarasvatī/*
> *narmade sindhu kāverī jale 'smin sannidhiṃ kuru.*
> Om! May the rivers Gaṅgā and Yamunā, and others like the Godāvarī, Sarasvatī, Narmadā, Sindhu, Kāverī come to this water.

Its fulfilment is enacted by the *dhenu* (cow) *mudrā* which is performed by holding the palms facing each other with the fingertips downwards. The *purohita* then intertwines his fingers so that the tips of the middle fingers of each hand join the index fingers of the other, while the ring fingers join with the other hand's little finger. The *mudrā* resembles a four-teated cow's udder. It orchestrates the successful transfer of sacred, spiritually nourishing waters from the Heavenly Cow (*surabhi*) into the *kośā* which is symbolically transformed into the Earth Cow (*dhenu* also means "the Earth"). The *kośā* is then covered with the *matsya* (fish) *mudrā*, made by holding the hands face down, one palm atop the back of the other. By then extending and moving the thumbs the *mudrā* resembles a fish swimming with the aid of its fins. The *mudrā* seals the ritual, marking its effective accomplishment. Fish that swim in those sacred rivers are now present in the consecrated vessel. The term *matsya* also recalls the first incarnation (*avatāra*) of Viṣṇu who, during a great deluge, is said to have only saved the seventh Manu and the Seven Sages from inundation. The symbol of the fish thus also connotes the salvific power of these waters.

Puṣpaśuddhi (Purification of Flowers)

Then, dipping *kuśa* grass into the *kośā*, the *purohita* sprinkles the consecrated water in different directions, purifying the objects in the room. He next purifies the flowers that will be used in the worship ceremony. For the Durgā Pūjā, it is common to include the red hibiscus or China rose (*japā*). Touching the flowers, which are kept in a plate set on a tripod to his right, he utters:

> *Om puṣpe puṣpe mahāpuṣpe supuṣpe puṣpasambhave/*
> *puṣpacayāvakirṇe ca huṃ phaṭ svāhā.*
>
> Om! [Through the utterance of the mystic syllables,] "Huṃ phaṭ" may flowers, small and big flowers, beautiful flowers, things born of flowers, and the space scattered over by heaps of flowers be purified.

Āsana Śuddhi (Purification of the Seat)

He next performs the ritual of purification of the seat (*āsana śuddhi*), by drawing a triangle with water from his fingers on the floor just in front of his mat. With hands crossed at the feet and offering a flower dipped in sandal paste, he utters:

> *Om hrīṃ ādharāśaktaye kamalāsanāya namaḥ.*

Then touching the seat he says:

> *āsanamantrasya meruprṣṭharṣiḥ sutalam chandaḥ kūrmodevatā āsanopaveśane viniyogaḥ.*

The approximate meaning of this combined act and utterance is:

> Om! Uttering "Hrīṃ" [I offer this flower] to this seat of lotus, the supreme supporting power [i.e., the Goddess]. Its sage is Meruprṣṭha, the meter is Sutala, the presiding deity is the Tortoise, and its application is the function of sitting.

Meruprṣṭha literally means the "the back/roof of Meru," the cosmic mountain. It stands for the sky or heavens. Kūrma, or tortoise, on which the cosmos rests, symbolically recalls the second incarnation of Viṣṇu who served as a "base support" for the cosmic mountain when the oceans were churned by the gods and demons to extract the nectar of immortality (*amṛta*). Among the many items to emerge from this churning was the goddess Śrī/Lakṣmī. *Sutāla* means "foundation," and is also the name of one of the seven nether regions (of which *pātāla* is the lowest). Heaven, earth, and the netherworlds are linked in the *āsana* which represents, through the symbolism of Meru and Kūrma, the cosmic ridgepole or *axis mundi*. Then with folded hands he recites:

> *Om pṛthvi tvayā dhṛta lokaḥ devī tvaṃ viṣṇunā dhṛtā/*
> *tvaṃ ca dhāraya māṃ nityaṃ pavitraṃ kuru cāsanam.*

> Om! O Earth, the worlds are borne by you. You, O Goddess, are borne by Viṣṇu. Please bear me eternally and thus purify this seat.

Bhūta Śuddhi (Purification of the Elements)

Next the *purohita* proceeds to purify the *bhūta*s. It is thought to be a cleansing of his constituent elements and his attachment to outward material things. Thus bodily and external matter to which the individual clings are both thought to constitute the physical being, and it is this gross body that is transformed in this purification ritual. It begins with ritual yogic breathing (*prāṇāyāma*) using various *mantra*s. In this *prāṇāyāma*, the sacred *mantra*, Om, is not used. Other seed syllables (*bīja*) are utilized. The energy vortices (*cakra*) within the body are purified with *mantra*s, so the dormant potential energy (*kuṇḍalinī*) can be activated and allowed to move up the bodily energy channels (*nādi*) smoothly. The baser elements are merged into the finer, until the *purohita*'s body is transformed into one of immaculate substance. The details of this purification are provided in the discussion of Durgā Pūjā that follows.

Nyāsa: Kara and *Aṅga* (Imprintment: Hand and Limb)

The *purohita* then performs *nyāsa*. This is a yogic ritual practice, likely of Tantric origin, in which the vibrational sounds that constitute the entire conceptualized universe, sounds which are contained in the alphabet of the Sanskrit language, are imprinted on various parts of the transformed body. Since all concepts are capable of being labeled with language composed of the vowels and consonants of the Sanskrit language, it is understood that the entire conceptualized cosmos can be symbolically reduced to this alphabet. By associating letters to body parts, the microcosm of the purified body is made to correspond to, to represent, to parallel, and even to contain the divine macrocosm. *Kara nyāsa*, through an act of meditative visualization, places these Sanskrit syllables in the fingers of the hand (*kara*), and then these syllables are placed in six parts (*aṅga*) of the body in a procedure called *aṅga nyāsa*. Appropriate *mantra*s are recited in conjunction with the *mudrā*s.

Some *purohitas* suggest that Ādya Śaṅkarācārya, the great eighth or ninth century C.E. reviver of Hinduism, founder of the Hindu monastic (*maṭha*) system, and proponent of a radical nondualistic philosophy (*advaita vedānta*) prescribed these *nyāsa* practices. Śaṅkara's name is often invoked to give a measure of legitimacy or orthodoxy to devotional and even Tantric ritual practices. For instance, his reputed composition of the *Saundaryalahari* (The Wave of Beauty), a devotional Goddess-centered text, links the devotional Śākta tradition to the orthodox Hinduism with which Śaṅkara is identified. The *Saundaryalahari* is frequently reproduced with numerous *yantras* appended, the ritual use of which is clearly Tantric. *Nyāsa*, however, does not always form part of Smārta/Vaidika *pūjā* (Bühnemann 1988:121) with which Śaṅkara is generally associated. The full details of the *nyāsa* ritual are found later in this study.

Dig Bandhana (Restraining the Directions)

The *purohita* restrains the directions (*dig bandhana*), establishing a perimeter around the space in which the ritual is to be performed. To do so he snaps his fingers in each of the ten directions (North, East, West, South, their midpoints, and the zenith and nadir).[6] Just as timing is crucial in ritual performance, with windows of sacred time appearing during the year (e.g., Navarātra), within which there are further subdivisions of sacredness (e.g., the conjunction of the eighth and ninth day), so too, the vast expanse of space must be divided and consecrated. The ritual must occur at a particular point in the space-time continuum, and thus the directional elements have to be held back. Within the sacred perimeter, a virtual "black hole" is created, where there is no time, no space, and no direction. The directions are restrained, held back, often with guardians placed at the cardinal points to prevent the untimely intrusion of the "created" into the "transcreated" primordium.

Bhūtāpasāraṇa (Dispersing the Agencies of Obstacles)

Finally he performs the ritual of *bhūtāpasāraṇa*, removing the agencies that might prove obstacles to the ritual. Such obstacles are twofold. They include the internal bad moods and dispositions that could result in failure or poor performance of the *pūjā*, as well as the outer agencies that may prevent one from proper performance. These outer agencies may be disembodied spirits of the recently dead (*bhūta*), ghosts (*preta*), vampires (*vetāla*), and a host (*gaṇa*) of other such pernicious beings. Details of this ritual will be presented in the Durgā Pūjā description that follows.

Offerings to *Brāhmaṇa* Attendants

Sometimes there is only one *purohita* performing the entire *pūjā*. But for elaborate *pūjās* such as Durgā Pūjā, it is not unusual to find a few *brāhmaṇas* assisting the priest. These may include the *tantradhāraka*, an important assistant or apprentice to the priest. Most *purohitas* begin learning their ritual art by serving as *tantradhārakas*. This is how Pandit Chakravarty first learned the Durgā Pūjā, with his father and uncle, and later with other *purohitas*. Although he may be an apprentice, the *tantradhāraka* coaches the *purohita* by pointing his finger along the written ritual script, prompting him at stages when he has lost his place, and so on. When the apprentice is ready to move to the stage of *purohita* himself, he may solicit the aid of his mentor as *tantradhāraka*. In complex rites, such as the Durgā Pūjā, the *tantradhāraka*, who might be either a novice or an expert, is an indispensable attendant. Other *brāhmaṇas*, friends or relatives of the *yajamāna,* may assist in the lighting of lamps or the placement of offerings. During the Mitra family's Durgā Pūjā, I witnessed as many as eight priests attending to the Devī.

Flowers, sandalwood paste, and a small quantity of washed, uncooked rice (*ātapa taṇdula*) are offered by the *purohita,* who pinches the offering with his thumb and fingers (as when moving a chess piece) and places them in the *tāmra pātra* (copper plate) in front of the *brāhmaṇas*.[7] He says three times:

> *Om kartavyesmin durgāpūjana karmaṇ/ om puṇyāhaṃ bhavanto bruvantu.*
>
> Om! On the occasion of this ritual to be performed for Durgā, would you please utter "*Om puṇyāham*" (Let auspiciousness be on me).

The *brāhmaṇas* are asked three times to repeat the request for auspicious benediction. If they are unable to repeat the *mantra* (e.g., not present at the time, or unable to utter the sacred Sanskrit *mantra*), the *purohita* will do it on their behalf. When offering flowers to them he says:

> *Om kartavyesmin durgāpūjana karmaṇ/ Om svasti bhavanto bruvantu.*
>
> Om! On the occasion of this ritual to be performed for Durgā, would you please utter "*Om svasti*" (Om! Approval).

And he, with fingers facing downward, gently tosses the flowers into the *tāmra pātra*. Then, again:

> *Om kartavyesmin durgāpūjana karmaṇ/ Om ṛddhiṃ bhavanto bruvantu*
>
> Om! . . . would you please utter "*Om ṛddhiṃ*" (Om! Prosperity).

The *brāhmaṇas* repeat:

> *Om ṛddhyatām. Om ṛddhyatām. Om ṛddhyatām.* (Om! Let there be prosperity.)

When finished, he says with folded hands:

> *Om sūryaḥ somo yamaḥ kālaḥ sandhye bhūtānyahaḥ kṣapāḥ/*
> *pavano dikpatir bhūmir ākāśaḥ khacarāmarāḥ/*
> *brāhmyaṃ śāsanam āsthāya kalpadhvam iha sannidhim.*
> *Om tat sat ayamārambhaḥ śubhāya bhavatu.*
>
> Om! The deities superintending over the sun, the moon, death, time, the two junctures of day and night, the waters and other elements, the wind, the guardians of the directions, the earth, the sky, those who move in the sky, the immortals, etc., properly following the rules/discipline as given by Brahmā, all of you should remain present here. May this beginning of ours be auspicious.

After having blessed and propitiated the *brāhmaṇas* and having invoked the celestial beings to attend the ritual and make the commencement auspicious, the *purohita* proceeds to the *svasti vācanam.*

Svasti Vācanam (Utterance of Approval)

Taking some rice from the plate, the purohita says:

> *Om somaṃ rājānaṃ varuṇam agnim anvārabhāmahe/*
> *ādityaṃ viṣṇuṃ sūryaṃ brāhmaṇanca bṛhaspatim.*
> *Om svasti, svasti, svasti.* [SV.1.91a; ŚB.5.1, 5.9]
>
> Om! I pray for the approval of the luminous moon, Varuṇa [the all-pervading moral force], and Fire. I [am going to proceed with my work and] pray for the approval of Āditya, Viṣṇu, Sūrya, and the *brāhmaṇa* Bṛhaspati. Om! Well-being, well-being, well-being.[8]

The plate (*tāmra pātra*) is placed on a tripod (*tripādikā*), which is placed in a big bowl. Should the *tāmra pātra* fill with water and overflow, the big bowl collects the overflow.

This *svasti vācanam* is described in the *Sāma Veda* fashion. There are also *Ṛg Veda* and *Yajur Veda* ways of performance according to the family's Vedic association. Public (*sārvajanīna*) *pūjā* normally follows the *Yajur Veda* method, unless the representative *yajamāna* is from a *Sāma Veda* or *Ṛg Veda brāhmaṇa* family. There is also a Tantric method of *svasti vācanam.* It is likely to be used if the *purohita* has special initiation, and if he so desires. It is a must if performing the *pūjā* of a Tantric deity. However, since Durgā is worshipped with a combination of Vedic, Purāṇic, and Tantric elements, the use of Tantric variants is left to the *purohita*'s discretion.

Saṅkalpa (Oath)

Saṅkalpa is the standard preliminary oath taken before the performance of any *pūjā* or vowed observance (*vrata*) of some duration. In it the *purohita* promises what he intends to do during the course of the *pūjā*. The *saṅkalpa* is a verbal testament of commitment to perform a series of ritual acts within the proper conventions. If these acts are carried out with the proper faith and ritual finesse, the desires wished for through the *pūjā* are expected to be realized. During the preliminary observances (*sāmānya vidhi*) prior to Durgā Pūjā, it runs as follows:

> *Viṣṇurom tat sadadya āśvine māsi kanyārāśisthe bhāskare śukle pakṣe saptamyām tithau ārabhya mahānavamīṃ yāvat amukagotra* [*kaśyapagotra* for the *purohita*s whom I consulted] *śrī . . . devaśarmā* [here varieties of desires wished for through the performance of the *pūjā* may be introduced] *sarvāpacchānti pūrvaka dīrghāyuṣṭva paramaiśvarya atula dhana dhānya putra pautrādya navacchinna santati mitra vardhana śatrukṣayottarottara rājasammānādyabhīṣṭa siddhaye paratra deviloka prāptaye ca (śrīdurgāprītikāmo vā) yathopakalpitopaharaiḥ devīpurāṇokta vidhinā saptamī vihita rambhādi navapatrikā snāna praveśa mṛṇmaya śrīdurgāpraveśa mahāsnāna gaṇapatyādi nānādevatā pūjāpūrvaka vārṣika śarat kālīna śrī bhagavaddurgāpūjā chchāga paśu balidāna mahāṣṭamī vihita mṛṇmaya śrīdurgāmahāsnāna gaṇapatyādi nānādevatā pūjāpūrvaka śrībhagavaddurgāpūjā chchāgapaṣu balidāna mahāṣṭamī mahānavamī sandhikāla vihita gaṇapatyādi nānādevatā pūjāpūrvaka śrī bhagavaddurgā pūjā chchāgapaśu balidāna mahānavamī vihita mṛṇmaya śrīdurgāmahāsnāna gaṇapatyādi nānādevatā pūjā chchāgapaśu balidāna pūrvaka śrī bhagavaddurgā pūjanamaham kariṣye.*[9]

The approximate translation is:

> Om Viṣṇu! Today, in the month of Āśvina, in the Kanyā (Virgo/virgin) constellation (*kanyā nakṣatra*), from the seventh to the ninth of the bright fortnight, I,________, of the ________ lineage, after allaying all obstacles, invoke peacefulness in order to obtain peacefulness and prosperity, wealth and food, sons and grandsons and an unbroken lineage, increasing numbers of friends, the destruction of my enemies, and to continue my association with endowments of honor from the overlord of the country, to obtain the results of my desires in this world and after my nonexistence in this world. (He may alternately only say "in order to procure the satisfaction of Śrī Durgā.")[10] What has been gathered by me following the tradition of the *Devī Purāṇa*, I shall follow all the rituals prescribed there. I shall perform the

> worship of Revered Goddess Durgā, as follows: on the seventh day, the installation of the *navapatrikā,* made of the Rambhā plant, and so on, getting the clay-molded Śrī Durgā to enter the temple, the great bath, and performing the rituals to Gaṇeśa and the other deities in the autumn season. After that a goat shall be offered (this is only said if an animal sacrifice will be performed). On the eighth day (*mahāṣṭamī*), the bathing of the clay-molded Śrī Durgā, the rites for Gaṇeśa, and other deities, and after that a goat sacrifice (*balidāna*) will be offered. Again at the juncture of the eighth and ninth *tithi* (*mahāṣṭamī mahānavamī sandhikāla*), Gaṇeśa and the other gods should be worshipped, and the clay image of Durgā bathed and worshipped, and a goat sacrifice offered. Again on the ninth day (*mahānavamī*) . . . (i.e., the whole process will be repeated)

Ghosha (1871:v–xv) speculates that Durgā's virginal persona is connected to the zodiacal sign of Virgo (Kanyā). The sun is positioned in Virgo at the autumnal equinox. He also notes that the constellations Leo and Centaur lie almost equidistant on opposite sides of Virgo. This heavenly triad may have inspired the myth in which the Devī (Virgo) and her lion mount (Leo) slay the demon who is half-man, half-buffalo (Centaur).

While reciting this *saṅkalpa*, the *purohita* places his right hand over the *kuśī,* which he holds in his left hand, and which has some water, rice, white flowers, sandal paste, *dūrvā* grass, and a yellow myrobalan (*harītakī*) fruit placed in it. At the critical moment, when he comes to the end of the *saṅkalpa*, on the word "*kariṣye*" he overturns the vessel on the floor to the right. This is a dramatic ritual gesture of commitment to the oath. He then sprinkles some rice while reciting the *saṅkalpa sūkta* verses from the *Ṛg Veda.*

Saṅkalpa Sūkta (Oath Hymn)

The *saṅkalpa sūkta* is a short hymn of praise (*sūkta*), which is offered up to assure the successful enactment of the oath. It is drawn from the *Ṛg Veda*, symbolically linking the entire ritual procedure (*pūjā*) to Vedic sacrificial (*yajña*) antecedents.

> *Om devo vo dravinodāḥ pūrnaṃ vivaṣṭāsicam udvā siñcadhvam upa vā pṛnadhvam ādidvo deva ohate/*
> *Om saṅkalpitārtha siddhirastu.* [RV.7.16.11a; SV.1.55a]
>
> Om! The God who gives your wealth demands a full libation poured to him. Pour ye it forth, then fill the vessel full again: then doth the God pay heed to you.[11]

The above mentioned rituals are preliminary to the celebrations of Durgā Pūjā proper, which begin on the sixth lunar day (*tithi*) of the nine lunar *tithi*s of Navarātra.[12] The two main rituals performed on the sixth (*ṣaṣṭhī)* day are *bodhana* and *adhivāsanam*. Due to a variance between the solar and lunar calendars, on certain years the sixth lunar day may not overlap satisfactorily with the sixth solar day. If the sixth *tithi* does not endure till after sunset (actually four o'clock in the evening) on the sixth solar day, *bodhana* will take place on the fifth day (*pañcamī*), and *adhivāsanam* on the sixth day.

4.2: Bodhana

Bodhana means "causing to awaken." It is commonly believed that the gods sleep for six months and are awake during the other six months, the full human year constituting a single night and day in their lives. Offerings made but once a year still reach them daily. During Āśvina Navarātra, Durgā needs to be woken up from her sleep, out of her normal awakening time. Thus, the ritual is sometimes called *akāla bodhana* (untimely awakening/awakening out of time). A myth cycle tells how prince Rāma performed a *pūjā* for Durgā to aid him in defeating the powerful and learned demon, Rāvaṇa, who had abducted Rāma's wife, Sītā. Rāma decided to wake up the Goddess in the month of Āśvina, performing her *pūjā* six months before the normal time of her worship in the spring month of Caitra. Durgā, propitiated, appeared to him and granted him victory. Most devotees with whom I spoke stated that Rāma's worship of the Devī during Āśvina was *the* precedent for such worship. However, in the *Devī Bhāgavata Purāṇa*, the sage (*ṛṣi*) Nārada tells Rāma how both semi-divine *ṛṣis* (Bṛghu, Viśvāmitra, etc.) and gods (Indra, Śiva, Nārāyaṇa, etc.) worshipped the Devī in this manner to defeat their enemies. Thus Rāma's worship must be regarded as the human precedent for this untimely awakening of the Devī.[1]

This rite of awakening is normally performed on the evening of Ṣaṣṭhī. If the *tithi* of Ṣaṣṭhī ends before four o'clock in the evening on the sixth solar day, the *bodhana* will be performed on the evening of the fifth day (*pañcamī*).

Bodhana Saṅkalpas (Oaths related to the Awakening Ritual)

This oath is not the same as the general *saṅkalpa* done previously.

> *Viṣṇurom tat sadadya, . . . , amuka gotram, . . ., vārṣika śarat kālīna śrī bhagavad durgā bodhana karmādhikāra pratibandhaka pāpāpanodana kāmaḥ om devi tvam ityādi mantrādvya japamaham kariṣye.*

> Om Viṣṇu! Today, . . . in the autumn season, during the ritual of awakening Durgā, with the desire of removal of obstacles, I shall recite two verses beginning with "*Om devi tvam*" (Om! O you lady divine).

Then immediately, with folded hands, he reads out these verses:

> *Om devi tvam prākṛtam cittam pāpākrāntam abhūnamama tanniḥ svāraya cittānme pāpam. Huṃ phaṭ ca te namaḥ!*
>
> *Om sūrya somo yamaḥ kālo mahābhūtani pañcavai, śubhāśubhāsyeha karmanoḥ navas sakṣinaḥ.*
>
> Om! O you lady divine, my heart is born of Prakṛti and full of sins. Please remove from my heart all these sins with my utterance of "Huṃ and Phaṭ."
>
> Om! The sun, the moon, the lord of death, time itself, and the five gross elements, these nine are the witnesses of deeds, which may be sinful or virtuous.

The *purohita* then looks down and to the sides with an angry glance (*krodhadṛṣṭi*), mimicking the witnesses in their action of destroying the obstacles.

He then sits quietly and taking the *kuśī* and putting *kuśa* grass, sesamum (*tila*), and flowers (*puṣpa*) in it, he makes another *saṅkalpa*. This is the same as the previous long *saṅkalpa* up to the phrase *yathopakalpitopahāraiḥ*, and it then proceeds as follows:

> *. . . devi purānoktavidhinā, bilva vṛkṣa, vāriṣika śarat kālīna, śrī bhagavad durgā pūjāṅgabhūta nānādevatā pūjā pūrvaka śrī durgāyāḥ bodhanamaham kariṣye.*
>
> . . . according to the method of the *Devī Purāṇa*, I will do the *bodhana* of Śrī Durgā into a wood-apple tree in the autumn season and perform the rituals of worship of other deities. It is one of the limbs of the *pūjā* to the glorious Goddess Durgā.

This *saṅkalpa* mentions that Durgā is to be invoked into a wood-apple (*bilva*) tree (*vṛkṣa*). This tree, also called the *bel*, has leaves in triads, resembling a trident (*triśūla*), and is sacred to Śiva. If a *bilva* tree is present close by, the ritual will take place there. If not, a branch from the *bilva* tree is removed and "planted" in an earthen pot (*ghaṭa*). Ideally, this branch should have two fruit on it of equal size, resembling and symbolizing the breasts of the Goddess. In front of this *bilva vṛkṣa*, the next set of rituals will take place.

The *purohita* now reads the *saṅkalpa sūkta,* previously given.

He then begins the installation of a jar (*ghaṭa*) in front of the *bilva* tree. Just as the *bilva* tree represents the Goddess, so does the jar (*ghaṭa*), which he is about to establish.

GHAṬASTHĀPANA (INSTALLATION OF THE JAR)

The jar (*ghaṭa* or *kalaśa*) is symbolic of the Devī, who will come to reside, or more accurately, be embodied in it.[2] While the composite structure will construe her final form, it is crucial to recognize that each element in the composition of the jar (*ghaṭa*) is one of her manifest forms. In compelling ways, one can observe in the *ghaṭasthāpana* the recreation of the body cosmos of the Devī herself.

First, a low altar of soft clay is built in front of the *bilva* tree over a *yantra*. Grain will be planted in this altar, which symbolizes the Goddess as earth and soil. While votaries in some homes will have drawn a very elaborate ritual diagram (*ālpanā*), more often it is the *purohita* who will draw an eight-petaled (*aṣṭadala*) lotus to serve as the *yantra*. On occasion, the *sarvatobhadra maṇḍala* (Diagram of All Auspiciousness) may be used. Among its various functions, the *yantra* denotes the Devī as the cosmic matrix from which this particular manifestation emerges. The *purohita* utters the following Vedic *mantra* while preparing the soil altar.

> *Om bhūrasi bhūmirasi aditirasi viśvadhāya viśvasya bhuvanasya dhartrī pṛthivī yaccha pṛthivīṃ dṛṇha pṛthivīm mān himsī.* [YV 13.18]
>
> Om! Thou art the earth, the ground, thou art the all-sustaining Aditi, she who supported the world. Control the earth, steady the earth, so the earth causes no injury.[3]

The symbolism of the clay altar is further expanded in this liturgical verse. The Earth goddess (Bhū Devī) and the goddess who supports the world (Jagaddhatrī) are symbolically linked. So is Aditi, the Vedic goddess who is often portrayed as the mother of the eight Ādityas, gods, of whom one is the Sun. Aditi is sometimes considered to be the mother or daughter of Dakṣa and either the wife or mother of Viṣṇu. In its broadest sense Aditi is the expansive heavens, thought to be the supporter of the earth. In this latter meaning, the altar also symbolizes the vast manifest cosmos of space and time in which the earth resides.

The *purohita* next sprinkles five grains (*dhānyamasi*) on the altar: paddy, wheat, barley, sesamum, and mustard. These grains will sprout within a few days and serve as an oracle to divine the quality of crops from the upcoming seasonal planting. The grains themselves represent the Goddess as germinal (*garbha*) forms of the expected harvest. He utters:

> *Om dhinuhi devān dhinuhi yajñam/*
> *dhinuhi yajña patim dhinuhi mām yajañyam.* [VS 1.20; ŚB 1.2.1.18]]
>
> Om! Nourish the gods, nourish the oblation,
> Nourish the lords of the oblation, nourish me the sacrificer also.[4]

The symbolism of nourishment resonates with the notions of the Goddess under her well-known epithets as Annapūrṇā (Replete with Sustenance) and Śākaṃbharī (Supporter with Vegetables). In the context of the cosmic recreation at the heart of the Durgā Pūjā ritual, the symbolism of the grain is noteworthy. Although in Śākta metaphysics all material reality is understood as possessing consciousness, the seeds sown into the clay altar add to the creation the dimension of life which is nourishing. Nourishment, then, is a vital aspect of the manifest cosmos and a crucial component of the nature of the Devī. Just as a mother gives birth to a child, whom she then feeds with her own breast milk, the Goddess begets the living creation out of her own being and then nourishes it with parts of her own body.

The jar (*ghaṭa*), particularly shaped with a wide circular mouth, narrow neck, and full round body, is placed on the altar as the *purohita* recites:

> *Om ājighra kalaśam mahyā tvā viśantvindavaḥ/*
> *punarūrjā nivarttasva sānaḥ sahasraṃ dhukṣvorudhārā payasvatī/*
> *pūnarmā viśatādṛayiḥ.* [VS 8.42a; ŚB 4.5.8.6]
>
> Om! Smell thou the vat. Let Soma drops pass into thee, O Mighty One. Return again with store of sap. Pour for us wealth in thousands with full broad streams and floods of milk. Let riches come again to me.[5]

The jar is supposed to be made of metal or clay, and represents the body of the Devī. It is the full orb of creation, or more microcosmically, the abundant earth itself. It is every container, ocean, lake, river, valley, cave, pond, tank, vessel, which holds treasures and life-nourishing elements.[6] It is the human body and particularly the female body.[7]

He next fills the jar to the neck with clean water, uttering:

> *Om varuṇasyotthambhanamasi varuṇasya skambha sarjanisthaḥ/*
> *varuṇasya ṛtasadanyasi varuṇasya ṛtasadanyasi varuṇasya ṛtasadanamasīda.*
> [VS 4.36; ŚB.3.3.4.25]
>
> Om! Thou art a prop for Varuṇa to rest on. Ye are the pins that strengthen Varuṇa's pillar. Thou art the lawful seat where Varuṇa sitteth. Sit on the lawful seat where Varuṇa sitteth.[8]

The water symbolizes all liquid elements in creation. It incorporates the symbolism of all the sacred female river goddesses, such as the Gaṅgā, Yamunā, and Sarasvatī. It is the sap of life that flows through all things.[9]

Ideally, in the next step, five jewels (*pañcaratna*) are to be placed into the water. Normally, five tiny filings of gold are sprinkled into it as a substitute. This procedure is occasionally completely omitted as the cost of staging such *pūjā*s escalates. The jewels symbolize the treasure and wealth within creation. In this manner, it recalls the goddess Śrī/Lakṣmī who is associated with material bounty and riches.

The mouth of the jar is then decorated with five leaf-bearing twigs (*pañcapallava*). These are the mango (*āmra*), banyan fig (*bhargata*), *pippala*, *aśoka*, and *yajñādumbara* (a twig commonly used in fire oblations). The number five used in the selection of grains, jewels, and leaf-bearing twigs symbolizes the diversity of creation. Most obvious is the notion of the five gross elements (*bhūta*, *tattva*), but there are numerous such collections in Hindu tradition. In an example of synecdochic substitution, many ritualists use only mango leaves instead of the prescribed variety. The leaf-bearing twigs identify the Goddess with all trees, not just the *bilva* tree into which she is invoked. The twigs and the sap that flows through them symbolize growth and fecundity in the life process. The *purohita* then utters:

> *Om dhanvanā gā dhanvanājim jayema/ tivrāḥ samado jayema/*
> *dhanuḥ śatrorapakāmam kṛṇoti dhanvanā sarvāḥ pradiśo jayema.*
> [RV.6.75.2a]
>
> Om! With Bow let us win kine, with Bow the battle, with Bow be victors in our hot encounters.
> The Bow brings grief and sorrow to the foeman: armed with the Bow may we subdue all regions.

He then places a fruit (*phala*), ideally a green coconut, on the jar. Often, a green coconut is unavailable, and a dried husked coconut is used as a substitute. Ideally, the coconut should possess the vine with which it is attached to the palm tree. This stem is regarded as a sign of the Devī's creative function (Östör 1991:193). The coconut serves as the head of the Goddess's body, which is being gradually constructed. The coconut represents the fruition of the growth initially symbolized by the twig-bearing leaves. The coconut is frequently offered to the Goddess in her temples. As such it has often been identified as a sacrificial substitute for a human or animal head. Yet, it is also evident that the coconut is a symbol of the Devī's own head, which is offered back to her. The notion of the Devī's self-decapitation is clearly illustrated in images of the Tantric goddess Chinnamastā, where streams of nourishing blood flow from the goddess's severed neck into her own mouth and into the mouths of her attendants. While placing the coconut, the *purohita* says:

> *Om yāḥ phalinī ryā aphalā apuspā yaśca puṣpinīḥ/*
> *bṛhaspatī prasūtāstā no muñcatvaṃ hasaḥ.* [RV.10.97.15]
>
> Om! Let fruitful Plants and fruitless, those that blossom, and the blossomless,
> Urged onward by Bṛhaspati, release us from our pain and grief.

Next, a vermillion (*sindūra*) diagram symbolizing the Goddess is drawn on the *ghaṭa*.[10] It resembles a stick drawing of a human being. This symbol of the Devī, which appears quite ancient, is found throughout India. It is also referred to as a *svāstika* (a symbol of well-being) or the *śrīvatsa*. There are many kinds of *svāstika*s. This Devī *svāstika* resembles a trident (*triśūla*) (or the Greek letter *psi*). It is even identified by some devotees with the *praṇava*, "Om." Vermillion, red like blood, may symbolize the ooze of sap or juice when a fruit is ripe. It is also blood, the sap of life, and the creatively potent menstrual blood of the matured female, all of which are evoked by his utterance:

> *Om sindhoriva prādhvane śūghanāso vātapramiyaḥ patayanti yahvāḥ/*
> *ghṛtasya dhārā aruṣo na vājī kaṣṭha bhindan nurmibhiḥ pinvamānaḥ.*
> [RV. 4.58.7]
>
> Om! As rushing down the rapids of a river, flow swifter than the wind the vigorous currents,
> The streams of oil in swelling fluctuation like a red courser bursting through the fences.

He then drapes a cloth (*vastra*) (often red, or red-bordered) over the coconut and the entire jar (*ghaṭa*), tying the edges snugly, so that it resembles a woman discreetly enshrouded in a *sārī*, and says:

> *Om yuvā suvāsāḥ parivīta āgāt sa u śreyān bhavati jāyamānaḥ/*
> *taṃ dhīrāsaḥ kavayaḥ unnayanti svādhyā manasā devayantaḥ.*
> [RV.3.8.4a]
>
> Om! Well-robed, enveloped he is come, the youthful: springing to life his glory waxeth greater. Contemplative in mind and God-adoring, sages of high intelligence upraise him.

He sprinkles the top of the Devī with *dūrvā* grass saying:

> *Om kāṇḍāt kāṇḍāt prarohanti paruṣaḥ paruṣaḥ pari/*
>
> *Evā no dūrve pratanu sahasreṇa śatena ca.* [VS.13.20a; ŚB.7.4.2.14; TA.10.1.7a]
>
> Om! From each stalk come forth thick joints from which emerge fine-limbed *dūrvā* grass in thousands and hundreds.[11]

And with flowers (*puṣpa*), saying:

> *Om śriśca te lakṣmiśca patnyāvahorātre pārśve nakṣatrāṇi rūpamaśivanau vyāttam/*
> *iṣṇanniṣaṇa mumma iṣāṇa sarvalokaṃ ma iṣāṇa.* [VS 31.22]

> Om! You are Śrī, you are beautiful, you are Lakṣmī's self by day, and by night, you are the stars as beautiful as the Āśvina, you are desired by us, loved by many, loved by all (Ghosha 1871:24).[12]

And with sandalwood paste (*gandha*), saying:

> *Om gandhadvārām dūrādharṣāṃ nityapuṣṭāṃ karīṣiṇīṃ/*
> *iśvarīṃ sarvabhūtānām tāmihopahvaye śriyam.* [TA.10.1]
>
> Om! I invoke the goddess Śrī, the superintending deity of all beings here in this abode which has doors of *gandha* (scent) and so on. It is impenetrable and is ever nourished and is surrounded by elephants.[13]

Sthirī Karaṇa (Giving Steadiness)

When the jar (*kalaśa*) is established, the *purohita* proceeds to the ritual of *sthirī karaṇa*, "giving steadiness to the jar." This rite firmly plants the jar in its location. It serves as a closure to the elaborate ritual of installation (*sthāpana*). To do so he recites:

> *Om sarvatīrthodbhavaṃ vāri sarvadeva samanvitam/*
> *imaṃ ghaṭam samāruhya tiṣṭha devagaṇaiḥ saha/*
> *sthāṃ sthīṃ sthiro bhava vidaṅga āśurbhava vājyarvan pṛthurbhava suṣadastvamagne purīṣavāhanaḥ.*
>
> Om! O water, you are born of water of sacred spots, being associated with all gods. Abide steadily and stay along with all gods in this jar. Be steady by the sound of *sthāṃ* and *sthīṃ*, O clever one, be swift-paced like a horse. Be bulky. You are seated on a nice seat, O fire, you are the carrier of rubbish.

Next, he recites the *Gāyatrī Mantra* one to ten times over the jar.

> *Om bhūr bhuvaḥ svaḥ tat savitur vareṇyaṃ bhargo devasya dhīmahi dhiyo yo naḥ pracodayāt. Om.*
>
> Om! Let us contemplate the wondrous spirit of the Divine Creator (Savitṛ) of the earthly, atmospheric, and celestial spheres. May he direct our minds toward the attainment of *dharma*, *artha*, *kāma*, and *mokṣa*. Om![14]

Kāṇḍā Ropaṇam (Erecting the Staffs)

Four sticks, slightly longer than the height of the *kalaśa*, and forked at the tops, are stuck in large lumps of clay and placed at four corners around

Figure 4.2.1 The Jar form of the Goddess is established atop the *sarvatobhadra maṇḍala* at the *purohita*'s home.

the jar. A red thread is then wrapped clockwise around the sticks making about seven to ten rounds from the bottom to the top (See Figure 4.2.1).The term "ropanam" means "to plant," suggestive of the method in which the *kāṇḍā*s are erected, implanted in balls of mud. I was told that the term *kāṇḍā* originally meant a length of branch between two knots. The forked tops of the *kāṇḍā*, together with the mud balls, conjure an image of young trees being propagated. When wrapped around with string, the sticks convey the image that a sacred space has been fenced or cordoned off. The jar-embodied Devī thus sits upon an earthen altar, seeded with grain, and surrounded by forked branches. While conducting this rite, the *purohita* utters:

> *Om kāṇḍāt kāṇḍāt prarohanti paruṣaḥ paruṣaḥ pari/*
> *evā no dūrve pratanuḥ sahasreṇa śatenaca.* [VS.13.20a; ŚB.7.4.2.14; TA.10.1.7a]
>
> Om! From each stalk come forth thick joints from which emerge fine-limbed *dūrvā* grass in thousands and hundreds.[15]

Tantric Method of *Ghaṭasthāpana*

Clearly, the aforementioned procedure of establishing the jar is both lengthy and complicated. The *purohita* may run the risk of making errors in the recitation of the Vedic *mantra*s or may run out of time. He may therefore opt for the Tantric method of *ghaṭasthāpana*, which is far simpler. Lengthy *mantra*s are replaced by seed syllables (*bīja*), which are said to encompass the potency and meaning of the expanded forms.

In the Tantric method, the *purohita* purifies the jar by uttering "*Klīṃ*," and then "*Aiṃ*." Placing the jar on the earth altar he utters "*Hrīṃ*" and fills it with water while uttering the *mantra* "*Hrīṃ*."[16] Then the *purohita* utters the *mantra*:

> *Om gaṅgādyāh saritaḥ sarvāḥ sarāṃsi jaladā nadāh/*
> *hradāḥ prasravanāḥ puṇyāḥ svarga pātāla bhūgatāḥ/*
> *sarva tirthānī puṇyāni ghaṭe kurvantu sannidhim.*
>
> Om! All rivers beginning with the Gaṅgā and all mighty water-givers, holy fountains, abiding in the heavens, netherworld or earth, all these auspicious and meritorious *tīrtha*s should abide in this jar.

When placing the leaf-bearing twigs on the jar, he utters "*Śrīṃ*." Uttering "*Huṃ*," he places the coconut on top of the *kalaśa*. To steady the *kalaśa*, he utters "*Strīṃ*." Anointing it with vermillion, he utters "*Raṃ*." Placing the flowers, he utters "*Yaṃ*." When placing the *dūrvā* grass, he utters the seed (*bīja*) syllable of Durgā, "*Duṃ*." Sprinkling the jar with water, he says "*Om*," and striking it with *kuśa* grass, he utters the *mantra*, "*Huṃ phaṭ svāhā*."

SĀMĀNYĀRGHA (COMMON OFFERING)

After establishing the jar (*ghaṭasthāpana*), the *purohita* proceeds to the common sacred offering (*sāmānyārgha*). Dipping his finger in water, he draws under the *kośā* a small downward pointing triangle, symbolic of the female generative organ (*yoni*),in which he writes the seed syllable (*bīja*) of Durgā, "*Duṃ*." He encircles the triangle with a circle (*maṇḍala*), and the circle is surrounded with a square (*bhūpura*). He has, in essence, created a *yantra*. Then some rice is taken from the plate of worship materials on his right-hand side. He scatters it on the *yantra*, saying:

Om ādhara śaktaye namaḥ/	Salutations to the Supporting Power
Om kūrmāya namaḥ/	Salutations to the Tortoise
Om anantāya namaḥ/	Salutations to the Endless Serpent
Om pṛthivyai namaḥ/	Salutations to the Earth.

All these references are to entities that support or bear the cosmos. Here again the *yantra* represents the cosmic matrix which is the Goddess. The scattered rice grains represent the coming into manifestation of the all-encompassing energy fundament, the mythic cosmic supports (i.e., tortoise and serpent), and the earth itself. The tortoise and cosmic serpent, often identified with Viṣṇu as one of his incarnations and the couch on which he reclines, respectively, are here identified with the Goddess.

He then washes the container (*argha pātra*) that will be used for the sacred offering, while uttering "*Phaṭ*."In the *argha* rituals that form part of the common preliminary duties (*sāmānya vidhi*), the smaller copper *kuśī* was used as the worship vessel. Here it is the larger *kośā* which is used. Both vessels resemble the female genitals, the vulva (*yoni*). He fills it with water, uttering "Om/Aum." Worshipping the water in the vessel, he utters:

Aṃ sūrya maṇḍalāya dvādaśa kalātmane namaḥ/
Uṃ soma maṇḍalāya soḍaśa kalātmane namaḥ/
Maṃ vahni maṇḍalāya daśa kalātmane namaḥ.

Aṃ! Salutations to the disc of the sun consisting of twelve divisional elements.
Uṃ! Salutations to the disc of the moon consisting of sixteen divisional elements.
Maṃ! Salutations to the disc of fire consisting of ten subtle elements (digits).

The *praṇava* or *omkāra*, "Aum," or "Om" is composed of the letters "A," "U," and "M," corresponding to the sun, the moon, and fire respectively. The essence of the *praṇava* is the Devī. The *argha* is often connected with sun worship, but here the sun, moon, and fire are linked, along with their constituent parts, and identified with the Devī.

At the head of the *kośā*, the *purohita* places *dūrvā* grass, flowers, and sandal paste. Then he stirs it well with his middle finger. The head of the *kośā*, which resembles the *yoni*, corresponds to the upper part of the vulva. *Dūrvā*, a hardy green grass, is common nutrition for grazing animals, such as cows, buffaloes, and goats. Its symbolic meaning again resonates with the nourishing aspects of the Goddess as Annapūrṇā or Śākambharī. It is also thought of as the hair on the goddess Earth (*pṛthivī*). The flower (often a red hibiscus, possessing four large red petals and prominent pistil) elicits identification with the labia and clitoris of the female genital organs. Both flower and sandalwood paste convey the sensory element of scent. He then performs the *mudrā*s of the goad (*aṅkuśa*), the cow (*dhenu*), and the fish (*matsya*) uttering:

> *Om gaṅge ca yamune ca godāvarī sarasvatī narmade sindhu kaverī jalesmin sannidhiṃ kuru.*
>
> Om! May the Gaṅgā, Yamunā, Godāvarī, Sarasvatī, Narmadā, Sindhu, and Kāverī come into this water's proximity.

When the induced flow and sanctification of the waters are complete, placing his hand over the *kośā* (also called the offering vessel, *argha pātra*), the *purohita* silently repeats "Om" ten times. He then sprinkles the consecrated water with a little *kuśa* grass over his own body, the worship materials, and the images (*mūrti*).

Bhūtāpasāraṇa (Removal of Inimical Spirits)

The *purohita* now takes either white mustard or rice, and uttering the following *mantra,* scatters the grain in various directions.

> *Om apasarpantu te bhūtāḥ ye bhūtaḥ bhuvisaṃsthitāḥ/*
> *ye bhūtāḥ vighna kartāraste naśyantu śivājñayā.*
>
> Om! May those ghosts be gone who are abiding in this earth, and those ghosts who are the makers of obstacles, by the command of Śiva, disappear.

He then draws a triangle (*trikoṇa*) with cow dung on the left-hand side of his seat and worships it with flowers and sandal paste while uttering the *mantra*:

Om ete gandha puṣpe/ om kṣetrapāladiḥ bhūtaganebhyoḥ namaḥ.

Om! These flowers and fragrances are offered with homage to the group of protectors of the field and the host of elemental spirits.

Placing some *māṣa* (pulse with its husk), curd, and turmeric (*haridrā*) powder in a wood-apple (*bilva*) leaf plate, the *purohita* mixes them together. Taking a small quantity of the mixture, he addresses it, purifying the offering:

Om eṣaḥ māṣabhaktabalaye namaḥ.

Om! Salutations to this sacrificial offering of a portion of pulse.

He then offers the mixture on the *bilva* plate (*pātra*) to the spirits, saying:

Om eṣaḥ māṣa bhakta baliḥ/ Om kṣetrapālādiḥ bhūtagaṇebyoḥ namaḥ.

Om! This sacrificial offering of a portion of pulse is offered with homage to the group of protectors of the field and the host of elemental spirits.

With folded hands, the *purohita* next prays:

Om bhūta preta piśācaścas dānavāh rākṣasāśca ye śāntim kurvantu te sarve imaṃ gṛhantu mad balim.

Om! The elemental spirits, departed souls, goblins, demons, and fiends should create an atmosphere of peace and receive this offering of mine.

And taking white mustard seed in his hand, he scatters it around the offering, saying:

Om vetālāśca piśācaśca rākṣasāśca sarīsṛpaḥ apasarpantu te sarve narasiṅghena tāḍitāḥ.

Om! May all of you vampires, goblins, fiends, and crawling entities be driven away by Narasiṅgha.

The inimical spirits include the guardians of the field. Through the offerings, they are both appeased and driven away. Śiva and Viṣṇu (in his fierce incarnation as the man-lion *avatāra*) are invoked to command away the malevolent beings.

Prāṇāyāma (Control of the Vital Energy)

After driving away the inimical spirits, the *purohita* performs the yogic control (*ayāma*: expansion and restraint) of the vital energy (*prāṇa*) in breath.

A single *prāṇāyāma* cycle consists of inhalation through one nostril (the other is kept shut with the thumb), retention of the breath (both nostrils are now closed with the thumb and index or ring finger), and exhalation through the other nostril. Then inhalation through the same nostril through which exhalation took place, retention, and exhalation through the other nostril. Once again inhalation, retention, and exhalation. Thus a single cycle, for example, is: in(r)-hold-out(l), in(l)-hold-out(r), and in(r)-hold-out(l). At a minimum, the inhalation may be done to a count of four, retention for a count of sixteen, and exhalation for a count of eight. Based on the expertise and desire of the *purohita*, the count may be altered in complex and lengthier ways. Three *prāṇāyāma* cycles are performed, and the seed syllables Hrīṃ, Klīṃ, Duṃ, or Om are uttered during the yogic activity (See Figure 3.1).

Bhūta Śuddhi (Purification of the Elements)

The *purohita* is now ready to embark upon the purification of the gross material elements of the body (*bhūtaśuddhi*).[17] The body is understood to be composed of five basic elements (*pañcamahābhūta*): earth, water, fire, air, and ether. These *bhūta*s are themselves composed of vibrational clusters expressed by certain seed syllables (*bīja*). Thus: Earth (*pṛthvī*) is made of the syllable *Laṃ*, Water (*jala*) of *Vaṃ*, Fire (*agni*) of *Raṃ*, Air (*vāyu*) of *Yaṃ*, and Ether (*ākāśa*) of *Haṃ*. Furthermore, these five *bhūta*s are connected with five of the body's energy vortices (*cakra*). Thus: *Mūlādhāra* is associated with *pṛthvī*, *Svādhiṣṭhana* with *jala*, *Manipura* with *agni*, *Anāhata* with *vāyu*, and *Viśuddhi* with *ākāśa*.

The *purohita* sits cross-legged, perhaps in the full-lotus posture (*padmāsana*), and taking water in the palm of his right hand, encircles his entire body conceiving it to be a wall of fire. He then places his right palm over the left on his lap. Uttering the *mantra*, "*So'ham* (I am this)," he conceptually and emotionally leads the limited self (*jīvātman*), which is said to abide in the center of the heart like the flame of a lamp (visualized as a bud of a flower), to the thousand-petalled lotus (*sahasrāra*) approximately located at the top of the head. He does this by arousing the coiled, serpentine energy (*kuṇḍalinī*) that abides in the *mūlādhāra cakra*. He allows the *kuṇḍalinī* to snake upwards along the central energy channel (*suṣumnā*). On its journey, the awakened *kuṇḍalinī* traverses the lower energy *cakra*s until it reaches the heart *cakra* (*anāhata*), from where the limited self (*jīvātman* or *jīvaśiva*) is carried up by her (*Kuṇḍalinī* is personified as a goddess) to the *sahasrāra*. The thousand-petalled lotus is conceived of as facing downwards, symbolizing in one conception the varied and manifold creation descending from the single supreme unmanifest reality. The limited self (*jīvātman*) is made to unite with that supreme Brahman (*parātman*) in the pericarp of that lotus.

During the raising of *kuṇḍalinī,* the *purohita* conceives that the (1) earth has been dissolved in water, (2) water in fire, (3) fire in air, (4) air in ether, (5) ether in sound, (6) sound in form, (7) form in taste, (8) taste in touch, (9) touch in smell, (10) smell goes to rest in the nose, (11) the nose goes to rest in the tongue, (12) the tongue goes to rest in the eye, (13) the eye goes to rest in the skin, (14) the skin goes to rest in the ear, (15) the ear goes to rest in (16) the mouth (organ of speech), which in turn dissolves into (17) the hands, (18) the feet, (19) the arms, (20) the generative organ, all of which rest in (21) matter or the sentient, primordial energy (*prakṛti*), then (22) mind (*manas*), (23) ego (*ahaṅkāra*), and (24) intellect (*buddhi*). The subtle essence of each of these twenty-four elements or states (*tattva*) are to be conceived as dissolved into the latter and finally into the supreme reality (*parātman, parabrahman*). This supreme reality may also be envisioned as the union of the goddess Kuṇḍalinī with the supreme Śiva (*paramaśiva*) or is thought of nondualistically as the Primal Power (*adiśakti*). This act is a deep and profound meditation, which is executed according to the capacity and yogic attainment of the *purohita*, who next proceeds to perform another *prāṇāyāma* as part of the *bhūta śuddhi* ritual.

Taking the seed syllable (*bīja*) "*Yaṃ,*" he exhales air from the left nostril thinking it to be smoky colored. He does similarly with exhalations from the right nostril with the same *bīja*, repeating the *prāṇāyāma* sixteen times. Next, taking the *bīja*, "*Raṃ*," he inhales it with the color red through the right nostril to a count of four. Holding the *bīja* "*Raṃ*" with the breath, he visualizes a sinful person (*pāpapuruṣa*) residing in his body. This *pāpapuruṣa* is generally visualized on the left side of the belly. Then he vividly imagines the *pāpapuruṣa* burned by the *bīja* "*Raṃ*," while the breath is held.[18] Upon exhalation to a count of eight, he visualizes the ashes of the destroyed sinful being ejected from the left nostril. Then, inhaling in from the left nostril, he manifests a white colored *bīja* of the moon, "*Yaṃ*." This moon he visualizes on his forehead (in the place of the third eye). He manifests the *bīja*, "*Vaṃ*" during the breath retention and "*Laṃ*" to steady his body.

This process is said to recompose the body. Originally made up of gross and subtle elements, the body is constituted of pure nectar as the goddess Kuṇḍalinī rises and unites with the supreme Śiva in the *sahasrāra*. This pure nectar then rains back down on the purified body like the discharge of sexual fluid from their union. When it reaches back down to the level of the lowest *cakra* (i.e., *mūlādhāra* or *pṛthivī*), it becomes solidified. The body is then regarded as immaculate and composed of adamantine substance.

Abbreviated Version of *Bhūta Śuddhi*

The *purohita* conceptually builds a wall of fire around himself as described above. He then proceeds to perform *prāṇāyāma*. During the period of breath retention, when both nostrils are held, he utters these four *mantras*:

> *Om mūla śṛṅgāṭā chiraḥ suṣumnā pathena jīvaśivam paramaśivapade yojayāmi svāhā.*
>
> Om! I unite the limited self (*jīvaśiva*) to the realm of the Supreme Self (*paramaśiva*) from the head of the basic triangle through the channel of *suṣumnā* with the utterance of *svāhā*.
>
> *Om yaṃ liṅgaśarīram śoṣaya śoṣaya svāhā.*
>
> Om! May the subtle body be burned up with the utterance of *yaṃ* and *svāhā*.
>
> *Om raṃ saṅkośā śarīram dāha dāha svāhā.*
>
> Om! May the limited body be burnt up with the utterance of *raṃ* and *svāhā*.
>
> *Om paramaśiva suṣumnā pathena mūla śṛṅgataṃ ullāsollasat ullasat jvala jvala prajvala prajvala haṃ saḥ so 'ham svāhā.*
>
> Om! Let Paramaśiva through the channel of *suṣumnā* make the base triangle radiate and radiate, get it inflamed, properly inflamed with the syllables *haṃ saḥ* to become reversed and take the form *so' ham* (I am that).

Every human being is thought to constantly utter "*so*" with the inhalation and "*ham*" with the exhalation, thus uttering "*so 'ham*" throughout life. When the "s" and the "h" vanish, all that remains is the sound "*aum/om*." This is said to occur naturally in fully realized beings, who have moved from the pulsating dualism of inhalation (life) and exhalation (death), to the state of singular vibration (*aum/om*), which transcends life and death.

These *mantras* are concerned with uniting the limited self (*jīvaśiva*) with the supreme self (*paramaśiva*) through the *suṣumnā,* which connects the *prāṇa* channels of the base and the head. They deal with the drying and burning of the subtle body and its sheaths (*kośā*). While uttering these *mantra*s, he should meditatively visualize the transformation of his body.

Nyāsa (Imprintments)

The *purohita* next moves to a series of rites in which various elements are imprinted (*nyāsa*) upon parts of his purified body.

Mātṛkā Nyāsa (Imprintment with the Alphabet)

The *purohita* begins with the ritual imprintment (*nyāsa*) of the Sanskrit alphabet (*mātṛkā*) upon his transformed body. There is a conceptual pun taking place here. The term *mātṛkā* means both alphabetic symbols, and mother. Consonants cannot be uttered without the aid of vowels. Thus when consonants combine with vowels, they are fertile mothers of sound vibration. In this process various charged syllables (*varṇa mayī*) are placed in different limbs of the gross body thus transforming it into a body composed of charged sound vibrations (*varṇa mayī tanu*).

One of the Goddess's manifestations is as Vāc, sound or speech vibration. Actually, *vāc* should be understood more comprehensively as the essential vibration of every conceptualization (thus every manifestation), which can be recognized through linguistic labels and thus uttered (*śabda*). By imprinting his immaculate body (transformed through *bhūtaśuddhi*) with the complete primary syllabary (i.e., it omits most conjunct consonants) of the Sanskrit language, the *purohita* transforms it into the vibrational body of the Goddess.

He begins by saying:

> *Asya mātṛkā mantrasya brahmaṛṣīḥ gāyatrīcchando mātṛkā sarasvatī devatā halo bījāni svarāḥ śaktayaḥ mātṛkā nyāse viniyogaḥ.*

This is a general statement of the presiding sage (*ṛṣi*), meter (*chandas*), deity (*devatā*), and application (*viniyoga*) of the procedure and is explained in his following utterances. The application (*viniyoga*) or purpose of the procedure is to perform the imprintment of syllables. The term "*hala*" refers to all the consonants, which are said to be seeds (*bīja*). The vowels are called *svara* and are said to be energy (*śakti*). The Tantric symbolism of Śiva-Śakti is apparent in this identification. The consonant (Śiva) is lifeless (*śava*) when separated from a vowel (Śakti). When combined with vowels (Śakti), consonants (Śiva) gain potency. Based on his comments that follow, one might also suggest that a Brahmā-Sarasvatī (the male and female cocreators) union is occurring, producing creative potential. An alternate interpretation, also suggested by Pandit Chakravarty (but not supported by these *mantras*), sees the collection of consonants as the generative source (*yoni*) and the vowels as the fertilizing seed.

Taking a flower from the right side and touching the top of his head with it, the *purohita* says:

Om brahmaṇe ṛṣaye namaḥ.	Om! Salutations to the sage Brahmā.

Touching his mouth, he says:

Om gāyatryai cchandase namaḥ. Om! Salutations to the meter Gāyatrī.

Touching his heart, he says:

Om mātṛkayai sarasvatyai devatāyai namaḥ.

Om! Salutations to the goddess mother Sarasvatī.

Touching himself at the lower back just above the region of the anus, he says:

Om halbhyoḥ bījebhyoḥ namaḥ. Om! Salutations to the seed consonants.

Touching the sides of his thighs and sweeping down to his ankles, he says:

Om svarebhyoḥ śaktibhyoḥ namaḥ. Om! Salutations to the energy vowels.

Then passing his hands over his whole body, palms facing forward he says:

Om klīṃ kīlakāya namaḥ. Om! Salutations to the bolt. *Klīṃ*!

This magical formula "*Klīṃ*" unleashes or unlocks the power of the *mantra*s, which have been fixed with a bolt/pin/nail (*kīlaka*) ("like a door shut with a bar," I was told). The notion of such a fastening pin is not uncommon in Tantric and Śākta ritual practices. An important appendage (*aṅga*) to the *Durgā Saptaśatī* called the *kīlaka* is recited just before the text itself. Normally the *kīlaka* is thought to release the power contained in the *mantra*s. In the context of the *nyāsa* ritual, where syllables are being imprinted on the body, the *kīlaka* is both releasing the power of these vibrations and fastening them onto the *purohita*'s body.

Kara Nyāsa (Imprintment on the Hands)

The *purohita* proceeds with the ritual placement of syllables in the fingers of the hand (*kara nyāsa*). He recites the following *mantra*s:

Om aṃ kaṃ khaṃ gaṃ ghaṃ ṅaṃ āṃ aṅguṣṭhabhyām namaḥ.
Om iṃ caṃ chaṃ jaṃ jhaṃ ñaṃ īṃ tarjanībhyām svāhā.
Om uṃ ṭaṃ ṭhaṃ ḍaṃ ḍhaṃ ṇaṃ ūṃ madhyāmabhyām vaṣat.
Om eṃ taṃ thaṃ daṃ dhaṃ naṃ aiṃ anāmikābhyām huṃ.
Om oṃ paṃ phaṃ baṃ bhaṃ muṃ auṃ kaniṣṭhābhyām vauṣat.
Om aṃ yaṃ raṃ laṃ vaṃ śaṃ ṣaṃ saṃ haṃ kṣaṃ aḥ karatala pṛṣṭhābhyām astrāya phaṭ.[19]

Aṅga Nyāsa (Imprintment of the Limbs)

The *purohita* proceeds to place the syllables in the limbs (*aṅga*) of his body. He uses the same combination of syllables but ends the *mantras* thus, while pointing to the appropriate body part.

> Pointing to the heart with the palm of the hand: . . . *hṛdayāya namaḥ.*
> Pointing to the head with the fingertips of the hand: . . . *śirase svāhā.*
> Pointing to the topknot with the tip of the thumb: . . . *śikhāyai vaṣaṭ.*
> With both hands embracing the body: . . . *kavacāya huṃ.*[20]
> With three fingers indicating the three eyes (middle finger pointing to the third eye): . . . *netratrayāya vauṣaṭ.*
> Moving his hands around each other and slapping the palm of the left hand briskly with the index and middle finger of the right hand, he says: . . . *karatala pṛṣṭābhyām astrāya phaṭ.*

The choice of limbs reflects the divine status of the *purohita*'s body. While the heart, head, topknot, divine armor (*kavaca*), and third eye are readily linked with the divine, the inclusion of the hands is interesting. The hands, it will be noted, were first imprinted with the syllables in *kara nyāsa* before these were transferred to the limbs. The hands (and body) could be seen to represent devotional service and action (*karma*), while heart and head (*manas*) symbolize feeling and loving devotion (*bhakti*), and the head and third eye correspond to intellect, knowledge (*jñāna*), and wisdom.

The *purohita* begins to imprint the syllables on the inner parts of his body. He begins at the energy vortex of sound and speech vibration (*viśuddhi cakra*), located at the base of the throat (*kaṇṭha mūla*). Visualizing a sixteen-petalled lotus there, he places all the fourteen vowels, *anusvara,* and *visarga* in the following manner. Sandwiching each between "Om" and "namaḥ," he proceeds saying:

> *Om aṃ namaḥ, om āṃ namaḥ, om iṃ namaḥ, om īṃ namaḥ, om uṃ namaḥ, om ūṃ namaḥ, om ṛṃ namaḥ, om ṝṃ namaḥ, om ḷṃ namaḥ, om ḹm namaḥ, om eṃ namaḥ, om aiṃ namaḥ, om oṃ namaḥ, om auṃ namaḥ, om aṃ namaḥ, om aḥ namaḥ*

Next at the energy plexus of the primal sound (*nāda*), *anāhata cakra*, the seat of the limited self (*jīvātman*) located in the region of the heart, he visualizes a twelve-petalled lotus. There he imprints the first twelve consonants, saying:

> *Om kaṃ namaḥ, om khaṃ namaḥ, om gaṃ namaḥ, om ghaṃ namaḥ, om ṅaṃ namaḥ, om caṃ namaḥ, om chaṃ namaḥ, om jaṃ namaḥ, om jhaṃ namaḥ, om ñaṃ namaḥ, om ṭaṃ namaḥ, om ṭhaṃ namaḥ.*

In the region of the navel, at the *maṇipūra cakra*, he visualizes a ten-petalled lotus and places the next ten consonants:

> *Om ḍaṃ namaḥ, om ḍhaṃ namaḥ, om ṇaṃ namaḥ, om taṃ namaḥ, om thaṃ namaḥ, om daṃ namaḥ, om dhaṃ namaḥ, om naṃ namaḥ, om paṃ namaḥ, om phaṃ namaḥ.*

In the region of the base of the male sexual organ, at the *svadhiṣṭhāna cakra*, he visualizes a six-petalled lotus, and places the next six consonants and semivowels:

> *Om baṃ namaḥ, om bhaṃ namaḥ, om maṃ namaḥ, om yaṃ namaḥ, om raṃ namaḥ, om laṃ namaḥ.*

At the base plexus (*mūlādhāra cakra*), the seat of the serpent energy (*kuṇḍalinī*), located in the region of the perineum between the genitals and the anus, he visualizes a four-petalled lotus and imprints the last semivowel and sibilants:

> *Om vaṃ namaḥ, om śaṃ namaḥ, om ṣaṃ namaḥ, om saṃ namaḥ.*

Then moving to the energy plexus at the region of the third eye at the joining point of the eyebrows, the seat of mind, the *ājñā cakra*, he visualizes a two-petalled lotus. There he places the aspirate syllable and the conjunct consonant.

> *Om haṃ namaḥ, om kṣaṃ namaḥ.*

Bahir/Bahya Mātṛkā Nyāsa (External Imprintment of Syllables)

Having completed this internal *nyāsa* through meditative visualization and *mantra*, the *purohita* proceeds to perform an external placement of syllables, with the aid of physical action. He begins with a meditative visualization and manifestation (*dhyāna*) of *mātṛkā*s thus:

> *Pañcāśallipibhir vibhakta mukha doḥ panamadhya vakṣasthalām/*
> *bhāsvan mauli nivaddha candraśakalām āpīna tuṅgastanīm/*
> *mudrām akṣa guṇam sudhāḍhya kalasam vidyāñca hastambujair vivhrāṇam*
> *viśada prabhām trinayanām vagdevatam āśraye.*

> I am taking recourse in the divinity of speech, who has her body made of fifty syllables differentiated, that have taken part in constituting the limbs of the deity like the face, the two arms, the middle portion, etc. She has decorated her head with the disc of the moon, and she has well-formed, large

breasts. In one of her hands she has taken a *mālā* of *rudrākṣa* [beads] and the *mudrā* (here the *purohita* assumes the *vaikhānasa mudrā,* where his index finger touches the thumb), and a jar and a replica of a book are held with her lotus hands. She is luminous, with three eyes, emanating clear light.

Then touching his forehead, he proceeds with the *nyāsa.*

Saṃhāra Mātṛkā Nyāsa (Enfolding/Compressing Imprintment of Syllables)

The *purohita* follows the same procedure as the external *mātṛkā nyāsa* but in reverse. Through this process he enfolds the vibrational body of the Goddess into his own.

Pīṭha Nyāsa (Imprintment of Seats)

The *purohita* now assigns the various seats or abodes (*pīṭha*) of the Goddess to appropriate body parts. The term, *pīṭha* (altar or seat), is commonly associated with the legend of the goddess Satī, the parts of whose body are scattered over the Indian subcontinent. The location of each of her body parts is a *pīṭha* of the Goddess, the most important one situated at Kāmarūpā where Satī's sexual organ (*yoni*) fell. D. C. Sircar (1973) notes the relationship between the *pīṭha* and the sexual organ of the Devī (symbolically akin to the *liṅga* of Śiva). Thus the *pīṭha* is conceptually the sexual organ (*yoni, bhāga*) of the Devī, from where all creation emerges. In her role as giver of spiritual attainments (e.g., as Siddhidātrī, one of the Nine Durgās of the *Devī Kavaca*), those seats of the Devī where *yogin*s are reputed to have attained perfection (*siddhi*) are called *siddha pīṭha*s. The Durgā Kuṇḍ temple in Banāras, for instance, is regarded as such a *siddha pīṭha*, and a stone lotus icon on its rear wall, which is reverentially touched by devotees as their most intimate contact point with the Devī, is also called the Devī *pīṭha*.

The *pīṭha nyāsa* will again be repeated during the special offering (*viśeṣa argha*) rite later in the Durgā Pūjā. The current set of *nyāsa*s, it should be remembered, although within the *bodhana* rituals, are fundamentally part of the general preliminary practices (*sāmānya vidhi*) prior to the actual awakening rite. During *viśeṣa argha* the *nyāsa* will be performed on a conch shell, which represents a *pīṭha* of the Goddess.

Touching his heart, the *purohita* says:

Om ādhara śaktaye namaḥ. Om kūrmāya namaḥ. Om anantāya namaḥ. Om pṛthivyai namaḥ. Om kṣīra samudrāya namaḥ. Om śvetadvīpāya namaḥ.

> *Om maṇimaṇḍapāya namaḥ. Om kalpavṛkṣāya namaḥ. Om maṇivedikāya namaḥ. Om ratnasiṃhāsanāya namaḥ.*
>
> Om! Salutations to the supreme supporting power, the tortoise, the endless serpent, the earth, the sea of milk, the white island, the jewelled pavilion, the wish-fulfilling tree, the jewelled altar, the jewelled throne.

The *pīṭha*s referred to here are not the commonly understood sacred places of the Goddess as enumerated in the *Pīṭhanirnaya* or certain Purāṇic texts. They are far more encompassing cosmic and divine entities. The term for "throne," *siṃhāsana*, literally means "lion seat" and informs our understanding of Durgā's mount (*vāhana*), the great lion, which is a symbol of her cosmic sovereignty. While reciting these *mantra*s, the *purohita* tries to visualize each of the abodes. He creatively visualizes the base, *ādhāraśakti*; next, the tortoise; then *ananta*, the great serpent upon whose hood the earth is supported. This is surrounded by the ocean of milk, within which sits the white island, upon which there is the jewelled pavilion, and so on.

Touching his right shoulder, he says: *Om dharmāya namaḥ*. For his left shoulder: *Om jñānāya namaḥ*. For his right thigh: *Om vairāgyāya namaḥ*. For his left thigh: *Om aiśvaryāya namaḥ*. For his mouth (opening of face): *Om adharmāya namaḥ*. For his left flank: *Om ajñānāya namaḥ*. For his navel: *Om avairagyāya namaḥ*. For his right flank: *Om anaiśvaryāya namaḥ*. And for his heart: *Om anantāya namaḥ* or *Om padmāya namaḥ*. These respectively mean:

> Om! Salutations to righteousness, knowledge, dispassion, royal power, wickedness, ignorance, passion, base weakness, the endless serpent, the lotus.

The Devī's ambivalent nature is clearly indicated in these abodes. Although it is commonly recognized that the Devī may be both benevolent and malevolent, it is evident here that her nature is trivalent. She encompasses the three qualities embodied in the Hindu metaphysical scheme of the *guṇa*s.

The *purohita* then says:

> *Aṃ arkamaṇḍalāya dvādaśa kalātmane namaḥ.*
> *Uṃ somamaṇḍalāya ṣodaśa kalātmane namaḥ.*
> *Maṃ vahnimaṇḍalāya daśa kalātmane namaḥ.*

In Indian philosophical categories, *arka* (sun) represents the *pramāṇa* aspect of reality (the instrument of knowledge), *soma* (moon) is the *prameya* aspect (the thing that is known, the knowable), and *vahni* (fire) is the *pramā* aspect (the knowing subject). All three are fused in the person of the *purohita*. Through the *pīṭha nyāsa*, the *purohita*'s body is itself transformed into a seat of the Devī.

Kara and *Aṅga Nyāsa*

The *purohita* repeats the imprintment on the hand and limbs.

Ṛṣyadi Nyāsa (Imprintment of the Revealer and Others)

He utters:

Śirasi brahmaṇe ṛṣāye namaḥ. Mukhe gāyatryai cchandase namaḥ. Hṛdāya durgāyai devatāyai namaḥ.
Guhye duṃ bījāya namaḥ. Pādayoḥ duṃ śaktaye namaḥ. Sarvaṅgeṣu klīṃ kīlakāya namaḥ.

Salutations to the revealer Brahmā in the head, to the meter Gāyatrī in the mouth, to the goddess Durgā in the heart, to the seed syllable Duṃ in the anus (literally, the hidden part, also understood as the *mūlādhāra*), to the śakti Duṃ in the two feet, and to the fastening pin Klīṃ in the entire body.

Vyāpaka Nyāsa (Pervasive Imprintment)

The *purohita* makes a general movement of his hands down the front of his body and back up over the head. He repeats it perhaps seven or nine times.

The *purohita* has finally completed the various *nyāsas* in this portion of the ritual. His body is not only transformed into pure substance through *bhūtaśuddhi*, but effectively imprinted with the vibrational capacity to bring about manifestation. It is also now a *pīṭha*, a creative abode and source of the Goddess.

Prāṇāyāma

He once again performs *prāṇāyāma*, this time with the *bīja* "Hrīṃ." This completes the *bodhana* rituals prior to actually awakening the Devī.

Gaṇeśa Pūjā

Now that the preliminaries have been finished, the *purohita* moves to the awakening (*bodhana*) of the Goddess. He starts with a *pūjā* to Gaṇeśa, who among all the deities must be propitiated first. The primacy in ritual worship afforded to Gaṇeśa is attributed to his role as a guardian deity and as the "Lord of Obstacles." His icon is often found on the portals of temples and recalls the mythic event in which he tried to prevent Śiva from entering Pārvatī's chambers. Taking a flower from the flower plate, the *purohita* performs the meditative visualization (*dhyāna*) of Gaṇeśa. I use the term "meditative visualization" to acknowledge the common translation of *dhyāna* (meditation). The *dhyāna*s performed during *pūjā* are perhaps better translated as creative visualizations, since they actually generate the matrices for the manifestation of the deities.

> *Om kharvam sthūlatanum gajendra vadnām lambodaram sundaram/*
> *praṣyandam madhugandha lubdha madhūpa/*
> *vyalola gaṇḍasthalam danta ghaṭa vidāritārirudhiraiḥ sindūra śobhākaram/*
> *vande śailasutāsutam gaṇapatim siddhipradam karmasu.*
>
> Om! I pay obeisance to the son of Pārvatī, the daughter of Himālaya. He is considered to be the lord of hosts [attending deities of Śiva]. In stature he is short; his body is robustly built. His face is that of an excellent elephant. He is a pot-bellied person, yet beautiful. His two cheeks are full of bees attracted by the scent of the ichor that oozes from them. He is beautiful because of being smeared with vermillion throughout his body and also with the flow of blood of the enemies who have been killed by the blow of his tusk. I pay obeisance to that god who is the giver of success in every effort.

This is the most commonly used *dhyāna* for Gaṇeśa. It identifies Gaṇeśa as Pārvatī's son (*śailasutāsutam*). It reinforces the identification between vermillion and blood. Vermillion (*sindūra*) is traditionally used to decorate elephants (*sindūratilaka*). The word *sindura* (with a short "u") also means elephant. Gaṇeśa is propitiated as the "remover of obstacles." Generally this *dhyāna* is performed twice. First a flower is placed in the palm of the *purohita*'s hand and with the *dhyāna mudrā* moved in front of his heart. The flower is then placed on the top of his head. Among the Tantric ritualists with whom I studied, the *dhyāna mudrā* was interchangeably referred to as the *yoni mudrā*. It is formed by bringing the tips of the thumbs, index and little fingers of both hands together, while the folded backs of the middle and ring fingers touch each other (see Figure 4.2.2).

The *purohita* then performs the *dhyāna* again with a flower placed on a tripod. The *purohita* uses the flower as the orifice through which the deity can manifest. By holding it in the *dhyāna/yoni mudrā* by his heart, Gaṇeśa is born through his heart-mind activity. The term *manas* is identified both with the heart and the mind, indicating an integrated mental and emotional faculty. The flowering forth or blossoming of the deity is frequently represented by images of the deity atop a flower, normally a lotus. When he places the flower on his head, the *purohita* is allowing his body to serve as the matrix for divine manifestation. He may include a mental offering (*mānasa upacāra*) to the deity. When he finally places the flower atop the tripod during the

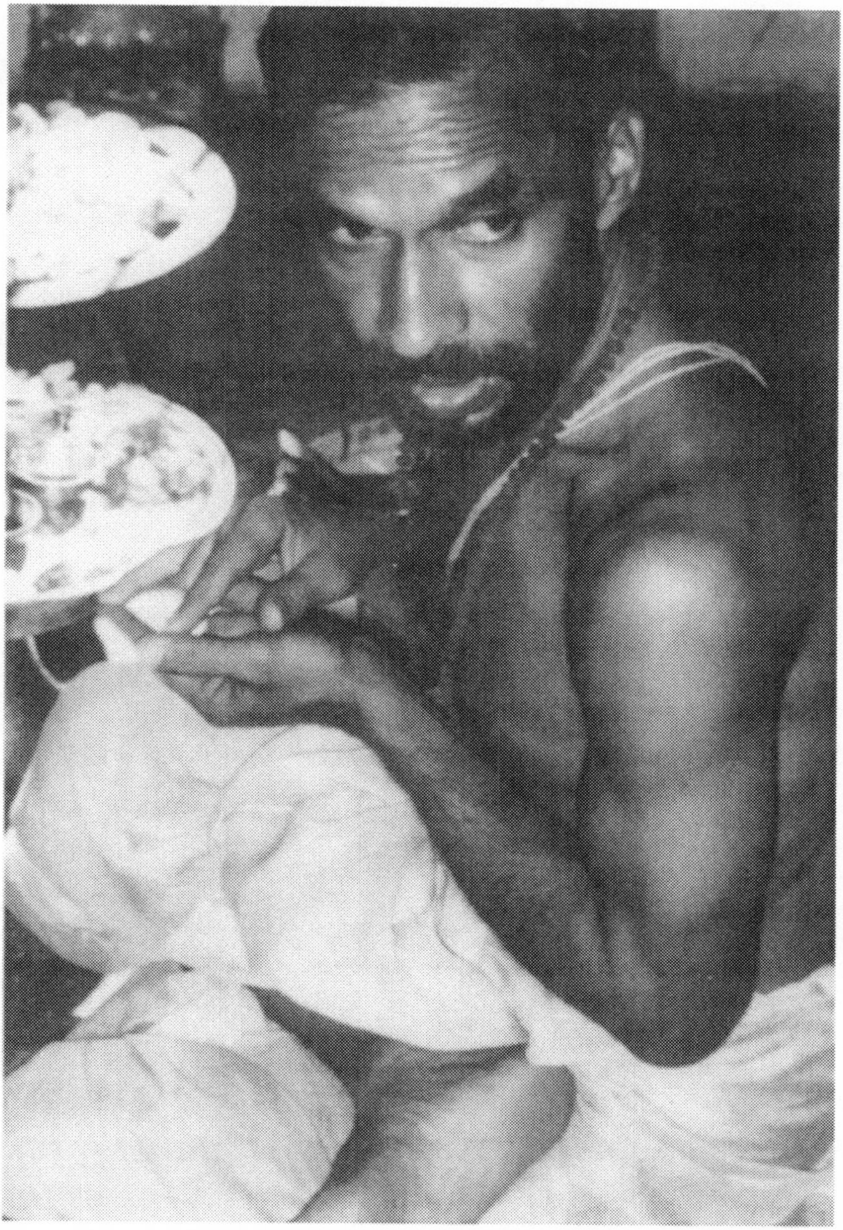

Figure 4.2.2 The *purohita* assumes the *dhyāna/yoni mudrā*, a ritual gesture that accompanies the meditative visualization of a deity.

second *dhyāna*, the *purohita* provides an independent locus for the deity's manifestation. This procedure is another characteristic of Tantric *pūjās* that is absent from Vaidik *pūjā*.

The *purohita* now worships Gaṇeśa with the commonly performed devotional ritual consisting of five offerings (*pañca upacāra pūjā*).

1. Taking a fragrant ointment (*gandha*) such as sandalwood paste, he offers it, saying "Om! Gāṃ! Obeisance to Ganeśa." "Gāṃ" is the seed syllable (*bīja*) of Gaṇeśa.

> *Eṣa gandhaḥ/ Om gāṃ gaṇeśāya namaḥ.*

2. Taking a most excellent flower (*sacandanam puṣpam*), he worships Gaṇeśa, saying:

> *Etat sacandanam puṣpam/ Om gāṃ gaṇeśāya namaḥ.*

3. Taking incense (*dhūpa*), such as camphor (*karpūra*), he offers it saying:

> *Eṣa dhūpah/ Om gāṃ gaṇeśāya namaḥ.*

4. He next worships with light from a flame, perhaps using a lamp (*dīpa*) of clarified butter/ghee (H: *ghi*), saying:

> *Eṣa dīpaḥ/ Om gāṃ gaṇeśāya namaḥ.*

5. And lastly he makes a small offering of food (*naivedyam*), such as a piece of sugarcane or banana, saying:

> *Etan naivedyam/ Om gāṃ gaṇeśāya namaḥ.*

He finishes the Gaṇeśa *pūjā* with:

> *Om devendra maulimandāra makarandakaṇaruṇāḥ vighnān harantu heramba caraṇambuja reṇavah.*
>
> Om! Let the red dust of *mandāra* flowers worn by Indra on his head (while he prostrates at the feet of Gaṇeśa) remove all obstacles of mine.

Pūjā to the Other Gods, Goddesses, and Celestial Beings

Prefacing his words of salutation with, "these flowers and fragrances (*ete gandhapuṣpe*)" the *purohita* makes offerings to all the other important deities as follows:

Ete gandhapuṣpe / *Om śivādi pañcadevatābhyo namaḥ.*
/ *Om ādityādi navagrahebhyo namaḥ.*
/ *Om indrādi daśadikpālebhyo namaḥ.*
/ *Om matsyādi daśāvatārebhyo namaḥ.*
/ *Om gaṅgāyai namaḥ.*

If he is performing the *pūjā* in Banāras, he adds:

/ *Om viśvanāthāya namaḥ.*
/ *Om annapūrṇāyai namaḥ.*
Continuing with: / *Om nārāyaṇāya namaḥ.*
/ *Om lakṣmyai namaḥ.*
/ *Om sarasvatyai namaḥ.*

Om! Obeisance to the five deities beginning with Śiva, to the nine planets beginning with Āditya, to the ten guardians of the directions beginning with Indra, to the ten incarnations beginning with Matsya, to Gaṅgā, to Viśvanātha, to Annapūrṇā, to Nārāyaṇa, to Lakṣmī, to Sarasvatī.

The *purohita* may add as many deities as he desires here, often including his chosen personal deity (*iṣṭadevatā*). He definitely makes offerings to all the deities present in the *yajamāna*'s home shrine. In certain *pūjā*s, such as at the Lahiris' home, there may be dozens of such morsels of food offerings (*naivedya*), which vary in size. Since this rite takes place in the family's shrine room, all the deities present are worshipped. A flower petal is often placed on each morsel, as it is offered to the deity by the *purohita* so as not to lose count. The large numbers of *naivedya*s not only correspond to the number of deities present in the *mūrti*s at the place of worship, but may also be offered to deities present in disembodied form. To offer *naivedya*s, the *purohita* sanctifies them with some water and with a flower offered to the superintending deity (e.g., Viṣṇu, Durgā). He then offers the morsels of food to the deities themselves.

Bhūtāpasāraṇa (Removal of Inimical Spirits)

Taking some white mustard seed, he utters the *mantra*:

Om vetālāśca piśācaśca rākṣasāśca sarīspāḥ/
apasarpantu te sarve ye cānye vighnakārakāḥ/
vināyakā vighnakarāḥ mahogrā yajñadviso piśitāsanāśca/
siddhārthakaiḥ vajrasamāna kalpaiḥ mayā nirastāḥ vidiśaḥ prayāntu.

Om! Vampires, goblins, fiends, and creeping entities be gone from this place, you and any others who are the creator of obstacles. Those who are the

> creators of obstructions and agents for misguiding people, very fierce by nature, inimical to oblations and sacrifice, eaters of raw meat, by the means of this white mustard that resembles thunderbolts (*vajra*), are removed by me.

And he disperses the mustard seed in different directions.

This passage serves as exemplary evidence of how the litany itself offers interpretations of ritual substance and activity. The white mustard (*siddhārthaka*) is compared to thunderbolts (*vajra*), which disperse the spirits. The preceding offerings to Śiva and a host of other deities has attracted a variety of unwanted entities, which have to be held at bay or dispersed.

Kara and *Aṅga Nyāsa*

The *purohita* now again performs *kara nyāsa* and *aṅga nyāsa* with the *bīja*, "Hrīṃ." These *nyāsa*s transform his body into the vibrational body of the Goddess, capable of manifestation.

Durgā Dhyāna (Meditative Visualization of Durgā)

Grasping a flower in the *yoni mudrā* by his heart, the *purohita* performs a meditative visualization (*dhyāna*) of Durgā. The *dhyāna* will be given in detail in a later section of the description.

Mānasa Upacāra (Heart-mind Devotional Service)

Placing the flower on his head, the *purohita*, with appropriate sentiments (*manas*), mentally visualizes offering various materials to Durgā. This may be the traditional five- (*pañca*), ten- (*daśa*), or possibly the sixteen- (*ṣodaśa*) item offering, since Durgā is the central deity in this *pūjā*. In Tantric worship the *mānasa pūjā* always precedes the outward worship of the deity in the form of an icon. The deity moves from the meditatively visualized and venerated image into the effigy. Yet although it is worshipped there, it still endures in the *purohita's* heart, like the original flame from which another has been ignited. The *Kulārṇavatantra* 6.75 states that since it is not possible to hold the form of a deity for long in one's heart-mind, the same form of the deity should also be worshipped externally.[21] Since the capacity for mental visualizations is unlimited, the deity may be provided numerous and opulent offerings, beyond the actual capacities of the votary. *Mānasa pūjā*, which is deemed extremely difficult, is held in higher regard than outer worship, since it requires the worshipper's fullest interior focus. Only advanced practitioners are thought to be capable of moving entirely beyond image worship.

Viśeṣa Argha (The Special Offering)

The *purohita* draws a square (*bhūpura*) with water from his finger on the floor to his left. Within this square he draws a circle (*maṇḍala*) and within that a triangle (*trikoṇa*). Inside the triangle he writes the *bīja*, "Duṃ." He worships this *yantra* with the words, "These flowers and fragrances (*ete gandhapuṣpe*)" preceding "Om! Obeisance to the Supporting Power, the Tortoise, the Endless Serpent, and the Earth," respectively. He offers sandal paste and flowers while making the utterances.

Ete gandhapuṣpe// *Om ādhara śaktaye namaḥ/ Om kūrmāya namaḥ/*
Om anantāya namaḥ/ Om pṛthivyai namaḥ.

He places a tripod on the diagram.The tripod is an important ritual apparatus and may be quite ornate. Among its symbolic referents are the various triads of primary qualities (*triguṇa*) through which the Devī as Prakṛti or Śakti manifests, namely the *sattva*, *rajas*, and *tamas guṇa*, or as *icchā*, *jñāna*, and *kriyā śakti*. The *viśeṣa argha* is not prepared in the *kośā* or *kuśī* as in the case of the *sāmānya argha*, but in a conch shell.

The conch shell has many symbolic associations. It emanates from the waters and possesses great beauty in form, color, and iridescence. It is rare, auspicious, and valuable. It is associated with Viṣṇu, the preserver of the cosmos, who in the widespread myth of the churning of the ocean for nectar, selected it when it appeared with thirteen other items. It is blown in battle, striking dread into the hearts of the enemy. It symbolizes victory in battle. When held to the ear, it produces a sound of the primordial ocean, the vibration of creation. Its shape of spiral expansion suggests the creative flowering of the cosmos. It is reminiscent of the female reproductive organ (*yoni*) (Eliade 1991:125ff). In Bengal, conch shell bangles are worn by women to indicate their married status. "The bride's father provides a pair of bangles, which are put on her wrists by a Śaṅkari (shell-maker)" (Fruzzetti 1982:69). The shell-maker caste claims a special relationship to Durgā (Östör 1980:34). In a related myth, Durgā is teased by her in-laws for not having any jewellery on her arms. Śiva, to appease her anger, appears disguised as a Śaṅkari, and provides her with conch-shell bangles. Since then, all Bengali brides wear conch-shell bangles as a sign of marriage (Fruzzetti 1982:70). Thus although the conch shell is also worshipped in other *pūjās*, for all the aforementioned associations, in particular those linked with the feminine, with creation, and with sound vibration, it seems appropriate that the next level of manifestation of the Goddess, should be the conch shell.

Unlike the conch shells used for blowing into (in worship and battle), these are left naturally sealed at one end. The conch (*saṅkha*) is purified with water and the *mantra*, "Huṃ phaṭ." The *purohita* then places it on the tripod worshipping both the conch and the tripod with flowers and sandalwood paste while uttering, "These flowers and fragrances (*ete gandhapuṣpe*)." He fills it with water saying:

Aṃ sūrya maṇḍalāya dvādaśa kalātmane namaḥ/
Uṃ soma maṇḍalāya śoḍaśa kalātmane namaḥ/
Maṃ vahni maṇḍalāya daśa kalātmane namaḥ.

Aṃ! Salutations to the disc of the sun consisting of twelve divisional elements.
Uṃ! Salutations to the disc of the moon consisting of sixteen divisional elements.
Maṃ! Salutations to the disc of fire consisting of ten subtle elements (digits).[22]

At the open end of the conch, he places flowers, *dūrvā* grass, *kuśa* grass, sandal paste, and washed rice, while uttering the Durgā *bīja*, "Duṃ." He covers the conch with *dhenu mudrā*, transforming the water into ambrosial nectar (*amṛta*) and with *matsya mudrā*, to signify its completion. Then inserting his middle finger into the conch, in the *aṅkuśa mudrā*, with a vigorous stirring motion he utters:

Om gaṅge ca yamune ca . . .

inducing the sacred rivers to flow into the vessel.[23] He then repeats the seed syllable of Durgā, "Duṃ," and invokes the deity from his heart into the conch and water. Among the diverse interpretations of the *argha* (*sāmānya* and *viśeṣa*) is that it is simply an offering made to the deity. Thus the water is purified, transformed into nectar, and given to the deity to drink. While this would seem appropriate for the *argha* within the sixteen-part offerings (*ṣodaśa upacāra*), a more compelling interpretation is that in this context the *argha* is the Devī herself. As previously stated, the Devī, through the matrix of the *yantra*, engenders the creative orifice (*yoni*) of the conch by means of the tripod on which it rests, through which she herself manifests.

Taking some water from the conch with *kuśa* grass, the *purohita* sprinkles it all around him and places a small quantity in the *prokṣani pātra*, the container from which water is offered to the deity. This is generally the *kośā*. It is clear that this water which is offered to the deity is different from the water in the *argha*, which could be thought of as the deity. A certain circularity is present in the conceptual symbols of the ritual, for ultimately, the Devī is offered nothing else but parts of her own manifest form.

Durgā Āvāhana (Invocation of Durgā)

Bhagavatī Durgā is then invoked (*āvāhana*) into the conch with this *mantra*:[24]

> *Hrīṃ bhagavati durge devi iha āgacchal iha tiṣṭha iha tiṣṭhal*
> *atra adhiṣṭhānam kurul mama pūjām gṛhaṇa.*
>
> Hrīṃ! O blessed goddess Durgā, come here, stay here, stay here, take up residence here, accept my worship.

Durgā Mantra

The *purohita* then worships Durgā with this *mantra*:

> *Om durge durge rakṣaṇi svāhāl hrīṃ durgāyai namaḥ.*
>
> Om! O Durgā, O Durgā, O protectress, Svāhā.[25] Hrīṃ! Obeisance to Durgā.

Ṣodaśa Upacāra (Sixteen-Part Devotional Service)

The *purohita* worships Durgā with sixteen aspects of devotional service (*ṣodaśa upacāra*) (See Figure 4.2.3). Each has an appropriate *mantra*.[26] They may be subdivided thus: 1. *āsana* (seating the Devī); 2. *svāgata* (welcoming the Devī); 3. *pādya* (washing the feet of the Devī); 4. *argha* (making a worship offering to the Devī); 5. *ācamanīya* (offering sips of water); 6. *punarācamanīya* (offering sips of water again); 7. *madhuparka* (offering a honeyed mixture); 8. *snāna* (bathing the Devī); 9. *vastraluttarīya* (offering an outer garment to the Devī); 10. *ābhūṣanalābharaṇa* (ornamenting the Devī); 11. *gandha* (anointing the Devī with fragrances); 12. *puṣpa* (offering flowers); 13. *dhūpa* (offering fragrances); 14. *dīpa* (worship with a flame offering); 15. *naivedya* (food offerings)[27]; 16. *praṇāmalvandana* (paying homage). The *purohita* pays homage by repeating the *mantra* of Durgā, "Duṃ," at least ten times.

Worship of the *Bilva* (Wood-apple) Tree

The *purohita* now worships the wood-apple (*bilva*) tree. The *bilva* grows large and is considered sacred to Śiva. Its leaves grow in triads, which resemble his trident (*triśūla*). The tree is reputed to have innumerable medicinal properties, and the fruit produces a refreshing beverage in the hot summer months.

Figure 4.2.3 The *purohita* performs *ārati* by ringing a bell and passing an honorific flame before Durgā during the awakening *(bodhana)* rite.

He utters the *mantra*:

Om bilva vṛkṣāya namaḥ. Om! Obeisance to the *bilva* tree.

He proceeds to perform the five-fold devotional service (*pañca upacāra*) to it. This consists of *gandha*, *puṣpa*, *dhūpa*, *dīpa*, and *naivedya*.

Bodhana of Durgā in the *Bilva* Tree

The *purohita* now prays:

Aiṃ rāvaṇasya vadhārthāya rāmasānugrahāyaca/
akāle brahmanā bodho devyāstvayi kṛtaḥ purā.

Aiṃ! For the purpose of killing Rāvaṇa and for showing grace to Rāma, the great Brahmā awakened you, divine lady, untimely, in the holy past.

Ahamapyāśvine tadvad bodhayāmi sureśvarīm/
dharmārtha kāma mokṣāya bhavaśobhane.

I, too, in the same way, awaken the lady of all divine beings in Āśvina for the purpose of righteousness, wealth, desire, and liberation (i.e., the four aims of existence). O beautiful one, be graceful (i.e., bestow boons on me.)

Śakreṇa saṃabodhya svarajyamāptam tasmādahamtvām pratibodhayāmi/
yathaiva rāmena hato daśāsyasthaiva śatrūn vinipātāyāmi/
devi caṇḍātmike caṇḍi caṇḍavigraha kāriṇi/
bilva śāktam samāsṛtya tiṣṭha devī yathāsukham.

After awakening you, Indra (Śakra) obtained his own domain once again. Therefore I also cause you to awaken.
As by Rāma, ten-headed Rāvaṇa was killed, in the same way, I shall also cause my enemies to fall.
O deity with the characteristic of dread, O dreadful one, who makes a very terrible war, taking this branch of the *bilva* tree as your abode, please remain here according to your pleasure.

The litany clearly makes references to particular myths. It articulates Rāma's worship of the Devī, as well as her untimely awakening. It is Brahmā who awakens her on Rāma's behalf for Rāvaṇa's destruction. Without specific reference to any particular incident, Indra's regaining of his sovereignty is attributed to the Devī. This could allude to a similar reference in the *Devī Bhāgavata Purāṇa* 3.30.25–26, where Indra's defeat of Vṛtra is attributed to the Āśvina Navarātra *pūjā*. While Rāma's untimely worship is that by a god incarnate as a human being on earth, Indra's worship is an earlier precedent purely among the gods. It reveals a cyclical pattern of worship developed in great theoretical detail by Mircea Eliade (1959a). The rite's precedent is first set by the gods and other divine beings themselves, then by the incarnate gods on earth, and finally by exceptional humans, who by the imitative act, themselves become godlike. While the second verse mentions the other reasons she is invoked, the martial purposes of awakening Durgā are stressed in the first and third verses. The Goddess is attributed with the characteristic of dread.

Offerings (*Bali*) to the *Kṣetrapālas* (Guardians of the Field)

The *purohita* now makes offerings to the guardians of the field (*kṣetrapāla*), deities who protect the sacred space in which the ritual is taking place. He prays with folded hands that they will accept the offerings made to them:

> *Om kṣetrapālādayaḥ sarve sarvaśānti phalapradāḥ pūjā vighnavināśāya mama gṛhnantvimam balim.*
>
> Let all the protectors of the field, the givers of all sorts of peacefulness for the purpose of the removal of obstacles regarding the ritual made by me, receive this offering.

Then he offers the mixture of unhusked pulse (Sanskrit/Hindi *māṣa/urad*) mixed with curd placed on a *bilva* leaf, which is placed on a *yantra* that he draws with cowdung on the floor. He says:

> *Eṣa māṣa bhakta baliḥ/ Om kṣetrapālādibhyoḥ namaḥ.*
>
> This is a sacrificial offering of a portion of pulse.
> Om! Homage to the guardians of the field and others.

Prayers to the Bhūtas (Elementals) and other Spirits

With folded hands he prays:

> *Om bhūta daitya piśācaśca gandharva rakṣāsām gaṇāḥ/*
> *siddhim kurvantu te sarve mama gṛhnantvimam balim.*
>
> Om! Elemental spirits, devils, goblins (literally "eaters of raw flesh"), and the host of heavenly musicians and demonic fiends you should give me successful attainment (*siddhi*) of my end and should receive my offering.

The spirits here are not dispersed as in *bhūtāpasāraṇa*, but are propitiated and enjoined to help the ritual succeed.[28] Their capacity to bestow attainment (*siddhi*) links them with the Devī, who possesses the epithet of Siddhidātrī (Bestower of Attainment).[29] Durgā is also referred to as the Great Demoness (*mahāsurī*) (*Durgā Saptaśatī* 1.58).[30] When making the actual offering of the leaf plate with pulse and curd (*dadhi*), the *purohita* says:

> *Eṣa māṣa bhakta baliḥ/ Om bhūtādibhyoḥ namaḥ.*
>
> This is a sacrificial offering of a portion of pulse.
> Om! Homage to the elemental spirits and others.

After each of these offerings, he washes his hands. These offerings bring a measure of ritual pollution onto the *purohita*, which he must remove through the purifying power of flowing water. Once again with folded hands, he prays:

> *Om ḍākinī yoginī caiva mātaro devayonayaḥ nānārūpadharānityam mama gṛhnantvimam balim.*
>
> Om! Ḍākinīs, yoginīs, mothers, and all those who are born of the divine (*devayoni*), who always assume different forms, you should receive my offering.

The *devayoni* are celestial beings who are divinely born and include among their ranks the fountainheads of sciences (*vidyādhara*), the heavenly damsels (*apsaras*), the *kinnara*s, and others. With the actual offering, he says:

> *Eṣa māṣa bhakta baliḥ/ Om ḍākinyādibhyoḥ namaḥ.*
>
> This is a sacrificial offering of a portion of pulse. Om! Homage to the ḍākinīs and others.

Next he prays:

> *Om ādityādi graha ca kuṣmāṇḍā rākṣasāśca indrādyāścaiva dikpālā mama gṛhnantvimam balim.*
>
> All the planets, beginning with the sun, those called *kuṣmāṇḍās*, *rākṣasas*, protectors of the quarters, like Indra and others should receive my offerings.

The inclusion of the term Kuṣmāṇḍā in this category of beings is noteworthy. It may suggest that *kuṣmāṇḍās*, like the planetary forces (*graha*), have the capacity to grab or affect people's psyches. The Durgā at the Durgā Kuṇḍ temple in Banāras is identified with the epithet Kuṣmāṇḍā Devī, who is one of the Nine Durgās of the *Devī Kavaca.* The title indicates her sovereignty over this ill-defined class of beings and also points to the controlling power in her nature. With the offering, he says:

> *Eṣa māṣa bhakta baliḥ/ Om ādityādibhyoḥ namaḥ.*
>
> This is a sacrificial offering of a portion of pulse.
> Om! Obeisance to the sun and others.

The entire set of foregoing offerings symbolically link the Devī to a range of spirits, demigods and demi-goddesses, and demons. It, too, resonates with Durgā's epithet of the great demoness (*mahāsurī*) in the *Durgā Saptaśatī.*

Invocation (*Avāhana*) of the *Bilva* Tree

The *purohita* now invokes the divine *bilva* tree to manifest within the *bilva* tree on the altar where it will be worshipped as Durgā.

> *Om meru mandara kailāsa himavat śikhare girau jātah śrī phalavṛkṣatvam ambikāyāh sadā priyaḥ śrī śaila śikhare jātah śrī phalaḥ śrī niketanaḥ netabyo 'si mayā gaccha pujyo durgā svarupataḥ.*
>
> Born from Meru, Mandara, and Kailāsa, at the top of the Himālaya Mountains, you tree called "*śrīphalavṛkṣa* (tree of the fruit of auspiciousness)" have always been a favorite to Ambikā (the consort of Śiva). You are born at the top of Śrī Śaila, and for this reason you are called "*śrī phala*" and the abode of auspiciousness. You are to be carried by me to the place of worship (altar) and be worshipped as Durgā there.

There are several symbols juxtaposed in this prayer, including a conceptual "pun." The tree is born at the top of the cosmic mountains Meru, etc., linking it with the *axis mundi*. Born at the top of Mount Śaila, it is equated with Śailaputrī (Daughter of the Mountain), an epithet of Durgā. As the favorite of Ambikā, the tree is equated with Śiva, whose name means "auspiciousness." The *bilva* is the abode of auspiciousness, and its fruit is "auspiciousness" (*śrī phala*). Of course, the term Śrī also links the tree and Durgā to the goddess Lakṣmī.

Kaṇḍā Ropaṇam (Erecting the Staffs)

He now proceeds to perform the ritual of closing off the sacred space, by placing four forked sticks, implanted in clay balls at four corners around the jar. He utters the *mantra*s:

Om kāṇḍāt kāṇḍāt . . .

And then circumscribes the sticks about seven times with red thread (see Figure 4.2.1).[31]

Durgā Japa (Repetition of the Durgā Mantra)

The *purohita* now begins to repeat (*japa*) the Durgā Mantra counting on the fingers (*kara japa*) in a special ritualized way. This ten-count is done at least ten times, and the repetition (*japa*) is offered to the left hand of the Goddess, saying:

> *Om guhyāti guyha goptrī tvam gṛhān asmat kṛtam japam siddhir bhavantu me devī tvat prasādam maheśvarī.*
>
> Om! You are the protector of the secret of all secrets, please receive my repetition of the *mantra,* and thus attainment may follow by your grace.

With this utterance, the *purohita* places consecrated water on the left-hand side of Durgā in her manifestation (*svarūpa*) as the *bilva* tree. In the worship of a male god the meritorious action of *japa* would be offered to the right side.

Worship of Durgā

Reciting what is known as the *namaskāra mantra* (sacred utterance of homage), the *purohita* says:

> *Om sarva maṅgala maṅgalye śive sarvārtha sadhike*
> *śaranye tryambake gaurī nārāyaṇī namo'stute.* [DSS.11.9]
>
> Om! You are the abode of all auspiciousness. O consort of Śiva, you are the giver of every kind of object (you are the means by which one can achieve all sorts of desired ends). You are the last resort, O mother of the three gods, salutations to you O Gaurī, O Nārāyaṇī.[32]

Ending of *Bodhana*

The *purohita* now places the right hand on the *kośā* with the left at his inner elbow and recites a statement of completion that complements the *saṅkalpa* oath he took at the beginning of the ritual.

> *Om viṣṇurom tat sadadya āṣvine māsi śukle pakśe śaṣṭhyām tithau kṛtaitat bhagavad durgāyāḥ bodhana karmaṇi yad vaiguṇyam jātam taddoṣa praśamanāya viṣṇu smaraṇamaham kariṣye.*
>
> Om! Whatever I have done regarding the *bodhana* rituals of goddess Durgā on this day of Ṣaṣṭhī on the bright fortnight in the month of Āśvina, whatever faults, flaws, and omissions have occurred, I shall repeat "Om Viṣṇu" ten times for allaying the defect.

Having done that, he says:

> *Om adya āśvine māsi śukle pakśe, ṣaṣṭhayam tithau kṛtaitat bodhana karmā acchidram astu*
>
> Om! Today, on this day of Ṣaṣṭhī, on the bright fortnight in the month of Āśvina, may this ritual called *bodhana* be free from all defects.

One of the attending *brāhmaṇas* may reply:

> *Astu!* So be it.

4.3: Adhivāsa

Adhivāsanam, interpretively translated, means "coloring the self with impressions." The *purohita* is said to "perfume the image." It is "teased with the color of his thought." The *adhivāsanam* (or *adhivāsa*) is the process through which the essence of the deity first and subtly permeates the image into which she will be invoked. An analogous process is used in the marriage ceremony. Prior to their meeting, the bride and groom are each anointed with turmeric (Skt/H: *haridra/haldi*) and mustard oil, which is rubbed on their bodies. Some remnants of the oil from the groom's anointing, "perfumed" with the subtle essences of his body, are mixed with oil with which the bride will be anointed (or vice versa). The term is also to describe the patient, persistent, and ultimately unignorable waiting by a person (e.g., a beggar) for audience with another. This dimension suggests the quality of the votary's beckoning and eager anticipation in the *adhivāsa* ritual process. The *adhivāsa* ritual is performed to the *ghaṭa* and the *bilva* tree, because the Devī has already been established in these forms. After finishing all the anointments, the *purohita* moves to the more elaborate clay images (*mūrti*) of the Devī and other deities, and at a minimum makes an offering of "flowers and fragrances (*anena gandhena puṣpena . . .*)." If time and energy permits, he may perform the entire *adhivāsa* anointings again to these *mūrtis*. The *adhivāsa* provides a preview of the many mediums through which Durgā manifests in the *pūjā*.

If the *ṣaṣṭhī tithi* does not extend past sunset (actually after 4:00 o'clock in the evening) of the sixth day of Navarātra, *bodhana* is performed on the fifth day (*pañcamī*). But if it does, then both *bodhana* and *adhivāsa* are done on the sixth day.

Preliminary Rituals

Svasti Vācanam (Utterance of Approval)

The *purohita* begins by taking some rice from the plate of worship materials and gently throwing them down says:

Om somaṃ rājānaṃ varuṇam agniṃ anvārabhāmahe/
ādityaṃ viṣṇuṃ sūryaṃ brāhmaṇanca bṛhaspatim/
Om svasti svasti svasti. [SV.191a]

Om! I pray for the approval of the luminous moon, Varuṇa (the all-pervading moral force), Fire;
I [am going to proceed with my work and] pray for the approval of Āditya, Viṣṇu, Sūrya, and the *brāhmaṇa* Bṛhaspati.
Om! Well-being, well-being, well-being.[1]

Adhivāsa Saṅkalpa (Anointment Oath)

This is the same as the long *saṅkalpa* of *bodhana* except at the end where it is changed as follows:

Om viṣṇurom, . . . , bhagavad durgāyāḥ śubhādhivāsana karamāham kariṣye/ kariṣyāmi.

Om Viṣṇu! . . . I shall perform the most auspicious deed of anointment with regards to Durgā.

Saṅkalpa Sūkta (Oath Hymn)

The *purohita* then recites a *saṅkalpa sūkta,* which differs from the one recited after the *bodhana* oath.

Om yajjāgrato dūram udaiti daivaṃ tadu suptasya tathaivaiti/
dūram gamaṃ jyotiṣāṃ jyotirekam tanme manaḥ śivasaṅkalpamastu.
[VS.34.1]

Om! Whatever shines to the awakened one, it shines at a distance, and when he remains asleep, it remains the same as arising. It is the light of all lights, and the light of it goes far. Let my mind remain awakened to the auspiciousness of that light.[2]

Bhūtāpasāraṇa (Removal of Inimical Spirits)

Taking some white mustard seed in his hand and saying:

Om vetālāśca . . .

the *purohita* scatters the seed in various directions dispersing the vampires and other spirits hostile to the ritual about to be performed. After scattering them, he propitiates the elementals and others (*bhūtagaṇa*) with *pādya* (water for washing the feet) and *argha* (*dūrvā* grass, flowers, and rice), saying:

Etat pādyam/ Om bhūtagaṇebhyoḥ namaḥ. Idam argham/ Om bhūtagaṇebhyoḥ namaḥ.

Then, taking a prepared mixture of unhusked pulse (*māṣa*), curd (*dadhi*), etc. (*māṣa bhakta bali*), he says:

Om bhūta preta piśācaśca ye vasantayatra bhūtale/
te gṛhnantu mayā datto balim eṣa prasādhitaḥ/
pūjitā gandhapuṣpādyair balibhistarpitāstathā/
deśād asmad viniḥ sṛtya pūjām pasyantu mat kṛtām.

Om! The elemental spirits, ghosts, and other goblins who stay on the surface of the earth should receive this offering of mine as has been prepared by me. Being worshipped with sandal paste, flowers, and other things, and having been satisfied by this special kind of offering, they should go away from this spot and should watch the ritual presented by me.

The spirits are not merely dispersed. They are subsequently propitiated and requested politely to attend the ritual from afar. When he finishes reciting this statement, he takes a small morsel of offering (*bali*) from the *bilva pātra*, saying:

Eṣa māṣa bhakta baliḥ/ Om bhūtebhyoḥ namaḥ.

Āsana Śuddhi

After washing his hands (*kara śuddhi*), he purifies his seat (*āsana*).

Bhūta Śuddhi

Through *prāṇāyāma* he performs *bhūta śuddhi*, transforming his body into immaculate substance into which the Devī can be embodied.

Sāmānyārgha

He then does the installation of the *sāmānyārgha*, creating the *yoni* through which she manifests.

Pīṭha Nyāsa

He next performs *pīṭha nyāsa*, manifesting the seats of the Goddess in various parts of his body, which is thus transformed into an abode and portal for the Devī.

Pañcopacāra Worship of the *Devas, Devīs,* and *Devatās*

With five devotional offerings (*pañcopacāra*: *gandha*, *puṣpa*, *dhūpa*, *dīpa*, and *naivedya*) he worships Gaṇeśa, the five gods beginning with Śiva, and others. He thus propitiates the lesser deities before worshipping Durgā herself.

Kara and *Aṅga Nyāsa*

He imprints his fingers and limbs with the Sanskrit syllables, transforming his body into the vibrational matrix of the Goddess as sound (*śabda*) or Vāc (thus, by implication, as the conceivable).

Durgā Dhyāna

The *purohita* now proceeds to perform the meditative visualization (*dhyāna*) of Durgā, aided by the verbal description (this *dhyāna* description will be provided later).

Adhivāsa of the Devī in *Bilva Tree* and *Ghaṭa*

The full array of anointing materials has been prepared in advance and placed on a large plate. A major activity of the *yajamāna*'s family, often months prior to the actual celebration of Durgā *pūjā*, is the acquisition of materials that will be used in worship of the Goddess. No item is too obscure or insignificant, and a tremendous anxiety may be felt if items have not yet been obtained as Durgā Pūjā approaches. Mr. and Mrs. Lahiri told me that they begin evaluating the year's celebration the moment it is over and think about what they wish to include/acquire for the next year's *pūjā*. Mrs. Lahiri said that she moves her preparations into high gear about a month before the celebration. Thus, however important the *purohita*'s role may appear in the actual performance of the *pūjā*, it is vital to remember that it is the climax of a much wider range of ritual activities by the patron's family or the communal body of worshippers.

The *purohita* utters a *mantra* to sanctify each item, which he then smears on the Devī Durgā embodied in the *bilva* tree. In one hand he holds a bell (*ghaṇṭa*), which he rings continuously. A special drum called the *dhāk* is also sounded continuously (See Figure 4.8.2). The overall effect during the *adhivāsa* is a "quickening" in the audience of worshippers that is parallelled by the arising of the Goddess. It soon grows apparent that the items are not merely devotional offerings of a royal and feminine nature, but subtle and varied forms of the Goddess. If *bodhana* was the awakening ritual, then *adhivāsa* could be understood as the "getting up" ritual causing the Devī to arise. The bells and drums figure in the process of enlivening the Goddess.

If it is inconvenient for the *purohita* to reach the Devī images (*bilva* tree, etc.), he may use a long piece of *kuśa* grass with which to touch the offerings, *ghaṭa*, and other images. The *purohita* prays:

> *Om adya prāptasi devītvam namaste śaṅkarapriye/*
> *durge devi samutiṣṭha aham tvam adhivāsaye.*
>
> Om! O dear consort of Śiva, O divine one, O Goddess Durgā, please arise properly. I shall anoint you with these articles.

1. Sandalwood paste (*gandha*).
   He reads the verse:

> *Om bhadrā indrasya rātayaḥ/ yo asya kāmam vidhato no raṣati mano dānāya codayan/*
> *anena gandhena bhagavad durgāyāḥ . . .* [RV.8.88.4]
>
> Om! Good are the gifts which Indra grants.
> He is not worth the one who satisfies his wish: he turns his mind to giving boons.

He then takes a small amount of sandal paste and touches the heart of the image.

2. Soil (*mahi*).
   Taking a bit of soil from its container in the large copper plate, he says:

> *Om mahi triṇāmavarastu dyuksam mitrasyāryamnaḥ/ durādharṣam varuṇasya/*
> *anayā mahyāḥ bhagavad durgāyāḥ . . .* [RV.10.185.1a]
>
> Om! Great, unassailable must be a heavenly favor of Three Gods, Varuṇa, Mitra, and Aryaman.

3. Sandalwood paste (*gandha*) again.

Om bhadrā indrasya rātayaḥ/ yo asya kāmam vidhato no raṣati mano dānāya codayan/
anena gandhena bhagavad durgāyāḥ . . . [RV.8.88]

Om! Good are the gifts which Indra grants.
He is not worth the one who satisfies his wish; he turns his mind to giving boons.

4. Small stone (*śilā*).

Om vi tvadāpo na parvatasya pṛṣṭhādukthebhi rindrānayanta yajñaiḥ/
tam tvā giraḥ suṣtutayo vājayantyajiṃ girvavāho jigyurasvāḥ/
anayā śilayā bhagavad durgāyāḥ . . . [RV.6.24.6a; SV.1.68a]

Om! By song and sacrifice men brought the waters from thee, as from a mountain's ridge, O Indra. Urging thy might, with these fair lauds, they seek thee, O theme of song, as horses rush to battle.

5. Unhusked rice (*dhānya*).

Om dhānāvantam karambhiṇam apūpavantam ukthinam/ indra prātarjuṣasvanaḥ/
anena dhānyena bhagavad durgāyāḥ . . . [RV.3.52.1a; SV.1.210a]

Om! Indra, accept at break of day our Soma mixt with roasted corn,
With groats, with cake, with eulogies.

6. *Dūrvā* grass.

Om yajjāyathā apūrvya maghavan vṛtrahatyāya/
tat pṛthivīmaprathaya tadastabhnā uto dyam/
anayā dūrvayā bhagavad durgāyāḥ . . . [SV.2.6.19.1.]

Om! When thou, unequalled Maghavan, wast born to smite the Vṛtras dead,
Thou spreadest out the spacious earth and didst support and prop the heavens.

7. Flower (*puṣpa*).

Om pavamāna vyaśnavat raśmibhi vājasātamaḥ/ dadhat stotre vāyam/
anena puṣpena bhagavad durgāyāḥ . . . [RV.9.66.27]

Om! May Pavamāna, best to win the booty, penetrate with rays,
Giving the singer-hero strength.

8. Fruit (*phala*) (e.g., myrobalan/gooseberry [*haritaki*]); dried fruit may be substituted.

Om indram naro nemadhitā havante yatpāryā yunajate dhiyastāḥ/
śūro nṛjātā śavasaśca kāma ā gomati vraje bhajā tvam naḥ/
anena phalena bhagavad durgāyāḥ . . . [RV.7.27.1a; SV.1.318a]

Om! Men call on Indra in the armed encounter that he may make the hymns they sing decisive.

Hero, rejoicing in thy might, in combat give us a portion of the stall of cattle.

9. Curd (*dadhi*) in a small container.

Om dadhikrāvno akāriṣam jiṣṇo raśvasya vājinah/
surabhi no mukhā karat praṇa āyumṣi tāriṣat/
anena dadhnā . . . [RV.4.39.6a; SV.1.358a]

Om! So have I glorified with praise strong Dadhikrāvan, conquering Steed. Sweet may he make our mouths; may he prolong the days we have to live.

10. Clarified butter/Ghee (*ghṛta*).

Om ghṛtavātī bhuvanānām abhiśriyorvī pṛthvī madhudughe supeśasā/
dyāvā pṛthvī varuṇasya dharmaṇā viṣkabhite ajare bhūriretasā/
anena ghṛtena bhagavad durgāyāḥ . . . [RV.6.70.1a]

Om! Filled full of fatness, compassing all things that be, wide, spacious, dropping meath [mead], beautiful in their form.
The Heaven and the Earth by Varuṇa's decree, unwasting, rich in germs, stand parted each from each.

11. Auspicious symbol (*svāstika*). This is often a cone-shaped (perhaps multicolored) item made of rice powder by the women of the household.

Om svasti na indro vṛddhaśravāḥ/ svasti naḥ pūṣā viśvavedāḥ/
svasti na stārkṣyo 'riṣṭanemiḥ/ svasti no bṛhaspatir dadhātu/
anena svastikena bhagavad durgāyāḥ . . . [RV.1.89.6a; SV.2.1225a]

Om! Illustrious far and wide, may Indra prosper us: may Pūṣan prosper us, the Master of all wealth. May Tārkṣya with uninjured fellies [wheels] prosper us: Bṛhaspati vouchsafe to us prosperity.

12. Vermillion (*sindūra*).

Om sindhorucchavāse patayantamukṣaṇam hiraṇyapāvāḥ paśumapsu gṛbhnate/
anena sindūrena bhagavad durgāyāḥ . . . [RV.9.86.43c; AV.18.3.18c; SV.1.564c]

Om! They seize the flying Steer at the stream's breathing-place: cleansing with gold, they grasp the animal herein.

13. Conch shell (*śaṅkha*).

Om sa sunve yo vasūnām yo rāyāmānetā ya idānām/ somo yaḥ sukṣitīnām/ anena śaṅkhena bhagavad durgāyāḥ . . . [RV.9.108.13a; SV.1.582a]

Om! Effused is he who brings good things, who brings us bounteous gifts and sweet refreshing food, Soma who brings us quiet homes.

14. Collyrium (*kajjala*).

Om añjate vyañjate samañjate kralūm rihanti madhvā bhañjate/ anena kajjalena bhagavad durgāyāḥ . . . [RV.9.86.43a; SV.18.3.18a; SV.1.564a]

Om! They balm him, balm him over, balm him thoroughly, caress the mighty strength and balm it with the meath [mead].

15. Bile of a cow (*rocanā* or *gorocanā*).

Om adha jno adho vā divo bṛhato rocanād adhi/
ayā bardhasva tanvā girā mamā jātā sukrato pṛṇa/
anayā rocanayā . . . [RV.8.1.18a; SV.1.52a]

Om! Whether thou come from earth, or from the luster of the lofty heaven, Wax stronger in thy body through my song of praise: fill full all creatures, O most Wise.

16. Yellow mustard (*siddhārtha*).

Om adha jno adho vā divo bṛhato rocanād adhi/
ayā bardhasva tanvā girā mamā jātā sukrato pṛṇa/
anena siddhārthena bhagavad durgāyāḥ . . . [RV.8.1.18a; SV.1.52a]

Om! Whither thou come from or from the luster of the holy heaven, wax stronger in thy body through my song of praise; fill full all creatures, O most Wise.

17. Gold (*kāñcana*).

Om yadvarco hiraṇyasya yadvāvarco gavāmuto/
satyasya brahmaṇo varca stena mām sam sṛjāmasi/
anena kāñcanena bhagavad durgāyāḥ . . . [ArS.4.10a]

Om! The brightness that is in gold or the splendor that is in the cows and the light in Brahman, let that strength be created in me.[3]

18. Silver (*raupya*).

> *Om yadvarco hiraṇyasya yadvāvarco gavāmuto/*
> *satyasya brahmaṇo varca stena mām sam sṛjāmasi/*
> *anena raupyena bhagavad durgāyāḥ . . .* [ArS.4.10a]
>
> Om! The brightness that is in gold or the splendor that is in the cows and the light in Brahman, let that strength be created in me.[4]

19. Copper (*tāmra*).

> *Om yadvarco hiraṇyasya yadvāvarco gavāmuto/*
> *satyasya brahmaṇo varca stena mām sam sṛjāmasi/*
> *anena tāmrena bhagavad durgāyāḥ . . .* [ArS.4.10a]
>
> Om! The brightness that is in gold or the splendor that is in the cows and the light in Brahman, let that strength be created in me.[5]

20. Whisk from yak's tail hair (*cāmara*). A *cāmari gai* (taken from a cow) may also be used. Nowadays, synthetic ones are also common. Unlike the full-sized *cāmara* used in other parts of the worship, the one used for *adhivāsa* is only a few inches long.

> *Om vāta ā vātu bheṣajam śambhu mayobhu no hṛde/ praṇa āyuṃṣi tariṣat/*
> *anena cāmarena bhagavad durgāyāḥ . . .*[RV.10.186.1a]
>
> Om! Filling our hearts with health and joy, may Vāta breathe his balm on us. May he prolong our days of life.

21. Mirror (*darpaṇa*).

> *Om āditpratnasya retaso jyotiḥ paśyanti vāsaram/ paro yadidhyate divā/*
> *anena darpaṇena bhagavad durgāyāḥ . . .* [RV.8.6.30a]
>
> Om! Then, verily, they see the light refulgent of primeval seed,
> Kindled on yonder side of heaven.

22. Lamp (*dīpa*).

> *Om āyurjyotiḥ ravijyotiḥ/ uhovā evārkajyotiḥ/*
> *anena dīpena bhagavad durgāyāḥ . . .*
>
> Om! The light of longevity, the light of the sun, or the light of *arka* [fire].[6]

The *purohita* now picks up the entire platter with worship materials (*praśasti pātra*) in his hand. On it he places a small burning lamp. He touches it to the earth and then to the Devī in her various forms. He repeats the process three times.

> *Om udyallikāmārocaya/ imāllokāmārocaya/*
> *prajābhūtamārocaya/ viśvambhūtamārocaya/*
> *anena praśastipātrena bhagavad durgāyāḥ . . .*
>
> Om! Illuminate the path of light. Illuminate this world.
> Let the world shine as your progeny. Let the universe shine in thy light.

A *dhunuci* (a large clay cup with pedestal and handle) is filled with coal or coconut husks and burned. *Dhuna* (incense powder) is added to it with sandalwood powder and *guggulu* (which produces a sweet smell). It burns continuously through the *adhivāsa*, filling the space with a pleasant sweet smoke, adding to the atmosphere of heightened expectancy. The *purohita* occasionally passes the *dhunuci* before the Devī.

Adhivāsa of the *Khaḍga* (Sword) and *Darpaṇa* (Mirror)

During this *adhivāsa* ritual, the *purohita* anoints the sword (*khaḍga*), which will be used for the blood sacrificial offering (*bali*) or its substitute (e.g., a type of melon [*kuṣmāṇḍā*]). He also anoints the mirror (*darpaṇa*), which is used later in the *pūjā* to worship (particularly bathe) the Devī in her form in the clay image. While it is possible to see this as merely a purification of worship items, it is more reasonable to recognize the sword and the mirror as the Devī herself. The potencies of both items are being aroused.

Adhivāsa of the *Navapatrikā* (Nine Plants)

The *purohita* has simultaneously been anointing the nine plants, one of which is the *bilva* tree, also called Śrīphala. Each of these plants symbolizes a constituent goddess form of the Great Goddess Durgā. The nine plants, on which more details will be provided in the section on invocation and worship, are:

1. Kadalī/Rambhā (plantain): It is a large tree about four to five feet tall. It should not be cut, but uprooted and its roots washed free of soil. It symbolizes the goddess Brahmāṇī.

2. Māna (a broad-leaved plant): Symbolizes the goddess Cāmuṇḍā.

3. Kacvī (or Kaccī) (a black-stalked plant): Symbolizes the goddess Kālikā (dark complexioned).

4. Haridrā (turmeric): Symbolizes Durgā (golden complexioned).
5. Jayantī (a kind of creeper, or barley): Symbolizes Kārtikī.
6. Śrīphala (a bilva branch containing two fruits resembling breasts): Symbolizing Śivā.
7. Dāḍimaḥ/mī (pomegranate): Symbolizing Raktadantikā.
8. Aśoka (a large shady tree; in the month of Caitra it blossoms with small red flowers): Symbolizes Śokarahitā.
9. Dhānya (rice paddy plant): Symbolizes the beneficence of Lakṣmī.

They are bound with the Aparājitā (*Clitora ternata*) creeper.

Namaskāra Mantra (Sacred Utterance of Homage)

The *purohita* now utters the *namaskāra mantra,* greeting and worshipping the Goddess after her anointment. He says:

> *Om sarva maṅgala maṅgalye śive sarvārtha sadhike*
> *śaranye tryambake gaurī nārāyaṇī namas' tute.* [DSS.11.9]
>
> Om! You are the abode of all auspiciousness. O consort of Śiva, you are the giver of every kind of object (you are the means by which one can achieve all sorts of desired ends). You are the last resort, O mother of the three gods, salutations to you O Gaurī, O Nārāyaṇī.

He now leaves the *bilva* tree and goes to the premises that will serve as the temple for the clay image of Durgā.

Preparing the Altar

The *purohita* draws a *yantra* on the floor of the shrine room (or temple). This is either an eight-petalled lotus (*aṣṭadala kamala*) or the *sarvatobhadra maṇḍala*.[7] He covers it with earth, and sprinkles it with five kinds of grain (*pañca śasya*). He establishes a jar (*ghaṭa*) atop the earth altar, filling it with clear water, placing mango twigs in its mouth and topping it with a green coconut. This he covers with a green coconut and ties it with a small red cloth (Hindi/Bengali: *aṅgoca/gamca*). Since this installation of the jar (*ghaṭasthāpana*) is done rapidly, he may use the Tantric method previously mentioned. The jar (*ghaṭa*) is set in the front of the earth altar, leaving room for the clay image.

The production of the clay image complex is itself an elaborate procedure. The Pals are regarded as the traditional family of image makers in Bengal. Bengali families, such as the Mitras of Chaukhamba, actually supported the migration of certain Pals to Banāras to serve as image makers.[8] Durgā Pūjā images are the occupational mainstay of the craftsmen, who also produce images for Kālī, Sarasvatī, Lakṣmī, and Viśvakarman Pūjās. Construction of the clay image complex begins on the second day of the bright fortnight of Āṣāḍha (June/July). This is Ratha Yātrā, the chariot festival to Jagannātha, Viṣṇu as Lord of the Universe. The skeletons of the images are built of bamboo and dried ulu grass (*imperata cylindrica*) and supported on a base of mango wood. The earthen dough is mixed with cow dung and rice husks, and skillfully molded onto the bamboo and grass substructure.[9] The *pratimā*, as the image complex is called, consists of Durgā atop her lion mount, engaged in the act of slaying the buffalo demon, Mahiṣa. She is flanked by images of Gaṇeśa and Lakṣmī to the right, and Kārtikeya and Sarasvatī to the left. Gaṇeśa's mouse, Lakṣmī's owl, Sarasvatī's swan, and Kārtikeya's peacock are also depicted beside them.[10]

There are two types of image clusters used in Durgā Pūjā. In the traditional Bengali type commonly used in Bengali homes and community celebrations, all the images are contained in a single unit called the *kaṭhamo*, which is topped by the *chal*, a decorated arch (see Figures 1.3, 4.3, 4.8.1, and 4.8.3). A host of other deities, including Śiva, Kālī, the ten *avatāras* of Viṣṇu, and the Mahāvidyās, ten forms of the Devī, may be painted on the *chal*. While in Bengal the *chal* is usually not painted by the Pals but by some other folk artists, in Banāras the Pals do the arch painting as well. The Pals and other artisans also produce the other type of image complex, popular among the non-Bengali community (*sārvajanīna*) *pūjās*. Since the trend has been toward larger images that cannot be contained in a single unit, the cluster has separate *mūrtis* of the gods (Gaṇeśa and Kārtikeya) and goddesses (Lakṣmī and Sarasvatī) with a central image of the triad, Durgā, Siṅgha, and Mahiṣāsura (see Figure 1.4). Certain families, such as the Mitras, include other deities in the complex, such as Rāma, Śiva, and the monkey deity, Hanumān (see Figure 2.1). The Bengali type of image leans toward an older customary style (i.e., forms, colors) of depicting the deities. The non-Bengali images, in contrast, opt for forms with wider public appeal. Artisans informed me that the Devī's alluring appearance in these images is inspired by popular Indian film actresses, while the demon's abundant musculature is derived from Greco-Roman sculpture, as well as comicbook superheroes and villains (see Figure 3.2).

After the clay images have dried for several weeks, they are intricately painted and varnished. They are carefully carried to the place of worship (See Figure 4.3). The Lahiri home is a three-storied quadrangle containing rooms surrounding a paved courtyard that is open to the sky. The ground-floor rooms that surround the courtyard are fronted by wide, high-roofed porches, whose stone pillars support corridor/verandahs on the upper floors. The place of worship is located on the porch on the north side of the quadrangle, and it is here that the image complex is brought and carefully placed. Family members, most of whom only now get their first view of the image, gather around with excitement. They comment on the details and beauty of the artful creation. The deities (including the demon, and the mounts) are already treated like the arriving family members and guests. "Durgā looks good; she seems to have gained weight since last year," said one of the Lahiri grandchildren.[11]

Adhivāsa of the Clay Image

The *purohita* may now repeat the entire elaborate *adhivāsa* ritual previously performed at the site of the *bilva* tree (see Figure 4.3). Sometimes he just makes a simple offering with flowers and sandalwood paste. In the elaborate *adhivāsa* he makes sure to touch the hearts of all the divine images, including Mahiṣāsura. The devotion paid to Mahiṣa during Durgā Pūjā contests superficial interpretations that the Goddess and the demon simply represent a struggle between good and evil.

Kāṇḍā Ropaṇam (Erecting the Staffs)

The *purohita* now places four forked sticks (*kāṇḍā*) around the image and wraps string seven or more times around them. This gesture of cordoning off sanctified space is done privately with the *yajamāna* in preparation for the rituals of the following day.

4.4 Saptamī

Varaṇa (Selection of the *Purohita*)

The *purohita* begins with his everyday (*nitya*) ritual actions (*kriyā*) on the seventh (*saptamī*) day. After finishing these (at his own home), he approaches the shrine of Durgā (in the *yajamāna*'s home), where the clay images were installed the day before and binds a red thread on the Devī's wrist while uttering the Durgā Gāyatrī Mantra.

Figure 4.3 The *purohita* prepares to perform the anointing *(adhivāsa)* rite of the clay image complex at the patron's home.

> *Om mahādevyai vidmahe/ durgāyai devyai dhīmahi/ tanno devī pracodayāt.*
>
> We know the Great Goddess. We make a meditation of the goddess Durgā. May that Goddess guide us (on the right path).[1]

He then takes his seat (*āsana*) and asks the *yajamāna* to present himself near the altar. The *yajamāna* sits facing north, and the *purohita* remains seated facing east. The *yajamāna* sips water thrice, wiping his lips with the cow's ear (*gokarṇa*) *mudrā*, and says:

> *Om viṣṇuḥ/ om viṣṇuḥ/ om viṣṇuḥ.*

The *yajamāna* then offers the *purohita* a red flower (*japā*), *dūrvā* grass, and washed uncooked rice in a copper vessel (possibly the *kuśī*), while uttering:

> *Om namo vivasvate brahman bhāsvate viṣṇutejase jagat savitre śucaye savitre karmadāyine idamargham/*
> *Om śrī sūryāya namaḥ.*
>
> Om! I pay obeisance to the Sun, associated with all glory, the supreme reality, shining, the progenitor and giver of fruits of actions; this offering of mine, which is given back to the universe, is always pure.

With this utterance he offers up the content on the plate, making an obeisance to the Sun:

> *Om javākusumasaṅkāśam kāśyapeyam mahādyutim/*
> *dhvāntārim sarvapāpaghnam praṇato 'smi divākaram.*
>
> Om! It is the color of the China rose (*javā*), exceedingly luminous, the son of Kaśyapa, remover of darkness, destroyer of all sins, I bow myself down to that maker of the day.[2]

Then looking at the *purohita*, he says:

> *Om sādhu bhavān āstam.* Om! May you be seated comfortably.

The *purohita* answers:

> *Om sādhvahamāse.* Om! I am well seated.

The *yajamāna* says:

> *Om arcayiṣyāmoḥ bhavantam.* Om! I shall pay reverence to you.

The *purohita* replies:

> *Om arcaya.* Om! You may go ahead.

The *yajamāna* then takes sandalwood paste, a flower, two pieces of cloth (an upper and lower garment made of silk, a cotton-silk blend, pure cotton, or artificial silk), a sacred thread (*yajña sūtra*), a seat (e.g., a woolen blanket), a *kuśāsana* (seat made of *kuśa* grass), a silver ring (*aṅgulīyaka*), betel leaf and nut (*pān*) and places these into the hands of the priest. It is progressively more common for patrons to provide *purohita*s with cash to purchase their personal essentials for the *pūjā*.

He asks the priest (the *purohita* is referred to as *ācārya* in these prayers) to uncover his knee and takes *dūrvā* grass, a flower, and washed rice in the *kuśī* in his left palm. Covering it with his right palm, he touches it to the knee of the *purohita* in a gesture of politeness and meek reverence. It parallels a gesture in the marriage ritual when the father of the bride touches the groom's knee. He then recites this oath (*saṅkalpa*):

> *Om viṣṇur namo 'dya āśvine māsi śukle pakṣe saptamī tithāvārabhya mahānavamim yāvat mat saṅkalpita durgāpūjāna karmaṇi ācārya karma karṇāya amuka gotram śrī amuka devaśarmāṇam gandhadibhir abhyarcya bhavantamaham vṛṇe.*
>
> Om Viṣṇu! From this day onward, in the bright fortnight in the month of Āṣvina, from the seventh lunar day to the great ninth, as has been desired by me for the purpose of performing Durgā Pūjā, I, after showing reverence to you by presenting sandalwood paste, etc., am selecting/appointing you, belonging to the *gotra* named _________ as my priest.

The *purohita* answers:

> *Om vṛto 'smi.* Om! I have been chosen.

The *yajamāna* says:

> *Om yathāvihitam ācārya karma kuru.*
>
> Om! Please perform the Durgā Pūjā ritual according to the method.

The *purohita* responds:

> *Om yathajñām karvāṇi.* Om! I shall do it according to my knowledge.

If the *tantradhāraka* is present, the same ritual is repeated for him. He will officially be referred to as the *tantradhāra karma karaṇa*.[3] These rites are curtailed at the Lahiri home (see Figure 4.4.1).

Figure 4.4.1 The purohita is formally commissioned by the patron *(yajamāna)*.

Saptamī *Sāmānya Vidhi* (Preliminary Common Rituals on the Seventh)

The *purohita* now occupies the seat again and sips water three times (*ācamana*). He then utters the *svasti vācanam*. He follows this with a call for the presence of the sun, moon, and so on, and for an auspicious beginning to the ritual.[4] He then makes a common offering (*sāmānya argha*), purifies the flowers (*puṣpa śuddhi*), and his seat (*āsana śuddhi*). He then makes a simple flower and fragrance offering to all major deities.

Main *Saṅkalpa* (Oath)

The *purohita* now utters the long *saṅkalpa* (oath), concerning all the rituals to be performed on Saptamī, Aṣṭamī, and Navamī. This is the same one uttered before the *bodhana* rituals on Ṣaṣṭhī. He does this while placing a piece of myrobalan/gooseberry (*haritaki*) into the *kuśī* (small copper ladle) along with water, flowers, and washed rice. He carries it in his left palm and covers it with his right. He places both hands on the right side. As he finishes the oath, he overturns the *kuśī* in a gesture of commitment.

Saṅkalpa Sūkta (Oath Hymn)

He now reads the *saṅkalpa sūkta*. While doing this, he takes washed rice in his hand and throws down the grain in small pinches saying: "*Om svasti, svasti, svasti.*"

Note: The rice grains and the *kuśī* are located to the Northeast (Īśana corner) of the *purohita*.

Cutting of the *Bilva* Tree Branch

The *purohita* now goes to the *bilva* tree and worships it with a ten-part devotional service (*daśopacāra*). These include washing of the feet (*pādya*), water for rinsing the mouth (*ācamana*), offerings (*argha*), and so on. Then with folded hands, he utters:

Om bilva vṛkṣa mahābhāga sadā tvam śaṅkara priyaḥ/
gṛhītvā tava śakāñca durgāpūjā karomyaham/
sakha cchedodbhavam duhkham nacakāryam tvayā prabho/
devai gṛhītvā teśākhām pujyā durgeti viśrutiḥ.

> Om! O great-souled *bilva* tree, you are always dear to Śaṅkara. Taking a branch of yours, I shall perform the worship ritual to Durgā. The pain born of the cutting of the branch should not be minded by you, O master. It is said that "taking the branch, it was worshipped as Durgā by the gods."

The prayer infers a divine precedent for the act of worshipping a branch of the *bilva* tree as a form of Durgā.

Then taking a knife, the *purohita* utters the *mantra*:

> *Chindi chindi phaṭ phaṭ svāhā.*

And cutting the branch (this is only a symbolic gesture since the selected branch has already been separated from the main branch earlier to avoid difficulties during the ritual), he says:

> *Om putrāyur dhana bṛdhyartham nesyāmi candikālayam/*
> *bilva śākhān samāsṛtya lakṣmīm rājyam prayacchame/*
> *āgacchacaṇḍike devi sarva kalyāṇa hetave/*
> *pūjān gṛhāṇa sumukhi namaste śaṅkara priye.*

> Om! For the purpose of the increase of sons and wealth, I shall take you to the temple of Caṇḍikā. After making your abode in the branch of the *bilva* tree, please endow me with wealth and kingship. Please, O Caṇḍikā, come along for the purpose of giving all sorts of auspiciousness/well-being. O nice-faced one, dear to Śaṅkara, please accept my offerings/worship.

With this *mantra* offering, and the beating of drums, blowing of conch shells, and ringing of bells, the branch is brought to the Devī shrine room and joined into the *navapatrikā*. The *bilva* branch, called Śrīphala, possesses two fruit that resemble breasts. It is lashed to the plantain (*kadalī*), which is also about three to five feet in height. These two plants give the *navapatrikā* body its form. The other plants are smaller and are wound like creepers around these and tied into place.

In this rite, the goddess Caṇḍikā is explicitly invoked into the *bilva* tree, which is to be worshipped as a form of Durgā. Caṇḍī or Caṇḍikā is the most common other name for Durgā. In fact, the *Durgā Saptaśatī* is often referred to as the *Caṇḍī*, or the *Caṇḍī Pāṭha* (Recitation [of Honorific Verses] to Caṇḍī). In contrast to the martial dimension of worship, where "defeat of one's enemies" is requested, here it is increase in sons, wealth, status (kingship), and auspiciousness. While the symbols and prayers that accompanied the *ghaṭa* rituals aimed to induce fertility, the *bilva* tree rituals seek to promote an increase in beneficence.

Bathing of the *Navapatrikā*

There is evidence to suggest that ritual bathing has ancient roots in Hindu social and religious behavior. Indus Valley civilization sites reveal the central position of what appear to be public baths in the layout of their cities. While we cannot be certain about the usages of those baths, ritual bathing for the purpose of purification is still common at temple tanks and sacred rivers throughout the subcontinent. "Archeologists generally agree that [the Great Bath at Mohenjo-daro] must have been associated with some sort of bathing ritual, and this strongly recalls later Hindu practices and concepts of pollution. A similar construction in Indian villages today catches and retains monsoon rains, and is used for practical as well as ritual bathing" (Craven 1976:11–12). It becomes clear that bathing does not simply serve the function of cleansing pollution but brings about a change in being. It is a transforming purification. This explains why baths are not merely conducted with cleansing agents such as water and soaps, but include anointments with materials of sacred purity such as the products of the cow. In the Vedic Rājasūya ritual, the king would be bathed in numerous materials and in the process undergo a form of spiritual rebirth into a pure, rejuvenated body (Heesterman 1957:7). Bathing someone else's feet is an act of loving service, such as honoring the king, queen, master, child, guest, or deity. Hindu deities are regularly bathed as part of the devotional service offered them. It is a combination of these notions and practices that inform the ritual activities of bathing which take place on Mahāsaptamī.

The *purohita* makes a preparation of turmeric (just a pinch) and oil and smears the body of the *navapatrikā* saying:

> *Om kosi katamosi kasmai tvā kāyatva suśloka sumaṅgala satyarājan*
>
> Om! Who are you? From where have you come? For whom are you here? Your body is auspicious and remains luminously manifest in truth.
>
> *Om nānārūpadhare devi divyavastrāvaguṇṭhite/*
> *tava lepana matreṇa sarva pāpam vinaśyati.*
>
> Om! O Goddess, you assume different forms. You are covered with divine clothes.
> Only by smearing your body with these unguents all kinds of sins disappear.

The questions asked in the first verse mirror the sort of speculative awe felt in the face of the mystery of existence voiced in the so-called Creation Hymn of the *Ṛg Veda* (10.129). In the second verse, the mysterious divine presence is identified as the Devī, who is recognized as assuming a variety of forms. The most common interpretation of bathing a divinity would be that although she is clothed in celestial garments, the process of manifestation (like the journey of a guest) has brought with it some material "pollution." These defilements are removed by anointing the Devī with the turmeric and oil mixture. However, the litany's use of the term *pāpam* suggests evildoing or sinfulness. Since the Devī is clearly not susceptible to such spiritual defilements, it is evident that the current anointing and the allusion to the upcoming bathing of the *navapatrikā* in a variety of substances is actually cleansing the votary and the manifest creation itself.

The Devī's manifest body, which is the created cosmos, including within it the *purohita* and the votaries, is progressively being vivified with the Devī's awakened presence. It is this manifest body that is being cleansed of impurities to make it a suitable receptacle for the Devī's immanent presence. Bathing cleanses the worshipper and the world, the physical form of the otherwise transcendent and immaculate Goddess.

Purification of the *Pañcagavya* (Five Products of the Cow)

The *navapatrikā* will first be bathed in five substances from the cow (*pañcagavya*). The *purohita* first purifies them with the following purification (*śodana*) *mantra*s:

1. For the cow urine he uses the Gāyatrī Mantra:

> *Om bhūr bhuvaḥ svaḥ tat savitur vareṇyam bhargo devasya dhīmahi dhiyo yoḥ naḥ pracodayāt.*
>
> Om! He who gives birth to the three worlds (*bhuḥ, bhuvaḥ, svaḥ*), the glorified light of that progenitor of the worlds, we meditate on that light, who may guide our intellect.[5]

2. For the cow dung:

> *Om gāvaścidghā sāmānyavaḥ sajātyena marutaḥ savandavaḥ rihate kakubho mithaḥ.* [RV.8.20.21a]
> Om! Allied by common ancestry, ye Maruts, even the Cows, alike in energy, Lick, all by turns, each other's head.

3. For the cow milk:

> *Om gavyoḥ ṣuṇo yathā purāsvayota rathayā varivasya mahāmaha.* [RV.8.46.10a]
>
> Om! Responding to our wish for cows, for steeds and chariots, as of old, Be gracious, Greatest of the Great!

4. For the cow curd (*dadhi*):

Om dadhikrāvno akāriṣam jiṣnoraśvasya vājinaḥ/
surabhi no mukhā karat praṇa āyuṃṣi tāriṣat. [RV.4.39.6a; SV.1.358a]

Om! So have I glorified with praise strong Dadhikrāvan, conquering Steed.
Sweet may he make our mouths; may he prolong the days we have to live.

5. For the ghee (*ghṛta*):

Om ghṛtavatī bhuvanānām abhiśriyorvī pṛthvī madhudughe supeśasā/
dyāvā pṛthvī varuṇasya dharmaṇā viṣkabhite ajare bhūriretasā.
[RV.6.70.1a]

Om! Filled full of fatness, compassing all things that be, wide, spacious, dropping meath [mead], beautiful in their form.
The Heaven and the Earth by Varuṇa's decree, unwasting, rich in germs, stand parted each from each.

Then he utters a *mantra* for the purification of the whole mixture.

Purification of the *Pañcāmṛta* (Five Nectars)

He also purifies the five nectars (*pañcāmṛta*) in the process, since it also consists of curd, milk, and ghee for which the same *mantra*s as above are used. For the two other ingredients, sugar (*śarkarā*) and honey (*madhu*), he recites:

For the sugar:

The *kuśodoka mantra*. This is the *mantra* for water infused with *kuśa* grass.

For the honey, he utters:

Om madhu vātā ṛtāyate madhu kṣaranti sindhavaḥ/ mādhvīr naḥ santrosadhiḥ/
om madhu naktamuto sasa madhu mat pārthivam rajah/
madhu dyaurastu naḥ pita/ madhu mānno vanaspatir madhumām astu sūryah/
mādhvīrgāvo bhavantu naḥ/ om madhu madhu madhu. [RV.1.90.6–8a]

Om! The winds waft sweets, the rivers pour sweets for the man who keeps the Law:
So may the plants be sweet for us.
Sweet be the night and sweet the dawns, sweet the terrestrial atmosphere;
Sweet be our Father Heaven to us.
May the tall tree be full of sweets for us and full of sweets the Sun:
May our milch-kine be sweet for us.
Om! Sweet, sweet, sweet.

Bathing the *Navapatrikā* in the *Pañcagavya*

The *purohita* holds the *navapatrikā* over a large vessel (to catch the bath fluids) and begins to bathe it by pouring consecrated substances over it while uttering appropriate *mantras* (See Figure 4.4.2).

When bathing it with consecrated cow urine, he says:

Om hrīṃ caṇḍikāyai namaḥ. Obeisance to Caṇḍikā!

With cow dung:

Om gāṃ gauryai namaḥ. Obeisance to Gaurī!

With milk:

Om hrīṃ triṇetrāyai namaḥ. Obeisance to She who Possesses the Third Eye!

With curd:

Om hrīṃ bhairavyai namaḥ. Obeisance to Bhairavī!

With ghee:

Om hrīṃ bhuvaneśvaryai namaḥ. Obeisance to Bhuvaneśvarī!

Then he bathes it in water touched with *kuśa* grass saying:

Om hrīṃ pārvatyai namaḥ. Obeisance to Pārvatī!

Bathing the *Navapatrikā* in Nine Kinds of Water

The *purohita* next bathes the *navapatrikā* in nine different kinds of water while uttering the following *mantras*. Each is directed to a particular plant in the *navapatrikā*.

1. In hot water, uttering:

Om kadalī tarusamsthāsi viṣṇūvakṣah sthalāśraye/
namaste navapatri tvam namaste caṇḍanāyike.

Om! You, who abides in the breast of Viṣṇu, are abiding in the plantain tree (*kadalī*). I bow to you, O divine nine plants. You are representing Caṇḍanāyikā (one of the forms of Caṇḍī).

Figure 4.4.2 The *purohita* bathes the Cluster of Nine Plants *(navapatrikā)*.

As the beloved of Śiva, the Devī is associated with Satī, Pārvatī, and the goddess Kālī. Here she is also identified with the *śrīvatsa*, an auspicious sign or curl of hair on Viṣṇu's breast (Narayanan 1982). The term *kadalī* is also used to describe a beautiful woman. A myth tells how the *yogi* Gorakhnāth rescued his master Matsyendranāth who was made a prisoner by the women of Kadalī. Gorakhnāth told his master that it was Durgā who had brought on the "forgetfulness" that had almost cost him immortality (see Eliade 1969:313/14). In this myth Durgā's power of delusion is implicitly linked to the beauty of women. The plantain tree, which is several feet high and gives the *navapatrikā* its main form, will later be draped in a *sārī* so that it resembles a woman.

2. Water from a tank:

> *Om kaccitvam sthāvarsthāsi sadā siddhi pradāyinī/*
> *durgārupeṇa sarvatra snānena vijayaṃ kuru.*
>
> Om! You are called *kacci.*[6] You remain in immovable objects, and you are the giver of all kinds of attainments in the form of Durgā. Through this bathing of yours bestow victory upon us.

This verse is an excellent example of how the litany provides us with clues about Durgā's nature. It clearly states that Durgā permeates immovable or stable objects (*sthāvarsthāsa*). This is extremely helpful in understanding why devotees identify structural integrity with the Devī's presence. While it is commonly stated that Śakti is the dynamic feminine energy that animates the creation, the static abiding nature of this power is often overlooked. For instance, the strength and impregnability of a fortress (*durga*) would depend on the presence of the Goddess, and this is why it is very common to find Durgā temples associated with fortresses, often within their very walls.[7] The Devī's solidifying presence extends to other constructions as well, such as bridges, which incorporate the soteriological notion of fording dangerous waters that are difficult (*dur*) to traverse (*ga*). Goddess temples, such as the one at Durgā Kuṇḍ, may themselves be identified as the Devī. The ideas of protection, indestructibility, and firm support extend to recognizing Durgā's presence in armor (*kavaca*), weapons (*āyudha*), rocks, mountains, altars, thrones, and so on. Thus, conceptions of Durgā's power (*śakti*) constitute a sacred physics. In addition to her presence as cosmic kinetic energy, the Devī is also present as a latent, static, potential, and bonding energy. Durgā's bonding power is further thought to permeate community groups, unifying and strengthening them.

3. Dew:

> *Om haridre hararūpāsi śaṅkarasya sadā priyā/*
> *rudrarūpāsi devi tvaṃ sarvasiddhiṃ prayacchame.*
>
> Om! You are called turmeric (*haridrā*). You represent the form of Hara (Śiva). You are always beloved by Śaṅkara. In the form of Rudra, O lady divine, bestow upon us all kinds of attainments.

4. Water mixed with flour:

> *Om jayanti jayarūpāsi jagatām jayahetave/*
> *namāṇi tvām mahādevi jayaṃ dehi gṛhe mama.*
>
> Om! Jayantī is the form of victory (*jaya*). She has assumed this form for the purpose of giving victory to worldly people. O great lady, I pay obeisance to you. Give me victory in my house.

5. *Sarvauṣadhi* water (mixture of powdered herbs purchased at a *pūjā* supply shop):

> *Om śriphala śrīniketo 'si sadā vijaya bardhana/*
> *dehi me hitakā māṃśca prasanno bhava sarvadā.*
>
> Om! You (*śrīphala*) are the abode of beauty and always increaser of victory. Please bestow upon me the desired well-being and remain satisfied all the time.

6. Ocean water:

Om dāḍimyaghavināśāya kṣunnāśāya ca vedhasā/
nirmitā phalakāmāya prasīda tvam harapriye.

Om! O you pomegranate (*dāḍimī*), for the purpose of removal of sins and of hunger, Lord Brahmā created you. You have been made for the purpose of fulfilment of the fruits of desire. O beloved of Hara, be pleased with me.

7. Scented, perfumed water:

Om sthirābhava sadā durge aśoke śokahāriṇi/
mayā tvām pūjitā durge sthirā bhava harapriye.

Om! The Aśoka tree is one which removes the sorrow of separation. O Durgā, remain steadily here. I have worshipped you, O beloved of Hara, for this purpose.

8. Water containing jewels:

Om mānamānyeṣu vṛkṣeṣu mānanīyaḥ surā suraiḥ/
snapayāmi mahādevīṃ mānam dehi namo'stute.

Om! O *māna*, among trees you *māna* are shown respect above all and even by gods and demons you are paid reverence. Obeisance to you Great Goddess.

9. Water mixed with sesamum oil:

Om lakṣmīstvam dhānyarūpāsi prāṇinām prāṇadāyinī/
sthirātyantam hi no bhūtva gṛhe kāmapradā bhava.

Om! You are Lakṣmī in the form of paddy (*dhānya*), and you are the giver of life to all living beings. While remaining steadily in my house, be the giver of fulfilment of all desires.

Bathing the *Navapatrikā* in Eight Waters

The *purohita* next bathes the *navapatrikā* with water from eight jars filled separately with different kinds of water. While the previous bathing was intended for each of the plants, this series represents homage paid to the Devī by various groups of divine beings.

1. Water from the Gaṅgā:

Om devyāstvāmabhiṣiñcantu brahmaviṣṇumaheśvarāḥ/
vyomagaṅgāmbupūrṇena ādyena kalasena tu.

Om! Let Brahmā, Viṣṇu, and Maheśvara bathe the divine Goddess with the first jar full of water that has fallen from the river Gaṅgā in the void/sky (*vyoma*).[8]

2. Rain water:

Om marutaścābhiṣiñcantu bhaktimantaḥ suresvarim/
meghāmbu paripūrṇena dvitīya kalasena tu.

Om! Let the heavenly air/wind gods (*maruta*) who are devoted to you, the monarch of the gods, bathe you with the second jarful of water collected from water falling from the cloud.[9]

3. Water from the Sarasvatī River (collected from Prayāga):[10]

Om sārasvatena toyena saṃpūrnena surottamām/
vidyādharāścabhiṣiñcantu tṛīya kalasena tu.

Om! Let Vidyādharas bathe you, the supreme of all divine ladies, with water form the third jar filled to the brim from the Sarasvatī River.[11]

4. Water from the sea:

Om śakrādyaścābhiṣiñcantu lokapālāḥ samāgatāḥ/
sāgarodakapūrṇena caturtha kalasena tu.

Om! Let Indra and the other guardians of the quarters who have come here bathe you with the fourth jar full of water filled with the water of the sea.

5. Water mixed with pollen from the lotus flower:

Om vāriṇā paripūrṇena padmareṇu sugandhinā/
pañcamenabhiṣiñcantu nāgāśca kalasena tu.

Om! May the serpents bathe you with the fifth jar of water, which has been made fragrant with pollen from the lotus flower.[12]

6. Water from a waterfall:

Om himvaddhemakūṭādyāścābhiṣiñcantu parvataḥ/
nirjharodaka pūrṇena saṣṭhena kalasena tu.

Om! May the mountains, beginning with the Himālaya, Hemakūtā, and others, bathe you with the sixth jar full of water collected from waterfalls (or fountains).

7. Water from different holy spots:

> *Om sarvatīrthāṃbupūrṇena kalasena sureśvarīm/*
> *saptamenābhiṣiñcantu ṛṣayaḥ sapta khecarāḥ.*
>
> Om! The seventh jar is filled with water collected from holy rivers and lakes. May the seven sages who roam about in the void/sky bathe you with this jar.

8. Water scented with sandalwood paste:

> *Om vāsavaścābhiṣiñcantu kalasenaṣṭamena tu/*
> *aṣṭamaṅgala saṃyukte durge devi namo'stute.*
>
> Om! May the Vasus bathe you with the eighth jar full of water, O Durgā, who are associated with the eight kinds of auspicious things.[13] I pay obeisance to you, O Goddess Durgā.

The *purohita* now removes the excess water from the body of the *navapatrikā* with a new cloth and wraps it in a red-bordered *sārī*, draping part of it over the top of the plantain leaves, so that it resembles a modest lady, her head and face concealed by the shroud. He places it on a raised altar near the Gaṇeśa image.

The *navapatrikā* form of the Devī elicits connections with traditions of *yakṣa* worship. *Yakṣa*s, and their female counterparts, *yakṣī*s, are supernatural beings who inhabit forests and wild areas. They are associated with the fecundity of nature and are often depicted beside trees or even melded with vegetation (see Coomaraswamy 1971:32).[14] The pairing of the *navapatrikā* with Gaṇeśa is thus appropriate, since the elephant-headed god "has his origins among the thick-set, fat-bellied, beneficent *yakṣa* deities, whose worship in India was prevalent long before the theistic worship of either Vishnu or Shiva came to the fore" (Eck 1982:182). However, the *navapatrikā*'s placement next to Gaṇeśa, makes Durgā's connection to Gaṇeśa more complex. Although most worshippers consider Gaṇeśa, in the clay image cluster, to be Durgā's child, in his association with Durgā as the *navapatrikā*, he is the Goddess's husband.

The *navapatrikā* is commonly called the *kalā bou* by Bengalis, a term that means a "newly married lady made of a banana plant." According to Pandit Chakravarty this is "the opinion of illiterate people since the *navapatrikā* represents Devī Durgā." However, from my questioning it was clear that most people thought of the *navapatrikā*, once it was clad in the *sārī*, as Gaṇeśa's wife.[15] Most did not know the details about the constituent plants of the *navapatrikā*, but generally identified it (particularly the *bilva* branch) as the Devī. Thus the *bilva* branch, regarded by all as a form of Durgā, undergoes a perceptual transformation among many votaries in the course of the ritual, as it is lashed to the banana and other plants. The *navapatrikā* is then ambiguously thought of both as Durgā herself and as the wife of Gaṇeśa.[16]

Gaṇeśa is often thought of as unmarried. At times he is paired with two wives, Buddhi/Ṛddhi and Siddhi, whose names mean intellect/prosperity and spiritual attainment, respectively.[17] Since these qualities are generally also attributed to the Goddess (e.g., under her epithets as Mahāvidyā, Śrī, and Siddhidātrī), it is appropriate to pair the *navapatrikā* with Gaṇeśa.[18] The Lahiri grandchildren told me a popular story about how Gaṇeśa wanted a wife and was tricked into marrying the *kalā bou*. Only later did he discover that she was a plant.[19] Gaṇeśa, with his potbelly and his ambivalent qualities of creating obstacles or being benevolent, mirrors, in form and character, Kubera, the god of the *yakṣa*s and of riches. The *navapatrikā* is very much a tree-sprite (*yakṣī*) form of the Goddess, and thus, too, is appropriately paired with Gaṇeśa. Early sculptures, such as a well-known example at Ellora, depict Gaṇeśa alongside groups of lesser goddesses.[20]

Formerly, in royal *pūjā*s, the king himself would wear the *navapatrikā*'s *sārī* on Vijayā Daśamī and parade around the town. His subjects and the women of the royal household would offer him homage with prostrations. The women would later wear the *sārī* themselves (Östör 1980:192). This rite forged an identification between the king, the royal women, and the Devī.

Mahāsnāna (Great Bathing) of the Goddess

The *purohita* now takes a large brass or earthenware pot and places a tripod in the center of it (See Figure 4.4.3). Upon the tripod he places a highly polished metal mirror (*darpaṇa*), arranging the apparatus so that the reflection (*pratibiṃba*) of the clay *mūrti* falls directly onto it. It would be impractical to bathe the earthen image due to its size and construction material (unbaked clay). The mirror is a practical alternative. However, it is also a symbolic device, for the mirror, in its use during self-adornment, is traditionally associated with the feminine. Also quite importantly, it suggests the illusory forms of manifest reality (i.e., the play of the Devī as Mahāmāyā) against the background of her unchanging self (i.e., as Brahman). The mirror, as an entity that has no intrinsic form or attributes, but which reflects all without itself being changed, is a symbol of the underlying essence of all reality.

In the Lahiri home, a large earthenware jar with a wide mouth is used. A triangular support made of sticks is placed over the mouth. The mirror is placed upon this support which is *yoni* shaped and carries the same triadic symbolism of the tripod. The mirror had been previously consecrated during

Figure 4.4.3 The place of worship *(pūjālaya)* on Saptamī. Visible ritual instruments include the copper *kośa* and *kuśī,* the yantric tripod over the Devī's jar form, and the clay pot in which water from the Great Bath *(mahāsnāna)* is collected.

the *adhivāsa* ritual. The *purohita* will proceed to bathe the image of Durgā in the mirror.

It is traditionally prescribed that particular musical pieces, known as *rāga*s, be performed during the Great Bath on Saptamī, Aṣṭamī, and Navamī. These may be sung or preferably played on the *shehnai* or the harmonium, although other instruments are not inappropriate. These performances may be accompanied by dancers and other musical accompaniment. The Lahiris do not include any music performance in their celebrations, but the Mitra family still continues the tradition of playing *rāga*s through much of the rite. They have, however, ended the exuberant entertainments, which included dancing girls, that were an integral part of their celebrations. The entertainment and music may also be used during the *navapatrikā* baths. During the bath in Gaṅgā water, the Mālava *rāga* is prescribed. For rain water, the Lalitā; for water from the Sarasvatī, the Vibhāsā; and the Bhairavī for ocean water. The Kedāra *rāga* is prescribed for water with lotus pollen; the Varadi for water from a fountain; the Vasanta *rāga* for water from all the sacred *tīrtha*s; and the Dhanasi *rāga* for cold water.

Taking a small twig from the *bilva* tree (from the *navapatrikā* or the main *bilva* tree) that is about the length of eight digits (*aṅguli*), the *purohita* places it on the mirror, implicitly forging a link between the Devī in these forms. It is for the Goddess to wash her mouth and teeth. Pouring hot water on the twig, he utters:

> *Om āyurbālam yaśovarcaḥ prajāḥ paśu vasūni ca/*
> *brahmā prajñāñca medhāñca tvanno dehi vanaspate.*
>
> Om! Longevity, strength, reputation, and inner stamina, progeny, animals, and wealth. Let Brahmā bestow upon me insight, wisdom, memory (*medhā*), and place upon me, O lord of the trees, all these things.

The *purohita* now rubs the surface of the mirror with rice powder, intimating that he is rubbing the whole body of the Devī, while uttering:

> *Om udvartayāmi devi tvām mṛṇmaye śrīphale 'pi ca/*
> *sthirātyantam hi no bhūtvā gṛhe kāmapradā bhava.*
>
> Om! I am rubbing your whole body in the earthen image and the *bilva* fruit. You should remain steady in this place and be the giver of desires.

In so doing, he explicitly links the Devī in the clay image and the *navapatrikā/ bilva* through their reflection in the mirror.

Bathing with *Pañcagavya*

Then, in the method used for the *navapatrikā*, he bathes the Goddess's body with the five products from the cow (*pañcagavya*), using the same *mantra*s.

Bathing with the *Bhṛṅgāra*

Taking water in a spouted water container (*bhṛṅgāra*) traditionally used for the consecration of royalty, the *purohita* utters these *mantra*s one after another, as he pours them on the mirror's surface. It represents honorific devotion to the Devī by a wide variety of divine beings.

> *Om ātreyī bhāratī gaṅgā yamunā ca sarasvatī/*
> *sarayur gaṇḍakī puṇyā śvetagaṅgā ca kauśikī/*
> *bhogavatī ca pātāle svarge mandākinī tathā/*
> *sarvāḥ sumanaso bhūtvā bhṛṅgāraiḥ snāpayantute.*
>
> Om! The river Ātreyī, Bhāratī, Gaṅgā, Yamunā, Sarasvatī, Sarayu, Gaṇḍakī, Śvetagaṅgā, Kauśikī, the river in the nether region (*pātāla*), Bhogavatī, and Mandākinī, all are very auspicious rivers. With all their attention concentrated towards the divine deity, may they bathe you with a *bhṛṅgāra*.

Om surāstvāmabhiṣiñcatu brahmaviṣṇumaheśvarāḥ/
vāsudeva jagannāthastathā saṅkarṣaṇaḥ prabhuḥ/
pradyumnaścāniruddhaśca bhavantu vijayāya te/
ākhaṇḍalo 'gnirbhagavān yamo vai naiṛtistathā/
varuṇa pavanaścaiva dhanādhyakśastathā śivaḥ/
brahmaṇā sahito śeṣo dikpālāḥ pāntu te sadā.

Om! Let all the heavenly beings, like Brahmā, Viṣṇu, and Maheśvara, Vāsudeva, who is the lord of the universe, and Saṅkarṣaṇa, the lord, Pradyumna, and Aniruddha bathe you and stand for your victory.[21] May the guardian deity of the east (i.e., Indra), Agni, Yama, Naiṛti, Varuṇa, and Pavana, the keeper of wealth (i.e., Kubera), and Śiva, Brahmā, along with Śeṣa, protect you all the time.

Om kīrtirlakṣmirdhṛtirmedhā puṣṭiḥ śraddhā kṣamā matiḥ/
buddhir lajjā vapuḥ śāntistuṣṭiḥ kāntiśca mātaraḥ/
etāstvāmabhiṣiñcantu rāhu ketuśca tarpitāḥ.

Om! May these Mothers (*mātṛ*), reputation (*kīrti*), wealth (*lakṣmi*), forbearance (*dhṛti*), memory (*medhā*), nourishment (*puṣṭi*), faith (*śraddhā*), forgiveness (*kṣamā*), intuition (*mati*), intellect (*buddhi*), bashfulness (*lajjā*), comeliness of form (*vapu*), peace (*śānti*), satisfaction (*tuṣṭi*), and delicate beauty (*kānti*) bathe you properly. And also Rāhu and Ketu.

Om ṛṣayo munayo gāvo devamātara eva ca/
devapatnyo dhruvā nāgā daityāścāpsarasāṃ gaṇāḥ/
astrāṇi sarvaśāstrāṇi rājāno vāhanāni ca/
auṣadhāni ca ratnāni kālasyāvayāśca ye/
Om saritaḥ sāgarāḥ sailāśtīrthāni jaladā nadāḥ/
devadānavagandharva yakṣarākṣasapannagāḥ/
ete tvāmambhiṣiñcantu dharmakāmartha siddhaye.

Om! Seers and sages, cows, the mothers of divine beings, their wives, the serpents, demons, the host of heavenly damsels, different kinds of weapons, all kinds of sacred texts, kings and their vehicles, medicinal herbs, jewels, the fractions of time, rivers, oceans, hills and mountains, givers of water (i.e., rivers and lakes), dwellers in heaven, demons, celestial musicians, *yakṣas*, *rākṣasas*, creeping animals, may these all bathe you properly for the attainment of the three worldly ends of life, righteousness (*dharma*), desires (*kāma*), and the means of their fulfilment (*artha*).

Om sindhu bhairavaśomādyā ye hradāḥ bhuvi saṃsthitāḥ/
sarve sumanaso bhūtvā bhṛṅgāraiḥ snāpayantu te.
Om kurukṣetraṃ prayāgaśca akṣayo vaṭasaṃjñakaḥ/
godāvarī viyadgaṅgā narmadā maṇikārnikā/
sarvāṇyetāni tīrthāni bhṛṅgāraiḥ snāpayantu te.
Om takṣakādyāśca ye nāgāḥ pātālatalavāsinaḥ/
sarve sumanaso bhūtvā bhṛṅgāraiḥ snāpayantu te.
Om durgā caṇḍeśvarī caṇḍi vārāhī kārtikī tathā/

> *harasiddhā tathā kālī indrāṇī vaiṣṇavī tathā/*
> *bhadrakālī viṣālākṣī bhairavī sarvarūpiṇī/*
> *etāḥ sumanaso bhūtvā bhṛṅgāraiḥ snāpayantu tāḥ.*

> Om! O the (male?) rivers Sindhu, Bhairava, Soma and other rivers that exist in this earth, after becoming mindful should bathe you with this *bhṛṅgāra*. Om! The sacred places like Kurukṣetra, Prayāga, where the deathless banyan tree exists, the river Godāvarī, the river in the sky, Narmadā, and the holy Maṇikarṇikā, after coming over here should bathe you with the *bhṛṅgāra*. Om! The serpents beginning with Takṣaka, who live in the nether world, with all willingness of their mind, should bathe you with the *bhṛṅgāra*. Om! Durgā, the most dreadful among the terrific forms, Vārāhī, Kārtikī, Harasiddhā, and Kālī, Indrānī, Vaiṣṇavī, Bhadrakālī, Viṣalakṣī, and Bhairavī, assuming all forms, having intentions of goodwill, should bathe you with this *bhṛṅgāra*.

This piece of the litany indicates that the Devī transcends even her epithet as Durgā, since Durgā is named as just one, albeit the supreme, of her fierce forms. Such usages of epithets suggest that the Devī *pūjā*, though called Durgā Pūjā is a composite of goddess-worship rites. It also suggests that although Durgā is the synonymous epithet of the Mahādevī (Great Goddess) in this *pūjā*, the Great Goddess is actually beyond all epithets.

Bathing with Waters Poured from the *Śaṅkha* (Conch Shell)

The *purohita* takes up a conch shell (*śaṅkha*) and bathes the mirror in different waters poured from it while reciting appropriate *mantras*. To save time and effort, this operation may be greatly curtailed by using Gaṅgā water alone, which serves as a metonymic equivalent for all waters.

Before each *mantra*, the *purohita* says, "This is a bath" (*etat snāniyam*).

Water from the Gaṅgā:

> *Om mandyākinyāstu yadvāri sarvapāpaharam śubham/*
> *svargasrotaśca vaiṣṇavyam snānam bhavatu tena te.*

> Om! The water of river Mandyākinī, auspicious and the remover of all kinds of sins, and the rivers of the heavens belonging to Viṣṇu, let your bathing be done by them.

Hot water:

> *Om pavitram paramam coṣṇam vahnijyoti samanvitam/*
> *jīvanaṃ sarvapāpaghnaṃ bhṛṅgāraiḥ snāpayantvimām.*

Om! The holy hot water housing the light of fire and life itself, and a remover of all sins, let it bathe you with *bhṛṅgāras*.

He also recites a Vedic verse:

Om āpo hi sṭhā mayo bhuvas tā na ūrje dadhātana/
mahe raṇāya cakṣase. [RV.10.9.1]

Om! Ye, Waters are beneficent: so help ye us to energy
That we may look on great delight.

Water mixed with gold:

Om pṛthivyām svarṇarūpeṇa devāṣṭhanti vai sadā/
sarvadoṣavināśārtham snāpayāmi maheśvarīm.

Om! Gods indeed remain always in the earth in the form of gold.
For the purpose of destruction of all kinds of defects/faults I am bathing this Great Goddess.

Water mixed with silver:

Om ambike tvam mahābhāge śārade pāpanāśinī/
snānenānena devi tvam varadā bhava suvrate.

Om! O you mother Ambikā, the most glorious one, you are known as Śāradā and the destroyer of sins. By this ritual bathing, O Goddess, you should become the giver of boons.

Plain water:

Om āpo hi sṭhā mayo bhuvastāna ūrje dadhātana/
mahe raṇāya cakṣase. [RV.10.9.1]

Om! Ye, Waters are beneficent: so help ye us to energy,
That we may look on great delight.

Water mixed with flowers:

Om agna āyāhi vītaye gṛṇāno havyadātaye nihotā satsi varhisi.
[SV.1.1a]

Om! Come, Agni, praised with song, to feast and sacrificial offering: sit
As Hotar [sacrificial priest] on the holy grass.[22]

Water mixed with fruit:

> *Om agna āyāhi vītaye gṛṇāno havyadātaye nihotā satsi varhisi.* [SV.1.1a]
>
> Om! Come, Agni, praised with song, to feast and sacrificial offering: sit
> As Hotar on the holy grass.[23]

Water with plain sugarcane juice:

> *Om nārāyaṇyai vidmahe bhagavatyai dhīmahi tanno gaurī pracodayāt.*
>
> Om! We know Nārāyaṇī. We make a meditation of the Goddess.
> May that goddess named Gaurī guide us (on the right path).

This is the Devī Gāyatrī Mantra. It is used as the consecration *mantra* for substances for which no specific *mantra* is prescribed. Alternately, the Durgā Gāyatrī Mantra may be used for the Durgā Pūjā.

> *Om mahādevyai vidmahe/ durgāyai devyai dhīmahi/ tanno devī pracodayāt.*
>
> We know the Great Goddess. We make a meditation of the goddess Durgā.
> May that Goddess guide us (on the right path).

With ocean water:

> *Devī /Durgā Gāyatrī Mantra.*

With *aguru* (a substance like sandalwood), camphor (*karpūra*), and silt from the banks of the Gaṅgā:

> *Devī /Durgā Gāyatrī Mantra.*

With sesame oil:

> *Om Hrīṃ cāmuṇḍāyai namaḥ.* Om! Hrīṃ! Obeisance to Cāmuṇḍā.

Then with a special oil (Viṣṇu *taila*) made by an Ayurvedic firm.

> *Om Hrīṃ cāmuṇḍāyai namaḥ.* Om! Hrīṃ! Obeisance to Cāmuṇḍā.

Then with water infused with five pungent flavors (*pañcakaṣāya*) obtained from the bark/fruit of five different trees:

> *Om Duṃ durgāyai namaḥ.* Om! Duṃ! Obeisance to Durgā.[24]

Water from a waterfall:

Om caṇḍavatyai namaḥ. Om! Obeisance to Caṇḍavatī.

Water from a coconut:

Devī Gāyatrī Mantra.

Dew:

Devī Gāyatrī Mantra.

Water from the sea:

Devī Gāyatrī Mantra.

Water infused with *sarvauṣadhī* (all herbs):

Om yāḥ oṣadhīḥ somarājñīrvahvīśata vicakṣaṇaḥ/ tāsāmtvamaśyuttamāraṃ kāmāya śamhṛde.

Om! The herbs, the Empress of Soma, and possessing the capacity of a hundred types of efficacy, among them you are the best. For the fulfilment of desire, I keep you in my heart.

Bathing with the *Sahasradhārā* (Thousandfold; Millifluent)

The *purohita* next bathes the mirror using a device like a shower head, called the *sahasradhārā* ("having a thousand"). Its openings shower the Devī with numerous distinct streams of water.

Om sāgarāḥ sarita . . .

Om! All the seas and rivers, the rivers of heaven and the big male rivers mixed with all sorts of herbs, which are the destroyer of sins, let them bathe you with their hundred openings. The oceans consisting of salt, sugar, wine, clarified butter, curd, milk, and water, should bathe you, the Great Goddess, with thousands of streams/flows.

He then utters the first verses from each of the four Vedas:

Om agnimīle purohitam yajñasya devamṛtvijam hotāram ratnadhātamam. [RV.1.1]

Om! I laud Agni, the chosen Priest, God, minister of sacrifice,
The Hotar, lavishest of wealth.

Om īṣe tvorje tvā vāyavasthā devovaḥ savitā prārpayatu śreṣṭhatamāya karmmaṇa. [YV.1.1]

Om! O, Lord, we resort to Thee for the supply of foodstuffs and vigour.[25]

Om agna āyāhi vītaye gṛṇāno havyadātaye nihotā satsi varhisi. [SV.1.1]

Om! Come Agni, praised with song, to feast and sacrificial offering:
As Hotar on the holy grass![26]

Om śamno devīrabhiṣṭaye śaṃyo bhavantu pitaye śamyorabhi śravantu naḥ. [AV.1.1; RV.10.9.4]

Om! The Water be to us for drink, Goddesses for our aid and bliss:
Let them stream to us health and strength.[27]

Bathing the Reflected Image with Eight Different Waters

After this, the *purohita* again bathes the Devī in the mirror with eight small jars full of different waters using the previously mentioned *mantras*. This is exactly the same process used on the *navapatrikā*.

Ending of the *Mahāsnāna*

Finally, after drying the surface of the mirror with a piece of white cloth, the *purohita* draws a disc with vermillion on the mirror and writes a seed syllable in the center.[28] The mirror, well covered with a piece of cloth, is then placed on the altar where the clay image is installed. The *mahāsnāna* is completed.

Bhūtāpasāraṇa (Appeasement of Inimical Spirits)

The *purohita* now commences an appeasement of the spirits, saying:

Etat pādyam/ etat sacandana puṣpam/ om bhūtebhyaḥ namaḥ.

This is an offering of water for the feet. This is an offering of a fragrant flower.
Om! Homage to the elemental spirits.

Om ghorarūpebhyo ghoratarebhyaḥ siddhibhyaḥ sādhyādibhyo bhūtebhyaḥ namaḥ.

Om! Obeisance to the dreadful, to the more dreadful, and to those who are called *siddhis* and *sādhyas*.

Then he recites these verses:

> *Om bhūtapreta piśācaśca* . . . (see *bodhana*)

And makes an offering of curd mixed with unhusked pulse on a *bilva* leaf (*māṣa bhakta bali*). This mixture, which is considered to be lowly, serves as a food offering (*naivedya*) for the spirits.

The *purohita* then takes fried rice (*lāja*), sandalwood paste, white mustard, sacred ashes, *dūrvā* and *kuśa* grass, and washed rice in his hand. He charges its with the *mantra* "Phaṭ" seven times and then utters the verses:

> *Om apasarpantu te bhūtaḥ ye bhūtā bhūmipālakāḥ/*
> *bhūtānāmavirodhena durgāpūjām karomyham.*
> *Om vetālāśca* . . . (see *bodhana*).
>
> Om! Let those elemental spirits and those who are protectors of the land be away. I shall worship Durgā without any opposition to those elemental spirits.
> Om! May all vampires, . . . (see *bodhana*).

He scatters the items held in his hand onto the floor and says:

> *Om bhūtebhyo namaḥ*. Om! Homage to the elemental spirits.

Worship of the *Bilva* Tree

The *purohita* now proceeds to worship the *bilva* tree either in its separate location or (more conveniently) as part of the *navapatrikā*. While offering flowers to it, he utters the *mantra*:

> *Om bilvasakavāsinyai durgāyai namaḥ.*
>
> Om! Obeisance to Durgā who abides in the *bilva* tree.

With the same *mantra* he proceeds to worship the *bilva*/*navapatrikā* with the ten-part devotional service (*daśopacāra*). Meditating on it to be a form of Durgā, he offers *dūrvā* grass and washed rice onto the "head" of the tree.

Invocation of Durgā into the *Pūjālaya* (Place of Worship)

Then, touching the altar of the clay image, as if directing the Devī from the *bilva*/*navapatrikā* to the place of worship, the *purohita* utters the *mantra*:

Om caṇḍike cala cala cālaya durge pūjālayam praviśa.

Om! O goddess Caṇḍī, please enter the place of worship without delay. You should please go to my abode with attendant deities, and please accept my rituals for the purpose of offering good to everybody.

Ghaṭasthāpana (Installation of the Jar)

Then a jar (*ghaṭa*) that was prepared beforehand is marked with curd and rice. While installing the jar in the method which he follows (Tantric or other), he utters the following *mantras*:

Om gaṅgādyāh saritaḥ . . .

(See the Tantric method of *ghaṭasthāpana* in the *bodhana* ritual.)

He then invokes the holy rivers into the water of the jar:

Om gaṅge ca yamunā . . .

(See the *jalaśuddhi* rite among the Preliminary Duties [*sāmānya vidhi*].)

And he stirs the water with his middle finger (*aṅkuśa mudrā*) inducing the salvific (*tīrtha*) streams to flow into the vessel. He places the leafed twigs, coconut, and cloth on the jar, completing the installation. If it has already been done, he performs it mentally.

General Preliminary Procedures

The *purohita* now purifies the flowers (*puṣpa śuddhi*), his seat (*āsana śuddhi*), and performs the common offering (*sāmānya argha*). He also performs the purificatory transformation (*bhūta śuddhi*) of the gross and subtle elements of his body.

Pūjā of Gaṇeśa and Other Deities

Purification of Worship Area and Materials

The *purohita* prepares to worship Gaṇeśa and the other deities before moving onto the worship of Durgā herself. He begins by uttering:

Haṃ Hiṃ Huṃ Phaṭ

and looks at all the materials present there with a fierce divine look (*krodhadṛṣṭi*, *divyadṛṣṭi*), purifying them.

Bhūtāpasāraṇa (Removal of Inimical Spirits)

Once again, taking the fried rice (*lāja*), sandalwood paste, white mustard seed, and so on, in his hand, charging it with the *bīja* "Phaṭ," he removes the *bhūtas* as before, uttering:

> *Om apasarpantu . . .* (see *bodhana*).

Removing the Obstacles of Earth and Sky

He strikes the floor with the heel of his left foot, while seated, removing the obstacles of the earth/soil. Then he snaps his fingers three times above his head, removing the obstacles of the sky (*antarikṣa*).

Worship of the *Gurus* (Spiritual Teachers)

The *purohita* then makes obeisance to three lines of spiritual teachers (*guru*). With his palms pressed together (*praṇāma*) and held by his left shoulder, he worships his human teachers with:

> *Om gurubhyo namaḥ/ Om paramagurubhyo namaḥ/ Om parāparagurubhyo namaḥ.*
>
> Om! Obeisance to the gurus, the most excellent gurus, and the greatest of the great gurus of the past.

Moving his folded palms to the right shoulder, he worships Gaṇeśa as *guru*:

> *Om parameṣṭhī gurubhyo namaḥ.* Om! Obeisance to the supreme one.

Thus the *purohita* pays homage to the lineage of spiritual teachers. And then with folded palms in the center, he makes a salutation to Durgā, as supreme teacher:

> *Om durgāyai devyai namaḥ.* Om! Obeisance to the Goddess Durgā.

Ṛṣyādi Nyāsa (Imprintment with the Sages and Others)

Next the *purohita* imprints (*nyāsa*) his body with a sage (or revealer) and others (*ṛṣyādi*) for the purpose (*viniyoga*) of worshipping Durgā. Placing his hand at the top of his head, he states:

Om śirasi nāradarṣaye namaḥ.

Om! Obeisance to the revealer/sage Nārada in the head.

On his lips:

Om mukhe gāyatrīcchandase namaḥ.

Om! Obeisance to the meter Gāyatrī in the mouth.

On his heart:

Om hrīṃ hṛdaye durgāyai devatāyai namaḥ.

Om! Hrīṃ! Obeisance to the goddess Durgā in the heart.

Kara Śuddhi (Purification of the Hands) and *Dig Bandhana*

After purifying both of his hands (*kara śuddhi*) with sandalwood paste and flowers by rubbing them in his palms and throwing them away, he snaps his fingers three times over his head. Again snapping ten times while circling his head, he arrests the ten directions (*dig bandhana*). Pandit Chakravarty explained that this ritual frees space from any directional or even spacial context. Since the center is regarded as the highest reality, it creates a sacred center without any perimeter.

Nyāsa (Imprintments)

The *purohita* next performs the imprintment with syllables (*mātṛkā nyāsa*). He performs *prāṇāyāma* with the seed syllable, "Hrīṃ." He then imprints his hands and limbs (*kara* and *aṅga nyāsa*) with the appropriate seed syllables. Next he performs *pīṭha nyāsa*, imprinting his body with the seats of the Devī.

Durgā Dhyāna (Meditative Visualization of Durgā)

He now makes a meditation (*dhyāna*) of Durgā holding a flower in the *dhyāna mudrā* close to his heart. Placing the flower on his head he mentally worships her with a sixteen-part devotional service (*mānasa ṣodaśopacāra*).

Viśeṣa Argha (Special Worship) in the Conch Shell

The *purohita* takes a special conch shell and places it on his left side (to the front of him). He draws a simple *yantra* in which is inscribed the seed syllable, "Huṃ." He follows the previously described procedure in worshipping the conch shell and the tripod on which it is placed. Then at the "head" of the conch shell, he places flowers with sandalwood paste, *dūrvā* grass, and washed rice. This being done, he shows *dhenu mudrā* over it. He covers it with *matsya mudrā*, and sanctifies the water with *aṅkuśa mudrā,* inducing the sacred rivers to join the water in the conch shell (*śaṅkha*). Next he repeats the Durgā seed (*bīja*) *mantra* "Duṃ" eight times over it.

He then utters:

> *Om ihāgaccha/ iha tiṣṭha/ iha sannidehi/ iha sannirudhyasva/ atrādhisthanam kuru mama pūjānam gṛhāna.*
>
> Om! Come here. Stay here. Come close by. Remain in my presence. Take up your abode here and accept my worship.

He simultaneously performs appropriate gestures. When saying "*ihāgaccha,*" his hands are cupped facing upwards calling the deity. When saying "*iha tiṣṭha,*" he closes his fingers towards the palms, as if taking hold of a person's hands. As he says "*iha sannidehi,*" he rolls his fists to face each other, clenched fingers touching each other, symbolizing closeness. And with "*iha sannirudhyasva,*" he moves the touching fists up and down in a pleading fashion. The interpretation offered to me was that in this combination of *mudrā* and *mantra,* "*āgaccha*" is the invocation (*āvāhana*); "*tiṣṭha*" brings about establishment or steadying of the deity (*sthāpanī*); "*sannidehi*" causes the deity to come near (*sannidhāpanī*); and "*sanniruddha*" arrests (*sanrodhanī*) the deity, causing it to remain face-to-face (*sanmukhikaraṇi*) with the ritualist and votary. The *mudrā*s and *mantra*s should always be accompanied by an intensely focused meditative visualization (*dhyāna*).

Worship of Gaṇeśa (as a *Ghaṭa*) and Other Deities

The *purohita* now places an installed jar called the Gaṇeśa *ghaṭa* in the northeast corner (i.e., in front of the Gaṇeśa image).This worship of Gaṇeśa as a *ghaṭa* links him to Kubera, to *yakṣa*s, to fertility, vegetation, and the Devī. The *ghaṭa* is shaped like the round belly of Gaṇeśa and its coconut head, a widely used sacrificial offering, may be implicitly connected to Gaṇeśa's decapitation. Next he performs the imprintment of hand and limbs (*aṅga* and *kara nyāsa*) with the following *mantra*s, while performing the appropriate *mudrā*s. He says

> *Gāṃ gīṃ gūṃ gaiṃ gauṃ*

while passing his hands over each other and finishes with a clap while uttering, "*gaḥ.*" He now performs the meditative visualization (*dhyāna*) of Gaṇeśa first with a flower clasped in the *dhyāna mudrā* by his heart. He places it on his head and mentally offers worship. He then places the flower before him (on the *ghaṭa*) and after repeating the *dhyāna* and the above *mantra* (*ihāgaccha/ iha tiṣṭha . . .*) performs an actual five- or ten-part devotional service (*pañca-* or *daśa-upacāra*). He concludes his worship of Gaṇeśa with an obeisance (*namaskāra*), uttering:

> *Om devendra maulimandāra makaranda kaṇārunaḥ/*
> *vighnān harantu herambe caraṇāmbuja reṇavaḥ.*
>
> Om! May the dust of your feet, O Heramba, remove all obstacles. These dusts have collected at your feet from the garland made of *mandara* flowers from the head of Indra and have become red and smeared with honey.

In that same *ghaṭa*, the five gods beginning with Śiva, the ten *avatāra*s of Viṣṇu, and the other deities, are worshipped separately with a five- or ten-part devotional service (*upacāra*).[29] The *purohita* then worships Brahmā, the directional guardians (*dikpāla*), and nine planets (*navagraha*) separately. Although there is no explicit invocation here, this ritual suggests that the cosmic bodies of all the deities that will be invoked into the clay images, or who will preside at the ritual, are first established in this jar. Thus Gaṇeśa is merely the first but not the only deity embodied in the jar.

PŪJĀ OF DURGĀ IN THE CENTRAL IMAGE

Invocation of Durgā into the Central Image

Moving to the central jar (*ghaṭa*), which was installed earlier in front of the clay images (*mūrti*), the *purohita* offers flowers. He follows the ritual of imprintment of his body with the seats of the Goddess (*pīṭha nyāsa*). Again he performs *kara* and *aṅga nyāsa*. In the *aṅga nyāsa* he imprints the words of the Durgā Mantra (*Om durge durge rakṣaṇi svāhā*) onto various parts of his body, which is undifferentiated from the body of the Goddess. He says:

> *Om durge hṛdayāya namaḥ. Om durge śirase svāhā. Om rakṣaṇi śikhāyai vaṣaṭ. Om svāhā kavachāya huṃ. Om durge durge rakṣaṇi netratrayāya vauṣāṭ. Om svāhā astrāya phaṭ.*

He now makes the pivotally consequential meditative visualization (*dhyāna*) of Durgā while holding a flower in the *dhyāna mudrā* close to his heart. He places it atop his head, transforming himself into the deity and mentally renders devotional service. Next he places the flower which was at the top of his head onto the top of the central jar. He again utters the *dhyāna*:

Om jaṭājūta samāyuktāmardhendukṛtaśekharām/
locanatraya saṃyuktāṃ pūrṇendu sadṛśānanām/
atasīpuṣpa (taptakāñcana) varṇabhām supratiṣṭhām sulocanām/
navayauvana sampannāṃ sarvābharaṇa bhūṣitām/
sucārudāśanām tadvat pīnonnatapayodharām/
tribhaṅgasthāna saṃsthānām mahiṣāsuramardinīm/
mṛṇālāyata saṃsparśā daśabāhusamanvitām/
triśūlaṃ dakṣiṇe dhyeyaṃ khaḍgaṃ cakraṃ kramādadhaḥ/
tikṣṇavāṇaṃ tathā śaktiṃ dakṣiṇeṣu vicintayet/
kheṭakaṃ pūrṇacāpañca pāśamaṅkuśameva ca/
ghaṇṭāṃ vā paraśuṃ vāpi vāmataḥ sanniveśayet/
śiraschedodbhavam tadvaddānavaṃ khaḍgapāṇinam/
hṛdi śūlena nirbhinnaṃ niryadantra vibhuṣitam/
raktāraktī kṛtaṅgañca raktaviṣphuritekṣaṇam/
veṣṭitaṃ nāgapaśena bhrūkuṭī bhiṣaṇānām/
sapāśavāmahastena dhṛtakeśañca durgayā/
vamadrudhiravaktrañca devyāḥ siṃhaṃ pradarśayet/
devyāstu dakṣinaṃ pādam samaṃ siṃhopariṣṭhitam/
kiñcid ūrdhvaṃ tathā vāmaṃ aṅguṣṭhaṃ mahiṣopari/
stūyamānanca tadrūpamaṃaraiḥ sanniveśayet/
ugracaṇḍā pracaṇḍā ca caṇḍogra caṇḍanāyikā/
caṇḍā caṇḍavatī caiva caṇḍarūpāti caṇḍikā/
aṣṭābhiḥ śaktibhistābhiḥ satatam pariveṣṭitam/
cintayet jagatām dhārīm dharma kāmārtha mokṣadām.

Om! The deity has matted hair. The top of it is adorned with the crescent moon. She has three eyes. Her face is like the beauty of the full moon. Her complexion is like the *atasī* flower (in some variants "like molten gold" [*tapta kāñcana*]).[30] She is well established having beautiful eyes, possesses all the beauty of early youth, decorated with all kinds of ornaments. Her teeth are nice-looking. Her breasts are well formed and heavy. She is standing in triple curve (*tribhaṅga*) form. She is crushing the demon Mahiṣa. Her arms are like the lotus stalk (in their tenderness of touch) extended. She has ten arms. She should be meditated upon as having a trident in the uppermost right hand and lower down gradually the weapons are the sword, the discus, the pointed arrow, and the *śakti* (a kind of weapon). These should be meditated upon as occupying her right hands. And one should place on the left side the *kheṭaka* (a staff), a bow, a noose, a goad, and a bell or axe. These are on the left-hand side. Down below the image of the Goddess, there is a buffalo shown whose head has been separated (beheaded) and emerging from the severed spot, a demon is seen bearing a sword in his hand. His chest has been pierced through by a spear, and together with that (spear) his body and limbs are smeared with entrails and blood. His angry red eyes are wide. His whole body is entwined with the noose in the form of a serpent. His frowning look is dreadful. With the left hand, Durgā has caught hold of his hair with her noose. The lion should be depicted vomiting blood from his mouth. The right foot of the Goddess is placed straight on the back of the lion. Slightly above that, the left toe of her left foot is placed on the demon. This form of the Goddess should be shown in such a way that she is praised by the various divinities. She is always surrounded by eight different *śakti*s (attendant feminine powers) named Ugracaṇḍā, Pracaṇḍā, Caṇḍogrā, Caṇḍānāyikā, Caṇḍā, Caṇḍavatī, Caṇḍarūpā, and Aticaṇḍikā. The aspirant should meditate on her as the protectress of the world and the bestower of virtue, fulfillment of desire, the desired end, and also liberation.

The *purohita* then utters:

Om bhūr bhuva svar bhagavati durge devi svagaṇasahite
ihāgaccha/ iha tiṣṭha/ iha sannidehi/ iha sannirudhasva/ mama pūjām gṛhāṇa.

Om! O Goddess Durgā, divine lady of the three worlds, with your own attendant, come, stay, approach, and remain here accepting my worship.

Passing his hands around each other in the *aṅguṣṭhādi sadaṅga nyāsa* (imprintment of the six limbs consisting of the five fingers and palms), he recites:

Hrāṃ hrīṃ hrūṃ hraiṃ hrauṃ

and ends by slapping the first few fingers of the right hand into the left palm while uttering, "*hraḥ*."

With his hands suitably charged, he places one on the image (or reaches it with a length of *kuśa* grass[31]) and prays:

Om āgaccha madgṛhe devi aṣṭābhiḥ śaktibhiḥ saha/ . . .

Om! O Goddess, come to my house with eight attending *śakti*s. O doer of all good, please accept my ritual (done according to the prescribed method, above).

Om ehyehi bhagavaddurge śatrukṣaya jayaprade/
bhaktitaḥ pūjāyāmi tvām navadurge surarcite.

Om! O goddess Durgā, the giver of victory and killer of enemies, I worship you, O nine-formed Durgā, with devotion, the one who is worshipped by gods.

Om durge devi samāgaccha sānnidhyamiha kalpaya/
yajñabhāga gṛhāṇa tvam aṣṭābhiḥ śaktibhiḥ saha.

Om! O goddess Durgā, come over here and show your presence beside me along with your eight *śakti*s. Please receive the share/portion of the oblation.

Om śāradīyāmimāṃ pūjām karomi kamalakṣṇe/
ājñāpaya mahādevi daityadarpa niṣūdani.

Om! O Great Goddess, give your leave/permission, O suppressor of the arrogance of demons, I shall perform this autumnal worship of yours, O lotus-eyed one.

Om saṃsārārṇava duṣpāre sarvāsura nikṛntani/
trāyasva varade devi namaste śaṅkarapriye.

Om! The worldly existence is like an ocean which is very difficult to cross. O destroyer of all sorts of demons, please rescue me, O giver of boons. I bow to you, the beloved of Śaṅkara.

Om ye devāḥ yāḥ hidevyāśca calitāḥ yāścalanti hi/
āvāhayāmi tān sarvān caṇḍike parameśvari.

Om! The gods and the goddesses that have moved towards us and those who are still on their way, I invite all of them here, O Great Goddess Caṇḍikā.

Om prāṇan rakṣa yaśo rakṣa putradārādhanaṃ sadā/
sarvarakṣākarī yasmād tasmāttvayi jagat priye.

Om! Protect our lives, and protect our good names, and always protect our sons and wives, as you are the protectress of all. The epithet, "The Beloved of the World," is right.

Om praviśāya tiṣṭha yajñe 'smin yāvat pūjām karomyaham/
śailānanda kare devi sarvasiddhiñca dehi me.

Om! Please enter the place of worship and remain steady there, so long as I make all my ritualistic offerings to you. You are the giver of happiness to the mountain (Himālaya). Please give us all kinds of attainments.

Om āgaccha caṇḍike devi sarvakalyāṇa hetave/
pūjām gṛhāṇa sumukhi namaste śaṅkarapriye.

Om! O goddess Caṇḍikā, please come for the purpose of well-being of all. O beautiful-faced one, the beloved of Śaṅkara, I pay obeisance to you, please receive our offering.

Om āvāhayāmi devi tvām mṛṇmaye śrīphale 'pi ca/
kailaśa śikharāddevi vindhyādrer himaparvatāt/
āgatya bilvaśākhāyām caṇḍike kuru sannidhim/
sthāpitāsi mayā devi pūjaye tvām prasīda me/
āyurārogyam aiśvaryaṃ dehi devi namo 'stute.

Om! I invite you, O Goddess, to abide in the image made of earth and also in the *bilva* fruit from the top of Mount Kailaśa and from Vindhya Hill or from the Himālaya. Come from those places, be present in the branch of this *bilva* tree. I have installed you here and should worship you. Be pleased. I pay obeisance to you, O Goddess. Give me strength, longevity, health, and wealth.

Om devi caṇḍātmike caṇḍi caṇḍavigraha kāriṇi/
bilvaśākhām samāśritya tiṣṭha devagaṇaiḥ saha.

Om! O Goddess, you are dread incarnate and make terrific battle against Caṇḍa, the demon. Abiding in the branch of the *bilva* tree, please remain along with the other divine beings.

The *purohita* next recites some Vedic verses:

Om haṃsaḥ śucisadvasurantarikṣa sad hotā vediṣad atithi duroṇa sat/
nṛṣad varasad vyomasad avjāgojā ṛtajā adrijā ṛtam bṛhat. [RV.4.40.5]

Om! The Haṃṣa homed in light, the Vasu in midair, the priest beside the altar, in the house the guest,
Dweller in noblest place, mid men, in truth, in sky, born of flood, kine, truth, mountain, he is holy Law.

Om pra tad viṣṇuh stavate vīryeṇa mṛgo na bhīmah kucaro giriṣṭhāḥ/
yasyoruṣu triṣu vikramaṇeṣvadhikṣiyanti bhuvanāni viśvā. [RV.1.154.2]

Om! For this mighty deed is Viṣṇu lauded, like some wild beast, dread, prowling, mountain-roaming;
He within whose three wide-extended paces all living creatures have their habitation.[32]

Om viṣṇur yoniṃ kalpayatu tvaṣṭā rūpāni piṃśatu/
ā siñcatu prajāpatir dhātā garbhaṃ dadhātu te. [RV.10.184.1]

Om! May Viṣṇu form and mould the womb, may Tvaṣṭar duly shape the forms,
Prajāpati infuse the stream, and Dhātar lay the germ for thee.[33]

Om tat savitur varenyam [RV.3.62.10]
Om! May we attain that excellent glory of Savitṛ the God.

Om tryambakam yajamahe sugandhim pustibardhanam urvarukamiva bandhanan mytyor murksiya ma mrtat. [RV.7.59.12]

Om! Tryambaka we worship, sweet augmenter of prosperity.
As from its stem the cucumber, so may I be released from death, not reft of immortality.

This Vedic verse serves as an interpretive resource. It refers to the removal of a seed-bearing fruit, the cucumber, from its stem. A cucumber or melon, is often offered to Durgā as a surrogate of the animal (or human) sacrifice. The head of the animal, which is the fruit of the body, is separated from the body (the stem) during the sacrifice, resulting not in death but immortality for the sacrificial victim.

The *purohita* then reads the Devī Gāyatrī. Following this he utters more verses:

Om devi tvam jagatāṃ mātaḥ sṛṣṭi saṃhārakāriṇi/
patrikāsu samastāsu sannidhyamiha kalpaya.

Om! O Goddess, you are the mother of the world and the agent of creation and dissolution. Make your presence here in all the plants and herbs.

Om pallavaiśca phalopetaiḥ śākhābhiḥ suranāyike/
pallave saṃsthite devi pūjām gṛhṇa prasīda me.

Om! In the twigs, branches attached with fruit, O Leader of the divine beings, abiding in the twigs, after receiving my ritual worship, be pleased with me.

Om āvāhayāni devi tvām mṛṇmaye śrīphale 'pi ca/
sthirātyantaṃ hi no bhūtvā ghṛe kāmapradā bhava.

Om! I invoke you, O Goddess, in the earthen image and also in the *bilva* fruit. Being steadily established here, be the giver of fulfillment of all desires.

Om caṇḍike caṇḍarūpāsi suratejomahāvale/
praviśya tiṣṭha yajñe 'smin yāvat pūjām karomyaham.

Om! O Caṇḍikā, you are terrific in form. You have enormous strength/might born of the divine energy (*tejas*) of the gods. Please enter in the altar of rituals (*yajña*), and stay here so long as I am engaged in worshipping you.

The Devī has been successfully invoked into all her representative forms, including the *navapatrikā* and *bilva* fruit, as well as the earthen image (*mṛṇmayi mūrti*).

Cakṣur Dāna (Giving Eyesight)

Now that the Devī has come to reside in the image, the *purohita* proceeds to give the image eyesight (*cakṣur dāna*). He takes collyrium (*kajjala*), which has been prepared and placed on a *bilva* leaf, and with the blunt end of another *bilva* leaf he applies it to the eyes of the image, while uttering:

1. For the right eye

Om citraṃ devānām udagādanīkam cak ṣurmitrasya varuṇasyāgne/
āprā dyāvā pṛthivīm cāntarik ṣamatho svaḥ. [RV.1.115.1]

Om! The brilliant presence of the Gods has risen, the eye of Mitra, Varuṇa, and Agni.
The soul of all that moveth not or moveth, the Sun hath filled the air and earth and heaven.

2. For the left eye

Om tac cakṣur devahitam śukramuccarat paśyema śaradaḥ satam/ jivema śaradaḥ śatam. [RV.7.66.16]

Om! A hundred autumns may we see that bright Eye, God-ordained, arise: A hundred autumns may we live.

3. For the third upper eye:

Devī Gāyatrī Mantra.

In the installation of any *mūrti* into a place of worship (*pūjālaya*) such as a temple, the ritual of giving eyesight (*cakṣur dāna*), along with the installation of vital energy (*prāṇa pratiṣṭhā*) which follows, is a climax point. The first rite activates the faculty of vision, so important for the lay worshipper's devotional interaction with the deity, where reciprocation of sight (*darśana*) is central. The second rite brings the image to life. The image and a designated space around it is thereafter treated with utmost reverence. In the Lahiri home, hereafter, the entire north porch that served as the shrine space, was off-limits to everyone except those directly involved in the worship rites.

Prāṇa Pratiṣṭhā **(Installation of Vital Energy)**

The *purohita* next installs vital life energy (*prāṇa*) into the image. He begins by touching the heart of the *mūrti* with a flower, saying:

Om aiṃ hrīṃ kroṃ gāṃ rāṃ lāṃ vāṃ śāṃ ṣāṃ sāṃ hauṃ hāṃ saḥ durgāyāḥ prāṇa iha prāṇaḥ.

Om! Let the vital energy (*prāṇa*) come through the utterance of these syllables.

Om aiṃ hrīṃ kroṃ, . . . , haṃ saḥ durgā devyaḥ jīva iha stitha.

Om! Let the soul (*jīva*) of Durgā come through the utterance of these syllables.

Om aiṃ hrīṃ kroṃ, . . . , haṃ saḥ durgā devyaḥ sarvendrīyāṇi iha stitha.

Om! Let all sense and motor organs come with the utterance of these syllables.

Om aiṃ hrīṃ kroṃ, . . . , haṃ saḥ durgā devyaḥ vākmanaścaksuḥ stvak śrotra ghṛāṇa prāṇa iha gatya sukhaṃ ciraṃ tiṣṭhantu svāhā.

Om! Let the speech, mind, eye, touch, hearing, organs of smell, and all the vital energies after coming over here remain comfortably in this body.

This ritual of installing life into the clay image is crucial in furthering our understanding of the Durgā Pūjā (or any *pūjā*). One clearly sees that the Devī is brought into material existence through the installation of various elements (*tattva*) of creation, such as life force, soul, sense organs, and vital energies into an image constructed of the gross elements. Through the activities of *pūjā*, however, devotees too engage in a process. From their initial purifications through to their devotional offerings, devotees elevate their own constituent elements in order to meet the deity (halfway so to speak) in a profound communion of substance.

The *purohita* then utters a Vedic verse:

Om mano jūtir juṣaṭāmājyasya bṛhaspatir yajñamimam tano tu/
aristam yajñam samimam dadhātu viśvedevāsa iha mādayantam om pratiṣṭha.
Asyai prāṇāḥ kṣarantu ca/ asyai devatā saṅkhyai svāhā.
[ŚB.1.7.4.22].

Om! Enjoy the pleasure of the essence of the mind in the form of clarified butter. May Bṛhaspati make this oblation wide and make this sacrifice auspicious. And may all the Viśvadevas (gods of the universe), after establishing themselves here, with the utterance of "Om" (signifying acceptance), enjoy.[34]

He recites this while touching the body of the image with the gesture of the lapping flame of fire (*leliha mudrā*) in which the thumb touches the bottom of the ring finger. Pandit Chakravarty explained that this *mudrā* symbolized/actualized the spark of vital energy, of life, taking flame in the image.

The *purohita* next repeats the procedure for each of the other clay images, including the demon, imbuing them with life.

Worship of Durgā Embodied in the Clay Image

Before offering anything to the Devī, the *purohita* sprinkles purified water from its vessel, consecrating his seat and the altar, uttering:

Vaṃ āsanāya namaḥ. Vaṃ! Homage to the seat.

Seating himself, he then offers a flower and sandalwood paste over the sacrificial offering vessel (*kośā*) saying:

Om adhipataye śriviṣṇave namaḥ. Om! Obeisance to the overlord Śrī Viṣṇu.
Idam āsanam/ Om durge durge durgāyai namaḥ.

This is a seat. Om! O Durgā, O Durgā. Obeisance to Durgā.[35]

He now proceeds to worship Durgā in the earthen image with an elaborated form of the sixteen-part devotional service (*ṣodaśopacāra*).[36]

1. *Āsana* (Seat)

With folded hands he says:

> *Om āsanaṃ gṛhna cārvaṅgī nānā ratna vinirmitam/*
> *gṛhāṇedam jaganmātaḥ prasīda bhagavatyume.*
>
> Om! Please receive this seat studded with various jewels, O Mother of the Universe, and be propitiated.

2. *Svāgatam* (Welcome)

Uttering the root *mantra* (*mūlamantra*) of the Goddess, he states:

> *Om duṃ durgāyai namaḥ. Om durge iha svāgatam? Svāgatam astu.*
>
> Om! Duṃ! Obeisance to Durgā.
> Om! Durgā, do you feel welcome here? Be welcome here.

3. *Pādya* (Water for Washing Feet)

Taking some water in the smaller copper ladle (*kuśī*), he offers it to Durgā for washing her feet:

> *Om pādyam gṛhna mahādevi sarva duhkhā pahārakam/*
> *trāyasva varade devi namaste śaṅkarapriye.*
>
> Om! Please, Great Goddess, receive this offering of a washing of your feet.
> It is the remover of all kinds of pain. Please protect me, O giver of boons.
> I offer my obeisance to the beloved of Śaṅkara, thus.

4. *Argha/Arghya* (Offering)

Placing some *dūrvā* grass, washed rice, and *bilva pātra* in a conch vessel (*śaṅkha*), he offers it to Durgā:

> *Om dūrvākṣata samāyuktam bilva pātram tathā param/*
> *śobhanaṃ śaṅkhapātrastham gṛhāṇārghyam harapriye/*
> *nānā tīrthodbhavam vāri kuṅkamādi suśītalam/*
> *gṛhāṇārghyam idam devi viśeṣvari namo'stute.*

Om! O beloved of Hara, accept my offering of this *dūrvā*, rice, *bilva* leaf, and placed in the most beautiful conch vessel. The water comes from many holy *tīrtha*s, has been made cool by adding saffron (*kuṅkuma*) and other things. Please accept this offering (*arghya*) from me, O Goddess. I am paying obeisance to you, O Mistress of the World.

5. *Ācamanīya* (Water for Sipping or Rinsing the Mouth)

Offering some water in the *kuśī*, he utters:

Om mandākinyāstu yadvāri sarvapāpaharaṃ śubham/
gṛhāṇācamaniyam tvam mayā bhaktyā niveditam/
idam āpo mayā bhaktya tava pānitale 'rpitā/
ācāmaya mahādevi prīta śāntim prayacchame.

Om! The water that has come from Mandākinī is auspicious and also the remover of all sins. Please accept this water for the purpose of sipping. This water has been presented by me into your hand out of devotion to you. You may wash your mouth and, thus satisfied, O Great Goddess, offer me peace.

6. *Madhuparka* (Honeyed Mixture)

He takes a fist-sized container (Hindi: *kaṭorā*) of brass or silver containing honey (*madhu*), ghee (*ghṛta*), and curd (*dadhi*). Since certain items (e.g., solids) require more purification than others (e.g., liquids), he first purifies it by saying:

Vaṃ madhuparkāya namaḥ. Vaṃ! Obeisance to the *madhuparka*.

He then utters:

Om madhuparkaṃ mahādevi brahmādyaiḥ parikalpitam/
mayā niveditam bhaktyā gṛhāṇa parameśvari.

Om! This honeyed mixture, O Great Goddess, was invented by Brahmā and others. It has been offered to you out of devotion. Please accept it, O Supreme Lady.

6a. *Punar Ācamanīya* (Again)

7. *Snānīyam* (Bathing)

The *purohita* offers Durgā water for bathing, saying:

Om jalañca śītalam svaccham idaṃ śuddhaṃ manoharam/
snānārthaṃ te mayā bhaktyā kalpitaṃ pratigṛhyatām.

Om! Cool, clear, pure, nice water I have arranged for your bath. Please accept it.

7a. *Punar Ācamanīya* (Again)

8. *Vastra* (Clothing)

Offering a new *sārī*, after purifying it (with the *bīja* "Vaṃ") he says:

Om bahutantu samāyuktam paṭṭa sūtrādi nirmitam/
vāso devi suśuklañca gṛhāṇavaravarṇini/
tantusantāna samyuktaṃ rañjitaṃ rāgavastunā/
durge devi bhaja prītiṃ vāsaste paridhīyatam.

Om! It is made of many threads and is composed of silken threads. It is white, and it is colored. O goddess Durgā, be satisfied after wearing it. It is one which has many stretched threads and is colored with dyes. O goddess Durgā, be satisfied and put this cloth on as your own.

8a. *Punar Ācamanīya* (Again)

9. *Alaṅkāra* (Ornamentation)

The ornaments are first purified and then offered. (A small silver ring may be offered as a token of ornaments):

Om divya ratna samāyuktāḥ vahnibhānusamaprabhāḥ/
gātrāṇi śobhayiṣyanti alaṅkārāḥ sureśvari.

These ornaments are studded with divine gems and shine like fire and the sun. They will adorn your limbs, O Queen of the Gods.

10. *Śaṅkha Alaṅkāra* (Ornamentation with Conch-shell Bangles)

He utters:

Om śaṅkhañca vividhaṃ citraṃ bāhunāñca vibhūṣaṇam/
mayā niveditaṃ bhaktyā śaṅkhañca pratigṛhyatām.

Om! The bangles made of conch shell are of various types. They decorate your arms and wrists. I have offered these with devotion. Please accept these conch-shell bangles.

During this time other items of jewelery and personal feminine ornamentation are offered. These may include a bottle of the red-colored dye (*lac*) with which women paint their feet (Sanskrit/Bengali *alaktaka/āltā*), combs, a small mirror, an iron bangle, which is the sign of a married woman (*sadhavā*), and a small basket. All such items offered to the Devī go to the *purohita,* who probably turns them over to his wife. In large religious community *pūjās* (e.g., Ānandamayī Mā Āśrama), where numerous items may be offered by wealthy patrons, these donations are often kept in trust and given to needy women (as a wedding *sārī*, for instance).

11. *Gandha* (Fragrant Ointment)

Taking some sandalwood paste in his fingers, the *purohita* says:

> *Om śarīrante na jānami ceṣṭāṃ naiva ca naiva ca/*
> *māṃ rakṣa sarvato devi gandhā netān gṛhāṇa ca.*
>
> Om! I do not know what form you have, and I am quite unknowing of your activity. Please protect me from all sides, and please accept this sandalwood paste.

This is another example of important insights conveyed by the litany. The prayers reveal that despite the myriad visible forms in which the Devī is to be embodied in this *pūjā*, the *purohita*/votary admits that her true form and activity is ultimately mysterious.

12. *Puṣpa* (Flowers)

While offering some flower garlands (*puṣpamāla*) to the Goddess, he says:

> *Om puṣpam manoharaṃ divyam sugandhaṃ devanirmitam/*
> *hṛdyam adbhūtam āghreyam devi dattaṃ pragṛhyatām.*
>
> Om! Flowers, fascinating, divine, fragrant, created by the divine hand, very lovely, unique (hard to obtain), worthy to be smelled, which are being offered to you, O Devī, please accept them.

13. *Dhūpa* (Fragrant Incense)

Since stick incense (Hindi: *agarbatti*) is considered unsuitably meager for such a grand *pūjā*, he makes an offering of powdered incense in a vessel, saying:

> *Om vanaspati rasa divyo gandhādhyaḥ sumanoharaḥ/*
> *mayā nivedito bhaktyā dhūpo 'yaṃ pratigṛhyatām.*
>
> Om! This incense is the sap/essence of big trees. It is a heavenly thing full of fragrance and pleasing to the mind. I have offered this to you with devotion. Please accept this incense.

14. *Dīpa* (Lamp)

Waving a ghee lamp (often multiwicked) in front of the Goddess, he says:

> *Om agnir jyotiravijyotiścandrajyotistathaiva ca/*
> *jyotiṣāmuttamo durge dīpo 'yaṃ pratigṛhyatām.*
>
> Om! The light of fire, the sun's light, the moon's light, among all of them this lamp is the best. O Durgā, please accept it.

15. *Sindūra* (Vermillion)

The *purohita* touches a small spot of vermillion (*sindūra*) on the forehead of the Goddess at the top of, but within a slightly larger spot of sandalwood paste (*candana*). He says:

> *Om candanena samāyuktaṃ sindūraṃ bhālabhūṣaṇam/*
> *rūpadyutikaraṃ devi caṇḍike gṛhṇa mastake.*
> *Om caṇḍikayai vidmahe bhagavatyai dhīmahi tanno gaurī pracodayāt.*
> *Om idaṃ sindūratilakam/*
> *Om durge durge rakṣaṇi svāhā/*
> *Hrīṃ durgāyai devyai namaḥ.*
>
> Om! This vermillion is associated with sandalwood paste. It decorates the forehead and manifests illumination of the form. O Caṇḍikā, please accept this on your forehead.
> Om! The Caṇḍī Gāyatrī
> Om! O Durgā, O Durgā, O Protectress Svāhā!
> Hrīṃ! Obeisance to Goddess Durgā.

16. *Kajjala* (Collyrium)

He offers collyrium on a *bilva* leaf to the Devī, saying:

> *Om namaste sarvadeveśi namaste śaṅkarapriye/*
> *cakṣusāmañjanaṃ hṛdyam devi dattam pragṛhyatām.*
>
> Om! O Goddess of all Gods, I bow to the beloved of Śaṅkara. This collyrium, which I offer to you, is pleasant to the eye. Please accept it.

17. *Naivedya* (Food Offering)

Washed rice heaped in a pile served in a spacious plate with fruits (bananas, etc.) on the top, and large, specially shaped pieces of coconut, sweet balls, etc. are offered. There might be special cakes (*tala*) made with palmyra palm fruit juice. The whole configuration resembles a mountain, at the base of which other fruits are placed. The *purohita* first purifies the food and then offers it saying:

> *Om āmānnam ghṛtasaṃyuktaṃ phalatāmbula saṃyuktam/*
> *mayā niveditaṃ bhaktyā āmānnaṃ pratigṛhyatām.*
>
> Om! This uncooked food (*āmānnam*) is associated with clarified butter, fruits, and betel nuts. This uncooked food which is offered by me, please accept it.

Next, another separate offering of fruits and other prepared but uncooked foods are offered:

> *Om phalamūlāni sarvāṇi grāmyāraṇyāni yāni ca/*
> *nānāvidhasugandhīni gṛhṇa devi mamāciram.*
>
> Om! Fruits and roots that have come from villages and grew in the forest, they have different smells. Please accept them as my offering.

The *naivedya* consists of uncooked or minimally cooked food. Fruits and roots, associated with villages and forests, are also offered to the Devī, linking her with agricultural and "gatherer" peoples. It supplements our understanding of her epithet, Vanadurgā (Durgā of the Forest), and her connection to such forest tribes as the Śabaras.

18. *Bilva Pātra* (Wood-apple Leaf)

Next he offers *bilva pātra*s to the Goddess while uttering the Durgā Mantra:

> *Om durge durge rakṣaṇi svāhā/ Hrīṃ durgāyai devyai namaḥ.*
>
> Om! O Durgā, O Durgā, O Protectress Svāhā!
> Hrīṃ! Obeisance to Goddess Durgā!

Throughout the *pūjā* one notes that such items as the conch shell (*śaṅkha*) and *bilva* leaf, which are unambiguously forms of the Devī, are offered back up to her. This observation naturally leads to the recognition that there is an implicit identification between each of the offered materials and the manifest form of Goddess herself.

19. *Pānārtha Jalam* (Water for Drinking)

The *purohita* offers clear water for drinking:

Om jalañca śītalaṃ svacchaṃ sugandhi sumanoharam/
mayā niveditaṃ bhaktyā pānīyam pratigṛhyatām.

Om! Water which is cool, clear, fragrant, pleasing to the mind, I have offered with devotion as drinking water. Please accept it.

20. *Tāmbula* (Betel)

Betel leaf and betel nut are offered separately (not mixed, as in the common preparation of *pān*):

Om phalapātra samāyuktam karpūreṇa suvāsitam/
mayā niveditaṃ bhaktyā tāmbulaṃ pratigṛhyatām.

Om! This betel, associated with betel nut and leaf, fragranced with camphor, is offered to you with devotion. Please accept it.

21. *Dūrvā* Grass

He offers *dūrvā* grass that has been woven into a thread:

Om namaste sarvadeveśi namaste sukha mokṣade/
dūrvāṃ gṛhāṇa devi tvaṃ māṃ nistāraya sarvataḥ.

Om! I bow to you supreme Goddess, the giver of happiness and liberation. Please accept this *dūrvā* grass, and rescue me from every quarter.

22. *Bilvapātramālā* (Garland of Wood-apple Leaves)

He presents a garland of *bilva* leaves to her:

Om amṛtodbhavaṃ śrīyuktaṃ mahādevapriyaṃ sadā/
pavitraṃ te prayacchāmi śrīphalīyaṃ sureśvari.

Om! I am giving you this pure, sacred thing born of the *bilva* (*śrīphala*) tree, O Goddess of all Gods. It emerged from nectar. It is associated with auspiciousness and has always been beloved to Śiva.

Bilva leaves are believed to contain *pārada* (mercury/quicksilver), which is understood to be the semen of Śiva. This adds to its medicinal potency.

23. *Puṣpamālā* (Flower Garland)

The *purohita* offers an exceptionally beautiful flower garland to the Devī, saying:

*Om sūtreṇa grathitaṃ mālyaṃ nānāpuṣpasamanvitam/
śrīyuktaṃ lambamānañca gṛhāṇa paramevṣari.*

Om! This garland has been woven by means of a thread (*sūtra*). It is associated with different kinds of flowers. It looks beautiful when it hangs on the neck. Please accept this, O Supreme Goddess.

23a. *Puṣpa*

He now recites the Gāyatrī Mantra while offering a handful of flowers three times to the Goddess.

23b. *Darpaṇa* (Mirror)

He then allows the Devī to see her reflection in the mirror.

23c. *Pādya, Argha, Punar Ācamanīya*

Again he offers water for her feet (*pādya*), *dūrvā* grass and washed rice (*argha*), and water for sipping (*ācamanīya*).

24. *Anna/Bhoga* (Cooked Food)

What follows is an extremely important participatory portion of the ritual, wherein someone, perhaps the woman who has herself prepared the cooked food, brings it directly from the kitchen to the place of worship. In the Lahiris' home, it was Mrs. Lahiri who used to carry the food down from the kitchen. Purified and purifying water was sprinkled before her, and her pathway was cleared of any persons who might defile the offering. As Mrs. Lahiri explained, there are three occasions for *bhoga* at the Lahiri home: "Balya bhog" in the morning, "Madhyana bhog" in the afternoon, and "Ratri bhog" at night. They consist of rice, many varieties of curry, sweets, and curd. Preparation and handling of the cooked-food offerings are restricted to married women who are not menstruating, or women who are past menopause. Furthermore, for the *pūjā* of Durgā and Kālī, these women must have received a special initiation (*dīkṣā*). Premenarche girls are pure and entitled to handle the uncooked food offerings.

One of Mr. Lahiri's son-in-laws told me that either men or women, provided they were *brāhmaṇa*s with initiation, could prepare the food, but "women have been preferred for so long that it has become a custom (*riti*)." Decades ago in Banāras there was apparently an abundance of such initiated women, often widows, who would volunteer their services to prepare the *bhoga* or do so for a fee. However, as the culture modernizes, and the conceptions of lifestyle options after widowhood have begun to change, there are far fewer initiated widows available. This, the Lahiris explained, is one of the factors that has led to a reduction in the elaborateness of the *bhoga* preparations of their *pūjā*. Nevertheless, since the Durgā Pūjā is the most important annual festival among Bengali Śāktas, the cook's preparations will surely include some of her finest dishes, such as special curries and sweets. The initiated postmenopausal woman's cooking activities in the kitchen are likely to be as elaborate as the *purohita*'s in the place of worship. The kitchen is an area of sanctity, restricted to the initiated. In the ritual of the cooked-food offerings, the activities of these two specialists connect.

The elaborate food preparations are consumed by the Devī in her manifest form. After she has consumed the food, it will be called *bhoga prasāda* (blessed food) and will be consumed by the votaries. The Lahiris distribute the *bhoga prasāda* to whomever is present regardless of their caste or relationship to the family. A portion of the *bhoga* is also delivered to the *purohita*'s home.

To conduct this offering the *purohita* clears the precincts in front of the Goddess and after drawing a *yantra,* places the cooked food (*anna/bhoga*) on it. The *purohita* now offers that cooked food to the Devī, the *navapatrikā*, and other deities present, praying:

> *Om annaṃ caturvidham devi rasaiḥ ṣadbhiḥ samanvitam/*
> *uttamaṃ prāṇadañcaiva gṛhāṇa mama bhāvataḥ.*
>
> Om! Food of four types, flavored with six kinds of tastes, it is excellent and the giver of life. Please accept it from my sincere sentiment (*bhāvataḥ*).[37]

25. *Paramānna* (Supreme Food)

Next he offers the Devī *paramānna* (i.e., rice cooked in milk, ghee, and sweetened with raisins, etc.), similar to the preparation known as *khīra* in Hindi.

> *Om gavyasarpiḥ samāyuktaṃ nānāmadhura saṃayuktam/*
> *mayā niveditaṃ bhaktyā paramānnam pragṛhyatām.*
>
> Om! The milk of the cow and a slight amount of ghee mixed with some other sweets, I have offered this supreme food with devotion.

26. *Piṣṭaka* (Cakes)

Then the *purohita* offers *piṣṭaka* (i.e., cakes of different kinds, always cooked):

> *Om amṛtayaiḥ racitaṃ divyaṃ nānārūpa vinirmitam/*
> *piṣṭakam vividhaṃ devi gṛhāṇa mama bhāvataḥ.*

Om! These cakes have been prepared as if with nectar. It is a heavenly delicacy made into different shapes. These varieties of cakes which I offer to you should be accepted.

27. *Modaka* (Sweet Balls)

Next he offers sweet balls (Sanskrit/Hindi: *modaka/laddu*), perhaps made from coconut or puffed rice mixed with molasses:

Om modakam svādu saṃyuktaṃ śarkarādi vimiśrītam/
suramyaṃ madhuraṃ bhojyaṃ devi dattaṃ pragṛhyatām.

Om! These very tasty sweet balls, mixed with sugar and other ingredients, are very sweet and edible. I have given them over to you. Please accept them.

27a. *Pānīyam Jalam* (Water for Drinking)

Again he offers drinking water (*pānīyam jalam*) to the Devī.

28. *Praṇāma/Vandana* (Homage/Obeisance)

The *purohita* finishes off the devotional service by reciting the *namaskāra mantra* as an obeisance to Durgā.

Om sarva maṅgala maṅgalye śive sarvārtha sadhike
śaranye tryambake gaurī nārāyaṇi namo'stute. [DSS.11.9]

You are the abode of all auspiciousness. O consort of Śiva, you are the giver of every kind of object (you are the means by which one can achieve all sorts of desired ends). You are the last resort, O mother of the three gods, salutations to you O Gaurī, O Nārāyaṇī.

Invocation and Worship of Nine Goddesses in the *Navapatrikā*

The *purohita* now commences worship of the *navapatrikā* separately. If there was an unambiguous underlying rationale for the choice of these specific nine plants to embody the corresponding goddesses, it has been lost. However, one discerns a variety of characteristics, sometimes the plant's name, appearance, or usefulness, which seems to be at the root of the choices.[38]

1. The *purohita* invokes the goddess Brahmāṇī in the plantain (*rambhā*).[39] Rambhā is the name of a heavenly damsel (*apsaras*) considered to be the

most beautiful woman in Indra's paradise. The term *kadalī* or plantain tree is commonly used to refer to a beautiful young woman, and as previously mentioned, the *navapatrikā* is often regarded as a young "banana wife "(*kala bou*). Perhaps it was selected in allusion to the Devī's feminine allure. Furthermore, virtually all parts of the plantain tree (including the fruit) are regarded as useful. For instance, the leaves are used as plates. This aspect of the plant could allude to the Devī's beneficence through providing nourishment, shelter, and so on.

The *purohita* utters:

> *Om rambhādhiṣṭhātri brahmāṇi*
> *ihāgaccha iha tiṣṭha atrādhiṣṭhanam kuru mama pūjām gṛhāṇa.*
> *Om rambhādhiṣṭhātryai brahmāṇyai namaḥ.*
>
> Om! O Brahmāṇī, who abides in the Rambhā (plantain), come here, stay here, take up residence here. Please accept my worship.
> Om! Obeisance to Brahmāṇī who abides in the Rambhā.

He offers a ten-part devotional service (*daśopacāra*) to her ending with an obeisance (*namaskāra*) in which she is worshipped as Durgā. He says:

> *Om durge devi samāgaccha sannidhyamiha kalpaya*
> *rambhārūpeṇa sarvatra śāntiṃ kuru namo'stute.*
>
> Om! O Goddess Durgā, come over here and remain close to this place in the form of the plantain (*rambha*) tree. Offer peace everywhere. I pay obeisance to you.

2. He repeats the procedure for the Kacvī (Edible Arum) (*Araceae colocasia antiquorum*) plant, invoking the goddess Kālikā. The *kacvi* is a black-stemmed plant, perhaps selected to allude to the dark skin of the goddess Kālikā. It is known for its fist-sized, succulent root, which when soft resembles meat. It may be prepared into a sweet. He utters:

> *Om kacvādhiṣṭhatri kālike*
> *ihāgaccha iha tiṣṭha atrādhiṣṭhanam kuru mama pūjām gṛhāṇa.*
> *Om kacvādhiṣṭhatryai kālikāyai namaḥ.*

and worshipping her with:

> *Om mahiṣāsura yuddheṣu kacvībhūtāsi suvrate/*
> *mama cānugrahārthāya āgatāsi harapriye.*
>
> Om! O Beloved of Hara, you turned yourself into Kacvī during the war with the demon Mahiṣa. You have come over here only to bestow favor on me.

3. In the turmeric (*haridrā*) he invokes Durgā. The deep yellow color of turmeric (*Curcuma longa*), an ubiquitous spice in Indian curries, may also allude to the color of Durgā's skin, which is often referred to as being like molten gold (*tapta kāñcana*). He utters:

> *Om haridrādhiṣṭhātri durge ihagāccha iha tiṣṭha . . .*
> *Om haridrādhiṣṭhātryai durgāyai namaḥ.*

and worships her with:

> *Om haridre varade devi umārūpāsi suvrate*
> *mama vighnavināśāya prasīda tvaṃ harapriye.*
>
> Om! O Turmeric, you have the characteristics of both Śiva and Umā, and for the removal of my obstacles, please accept my offering and be pleased, O beloved of Hara.

4. In the Jayantī creeper he invokes the goddess Kārtikī.[40] Jayantī is the feminine form of Jayanta, meaning "victorious one," an epithet of Kārtikeya, the war god. Perhaps this is why the plant is chosen to represent the goddess Kārtikī. Durgā is herself linked with Kārtikeya in the clay images complex of the Durgā Pūjā, where she is regarded by most devotees as his mother. In the *Devī Kavaca*, an appendage of the *Durgā Saptaśatī*, Durgā is known by the epithet, Skandamātā (Mother of Skanda/Kārtikeya), the fifth of her nine forms. Jayantī also refers to the sprouted grain planted on the earthen altar during Navarātra, which is harvested on the last day. The leaves of the Jayantī plant are used to treat fevers.

> *Om jayantyadhiṣṭhātri kārtiki ihāgaccha . . .*
> *Om jayantyadhiṣṭhātryai kārtikyai namaḥ.*

He worships her saying:

> *Om niśumbha śumbhamathane sendraiḥ devagaṇaiḥ saha/*
> *jayanti pūjitāsi tvam asmākaṃ varadā bhava.*
>
> Om! In the war of Śumbha and Niśumbha with Indra and the other gods, she who killed them is Jayantī. O Jayantī, you have been worshipped here. Be the bestower of boons to us.[41]

5. In the wood-apple (*bilva*) tree (*Aegle marmelos*), he invokes the goddess Śivā. The *bilva* fruit is associated with Śiva for a number of reasons. For instance, its trifoliate leaves resemble his trident, and its leaves are believed to contain mercury, which is his semen. So it is appropriately linked to the

goddess Śivā. The fruit of the *bilva* tree, which has many medicinal properties, is also prepared into a beverage renowned for its cooling effect in the summer heat. It is also used to treat digestive problems. The *purohita* utters:

> *Om bilvavṛkṣādhiṣṭhātri śive ihāgaccha . . .*
> *Om bilvavṛkṣādhiṣṭhātryai śivāyai namaḥ*

offering obeisance with:

> *Om mahādevapriyakaro vāsudevapriyaḥ sadā/*
> *umāprītikaro vṛkṣa bilvarūpo namo 'stute.*
>
> Om! Whatever you do is always favored by Śiva and Vāsudeva. O tree, you cause delight to Umā. I pay obeisance to you who are in the form of the *bilva.*

Here the *bilva* (*śrīphala*), and thus the Devī, is explicitly connected to both Śiva and Viṣṇu (as Vāsudeva).

6. He invokes the goddess Raktadantikā (She whose Teeth are Bloodied) in the pomegranate (*dādimi*). The numerous succulent red pods of the pomegranate (*Punica granatum*) fruit and the plant's red flowers, forge an obvious connection with the red teeth of Raktadantikā. He utters:

> *Om dādimyadhiṣṭhātri raktadantike ihāgaccha . . .*
> *Om dādimyadhiṣṭhātryai raktadantikāyai namaḥ.*

worshipping her with:

> *Om dādimi tvaṃ purā yuddhe raktabījasya sammukhe/*
> *umākāryaṃ kṛtaṃ yasmādasmākaṃ varadā bhava.*
>
> Om! O Pomegranate (*dādimi*), in former times, while warring against Raktabīja you have done the duty handed over by Umā well. Therefore, please be the bestower of boons on us.[42]

7. In the Aśoka (*Jonesia aśoka*) tree, he invokes the goddess Śokarahitā (She who Frees from Grief).The word *aśoka* which means "without grief," is itself a near synonym for Śokarahitā and perhaps figures strongly in the reason behind the choice. The Aśoka tree produces red flowers and can be induced to blossom, according to legend, when struck by the red-lacquered feet of a maiden wearing jingling anklets. According to Östör (1980:191), the Aśoka is Viṣṇu's tree and has medicinal properties. Barren women are said to become fertile if they eat its leaves during certain rituals. The leaves are customarily hung in clusters as decorations. The *purohita* utters:

Om aśokādhiṣṭhātri śokarahite ihāgaccha . . .
Om aśokādhiṣṭhātryai śokarahitāyai namaḥ

paying obeisance with:

Om haraprītikaro vṛkṣa hyaśoka śokanāśanaḥ/
durgāprītikaro yasmān māmaśokam sadā kuru.

Om! O Tree, you had always been doing deeds favored by Śiva. O Tree, you are called Aśoka, the remover of the pangs of separation. As you cause delight in Durgā, please get me free from grief (the sadness of bereavement).

8. He invokes Cāmuṇḍā in the Māna, a long-stemmed, broad-leaved plant (perhaps a variety of Kacvi). The thick stem (six to eight inches in diameter) is the source of delicious food preparations, and the leaves are used for protection from rain. He utters:

Om mānādhiṣṭhātri cāmuṇḍe ihāgaccha . . .
Om mānādhiṣṭhātryai cāmuṇḍyai namaḥ

and propitiates her with:

Om yasya patre vaseddevi mānavṛkṣaḥ śacīpriyaḥ/
mama cānugrahārthāya pūjām gṛhāṇa praśīda me.

Om! The Māna plant is favoured by Śacī, the beloved of Indra. Here the Goddess abides in the leaf. For bestowing grace to me, please accept my offering and be pleased.[43]

9. In the rice paddy (*dhānya*), he invokes Lakṣmī. The identification of Lakṣmī, the Goddess of Fortune, with rice (*Oryza sativa*) is obvious. Rice is the staple food of most Hindus. Bengalis quip that without rice in a meal, one has not eaten at all. The *purohita* utters:

Om dhānyādhiṣṭhātri lakṣmi ihāgaccha . . .
Om dhānyādhiṣṭhātryai lakṣmyai namaḥ

worshipping her with:

Om jagataḥ prāṇa rakṣārtham brahmaṇā nirmitaṃ purā/
umāprīti karaṃ dhānyaṃ tasmāttvam rakṣa mām sadā.

Om! For keeping the world alive, O paddy, you have been created by Brahmā in ancient times. It is favored by Umā. Please protect us for this reason.

Lastly, he worships the *navapatrikā* as a whole with the following *mantra*:

> *Om navapatrikāvasinyai durgāyai namaḥ.*
> *Om patrike navadurge tvam mahādeva manorame/*
> *pūjāṃ samastāṃ saṇigṛhya rakṣa māṃ tridaśeśvari.*
>
> Om! O the divine Goddess of all the gods, you have assumed these nine forms of Durgā in nine different plants and leaves. You are dear to Lord Śiva. After accepting all my offerings, please protect us.

Offerings to the *Dikpālas* (Directional Guardians)

The *purohita* now offers flowers to the lords of the directions (*dikpāla*):

In the	East,	Indra: *Ete gandhapuṣpe/*	*Om indrāya namaḥ.*
In the	SE,	Agni:	*Om agnaye namaḥ.*
	South,	Yama:	*Om yamāya namaḥ.*
	SW,	Nirṛti:	*Om nirṛtaye namaḥ.*
	West,	Varuṇa:	*Om varuṇāya namaḥ.*
	NW,	Vāyu:	*Om vāyave namaḥ.*
	North,	Kubera:	*Om kuverāya namaḥ.*
	NE,	Īśāna:	*Om īśānāya namaḥ.*
	Zenith, ENE,	Brahmā:	*Om brahmaṇe namaḥ.*
	Nadir, WSW,	Ananta:	*Om anantāya namaḥ.*

Invocation and Worship of the Clay Images of the Attending Deities

The *purohita* proceeds to worship the deities attending Durgā in the clay image cluster. He proceeds in the standard manner, first grasping a flower in the *dhyāna mudrā* by his heart, meditating on the deity, placing the flower on his head, worshipping the deity by mentally devotional service (*mānasopacāra*), and finally by placing the flower in front of the image and repeating the meditation. He then invokes the deity into the image and worships it with devotional service (*upacāra*). He ends the service by uttering an obeisance (*praṇāma*) *mantra,* while making a deeply respectful bow in which both hands and his forehead touch the ground. Generally, on Saptamī, a five-part service (*pañcopacāra*) is used. The lengthy *mantra*s that accompany offerings are not uttered here. The *purohita* merely offers up the various items quickly, saying, "This is an offering of flowers (for instance). Om! Obeisance to Gaṇeśa. (*Ete gandhapuṣpe/ om gaṇeśāya namaḥ*)." The attending deities venerated in this rite will each be worshipped at least once during the subsequent days with a full sixteen-part devotional service (*ṣodaśopacāra*).

Gaṇeśa

The *purohita* begins with Gaṇeśa, meditating thus:

Om kharevaṃ sthūlatanuṃ gajendra vadanaṃ lambodaram sundaram/ . . .

(See the *bodhana* rite for full details)

He invokes Gaṇeśa into the image with:

Om gaṇeśa
ihāgaccha/ iha tiṣṭha/ iha sannidehi/ iha sannirudhasva/ mama pūjām gṛhāṇa.

completing the invocation with:

Om gāṃ gaṇeśāya namaḥ.

He gives eyesight (*cakṣur dāna*) to the deity and installs vital energy (*prāṇa pratiṣṭha*). He worships Gaṇeśa with devotional service ending with an obeisance (*praṇāma*) *mantra.*

Om devendra maulimandāra karakanda kaṇāruṇaḥ
vighnān harantu heramba caraṇāmbuja reṇavah.

Om! May the dust of your feet, O Heramba, remove all obstacles. These dusts have collected at your feet from the garland made of *mandāra* flowers from the head of Indra and have become red and smeared with honey.

Nārāyaṇa and Śiva

In certain performances of Durgā Pūjā, the deities Nārāyaṇa and Śiva are invoked and worshipped. Śiva's image often appears painted on the arch (*cala*), which rests over single-piece clay image clusters. In the Mitra family's *pūjā*, each deity's image is housed in a separate shrine, and Śiva and Rāma (an incarnation [*avatāra*] of Viṣṇu) are included among them. Nārāyaṇa may be invoked and worshipped in homes of families having Vaiṣṇava leanings. In the Lahiri home, the family deities are brought down from the shrine room on the second floor to the *pūjālaya* on the ground floor. Visṇu/Nārāyaṇa is worshipped as a *śālagrāma* (a black, fossilized mollusk found in the Himālayas). Viṣṇu and Śiva (neither of whom necessarily have a tangible presence during the ritual in other locales) are linked to the Devī in a hierarchically ambiguous fashion. Viṣṇu/Nārāyaṇa is sometimes considered to be the deity who presides over the ritual, and Durgā is often referred to as the beloved of Śiva (*Śaṅkarapriyā*).

Nārāyaṇa

Nārāyaṇa is invoked and meditated on with the *dhyāna*:

Om śaṅkhacakragadāpadmadharaṃ kamalalocanam/
śuddhasphaṭikaśaṅkāśam kvacinnīlāmbujacchavim/
garuḍopari ca dhyāyet śuklapadmāsanaṃ harim/
śrīvatsavakṣasaṃ śāntam vanamālādharaṃ param/
keyūrakuṇḍaladharaṃ kirīṭa mukuṭojjvalaṃ/
lakṣmī sarasvatī kāntam sūryamaṇḍala madhyagam.

Om! Nārāyaṇa, with lotus eyes, having the color of pure crystal, is holding the conch shell, the discus, the club, and lotus. Or he may be meditated on as shining like a blue lotus sitting on Garuḍa. And this Hari should be meditated upon as seated on a white lotus. His chest is covered with a *śrīvatsa* sign. He is very tranquil in appearance. A forest garland (*vanamālā*) is hanging on his chest.[44] He is wearing an armlet (*kayūra*) and shining with a crown and diadem (*kirīta*). He is the beloved of Lakṣmī and Sarasvatī and is seen inside the orb of the moon.

His devotional service ends with this obeisance (*praṇāma*) *mantra*:

Om namo brahmaṇyadevāya go brāhmaṇahitāya ca/
jagaddhitāya kṛṣṇaya govindāya namo namaḥ.

Om! I pay obeisance to Nārāyaṇa who is always engaged for the good of the universe. He is the person doing good to cattle and *brāhmaṇas*. He is very awe-inspiring. I pay obeisance to Kṛṣṇa and Govinda repeatedly.

Śiva

Śiva is invoked and meditated upon with this *dhyāna*:

Om dhyānenityaṃ maheśaṃ rajatagirinibham/
cārucandrāvataṃsaṃ ratnākalpojjvalāṅgam/
paraśumṛgavarābhītihastaṃ prasannam
padmāsīnaṃ samantāt stutamamaragaṇaiḥ
vyāghrakṛttivāsānaṃ viśvādyaṃ viśvabījam
nikhilabhayaharaṃ pañcavaktraṃ triṇetram.

Om! One should always meditate on Śiva, the Lord of gods. He is white like the color of the silver mountain, having the disc of the moon as the ornament of his crest. His limbs are very bright like heaps of shining jewels. In his four hands he holds an axe, a deer, and in the lower right, the gesture of the boon, and in the lower left, assurance. He appears to be very graceful, sitting in lotus posture, and from every side he is praised by a good number of divinities. He is wearing the skin of a tiger. He is the primary cause and the seed of the universe. He is the remover of all sorts of misery. He has five faces with three eyes in each.

His devotional service ends with this obeisance *mantra*:

Om śivāya śāntāya kāraṇatrāyahetave/
nivedayāmi cātmānaṃ tvam gatiḥ parameśvaraḥ.

Om! I pay obeisance to Śiva, the tranquil one. He is the cause of three causes. I surrender myself, realizing that you are our ultimate resort.

Kārtikeya

Next the *purohita* proceeds to meditate (*dhyāna*) on Kārtikeya:

Om śambhornandanam agnivarcasamudāradīndraputrīsutam/
śāntaṃ śaktidharaṃ sadānanamalaṃ kṛtam/
bhāsā nirjita hemakuṅkumagarudgorocanā śailajam/
dhyāyeddaitya kulārdanaṃ suramudaṃ taṃ kārtikeyaṃ mahaḥ.

Om! The son of Śiva is bright like the flames of fire. He is also called the son of the daughters of Indra. He is quiet in appearance, holding the *śakti* weapon in his hand. He has six faces and is well decorated with ornaments. By his brightness, he has surpassed the brightness of gold, saffron (*kuṅkuma*), cow's bile (*gorocanā*), and resin (*śailaja*). One should meditate on him as the defeater of the host of demons. He who elates the hearts of gods is Kārtikeya.

He finishes the devotional service with this obeisance *mantra*:

Om kārtikeya mahābaga gaurīhṛdaya nandana/
kumāra rakṣa māṃ deva daityārdana namo 'stute.

Om! O great Kārtikeya, you are the giver of delight to the heart of Gaurī. O Kumāra, please protect us. I pay obeisance to you who are the killer of demons.

There are several points worth noting. Although this *dhyāna* depicts Kārtikeya with six faces, the clay *mūrtis* used for Durgā Pūjā portray him as a single-faced, handsome prince (*kumāra*). He is considered by many devotees to be the youngest child of Durgā (Gaṇeśa is the eldest).[45] If a male child is born slim and comely, he is said to be like Kārtikeya; if stout and charming, he is like Gaṇeśa. Kārtikeya's traditional weapon is the *śakti*, which means energy or power. The term *śakti* is most commonly used to refer to the feminine divine energy that activates the cosmos. The feminine form of *śailaja* (i.e., *sailajā*) is an epithet of Pārvatī/Durgā (born of the mountain). In this context the word appears to refer to a yellow substance found in the mountains. Most likely, it is benzoin, a hard, fragrant, yellowish, balsamic resin from trees (genus *Styrax*) used in incense preparations and medications.

The male deities are given ritual precedence over the female deities, and Gaṇeśa is always invoked and propitiated first. Having finished with them, he now proceeds to invoke the female goddesses.

Lakṣmī

Then Lakṣmī is meditated upon:

> *Om kāntyā kañcana sannibhāṃ himagiriprakhyaiścaturbhi gajaiḥ/*
> *hastat kṣipta hiraṇmayāmṛtaghaṭair āsicyamānām śriyam/*
> *vibhrāṇāṃ varam abjayugmam abhayaṃ hastaiḥ kirītojjvalām/*
> *kṣaumābaddhanitambabimbalalitāṃ vande 'ravindasthitām.*

> Om! In beauty she resembles gold. She is seen bathed by four elephants resembling the Himālaya mountains, with their trunks holding golden jars raising them above. She bears two lotuses, the boon-giving (*vara*), and assurance (*abhaya*) gestures. She is resplendent with her crown. Her buttocks are nice, reflecting the brightness of the silken cloth. We pay obeisance to the one who is seated on a red lotus.

This *dhyāna* corresponds to the form of Lakṣmī more commonly called Gajalakṣmī (Lakṣmī with Elephants). It perhaps supports the placement of the elephant-headed god Gaṇeśa beside her in the Durgā Pūjā image cluster.[46] She is invoked into the image, worshipped, and rendered obeisance with the *mantra*:

> *Om dhanaṃ dhānyam dharām dharmaṃ kīrtimāyuryaśah śriyam/*
> *turagān dantiputrānśca mahālakṣmi prayacchame.*

> Om! Give us wealth, crops, land, right morals (*dharma*), fame, longevity, good name, and beauty. Give us horses and elephants. O Mahālakṣmī, give me all.

Sarasvatī

Next Sarasvatī is meditated upon with the *dhyāna*:

> *Om taruṇaśakalamindorvibhratī śubhrakāntiḥ/*
> *kucabharanamitāṅgī sanniṣannā sitābje/*
> *nijakara kamalodyallekhani pustaka śrīḥ/*
> *sakalavibhavasiddhaiḥ pātu vāgdevatā naḥ.*

Om! Bearing the disc of the young moon (on her head), white in complexion, bent by the burden of her breasts, seated on a white lotus, she shines beautifully with a pen and a book in her hands. May the goddess of speech protect us and help us for the attainment of all wealth.

She is invoked into the image, imbued with eyesight and vital energy, and worshipped. The devotional service ends with this obeisance *mantra*:

Om sarasvatī mahābhāge vidye kamala locane/
viśvarūpe viśālakṣi vidyāṃ dehi namo 'stute.

Om! O eminent Sarasvatī, learning personified, with eyes like a lotus, who assumes multifarious forms and has long eyes, I pay obeisance to you. Give us learning.

Vāhanas (Mounts) and *Nāga* (Snake)

The *purohita* then offers three handfuls of flowers, one after the other, worshipping all the mounts and Durgā's snake noose (*nāgapāśa*) saying:

Om sāṅgo pāṅgāyai savāhanāyai durgāyai namaḥ.

Om! Obeisance to Durgā, and to the group of mud images, with their vehicles.

He then makes quick offerings to the snake (*sarpa*), peacock (*mayura*), and the mouse (*muṣika*), saying:

Om sarpāya namaḥ/ Om mayurāya namaḥ/ Om muṣikāya namaḥ.

The peacock is the *vāhana* of Kārtikeya, though it is also associated with Sarasvatī. The mouse is the mount of Gaṇeśa. The snake is a noose that is wrapped around the limbs of the demon Mahiṣa. If Sarasvatī's swan mount and Lakṣmī's owl are present in the image cluster, the purohita will quickly worship them as well.

Mahāsiṅgha/Mahāsiṃha and Mahiṣāsura

Both the great lion (*mahāsiṅgha*) mount of Durgā and the demon Mahiṣa have already been meditated upon and brought to life in the Durgā *dhyāna* (see before). He reinvokes the lion with:

Om vajranakha daṃṣṭrāyudhāya mahāsiṃhāya huṃ phaṭ namaḥ.

Om! Obeisance to the great lion, armed with teeth and nails like thunderbolts. *Huṃ*! *Phaṭ*!

He makes offerings to Mahāsiṃha, ending with the *mantras*:

> *Om siṃha tvam sarvajantūnām adhipo 'si mahābala/*
> *pārvatīvāhana śriman varaṃ dehi namo 'stute.*
> *Om āsanañcāsi bhūtānām nānālaṅkāra bhūṣitam/*
> *merusṛṅga pratīkāsam siṃhāsana namo 'stute.*
>
> Om! You are the lord of all creatures (living beings), enormously mighty lion. You, auspicious one, are the vehicle of Pārvatī. Please bestow blessings on us. I pay obeisance to you.
> Om! You are the seat of all beings and decorated variously with different ornaments. You are like the pinnacle of Mount Meru. I pay homage to the seat in the form of a lion.[47]

The *purohita* then offers devotional service to Mahiṣāsura, paying homage to him with the *mantra*:

> *Om mahiṣāsurāya namaḥ.* Om! Homage to Mahiṣāsura.

ADORATION OF DURGĀ

Durgā Japa

Now that the entire image cluster is alive and active, the *purohita* repeats a *mantra* of Durgā, at least ten times.

> *Om duṃ durgāyai namaḥ.* Om! Duṃ! Obeisance to Durgā!

Ārati

Next he performs an *ārati* to Durgā using the following items. The term "*ārati*" is often used synonymously with "*dīpopacāra*" (devotional service with a lamp). It is related to (even possibly derived from) the word "*ārātrika*" which refers to worship at night (*rātrī*), in which light is waved in front of the image. *Ārati* may also be derived from the verbal root, *aram*, meaning "to take delight." This latter connotation seems appropriate for the activity described here, since it is not just light but a number of honorific items that are passed before the Devī.

The *purohita* waves before the Devī:

1. Incense (*dhūpa*) in a container.

2. A lamp (*dīpa*) with at least five wicks.

3. A conch shell (*śaṅkha*) with water in it.

4. Washed clothes (*vastra*). Normally these are new items of clothing (Hindi: *sārī* or *dhoti*) which have been previously washed. It deserves some reflection, since new clothes (many of which are worn by the patron's family during Durgā Pūjā) are not generally prewashed. Perhaps the offering points to the purificatory power of water.

5. A large yak's tail whisk (*cāmara*). A tiny symbolic form of the *cāmara* was used during *adhivāsa* ritual, but an elaborate full-sized version was used in the devotional service and in this *ārati*. The *cāmara* serves as a fan, wafting cooling air towards the deity and keeping insects away. There is something extremely moving in this ritual, which exudes a combination of majestic pomp and hallowed atmosphere. The *pūjālaya* is thick with fragrant smoke, as the incense, lamp, and other items are offered to the Devī. Despite the steady decline in the scale of the domestic celebrations, both the Mitra and Lahiri families continue to utilize heirloom items of substance. There are enormous brass and copper containers, tripods, and other items that are used primarily, if not exclusively, for the family's *pūjās*. The large ornate *cāmara* is merely one such item.

6. He offers flowers (*puṣpa*) to the Devī.

7. He again waves the *śaṅkha*, this time sprinkling some water from the shell, providing a pleasing, cooling effect.

8. He bows before the Goddess (*namaskāra*).

Durgā Stuti

The *purohita* follows the *ārati* by reciting a hymn of adoration (*stuti*) to Durgā. He may opt instead to recite the *Devī Kavaca* (Armor of the Goddess), one of the sections appended (*aṅga*) to the *Durgā Saptaśatī* (see Coburn [1991] for an excellent translation) or the *Durgā Stava*, a *Mahābhārata* hymn attributed to Yudhiṣṭhira.

> *Om durgāṃ śivāṃ śāntikarīṃ brahmāṇīṃ brahmaṇapriyām/*
> *sarvaloka praṇetrīñca praṇamāmi sadā śivām/*
> *maṅgalāṃ śobhanāṃ śuddhāṃ niṣkalāṃ paramām kalām/*
> *viśveśvarīṃ viśvamātām caṇḍikāṃ praṇamāmyaham/*
> *sarvadevamayīm devīṃ sarvalokabhayāpahām/*
> *brahmeśa viṣṇunamitāṃ praṇamāmi sadā umām/*
> *vindhyasthāṃ vindhyanilayām divyasthāna nivāsinīm/*

yoginīṃ yogamātāñca caṇḍikāṃ praṇamamyaham/
īśānamātaraṃ devīm īśvarīm īśvarapriyām/
praṇato 'smi sadā durgām saṃsārārīṇavatāriṇīm/
ya idaṃ paṭhati stotroṃ śṛṇuyād vāpi yo naraḥ/
sa muktaḥ sarvapāpebhyo modate durgayā saha.

Om! I always pay obeisance to you, the consort of Śiva. You are Durgā (the one who saves persons in danger). You are Śivā (auspicious), giver of peace. You are also called Brahmāṇī, the dynamic aspect of Brahmā and lovingly attached to Brahmā. You are the creatrix of all worlds.
You are well-being itself, beautiful to look at, pure. You do not have any parts, and at the same time you are the ultimate division (*kalā*). You are the lady of this universe. I pay obeisance to your terrific form.
You, O Goddess, are made of the essence of the gods. You are the remover of fears arising from all quarters. You are shown reverence by Brahmā, Viṣṇu, and Śiva. I pay obeisance to you, O Umā.
You are steadily established in the Vindhya Mountains, and having an abode in the Vindhyas, you live in the divine level. To *yogins*, you are the mother of Yoga. O Terrific one, I pay obeisance to you.
You are the mother of Īśāna (Śiva). You are the lady and beloved of the superintending agent (Īśvara). O Durgā, I always pay obeisance to you, who are the rescuer of worldly existence.
Whoever reads this verse praising Durgā, or the person who listens to it, becomes liberated from all sins and lives happily with Durgā afterwards.

In another example of the importance of the litany in revealing perceptions about the nature of the Great Goddess, one notes the epithet Īśānamātā (Mother of Īśāna/Śiva). The epithet explicitly extends the conceptualization of Durgā beyond a spousal affiliation with Śiva/Śaṅkara. Although she is frequently addressed as the beloved of Śaṅkara, here she is the mother or source of the supreme male deity Śiva (under a subordinate epithet of Īśāna) himself.

Puṣpāñjali (Adoration with Flowers)

The *purohita* now asks devotees to come up and offer flowers. This is a participatory portion of the ritual to which the worshippers greatly look forward. Everyone wants to make an offering to the Devī, and passive members are encouraged to participate. If a large group is present, a helper passes out flowers and *bilva pātra*s from a basket. The people wash their hands first, or the *purohita* sprinkles water on their bodies for purification. They then pray aloud, with great reverence, following the *purohita*, who may dictate some of these or other appropriate *mantra*s to them. First, the *purohita* utters:

Mahiṣaghni mahāmāye cāmuṇḍe muṇḍamālini/
āyurārogya vijayam dehi devi namo 'stute.

O Cāmuṇḍā, the great deluder, bearing the garland of skulls, you are the slayer of Mahiṣāsura. Bestow on me longevity, health, and victory. I pay obeisance to you.

And finishes with:

Eṣaḥ sacandanabilvapatrapuṣpañjaliḥ/
namo bhagavatyai durgāyai devyai namaḥ.

This is an adoration with fragrant flowers and bilva leaves.
Obeisance to the Goddess Bhagavatī Durgā.

Since the caste composition of the audience is unknown, and since many people in the audience are not initiated, Pandit Chakravarty explained that the *purohita* may feel they have not earned the right to say "Om" or "Aiṃ." Normally women and *śūdra*s (even if initiated), and the uninitiated, are not supposed to say "Om." Thus the more general "Namaḥ" is used.

When this is complete, the devotees throw the flowers towards the image. Often a large copper plate is used in front of the image with a sandal (*pāduka*), a symbol of the Devī's footprint, in it. This prevents the clay image from being damaged by the overenthusiastic throwing of flowers. The term *añjali* generally refers to the classic gesture of prayer made by pressing the palms together, fingers extended upwards. In *puṣpāñjali* the flowers are held between the palms. The palms are then raised over and behind the head and the flowers thrown with both hands.

Second:

Candanena samālabdhe kuṅkumena vilepite/
bilva patra kṛtā pīḍe durge ham śaraṇaṃ gataḥ.
Eṣaḥ sacandena bilvapatra . . . namaḥ.

Being anointed with sandalwoodpaste and smeared with saffron (*kuṅkuma*), being overlaid by *bilva* leaves, I am surrendering myself to Durgā.

Third, he utters:

Puṣpam manoharaṃ divyaṃ sugandhaṃ devanirmitam/
hṛdayaṃ adbhūtaṃ āghreyaṃ devi dattaṃ pragṛhyatām.
Eṣaḥ sacandena bilvapatra . . .namaḥ.

Flowers, fascinating, divine, fragrant, created by the divine hand, very lovely, unique (hard to obtain), worthy to be smelled, which are being offered to you, O Devī, please accept them.

He may now utter portions of the *Durgā Stuti* for people to repeat. He then utters:

Āyurdehi yaśodehi bhāgyam bhagavati dahime/
putrān dehi dhanaṃ dehi sarvān kāmāṃśca dehime.
Bhagavati bhayocchede bhava bhavāni kāmade/
śaṅkari kauśiki tvam he kātyāyani namo 'stute.
Harapāpaṃ hara kleśaṃ hara śokaṃ harāśubham/
hara rogam hara ksobhaṃ hara devi harapriye.

Give me longevity. Endow me with reputation. Please give me good fortune. Give me sons, wealth, and all sorts of desires.
O divine lady, you are the uprooter of all fears, O consort of Bhava (Śiva), giver of all desires, you are Śaṅkarī, Kauśikī, and Kātyāyanī. I pay obeisance to you.
Please remove sins, remove affliction, remove the pain of separation, remove all sorts of inauspiciousness, remove illness, remove agitation of the mind, O beloved of Hara (Śiva).

Finishing this, he asks them to repeat the *namaskāra mantra*, which is sometimes the only prayer utilized:

Sarva maṅgala maṅgalye sive sarvārtha sādhike/
śaraṇye tryambake gauri nārāyaṇi namo 'stute.

You are the source of all auspiciousness, O consort of Śiva. You are the fulfiller of all desired ends. You are the last refuge of all. You are the three-formed mother[48], O Gaurī, O Nārāyaṇī, I pay obeisance to you.

This brings an end to the rituals belonging to the seventh day of Navarātra (Mahāsaptamī). The *purohita* returns home. Sometime during the night he may return to the place of worship (*pūjālaya*) to prepare the *maṇḍala,* which will constitute a major part of the worship ritual on the following day, Mahāṣṭamī. According to Pandit Chakravarty, the prescription for drawing this *maṇḍala* is found in the *Devī Purāṇa*. The *purohita* draws it using a chalk line (string covered with powdered chalk, as used on construction sites). Since it is a complex procedure, *purohita*s such as Pandit Nitai use a *maṇḍala* that they have previously drawn and that is repeatedly reused for this purpose.

4.5: Mahāṣṭamī

The worship on the eighth day (*aṣṭamī*) of Navarātra is essentially a repetition of the rituals performed on the previous day (*saptamī*). The significant difference lies in the worship of Durgā in the form of a complex *maṇḍala*. This Maṇḍala of All Auspiciousness (*sarvatobhadra maṇḍala*) (see Figure 4.5) is a diagram that consists of a large square and encloses several smaller squares, a circle, and an eight-petalled lotus.[1] The small squares are filled with five colors of powdered dust (white, green, yellow, red, and black). In the eight-petalled lotus, the eight *śakti*s that were mentioned in the Durgā *dhyāna*, namely, Ugracaṇḍā and other goddesses, are worshipped.

The *purohita* arrives at the place of worship (*pūjālaya*) and, sipping water three times (*ācamana*), makes himself pure. He makes a frowning glance (*krodha/divyadṛṣṭi*) to everything around uttering, "*Raṃ riṃ ruṃ phaṭ.*" He proceeds by doing everything that was done during Saptamī, including: 1. *sāmānyārgha*; 2. *āsanaśuddhi*; 3. *puṣpaśuddhi*; 4. offering at least flowers and fragrances to Gaṇeśa, Śiva and the other gods, Aditya and the other *navagraha*s, the *daśāvatāra*, etc.; 5. *bhūtaśuddhi*; 6. *nyāsa*s; 7. *prāṇāyāma*; 8. *pīṭhanyāsa*; and 9. *Durgā dhyāna*. 10. He then takes the mirror (*darpaṇa*) from its place on the pedestal of the clay images. Placing it in front of the image, he offers three handfuls of flowers to the reflection, pouring them onto the mirror, saying:

Ete gandhapuṣpe/ duṃ durgāyai namaḥ.

With these fragrant flowers, Duṃ, I offer obeisance to Durgā.

He then moves the mirror with some petals on it gently beside him onto a tripod, which is situated inside a large container. He smears the surface of the mirror with mustard oil and turmeric, a combination also used in the *adhivāsa* ritual used to remove blemishes and to give a golden hue to the skin.

11. He performs the *mahāsnāna* in the same manner as on Saptamī.

12. He dries the mirror. He then writes the *mantra*, "Hrīṃ," in vermillion on the mirror and places it on the altar (pedestal) of the clay image cluster.

13. He offers *māśabhaktabali* to pacify the entities that may create disturbances.

Note: There is no *ghaṭasthāpana* performed on Aṣṭamī.

14. He invokes Gaṇeśa again, and after making a *dhyāna* of him, he proceeds to worship him with *daśopacāra*.

15. He follows this with *Śivādi pañcadevatā* worship; 16. *prāṇāyāma* again; 17. *ṛṣyādi nyāsa*; 18. *karanyāsa*; 19. *aṅganyāsa*; 20. *Durgā dhyāna* again (internal); 21. *viśeṣārgha* (conch-shell worship); 22. *pīṭhanyāsa*; 23. *karanyāsa*; 24. *aṅganyāsa*; and 25. *Durgā dhyāna* again (external).

*Dhyāna*s are normally performed twice: first, internally, with a flower held in *dhyāna mudrā* by the heart, and second, externally, with the flower placed before the image (e.g., *ghaṭa*, plant, *mūrti*, *yantra*) to be worshipped.

In this ritual the *purohita* places the flower at the feet of the clay image. Air that escapes the nostrils during the *dhyāna* is thought to transfer the internally meditated deity to the external image.

Note: There is no *prāṇa pratiṣṭha* performed on Aṣṭamī, since the images are already imbued with life.

26. The *purohita* now worships the Devī with *ṣodaśopacāra*, as on Saptamī.

27. He performs *śadaṅganyāsa* and worships the *bilva* tree and the *navapatrikā*.

28. The *purohita* next performs the practice of the *maṇḍala*.

Sarvatobhadra Maṇḍala

The *purohita* has drawn the *maṇḍala* the previous night on the floor in front of the image. Alternately, he may bring a previously drawn *maṇḍala* to use for this purpose. Truly adept ritual specialists may perform the invocations while drawing the relevant parts of the *maṇḍala*. On occasion, the entire clay image cluster sits upon the *sarvatobhadra maṇḍala*. Pandit Nitai constructs such a *maṇḍala* using powders made from wood-apple leaves (*bilva patra*) for the green color, turmeric (*haldi*) for the yellow color, *palash* (a lotus-like flower that only blooms in autumn) for the red color, and rice for the white color. The *maṇḍala*, which enjoys such an eminent position in the worship ritual, is clearly an important embodiment of the deity. Śāstric injunctions, Pandit Chakravarty explained, normally prohibit the worship of images and *yantra*s or *maṇḍala*s in the same ritual. However, the Durgā Pūjā disregards this strict formality and opts to worship the Devī in a plethora of forms.

Worship of Durgā's Eight *Śakti*s

The *purohita* turns his attention to the eight-petalled lotus in the center of the diagram. He begins by invoking and worshipping the eight *śakti*s referred to in the Durgā *dhyāna*, who are said to accompany the Goddess always. The *purohita* may visualize these *śakti*s if he is aware of their forms. Their colors are as follows: Pracaṇḍā is black; Caṇḍogrā is blue; Caṇḍanāyikā is white; Caṇḍā is smoky-colored; Caṇḍavatī is blue; Caṇḍarūpā is black; Aticaṇḍikā is white; and Ugracaṇḍā is bright (like the noonday sun).

Figure 4.5 The Diagram of All Auspiciousness *(sarvatobhadra maṇḍala).*

Ugracaṇḍā

The petal facing east is for the *śakti* Ugracaṇḍā. He invokes her there with:

Om hrīṃ śrīṃ ugracaṇḍe/
ihāgaccha ihāgaccha/ iha tiṣṭha iha tiṣṭha/
iha sannidehi iha sannidehi/ iha sannirudhyasva iha sannirudhyasva
mama pūjāṃ gṛhāṇa

Om! Hrīṃ! Śrīṃ! O Ugracaṇḍā. Come here, come here. Stay here, stay here. Remain here, remain here. Take up residence here, take up residence here. Please accept my worship.

He worships her with *pañca* or *daśopacāra*, uttering her *mantra*:

> *Eṣa gandha/ Om hrīṃ śrīṃ ugracaṇḍāyai namaḥ.* (Om! Hrīṃ! Śrīṃ! Obeisance to Ugracaṇḍā . . .)
>
> *Etat puṣpam/ . . .; Eṣa dhūpaḥ/ . . .; Eṣa dīpaḥ/ . . .; Etan naivedyam/ . . .*

and ends with a gesture and *mantra* of obeisance (*praṇāma*):

> *Om ugracaṇḍā tu varadā madhyāhnārka samaprabhā/*
> *sāme sadāstu varadā tasyai nityaṃ namo namaḥ.*
>
> Om! O Ugracaṇḍā, having the brilliance of the noonday sun, is the bestower of blessings. May she be a giver of boons to me. I pay obeisance to her everyday.

Pracaṇḍā

In the southeast petal, Pracaṇḍā is invoked and worshipped similarly. Her *praṇāma mantra* is:

> *Om pracaṇḍe putrade nitye pracaṇḍa gaṇa saṃsthite/*
> *sarvā nanda kare devi tubhyaṃ nityaṃ namo namaḥ.*
>
> Om! O Pracaṇḍā, eternally surrounded by dreadful groups (*gaṇa*), you are the giver of boons. You are the source of all happiness. I pay obeisance to you everyday.

Caṇḍogrā

In the south petal, Caṇḍogrā is invoked and worshipped. Her *praṇāma mantra* is:

> *Om lakṣmistvaṃ sarvabhūtānāṃ sarvabhūtābhayapradā/*
> *devi tvam sarva kāryesuvaradā bhava śobhane.*
>
> Om! Your beauty/affluence (*lakṣmi*) is present in all beings, and you are the giver of assurance to all beings. O divine deity, we hope that in every effort of ours you should be the giver of blessings (boons). You are the beautiful one.

Caṇḍanāyikā

In the southwest petal, Caṇḍanāyikā is invoked and worshipped with the *praṇāma*:

> *Om yā sṛṣṭi sthitināṃ nāca deveśa varadāyinī/*
> *kalikalmaṣanāśāya namāmi caṇḍanāyikām.*

Om! The one who is the giver of boons to the Lord of gods of creation and preservation, for the purpose of removal of sins of Kali (i.e., *kaliyuga*), we pay worship to Caṇḍanāyikā.

Caṇḍā

In the west, the *śakti* Caṇḍā is invoked and worshipped:

Om devi caṇḍātmike caṇḍi caṇḍārivijayaprade/
dharmārthamokṣade durge nityaṃ me varadā bhava.

Om! O Goddess, you have assumed the form of Caṇḍā, who is the giver of victory over the enemy called Caṇḍa.[2] You are the bestower of *dharma*, *artha*, and *mokṣa*. O Durgā, always be the giver of boons to me.

Caṇḍavatī

In the northwest, Caṇḍavatī is invoked and worshipped.

Om yā sṛṣṭi sthiti saṃahāra guṇa traya samanvitā/
yā parāḥ śaktayas tasyai caṇḍavatyai namo namaḥ.

Om! The one who is associated with the three attributes of creation, preservation, and dissolution and the one who transcends those powers (*śakti*s), I pay obeisance to that Caṇḍavatī.

Caṇḍarūpā

In the north, Caṇḍarūpā:

Om caṇḍarūpātmikā caṇḍā caṇḍikā caṇḍanāyikā/
sarva siddhi prade devi tasyai nityaṃ namo namaḥ.

Om! All the forms of Caṇḍā, Caṇḍikā, and Caṇḍanāyikā have assumed the form of Caṇḍarūpā. She is the bestower of all attainments. I always pay obeisance to her.

Aticaṇḍikā

In the northeast, Aticaṇḍikā:

Om bālārka nayanā caṇḍā sarvadā bhaktavatsalā/
caṇḍāsurasya mathani varadastvaticaṇḍika.

Om! Aticaṇḍikā has eyes like the morning sun. She looks tenderly on her devotees. She who has trampled down the demon Caṇḍa is the giver of boons.

Invocation and Worship of the (Sixty-four) Yoginīs

In the center of the lotus, the *purohita* now invokes the Sixty-four Yoginīs thus:

Om catuṣaṣṭayogini/ ihāgaccha ihāgaccha . . .

He then worships each of them saying:

Ete gandapuṣpe, etc./ Om hrīṃ klīṃ nārāyaṇyai namaḥ.

(He repeats the procedure for each of the sixty-four names).

The listings of the *yoginīs* vary considerably. The *purohita* selects his own tradition's count or that of the *yajamāna*'s family. The list given in the *Bṛhannandikeśvara Purāṇa* is: Nārāyaṇī, Gaurī, Śākambharī, Bhimā, Raktadantikā, Bhrāmarī, Pārvatī, Durgā, Kātyāyanī, Mahādevī, Caṇḍaghantā, Mahāvidyā, Mahātapā, Sāvitrī, Brahmavādinī, Bhadrakālī, Viśālakṣī, Rudrāṇī, Kṛṣṇā, Piṅgalā, Agnijvālā, Raudramukhī, Kālarātrī, Tapasvinī, Medhasvanā, Sahasrākṣī, Viṣṇumāyā(1), Jalodarī, Mahodarī, Muktakeśī, Ghorarūpā, Mahāvāyū, Śrūtī, Smṛtī, Dhṛtī, Tuṣṭī, Puṣṭī, Medhā, Vidyā, Lakṣmī, Sarasvatī, Aparnā, Ambikā, Yoginī, Ḍākinī, Sākinī, Hākinī, Nākinī, Lākinī, Tridaśeśvarī, Mahāṣaṣṭhī, Sarvamaṅgalā, Lajjā, Kauśikī, Brahmāṇī, Maheśvarī, Kaumārī, Vaiṣṇavī, Aindrī, Nārasiṃhī, Vārāhī, Cāmuṇḍā, Śivadūtī, Viṣṇumāyā(2), and Mātṛkā.[3]

The *purohita* finally invokes the group of them together:[4]

Om koṭi yoginīgaṇaḥ/ ihāgaccha ihāgaccha . . .

Worship of Deities from other Regions

The *purohita* utters:

Om hrīṃ śrīṃ nānādeśanivāsinibhyoḥ devibhyoḥ namaḥ.

Om! Hrīṃ! Śrīṃ! Salutation to other deities residing in other regions/countries.

Invocation and Worship of the Mātṛs (Mothers)

The Mothers (*mātṛ*, *mātṛkā*) are a group of female deities who are first mentioned about the first century C.E. While the number of members in the groups and their constituent members vary widely, one of the best-known groups belongs to the third episode of the *Durgā Saptaśatī*. There, in order to aid the Devī, who is engaged in battle with the demons Śumbha and

Niśumbha, the male gods produce *śaktis*, female counterparts of themselves. Seven such female energy manifestations are produced, and the text (DSS 8.38, 44, 49, 62) refers to them collectively as the Mātṛkās. They are: Brahmāṇī, created from Brahmā, Māheśvarī, created from Śiva (Maheśvara), Kaumārī, created from Kārtikeya (Kumāra), Vaiṣṇavī, created from Viṣṇu, Vārāhī, created from Varāha (Viṣṇu's boar incarnation), Nārasiṃhī, created from Narasiṃha (Viṣṇu's man-lion *avatāra*), and Aindrī, who is created from Indra. As a group, they rush into battle, accompanied by Cāmuṇḍā (an epithet of Kālī). Despite their origins, names, and appearances, the *Durgā Saptaśati* emphasizes that they are not primarily consorts of the male gods, but are in actuality manifestations of the Great Goddess herself. She explicitly refers to them that way as she draws them back into herself at one point in the battle (DSS 10.2–5). It is precisely this cluster of seven Mātṛkās, together with Cāmuṇḍā (also included as a Mother), who are invoked in this segment of the *maṇḍala* rite. The goddess Kātyāyanī is also worshipped as a *mātṛ*, but at the center of the *maṇḍala*, suggesting that she is the aspect of the Great Goddess from whom the other Mothers emerge.

Brahmāṇī

The *purohita* invokes and worships Brahmāṇī at the northeast of the *maṇḍala*:

> *Om hrīṃ śrīṃ brahmāṇyai namaḥ.*

and pays obeisance with this *mantra*:

> *Om caturamukhiṃ jagaddhātriṃ haṃsārudhām varapradāṃ*
> *sṛṣṭi rūpāṃ mahābhāgāṃ brahmaṇīṃ tām namamyaham.*
>
> Om! She has four faces, is seated on a swan, and is the giver of boons. She is the protector of the world. She is the form of creation. She is noble hearted. I pay my obeisance to you.

Māheśvarī

He also invokes Māheśvarī in the northeast:

> *Om hrīṃ śrīṃ māheśvaryai namaḥ.*

and pays obeisance with:

> *Om vṛṣārudhāṃ śubhaṃ śuklāṃ trinetrāṃ varadāṃ śivaṃ/*
> *māheśvarīṃ namamyadya sṛṣṭi saṃhārakārinīm.*

Om! Māheśvarī is atop the bull. She is auspicious, white, with three eyes. She is the giver of boons and is known as the consort of Śiva. I pay obeisance today to Māheśvarī, who is the agent of creation and destruction.

Kaumārī

In the southeast, he invokes Kaumārī:

Om hrīṃ śrīṃ kaumāryai namaḥ.

and pays obeisance with:

Om kaumārīṃ pītavāsanāṃ mayūrvāhanām/
śakti hastāṃ sitāṅgiṃ tāṃ namāmi varadāṃ sadā.

Om! Kaumārī is wearing yellow clothes and has a peacock as her vehicle. The weapon she bears is called *śakti*. Her limbs are white. I always pay obeisance to her, the giver of boons.

Vaiṣṇavī

Vaiṣṇavī is also invoked in the southeast corner:

Om hrīṃ klīṃ vaiṣṇavyai namaḥ.[5]

and paid obeisance with:

Om śaṅkha cakra gadā padmadhāriṇīṃ kṛṣṇarūpinīm/
stithi rūpāṃ khagendrasthāṃ vaiṣṇavīṃ tām namāmyaham.

Om! Vaiṣṇavā bears the conch, discus, club, and lotus. She is of the form of Kṛṣṇa. She signifies maintenance. She is seated on Garuḍa (lord of birds). I pay obeisance to Vaiṣṇavī.

Vārāhī

In Banāras, Vārāhī is invoked into the southwest corner.

Om hrīṃ klīṃ vārāhyai namaḥ.

and paid homage with:

Om vārāha rupinīṃ devīṃ daṃstrodhṛta vasundharām/
subhadāṃ pītavāsanāṃ vārāhīṃ tām namāmyaham.

Om! She is of the form of a boar, who by her tusk holds up the earth. She is the giver of well-being. She puts on yellow clothes. I pay obeisance to that Vārāhī.

Nārasiṃhī

Again in the southwest corner, he invokes Nārasiṃhī.

Om hrīṃ klīṃ nārasiṃhyai namaḥ.

and pays obeisance with:

Om nṛsiṃharūpinīṃ devīṃ daitya dānava darpahām/
śubhām śubhapradām nārasimhim namāmyham.

Om! She is of the form of a lion-person. The goddess is the destroyer of the arrogance of demons. She is auspicious, the giver of auspiciousness, white in color. I pay obeisance to that Nārasiṃhī.

Indrāṇī

In the northwest corner of the *maṇḍala*, Indrāṇī is invoked.

Om hrīṃ śrīṃ indrāṇyai namaḥ.

and paid obeisance with:

Om indrāṇī gajakumbhasthāṃ sahasaranayanojjvalām/
namāmi varadām deviṃ sarva deva namaskṛtām.

Om! Indrāṇī is seated between the two lumps of an elephant's temples. She is bright with one thousand eyes. I bow to that giver of boons who is paid obeisance by the gods.

Cāmuṇḍā

Cāmuṇḍā is also invoked in the northwest corner.

Om hrīṃ śrīṃ cāmuṇḍāyai namaḥ.

and worshipped with:

Om cāmuṇḍāmuṇḍamathaniṃ muṇḍamālāpośobhitām
aṭītahāsa muditāṃ namāmyātma vibhūtaye.

Om! Cāmuṇḍā is the destroyer of the demon Muṇḍa. She is wearing a garland of skulls. She laughs loudly and thus shows her inner delight for proper attainment of power of the self. I bow to her.

Kātyāyanī

And in the center of all these goddesses he invokes Kātyāyanī.

Om hrīṃ śrīṃ kātyāyanyai namaḥ.

paying her obeisance with:

Om kātyāyanīṃ daśabhujāṃ mahiṣāsuramardiniṃ
prasanna vadanām devīṃ varadāṃ tām namāmyaham.

Om! Kātyāyanī, possessing ten arms, crushed the demon called Mahiṣa. She has a smiling face and is the giver of boons. I pay obeisance to her.

Caṇḍikā and the Nine Durgās

Then taking flowers, the *purohita* utters this verse:

Om caṇḍike navadurge tvam mahādevamanorame
pūjāṃ samastāṃ saṅgrihya rakṣamāṃ tridaśeśvarī.

Om! O Caṇḍikā, you are the Nine Durgās. You are dear to Śiva. After receiving my worship, O goddess of the heaven, please protect me.

And he offers these flowers three times to the center of the *maṇḍala* with the *mantra*:

Om hrīṃ śrīṃ navadurgāyai namaḥ.

Om! Hrīṃ! Śrīṃ! Obeisance to the Nine Durgās.

Jayantī and other Goddesses

The *purohita* now invokes Jayantī and other goddesses with:

Om hrīṃ śrīṃ jayantyai namaḥ. (Repeated for each of the other goddesses)

He does so for Maṅgalā, Kālī, Bhadrakālī, Kapālinī, Durgā, Śivā, Kṣamā, Dhātrī, Svāhā, and Svadhā.

It is important to note that the inner portion of the *sarvatobhadra maṇḍala,* consisting of the eight-petalled lotus and surrounding square elements, is further circumscribed by a square border. This border is decorated with a leaf and floral creeper, beyond which the *liṅga/yoni* features of the *maṇḍala* reappear. The goddesses are all invoked into the inner portion of the *maṇḍala*, with its lotus center and vegetative boundary. Male deities, except for the guardians of the field, are invoked beyond the creeper boundary, and Durgā is finally worshipped as the entire *maṇḍala*.

Worship of the Weapons

The *purohita* now leaves the *maṇḍala* temporarily to perform the worship of Durgā's weapons. These are fashioned out of thin sheets of tin.[6] He begins with the weapons in her right hands.

Triśūla (Trident)

He invokes the *triśūla* with:

Om triśūlāya namaḥ.

and then pays homage:

Om sarvāyudhānāṃ prathamo nirmitastvaṃ pinākinā
śūlat śulaṃ samākṛṣa krtvā muṣṭigrahaṃ śubham.

Om! You have been made as the first of all weapons by Śiva himself. He has made you by making it emerge from his trident by means of his auspicious grasping fist.[7]

Khaḍga (Sword)

Om khaḍgāya namaḥ.
Om asirviśāsanaḥ khadga stīkṣṇadhārodurāsadaḥ/
śrīgarbho vijayaścaiva dharmapāla namo 'stute.

Om! The sword is that which causes death. This sword is very sharp and cannot be overpowered. I pay homage to you who is named as Śrīgarbha, Vijaya, and Dharmapāla.

Cakra (Discus)

Om cakrāya namaḥ.
Om cakra tvam viṣṇurupo 'si viṣṇu pāṇau sadā sthitaḥ/
devi hastasthito nityam sudarśana namo 'stute.

Om! O discus, you are of the form of Viṣṇū and always remain in his hand. Now you are in the hand of the Goddess and remain there eternally. I pay homage to this discus named Sudarśana.

Tīkṣṇavāna (Sharp Arrow)

Om tīkṣṇavānāya namaḥ.
Om sarvāyudhānām śreṣṭo 'si daityasenānisūdana
bhayebhyaḥ sarvato rakṣaḥ tīkṣṇavāna namo 'stute.

Om! This sharp arrow excels among all weapons. It is the key destroyer of the army of the demons. Please protect us from everything. I pay homage to you.

Śakti Weapon

Om śaktaye namaḥ.
Om śaktistvam sarvadevānām guhasyaca viśeṣataḥ/
śaktirūpeṇa sarvatra rakṣām kuru namo 'stute.

Om! You are the *śakti* of all gods, particularly of Guha (Kārtikeya).[8] I pay homage to you, and you should protect us from all sides.

The *purohita* now worships the weapons in the left hands of the Devī.

Kheṭaka (Club/Staff)

Om kheṭakāya namaḥ.
Om yaṣṭi rūpeṇa kheṭatvaṃ vairisaṃhāra kārakaḥ/
devīhasta sthithonityaṃ mama rakṣaṃ kurusvaca.

Om! You are the destroyer of enemies in the form of a club/staff.[9] Remaining in the hands of the Goddess, please protect me.

Pūrṇacāpa (Fully drawn Bow)

Om pūrṇacāpāya namaḥ.
Om sarvāyudha mahāmātra sarvadevārisūdanaḥ/
cāpam mām sarvataḥ rakśa sākam sāyaka sattamaiḥ.

Om! The bow and arrow of yours is the destroyer of the enemies of the gods and the chief (minister) of weapons. The strung bow along with excellent arrows should protect me from all sides.

Aṅkuśa (Goad)

Om aṅkuśāya namaḥ.
Om aṅkuśo 'si namastubhyam gajānām niyamaḥ sadā/
lokānāṃ sarva rakśārthaṃ vidhṛtaḥ pārvatī kare.

Om! O goad, you are the restrainer of elephants. I pay homage to you. For the protection of the world, it is held by the hands of Pārvatī.

Ghaṇṭa (Bell)

Om ghaṇṭāya namaḥ.
Om hinasti daityatejāṃsi svanenāpūrya yā jagat/
sa ghaṇṭā pātuno devi pāpebhyoḥ naḥ sūtāniva.

Om! By the sound of the bell which fills the whole world and overturns the vigor of the demons, may that bell, like sons, protect us from sins.

Paraśu (Axe)

Om paraśave namaḥ.
Om paraśu tvaṃ mahātīkṣṇa sarvadevāri sūdanaḥ/
devihastasthithonityaṃ śatrukṣāya namo 'stute.

Om! O axe, you are very sharp. You are the destroyer of the enemies of the gods. You always remain in the hand of the Goddess. I pay homage to you, the destroyer of enemies.

Nāgapāśa (Serpent Noose)

The *purohita* now worships the serpent-noose weapon, which is wrapped around the image of the demon Mahiṣa.

Om nāgapāśāya namaḥ.
Om pāśatvaṃ nāgarūpo 'si viṣapūrṇo viṣodaraḥ/
śatrūṇaṃ duhsahahonityaṃ nāgapāśaṃ namo 'stute.

Om! You are of the form of the serpent, O noose, full of poison. Your stomach is full of poison. It is quite unbearable to the enemies. I pay homage to you all the time.

Worship of Caṇḍikā as Bearer of All Weapons (*Sarvāyudhadhāriṇī*)

He pays obeisance to Caṇḍikā herself with the *mantra*:

Om hrīṃ śrīṃ sarvāyudhadhāriṇyai namaḥ.
Om sarvādhānaṃ śreṣṭhāni yāni yāni tripistape/
tāni tāni dadhatyai caṇḍikāyai namo namaḥ.

Om! You are the bearer of all those excellent weapons that exist in heaven. I pay obeisance to that Caṇḍikā over and over again.

Worship of the Devī's Ornaments

Then he worships the ornaments worn by the Goddess. On the clay image these are mock ornaments intricately cut from thin sheets of *sola*, a white cork which is also extensively used for decorating the place of worship. The *purohita* utters:

> *Om kirīṭādi devyaṅgabhūṣanebhyoḥ namaḥ.*
>
> Om! I pay homage to all the ornaments on the Goddess's body, beginning with the crown, and so on.

Worship of the Baṭukas (Young Lads)

Once again the *purohita* goes to the *maṇḍala* and offers flowers to the Baṭukas. The Baṭukas, or Baṭuka Bhairavas, are fierce boy-forms of Śiva. Their numbers vary in Purāṇic accounts. They could be considered male counterparts of the Kumārīs. Baṭuka, in *sattva* (pure) form, is white like crystal. He removes untimely death, offers longevity and liberation. In *rajas* (passionate) form he is red and offers *dharma*, *artha*, and *kāma*. The *tamas* (turbid) form is blue and removes fear from enemies and the inimical effects of the planets. Offering flowers to the eastern side, the *purohita* says:

> *Om śrīṃ siddhaputra baṭukāya namaḥ.*
>
> Om! Śrīṃ! Obeisance to Baṭuka, son of Siddha (Attainment).

On the South:

> *Om śrīṃ jñānaputrabaṭukāya namaḥ.*
>
> Om! Śrīṃ! Obeisance to Baṭuka, son of Jñāna (Knowledge).

West:

> *Om śrīṃ sahajaputrabaṭukāya namaḥ.*
>
> Om! Śrīṃ! Obeisance to Baṭuka, son of Sahaja (Friendship).

North:

> *Om śrīṃ samayaputrabaṭukāya namaḥ.*
>
> Om! Śrīṃ! Obeisance to Baṭuka, son of Samaya (Togetherness).

Worship of the *Kṣetrapālas* (Guardians of the Field)

Then he worships eight *kṣetrapāla*s (i.e., Hetuka, Tripuraghna, Agnijihva, Agnivetāla, Kāla, Karāla, Ekapāda, and Bhīmanātha) between the lotus petals and the filament (*keśara*) of the lotus.

North:	*Om hetukāya kṣetrapālāya namaḥ.*
NE:	*Om tripuraghnāya kṣetrapālāya namaḥ.*
East:	*Om agnijihvāya kṣetrapālāya namaḥ.*
SE:	*Om agnivetālāya kṣetrapālāya namaḥ.*
South:	*Om kālāya kṣetrapālāya namaḥ.*
SW:	*Om karālāya kṣetrapālāya namaḥ.*
West:	*Om ekapādāya kṣetrapālāya namaḥ.*
NW:	*Om bhīmanāthāya kṣetrapālāya namaḥ.*

Worship of the Bhairavas

The Bhairavas are fierce forms of Śiva. In this rite they are Asitāṅga, Ruru, Caṇḍa, Krodha, Unmatta, Bhayaṅkara, Kapālin, Bhīṣaṇa, and Saṃhārin. The *purohita* invokes them into sections of the *maṇḍala* and worships them as follows:

East:	a)	*Om asitāṅgāya*	*bhairavāya*	*namaḥ.*
	b)	*Om rurave*	"	"
South:	a)	*Om caṇḍāya*	"	"
	b)	*Om krodhāya*	"	"
West:	a)	*Om unmattāya*	"	"
	b)	*Om bhayaṅkarāya*	"	"
North:	a)	*Om kapāline*	"	"
	b)	*Om bhīṣaṇāya*	"	"
Center:		*Om saṃhārine*	"	"

This completes the invocations and worship of deities in the *maṇḍala.*[10]

Worship of Durgā

The *purohita* once again worships the Devī as a whole, in all her forms, by repeating her *mantra* according to his mood and capacity. He offers the fruit of this worship back to her if the *pūjā* is *niṣkāmya* (without desire). He may offer her and the companion deities cooked food (*bhoga/annam*) and perform *ārati*. He pays obeisance to her with a full prostration (*aṣṭaṅga praṇāma*). He may then again recite the *Durgā Stuti*. This completes the rituals of Mahāṣṭamī.

4.6: Sandhi Pūjā

The *purohita* must finish the Mahāṣṭamī *pūjā* before Sandhi *pūjā*, a requirement that may greatly reduce the time and ritual elaboration of the Aṣṭamī worship. The Sandhi *pūjā* occurs at the point of confluence of the eighth (*aṣṭamī*) and ninth (*navamī*) lunar days (*tithi*). A *tithi* is divided into equal divisions called *daṇḍas*. Twenty-four minutes is the duration of one *daṇḍa*. The Sandhi juncture's duration is forty-eight minutes, composed of the last twenty-four minutes (i.e., *daṇḍa*) of the *aṣṭamī tithi* and the first twenty-four minutes of the *navamī tithi*. The juncture, which may occur at day or night, is considered highly auspicious. The entire *pūjā* must be performed during this interval. Traditionally, the climax occurs with the offering of a blood sacrifice (*bali dāna*) to the Goddess.[1]

To expedite matters, everything that is to be offered to Durgā is prepared beforehand. The *purohita* sits on his *āsana*. He sips water three times (*ācamana*), utters the *svasti vācanam*, performs *āsanaśuddhi*, and offers flowers to Gaṇeśa and other deities. Then making a *nyāsa* of the *mātṛkās*, followed by *prāṇāyāma*, he worships Durgā as Cāmuṇḍā. To do so, he takes a flower in his hands in *dhyāna mudrā* and meditates:

> *Om kālī karāla vadanā viniskrāntāsi pāśinī/*
> *vicitra khaṭvaṅgadharā naramālā vibhūṣanā/*
> *dvīpi caramaparīdhānā śuskamāṃsāḥ bhairavā/*
> *ativistāravadanā jihvā lalannbhiṣā/*
> *nimagnā rakta nayanā nādā pūrita dinamukhā.*

> Om! She is Kālī, deadly black, very dreadful faced, emerging with a sword and noose in her hands, holding a strange staff (*khaṭvaṅga*) in her hand, adorned with a garland of human bodies, wearing the hide of an elephant. The flesh of her body has become withered (emaciated) and is exceedingly dreadful. Her exceedingly expanded mouth has a dreadful lolling tongue. Her eyes are deeply set but very red in color. The sound which is emanating from her is of such a high pitch that it has filled all the quarters.

Since this *dhyāna* is short, it is more appropriate for Sandhi *pūjā* than the long *dhyāna* of Durgā previously cited. There are variations in the *dhyāna* of Cāmuṇḍā. Cāmuṇḍā is then worshipped mentally according to regional differences. Most significant here is the decision regarding the inclusion of a blood sacrifice. In Banāras, for instance, blood sacrifice during these *pūjās* has for the most part vanished entirely.

The *purohita* then performs a *viśeṣārgha* (conch-shell worship) in the same manner as performed on Saptamī. He repeats the *dhyāna* of Durgā as Cāmuṇḍā and offers the sixteen-part devotional service (*ṣodaśopacāra*), of which the blood sacrifice may be a part, with this *mantra*:

Om krīṃ hrīṃ cāmuṇḍārūpāyai namaḥ.

Om! Krīṃ! Hrīṃ! Obeisance to the form of Cāmuṇḍā.

Due to time limitations, the *purohita* does not recite the lengthy *mantra*s normally used in these devotional services on the other days.

Balidāna (Sacrificial Offering)

If a blood sacrifice is to be offered, it will be done now. The blood sacrifice occurs just after the Devī is shown her own reflection in the mirror (*darpaṇa*). The shining blade of the sacrificial sword is often used in lieu of the mirror. To conduct the *balidāna*, the sacrificial animal, normally an uncastrated dark male goat, is bathed.[2] The *yajamāna* places a red garland on its neck and puts vermillion marks on its horns. Then it is brought before the *purohita*. Its face should be directed towards the east. The Tantric form of the ritual is described below. It is shorter, focuses more on the sword (i.e., the Devī) than on the animal, and is more commonly used, since it is shorter and fits well within the limited time period. The Vedic form follows for reference.

The *purohita* sprinkles the animal with water from his vessel, purifying it simply by uttering "Huṃ." He shows it the *dhenumudrā*. He offers consecrated water onto its feet (*pādya*), saying:

Etat pādyaṃ/ om chagapaśave namaḥ.

This is *pādyam*. Om! Homage to the goat animal.

He utters this Vedic *mantra*, a sort of Sacrificial Animal Gāyatrī, in its ears:

Om paśupāśāya vidmahe viśvakarmaṇe dhīmahi tanno jīva pracodayāt.

Om! We know the bonds which bind the beast/soul.
We make a meditation of the Supreme Creator.
May that Soul guide us (on the right path).

Then the sword is brought before the animal, washed and cleaned. He marks it with a disk of red vermillion. He then writes with the stem of a *bilva* leaf, the word, "Hrīṃ," on the vermilion using a secret script.[3] He worships the iron sword with the *mantra*:

Om hrīṃ kāli kāli vajreśvari lauha daṇḍa namaḥ.

Om! Hrīṃ! O Kālī, O Kālī, thunderbolt goddess, iron staff, homage.

Then he utters this *mantra* and offers flowers to the top of the sword.

> *Huṃ vāgiśvarībrahmābhyāṃ namaḥ.*
>
> Huṃ! Obeisance to Vāgīśvarī (the goddess of speech) and Brahmā.

To the middle:

> *Huṃ lakṣmīnārāyaṇābhyāṃ namaḥ.*
>
> Huṃ! Obeisance to Lakṣmī and Nārāyaṇa.

To the hilt:

> *Huṃ umāmaheśvarābhyāṃ namaḥ.*
>
> Huṃ! Obeisance to Umā and Maheśvara.

Then to the entire body of the sword:

> *Om brahmāviṣṇuśivaśaktiyuktāya khaḍgāya namaḥ.*
>
> Om! Homage to the sword, united with Brahmā, Viṣṇu, Śiva, and Śakti.

Then the priest makes a *praṇāma* to the sword, saying:

> *Om khaḍgāya kharadhārāya śakti kāryārthatatparal*
> *paśuschedyastvayā sīghraṃ khaḍganātha namo 'stute.*
>
> Om! I pay homage to the sword and the bearer of the sword. O you who is engaged in performing the duty toward Śakti, you cut the animal at once. I pay homage to you the bearer of the sword.

Then placing some sesamum, *tulasi* leaf, and *kuśa* grass in the *kuśī*, he reads an oath:

> *Om viṣṇur namo adya āśvine māsi śukle pakśe vārāṇasī kṣetre sandhyam tithau amuka gotra amuka devaśarmā amuka gotrasya amuka devaśarmaṇaḥ śrī durgā prīti kāmaḥ imam chāgapaśuṃ vahni daivatāṃ durgā devatāyai tubhyam ghāṭaiṣve.*
>
> Om! . . . I shall slaughter this animal in the form of the goat to the fire, the superintending deity, for you, the divine Goddess Durgā.

And with folded hands he prays:

> *Om balim gṛhṇa mahādevi paśuṃ sarvaguṇānvitaṃl*
> *yathoktena vidhānena tubhyam astu samarpitam.*

> Om! Please accept my offering, O great deity. This offering is an animal having all good qualities. I have presented this to you according to the right procedure. Let it go to you.

Then taking up the sword in both his hands and uttering:

> *Aiṃ Huṃ Phaṭ*

he severs the neck of the goat with a single stroke. He may alternately release the goat with a small release of blood from a cut made in its ear.

There are numerous associations between the Devī and swords. The *Devī Purāṇa* states that the Goddess may be venerated as a sword (Kinsley 1986:109). In legends of the seventeenth-century Maratha military hero, Shivaji, the goddess Bhavānī identifies herself with his sword or enters it before battle. The Devī often bestows her devotees with weapons, which in turn may be venerated during Navarātra.[4]

Vedic Procedure of *Balidāna*

> *Om vārāhī yamunā gaṅgā karatoyā sarasvatī/*
> *kāverī candrabhāgāca sindhu bhairava śoṇagaḥ/*
> *ajāsnāne maheśāni sānnidhyamiha kalpaya/*
> *Om pṛṣṭhe pucche lalāṭe ca karṇayoḥ jaṅghayostathā*
> *meḍhre ca sarva gātreṣu muñcantu paśudevatāḥ.*

> Om! O rivers, Vārāhī, Yamunā, Gaṅgā, Karatoyā, Sarasvatī, Kaverī, Candrabhāgā, Sindhu, Bhairava, and Śonagā, be present when we bathe this goat. The deities present in the limbs of the goat, namely in the back, the tail, forehead, ears, shanks, and genitals, and his limbs should help the animal to attain release.

Sprinkling the beast (*paśu*) with water (with the aid of a length of *kuśa* grass), he utters Vedic verses:

1. *Om agniḥ paśurāsīt tenāyajanta sa etaṃ lokam ajayat/*
   yasminn agniḥ sa te loko bhaviṣyati taṃ jeṣyasi pibaitā apaḥ.
   [VS.23.17; ŚB.13.2.7.13]

   Om! In the beginning, Fire was an animal. It has made sacrifices/oblations and made a victory over this region in which it now abides. It will be your domain. You will be able to win it, so drink this water.[5]

2. *Om vāyuḥ . . ./ yasmin vāyuḥ . . .*

   Om! In the beginning, Wind was an animal, . . .

3. *Om sūryaḥ . . ./* *yasmin sūryaḥ. . .*

Om! In the beginning, the Sun was an animal, . . .

Then he utters:

Om	*vācaṃ*	*te*	*sundhāmi*	Om! I purify your speech.
Om	*prāṇa*	*te*	*sundhāmi*	Om! I purify your vital breath.
Om	*cakṣus*	*te*	*sundhāmi*	Om! I purify your eyes.
Om	*śrotraṃ*	*te*	*sundhāmi*	Om! I purify your ears.
Om	*nabhiṃ*	*te*	*sundhāmi*	Om! I purify your navel.
Om	*medhram*	*te*	*sundhāmi*	Om! I purify your penis.
Om	*payum*	*te*	*sundhāmi*	Om! I purify your anus.
Om	*caritram*	*te*	*sundhāmi*	Om! I purify your character.
Om	*vāk*	*ta*	*āpyāyatām*	Om! Let your speech be refreshed.
Om	*manas*	*ta*	*āpyāyatām*	Om! Let your mind be refreshed.
Om	*cakṣus*	*ta*	*āpyāyatām*	Om! Let your eyes be refreshed.
Om	*strotram*	*ta*	*āpyāyatām*	Om! Let your ears be refreshed.

Yat te krūramyadāsṭhitam/ sṭhitam tat te āpyāyatām/
tat te niṣṭhāyatam/ tat te śuddhatu/ sama hobhyaḥ svāhā

May whatever cruelties there are or are absent within you be satisfied.
May they steadily abide there. May they become pure. I utter *svāhā* for them.

Om aiṃ hrīṃ śrīṃ candramaṇḍalādhithita vigrahāyai/
paśurūpa caṇḍikāyai imaṃ paśuṃ prokṣayāmi svāhā.
Om paśupāśāya vidmahe śiraścchedāya dhīmahi/
tannaḥ paśuḥ pracodayāt.
Om paśupāśa vināśāya hemakūṭa sthitāya ca/
parāparāya parameṣṭhine huṅkārāya ca mūrtaye.

Om! Aiṃ! Hrīṃ! Śrīṃ! I offer to the form that is in the disc of the moon and that is in the shape of this animal. I sprinkle water unto this and utter *svāhā*.
Om! We know the bonds that bind this beast/soul.
We meditate upon the decapitation.
May that beast/soul guide us (on the right path).
Om! For the purpose of cutting the knot of the bond of this animal, I offer this animal to the deity who lives on the golden peak, who is the transcendent and nontranscendent and the fourth[6] who assumes the form of "Huṃ."

Then he binds the animal to a sacrificial stake (Y-shaped at the top), placing its neck in the V, and says:

Om meghākāra sthambha madhye paśuṃ bandhaya bandhaya sasṛṇga sarvā vayavaṃ paśuṃ bandhaya brahmāṇḍa khaṇḍarūpiṇaṃ paśum bandhaya bandhaya.

> Om! Between two pillars with the shape of a cloud, fix the animal, and fix, fix the animal having all its limbs intact. Bind, bind the animal, which is only a small portion of the whole cosmic egg.

He severs its head in a single stroke saying:

> *Aiṃ huṃ phaṭ svāhā.*

Surrogate Offerings

The blood sacrifice, a crucial part of the Durgā Pūjā, is rapidly disappearing in Banāras. It is no longer performed by the few homes in the city that continue the tradition of elaborate domestic *pūjā*s. Most of these homes, and all public *pūjā*s, have eliminated the blood sacrifice altogether from the celebration, while others offer a vegetable substitute in place of the animal. In the not-too-distant past, however, groups, such as the Mitra family, that did perform blood offerings had the sacrifices performed at the city's Durgā Kuṇḍ temple, which bears a plaque testifying to the family's patronage. The scale of these sacrifices probably never equaled those at the Caṇḍī temple in Cuttack, where in 1978 over a thousand goats were sacrificed.[7] However, I have still seen the blood of sacrificed goats attain enough volume to trickle (where in the past it "flowed") from the sacrificial pit into the waters of Durgā Kuṇḍ, some twenty meters away.

The comments of Sudarshan Chowdhury, one of the organizers of the Durgotsav Sammilini *pūjā*, were typical of the prevailing view in Banāras. The sacrificial offering, he said, "is a ghastly affair, and should be avoided by substitution."[8] In response to why a surrogate is used, he replied, "Ram and Ravan both sacrificed, so it is necessary, but in the modern era we can do it by amending the rituals." He did not feel that the substitution weakened the rite, pointing out that "amendment is not abolition," and inferring that the spirit of the ritual was maintained resulting in no loss of efficacy. Pandit Chakravarty's explanations echoed the same sentiment. To him, "killing animals is simply not nice, so people refrain from it. However, blood sacrifice is an age-long tradition and one doesn't like to violate tradition."[9] He remembered frequently witnessing goat sacrifices, and once even a buffalo sacrifice in his village, although he himself has never performed a blood sacrifice. He called these *rajas* and *tamas* types of blood sacrifice. Even in those cases, the *purohita* performed the rites to consecrate and symbolically kill the animal, while the actual slaughter was performed by a specialist. Pandit Chakravarty does not object to performing *balidāna* as part of the Durgā Pūjā if it is of the *sattva* form, in which no living things are offered. As a substitute, a *kuṣmāṇḍa* melon, sugarcane (*ikṣudaṇḍa*), a plantain (*kadaliphala*), a cucumber, etc., may be offered.[10]

To sanctify these offerings, the *purohita* may say:

> *Om kuṣmāṇḍa balaye namaḥ. Om ikṣudaṇḍa balaye namaḥ. Om kadaliphala balaye namaḥ.* Etc.

An effigy (also sometimes called a *svāstika*) of a human figure is drawn on the fruit using red vermillion or rice paste, and this is then severed with a single stroke across its "throat." According to Pandit Chakravarty, this symbol represents the enemy, the demon, or any inimical force, and the substitute fruit must be meditatively visualized as the sacrificial animal.[11] As to the effectiveness of this substitution, he was less clear. "Who knows whether the enemy is actually thus destroyed. You have heard of the five Ma's in Tantric forms of worship. *Madhya* (wine), *māmsa* (meat), and sex have their substitutes. So why not the *bali*?"[12]

Since they belong to a *brāhmaṇa* family, Mrs. Lahiri emphasized that "*balidāna* has never been a part of our system."[13] Despite Mrs. Lahiri's perception that no blood sacrifice is performed, her granddaughter explained about a special rite which, although conducted in the kitchen, is an evident example of a surrogate sacrificial offering.

> Men, too, feel special at this time. A special squash is eaten at this time, predominant at Durgā Pūjā time. Only the men can cut it, and then the women cook it up. It is called Chal Kumru. It is white, and looks a bit like *kaddu*. It looks like cucumber. Large, green outside, white inside. Males are the primary activators of the food preparation.[14]

The "squash" in this description is very likely a *kuṣmāṇḍa* melon, which is "sacrificed" not in the main *pūjālaya*, but in the kitchen. The males of the household, in conjunction with the *purohita*, perform the sacrifice, at which point the women prepare the cooked food (*bhog*) offering with it. This displacement of the sacrificial venue is not unusual, for other Banāras families often performed blood sacrifices at the Durgā Kuṇḍ temple and not in front of the clay image. However, the rite iterates the place of the kitchen as a prominent ritual arena.[15]

Offering of the Head to Durgā

In Banāras, the actual slaughter of the goat may take place at the Durgā Kuṇḍ temple, and is performed by another person, such as a worker at the temple. Up to a dozen goats may still be sacrificed at the Durgā Kuṇḍ temple on any given day during Navarātra. Even there, most of the *pūjāri*s and

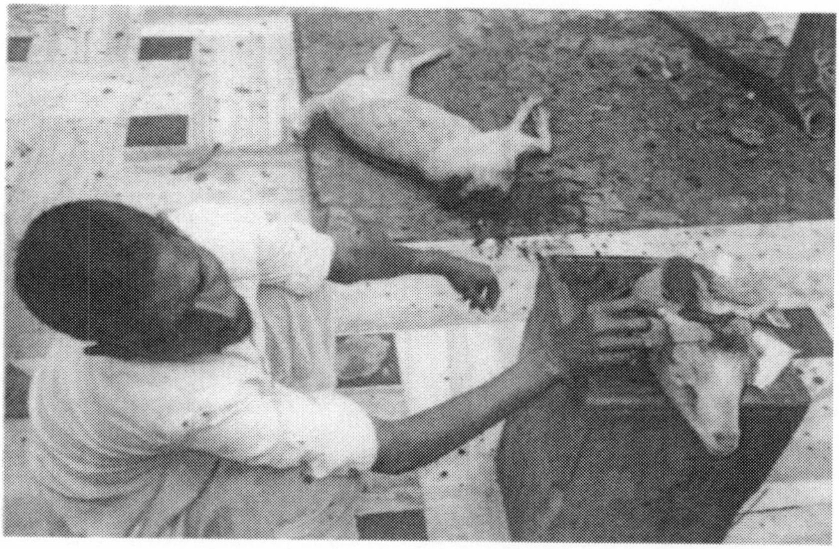

Figure 4.6.1 Animal sacrifice *(balidāna)* at Durgā Kuṇḍ temple. The goat's head, blood, and an honorific flame are placed on the sacrificial pillar altar before the image of Durgā.

workers find the task repulsive and try to avoid it. Nevertheless they do perform the ritual blessing of the goat, sword, and offering of the severed head to the Devī, while leaving the actual killing to one or two designated "priests." At the Durgā Kuṇḍ temple the goat faces north when being beheaded. The severed head is then placed atop the sacrificial pillar facing east (and the Devī) (see Figure 4.6.1).

After the head of the goat is cut, the head is brought back near the *purohita*, with some blood, and placed before the altar facing north. A ghee lamp is lit atop the head and the *purohita* says:

> *Eśa sapradīpa cchāga sirṣa baliḥ/ om durgā devatāyai namaḥ.*
>
> This is a sacrificial offering of a goat's head with a lamp.
> Om! Obeisance to Goddess Durgā.

Offering the Flesh and Blood to Durgā and Other Deities

The *Kālikā Purāṇa* states that Durgā partakes of both the head and flesh of the victim, but that the adept worshipper should offer flesh rarely, except for blood and the head, which together become nectar (Kane:5.165–166). The *purohita* offers the blood (with a portion of flesh) thus:

> *Eṣa samaṃsa rudhira baliḥ/ om durgā devatāyai namaḥ.*
>
> This is a sacrificial offering of blood with flesh.
> Om! Obeisance to Goddess Durgā.

He offers about a half portion to Durgā and divides the remaining half into four portions, which he offers to other deities who partake of blood sacrifices.

He offers flowers to Baṭuka:

> *Ete gandhapuṣpe/ om huṃ vaṃ baṭukāya namaḥ.*

and then one of the portions:

> *Eṣa samaṃsarudhira baliḥ/ om huṃ yāṃ baṭukāya namaḥ.*

The second portion to the Yoginīs:

> *. . ./ om huṃ yāṃ yoginibhyoḥ namaḥ.*

The third to the Kṣetrapālas:

> *. . ./ om huṃ kṣetrapālāya namaḥ.*

And the last to Gaṇapati (Gaṇeśa), who accepts blood sacrifice, and who, although propitiated first, is fed last.

> *. . ./Om huṃ gāṃ gaṇapataye namaḥ.*

The *purohita* concludes the blood sacrifice ritual with:

> *Om aiṃ hrīṃ śrīṃ kauśiki rudhireṇa āpyāyatām.*
>
> Om! Aiṃ! Hrīṃ! Śrīṃ! O Kauśikī, please be satisfied with this blood.

When Pandit Chakravarty was young, he attended *pūjās* where goats were sacrificed on Saptamī, Aṣtamī, and Navamī, as well as during the Sandhi *pūjā*. The meat of the sacrificed offering, consecrated after being consumed by the Devī, was cooked and distributed as *bhoga prasāda* (blessed cooked food) to the invited guests and relatives. I, too, watched the decapitation and preparation (at their home) of a goat sacrificed by some Nepalī soldiers at the Durgā Kuṇḍ temple. I later consumed (with large quantities of rum) the *bhoga prasāda*. The head, blood, and some inner organs were first prepared into a spicy fried/grilled snack, which was consumed with reverence, and the meat cooked into a curry served with rice with great festivity.

Offering of 108 Lamps

The *yajamāna* or members of his family set about lighting 108 ghee lamps (see Figure 4.6.2). These may be set in a large candelabra suspended from a chain. Otherwise, individual clay lamps may be placed on a large platter or arranged in some yantric pattern. At the Mitra family *pūjā* I observed a pattern of intersecting upward and downward pointing equilateral triangles, with a *svāstika* figure in the hexagon formed at the center. The procedure requires patience and excellent timing, since it is not easy to keep all lamps lit simultaneously. The effect is impressive. This ritual is essentially an elaborate variation of the *ārati* worship to the Devī. The *purohita* offers the 108 lamps to Durgā, uttering:

> *Om viṣṇurom tat sadadya āśvine māse śukle pakṣe avimukta vārāṇasī kṣetra amuka gotra śrīamuka devaśarma śrī durgā pritikāmaḥ/ Etan aṣṭodara śata saṅkhyakan prajjvalitān dīpān śrī cāmuṇḍarūpāyai durgāyai tubhyamaham saṃpradade.*
>
> Om! . . ., I am offering these 108 lamps to you, O Durgā, in the form of Cāmuṇḍa.

Kumārī Pūjā (Worship of Virgins)

This *pūjā* generally follows the blood sacrifice. The blood sacrifice is almost always performed, if at all, during the Sandhi *pūjā*. However, the short time interval of the Sandhi is also the prescribed time for *kumārī* worship. Thus, in reality, for the sake of convenience, the *kumārī pūjā* is often performed on Aṣṭamī or Navamī. Young girls before the age of puberty are invited to the place of worship.The girls are normally *brāhmaṇa*s, although this varies according to the family tradition. The Mitra family, for instance, celebrates the *kumārī pūjā* on Saptamī, Aṣṭamī, and Navamī due to the larger number of girls, not exclusively *brāhmaṇa*s, who are venerated as *kumārī*s. They come from the *yajamāna*'s immediate family or from the families of relatives, friends, or neighbors. They are to be worshipped as living forms of the Devī. The theological or philosophical symbolism of the virgin is suggested in Kashmir Śaivism, where one encounters the phrase: *icchā śakti umā kumārī* (Kaviraj 1986). Umā is an epithet of Pārvatī/Durgā. The *icchā* spoken

Figure 4.6.2 The patron's family members assist in lighting the 108 lamps offered as an *ārati par excellence* during the Sandhi Pūjā. (Photo: Ruth Rickard)

of here transcends the triad of manifest *śakti*s, namely, conscious will (*icchā*), knowledge (*jñāna*), and action (*kriyā*). It is *svatantra śakti*, the autonomous will, which is equated with the supreme Śakti. Thus the virgin (*kumārī*) symbolizes the uncreated, active potential to manifest. In Nepal, premenarche girls, in whom Durgā is thought to manifest, are selected at the age of three or four to serve as living embodiments of the Goddess. The most important of these, the Rāj-Kumārī, annually renews the king's sanction to rule through her divine blessing. With the onset of menstruation (or if any of her blood is spilled), she is divested of her divinity, since the Devī is believed to have left her.[16]

The *purohita* makes an oath (*saṅkalpa*):

> *Om viṣṇurom tat sadadya . . . . śukle pakṣe . . . amuka gotra, amuka devaśarma gauri prītikāmaḥ gaṇapatyādi nānādevatā pūjā pūrvaka kumārīpūjānamaham kariṣye.*
>
> Om! . . ., in order to please Gaurī, after worshipping Gaṇeśa and other deities, I shall worship a virgin representing the consort of Śiva.

He then reads the oath hymn (*saṅkalpa sūkta*) and performs all the preliminary worship rituals (*sāmānya vidhi*) such as *sāmānyārgha*, *āsanaśuddhi*, and so on. He performs *mātṛkā nyāsa* and offers flowers to Gaṇeśa and other deities. He places a maiden girl (generally below eleven years of age) adorned with clothes, ornaments, garlands and decorated with sandalwood paste (spots placed on the face for beauty) on a large brass plate. He washes her feet and offers a flower with the *mantra*:

> *Om śrīṃ kumāryai namaḥ*. Om! Śrīṃ! Obeisance to Kumārī.

He does *prāṇāyāma*, *aṅganyāsa*, *karanyāsa*, and then does a *dhyāna* of the goddess Kumārī.

> *Om kumārīṃ kamalārudhāṃ trinetrāṃ candraśekharāṃ/*
> *tapta kāṇcana varnādhyām nānālaṅkara bhūṣitāṃ/*
> *raktāmbara paridhānāṃ raktamālyānulepanām/*
> *vamenābhayadāṃ dhyāyet dakṣiṇena varapradām.*
>
> Om! The maiden is standing on a bloomed lotus. She has three eyes, with the moon on her forehead. Her complexion is like molten gold, and she is adorned with different kinds of ornaments. She wears a red cloth, and on her neck there is a red garland. She is smeared with red sandalwoodpaste (unguents). Her left hand is offering assurance. And with her right hand she is giving boons.

This description most closely resembles the forms in which the Devī frequently appears in temple images. There she is often portrayed with a golden mask and draped in a red cloth. He offers worship mentally and then repeats the *dhyāna* actually performing the sixteen-part devotional service (*ṣodaśopacāra*).

The *purohita* next offers flowers to Kauśikī, Gaṅgā, Sarasvatī, Yamunā, Vegavatī, Nāradā, Vaiṣṇavī, Viṣṇū, Padmā, Śaṅkhā, Śvetadīpā, Pavanā, Ghorā, Ghorarūpā, Menakā, Kamalā, Siṃhāsanā, and Cakrā. He then recites the verse:

> *Om! āyurbalam yaśo dehi dhanam dehi kumārike/*
> *sarvaṃ sukhaṃ ca me dehi prasīda parameśvari/*
> *namaste sarvato devi sarva papapraṇāśini/*
> *saubhāgyam santatim dehi namastute kumārike/*
> *sarva bhiṣṭa prade devi sarvapat vinivārini/*
> *sarvaśānti kare devi namastestu kumārike/*
> *brāhmī maheśvarī raudrī rīpatritayadhāriṇī/*
> *abhayañca varam dehi narāyaṇi namo 'stute.*
>
> Om! Give me, O maiden mother, longevity, vigor, fame, and wealth. Give me all kinds of happiness and be pleased with me. I pay obeisance to you in every respect. You are the remover of all sins. Give me prosperity, sons

and daughters. I pay obeisance to you, O maiden mother. You are the bestower of all sorts of desired objects. You are the remover of all sins. You are the giver of peace. I pay obeisance to you, mother. You are of the form of Brahmā, Maheśvara, and Rudra in female aspect. You assume these three forms. Give me fearlessness and blessing. I pay obeisance to Nārāyaṇī.

Dakṣiṇā (Offering of Money)

The *purohita* then makes a prayer of the monetary donation (*dakṣiṇā*) to be given to him for the services rendered. He begins with the *saṅkalpa*:

> *Om viṣṇurom tad sadadya, . . . , amuka gotra amuka devaśarma kumārīpūjā sāṅgatārtham dakṣiṇāmidam kañcana mūlyam śrī viṣṇu daivatam yathā sambhava gotra nāmne brahmaṇayā aham dadāmi.*

He finishes with:

> *kṛtaitat kumārī pūjācchidramastu.*
>
> Om! . . . , a value of gold is given to the *brāhmaṇa* for fulfilling this *kumārī pūjā*.

The traditionally recommended numbers of virgins to be worshipped are 1, 9, 17, 108 or more. When performed to such a large number of girls it is an imposing spectacle. However, there is often just one *kumārī* chosen to represent all others who are present. The rituals are performed to her. The maiden is then fed with dainties or well-cooked food and sent away.

Sandhi, Pandit Chakravarty explained, is regarded as the climax of the *pūjā*, since due to its auspicious astrological configuration, it is when the "inner light may be received." The Devī is most accessible during this period, and this is why ideally, the blood sacrifice, virgin worship, and the 108-lamp *ārati* is performed. Since it is difficult to conduct all rites within the short interval of time, the *tantradhāraka* is often invested with the task of conducting the *kumārī pūjā*. In many non-Bengali *brāhmaṇa* homes, the *kumārī pūjā* is performed on Navamī "for women, by women," as one *brāhmaṇa* woman in Banāras explained. It is evident that the virgin worship rite belongs to a women's tradition in which the male *purohita* originally played no part. By contrast, the male *purohita* is indispensable in the Bengali Durgā Pūjā *kumārī* worship, although many Bengali groups no longer conduct the blood sacrifice, and some even forego the *kumārī pūjā*. Since the Durgā Pūjā plays a role in orchestrating feminine energy, a group's decision to waive the *kumārī pūjā* may reflect a shift in emphasis in the *pūjā's* many functions. Certainly, the revival of the autumn Durgā Pūjā appears to have been motivated more for purposes of empowerment than fertility, the latter being a function character-

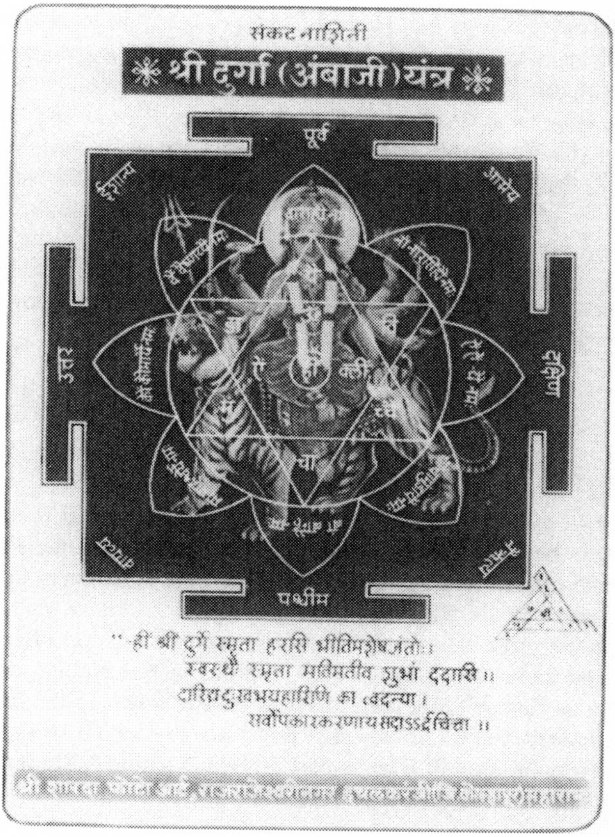

Figure 4.7.1 Durgā within her *yantra*. Contemporary lithograph.

istic of the spring Navarātra rites. However, by structurally building upon the spring worship rituals (e.g., the establishment of a jar form of the Devī is widely practiced during the spring Navarātra), the autumn Durgā Pūjā carries a larger amalgam of functions.

Regarding the substitutions or eliminations of what appear to be important ritual acts, Pandit Chakravarty explained that such variations do not seriously weaken the *pūjā*, since the *pūjā* itself is most important, not its individual elements. He initially speculated that perhaps the grosser elements were disappearing, while finer ones were beginning to take their place. However, after reflecting on the blaring music and theatrical trends at the large public shrines, he suggested that perhaps, while the *pūjā* itself is not weakened, its reverential spirit had declined in favor of amusement and entertainment. He frequently stressed that "nothing is more important than the divine concept. Nothing (i.e., no individual rite or image of the Devī) is great or divine without relating each one of them with the light of the Divine."[17]

Although substitutions and eliminations are obviously permitted, there is no flexibility with the timing of the Sandhi Pūjā. Since Pandit Nitai performs the *pujā* at both the Lahiris' home (where I observed him) and the Durgotsava Sammilini, I wondered if he conducted the Sandhi Pūjā for the club at another time. However, I was informed that this is never the case. There is always someone else (e.g., Pandit Nitai's brother) who will perform the Sandhi Pūjā at its appointed time.

4.7 Mahānavamī

The Mahānavamī rituals are identical to those performed on Saptamī, differing primarily by their inclusion of a fire oblation ritual (*homa*). Everyday, before going to the place of worship, the *purohita* has made some small offerings and offered homage to the *bilva* tree. He then enters the *pūjālaya*, begins as usual performing the *ācamana*, *svasti vācanam*, and so on and proceeds to the great bath of the Goddess (*mahāsnāna*). He offers her *bilva* twigs as tooth cleansers (*dantakāṣṭhā*), completing the bathing ritual just as it was done on Saptamī. He then offers *māśabhaktabali* to the *bhūta*s. Next he offers flowers and other worship materials to Gaṇeśa, Śiva, and other deities, performing the full sixteen-part service if inclined. He now proceeds to worship Durgā through the fire oblation.

Homa (Fire Oblation)

The fire pit (*kuṇḍa*) where the oblation is to be held is called the *sthaṇḍila*. Its area is one square cubit, a cubit being the length from elbow to fingertip. It should be four fingers (*aṅguli*) in height and could be made of bricks and mud. In the Lahiri home, a copper *sthaṇḍila* is used, set right upon the stone paving in the home. Fine sand is spread over it. A *yantra* consisting of an ascending triangle intersected by a descending triangle is drawn with *kuśa* grass in the middle and a point (*bindu*) placed in the center of it. The triangles are surrounded by a circle, and then eight lotus petals emanate from the circle. This is surrounded by a *bhūpura*, a square with symbolic gateways at the cardinal directions. A *bīja mantra*, such as "Duṃ," may be drawn on the *bindu*. This diagram is the Durgā Yantra (see Figure 4.7.1).

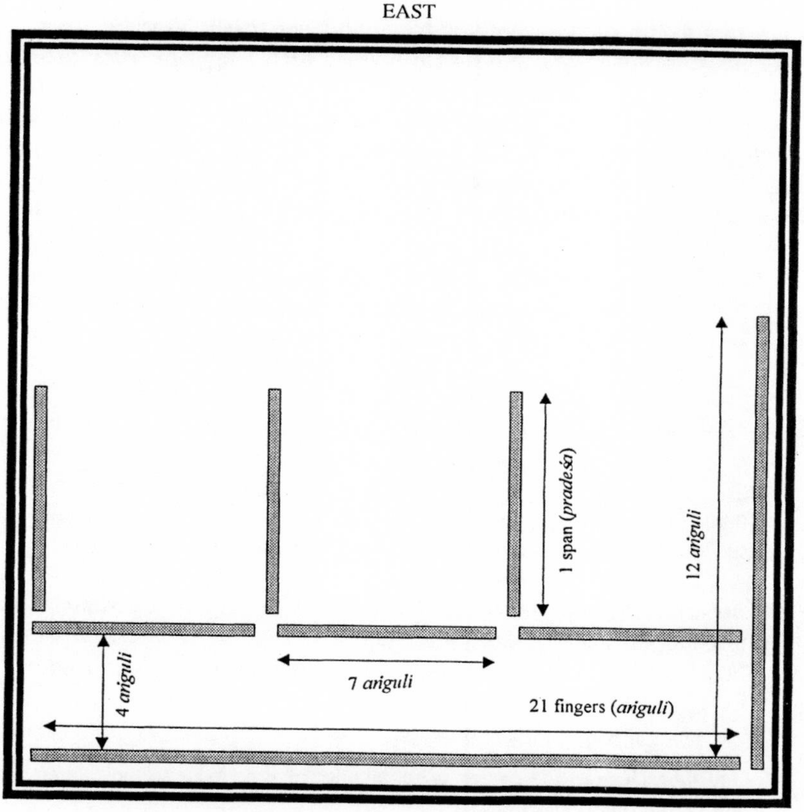

Figure 4.7.2 Layout of the Fire Pit *(sthaṇḍila)* in the Durgā Pūjā.

Thus, in the *homa* ritual the *sthaṇḍila* is identified as the *yantra* of the Devī, and the offerings made into the fire are symbolic of the reconstitution or reintegration of the cosmos. The Devī's manifest form is offered back to her. The gross elements of the creation, through the medium of the fire, are transformed into more subtle elements and through the symbolism inherent in the smoke, flame, and ashes are reunited with the Devī in her most sublime essence.

The *purohita* looks at the *sthaṇḍila* while uttering Durgā's *mūlamantra,* and he strikes it with *kuśa* grass saying "Phaṭ" and sprinkles it with water saying "Huṃ." Again uttering the *mūlamantra*, he says:

Om kuṇḍāya namaḥ.

He sits on the *sthaṇḍila's* west side, facing east and places fine lengths of *kuśa* grass in the *kuṇḍa* according to a particular pattern (see Figure 4.7.2) using his ring finger and thumb. He presses each length of grass to make indentations in the sand. If any sand is to be removed, he does so with the ring finger and thumb of his right hand and discards this *utkara* in the northeast direction. When this is done, he again purifies the *sthaṇḍila* with sprinkling (*prokṣana*), striking (*tāḍana*), and spreading of water in it (*abhyukṣana*). He proceeds to worship the three lines of *kuśa* grass pointing east with:

First	*Om mukundāya namaḥ*	Om! Obeisance to Mukunda (Viṣṇu)
Middle	*Om īśānāya namaḥ*	Om! Obeisance to Īśāna (Śiva)
Last	*Om purandarāya namaḥ*	Om! Obeisance to Purandara (Indra, "Destroyer of Forts")

To the three lines facing north, he pays obeisance with:

First	*Om brahmaṇe namaḥ*	Om! Obeisance to Brahmā
Middle	*Om vaivasvte namaḥ*	Om! Obeisance to Vivasvan (Agni)
Last	*Om indave namaḥ*	Om! Obeisance to Indu (Moon)

Next, he offers flowers to Durgā five times, after which he examines the oblation materials silently repeating, "Om."

Then, offering flowers into the center of the pit, the *purohita* utters:

> *Om ādhāraśaktyādi piṭhadevatābhyo namaḥ.*
>
> Om! Obeisance to the deities of the abodes of the Goddess, the Supreme Supporting Śakti, and others.

Facing east, he worships aspects of the Devī in the various corners:

SE	*Om dharmāya namaḥ*	Om! Obeisance to [the Goddess as] righteousness
SW	*Om jñānāya namaḥ*	Om! Obeisance to [the Goddess as] knowledge
NW	*Om vairāgyāya namaḥ*	Om! Obeisance to [the Goddess as] dispassion
NE	*Om aiśvāryāya namaḥ*	Om! Obeisance to [the Goddess as] royal power

and in the sides:

E	*Om adharmāya namaḥ*	Om! Obeisance to [the Goddess as] wickedness

S	*Om ajñānāya namaḥ*	Om! Obeisance to [the Goddess as] nescience
W	*Om avairāgyāya namaḥ*	Om! Obeisance to [the Goddess as] passion
N	*Om anaisvāryāya namaḥ*	Om! Obeisance to [the Goddess as] ingloriousness

and to the middle:

Om anantāya namaḥ	Om! Obeisance to [the Goddess as] the endless serpent
Om padmāya namaḥ	Om! Obeisance to [the Goddess as] the lotus flower

Then, also to the center, he utters obeisance to the solar, lunar, and fire spheres and their divisional components:

Aṃ arkamaṇḍalāya dvadaśakalātmane namaḥ
Uṃ somamaṇḍalāya ṣodaśakalātmane namaḥ
Maṃ vahnimaṇḍalāya daśakalātmane namaḥ

Next, he offers flowers to the center, paying homage to each of the component parts of fire, saying:

Om pītāyai namaḥ	Om! Homage to [fire's quality of] yellow
Om śvetāyai namaḥ	Om! Homage to [fire's quality of] white
Om aruṇāyai namaḥ	Om! Homage to [fire's quality of] rose pink
Om dhūmrāyai namaḥ	Om! Homage to [fire's component of] smoke
Om kṛṣṇāyai namaḥ	Om! Homage to [fire's component of] black
Om tibrāyai namaḥ	Om! Homage to [fire's component of] ferocity
Om sphuliṅganyai namaḥ	Om! Homage to [fire's quality of] sparkle
Om rucirāyai namaḥ	Om! Homage to [fire's quality of] loveliness
Om jvālinyai namaḥ	Om! Homage to [fire's quality of] ripening
Om vahni āsanāyaī namaḥ	Om! Homage to fire as the seat

He next makes a *dhyāna* of the goddess of speech, Vāgīśvarī:

Om vāgīśvarīṃ ṛtusnātāṃ nīlendī vara locanām vāgīśvareṇa saṃyuktām krīḍa bhāva samanvitām.

Om! Vāgīśvarī is the lady of speech, who has eyes like a blue lotus. She has just completed her menstrual cycle and properly bathed, and now has entered into playful union with the lord of speech.

This *dhyāna* clearly implies sexual playfulness. Fire is perceived to be the play (*krīḍa*) of the divine, conceived of as the copulation between male and female polarities of divinity at the threshold of manifestation (symbolized by

Vāc, "speech," which represents "vibration.") This sexual union appears to be essentially for pleasure, not primarily for reproduction.

And he offers flowers and obeisance with:

> *Om hrīṃ vāgīśvara sahita vāgīśvaryai namaḥ.*
>
> Om! Hrīṃ! Obeisance to the Lord of Speech united with the Lady of Speech.

The *purohita* then collects fire (from an ember) with the *mantra* "Vauṣaṭ" and invokes/kindles the tinder with "*astrāya phaṭ.*" Saying:

> *Huṃ phaṭ kravyādevyaḥ svāhā*

he takes a small amount of fire and offers it to the deities who are eaters of raw flesh (*kravya*). He then waves the flame around the *kuṇḍā* three times, kneels down with both knees touching the earth, and places it with both hands into the *sthaṇḍila*. He offers it flowers, saying:

> *Om hrīṃ vahni mūrtaye namaḥ/ Om vaṃ vahni cetanāya namaḥ*
> *Om cit piṅgala hana hana daha daha paca paca sarvajñā ājñā paya svāhā.*
>
> Om! Hrīṃ! I pay homage to the form of the blazing fire.
> Om! Vaṃ! I pay homage to the consciousness that pulsates in the fire.
> Om! O consciousness with the color of gold, kill, kill, burn and burn, consume and consume, O omniscient one, please command. Svāhā!

and now places kindling on it causing the fire to blaze properly. Then with folded hands he says:

> *Om agniṃ prajjvalitaṃ vande jāta vedaṃ hutāśanaṃ suvaraṇam amalam viśvāto 'mukham/ agneh tvam valadanāma āsi.*
>
> Om! I pay homage to the fire that is ablaze, who knows everything after birth, whose color is of pure gold. It has its outlets in all directions. You fire, you are named Valada.
>
> *Om vaiśvānara jātaveda ihāvaha lohitākaṣa sarvakarmāṇi sādhaya svāhā.*
>
> Om! O fire, the inborn knower of everything, having red eyes, fulfil the result of every act of mine.

He next offers homage to the fire with flowers and sandalwood paste:

> *Etat sacandanapuṣpam/ om agnaye namaḥ*

and worships the aspects of fire and other deities with flowers:

Ete gandhapuṣpe/

Om agner 'hiraṇyādi sapta jivhābhyoḥ namaḥ
Om agner saḍaṅgebhyoḥ namaḥ
Om agnaye jātavedase aṣṭamūrtibhyoḥ namaḥ
Om brāhmyādyāṣṭaśaktibhyoḥ namaḥ
Om padmādyāṣṭanidhibhyoḥ namaḥ
Om indrādi lokapālebhyoḥ namaḥ
Om dhvajādyastrebhyoḥ namaḥ

Om! I pay homage to the seven tongues of fire.
Om! I pay homage to the six limbs of fire.
Om! I pay homage to fire, who has inborn omniscient intuition, who has eight forms like Śiva.[1]
Om! I pay homage to eight *śakti*s, beginning with Brāhmī.
Om! I pay homage to eight kinds of wealth, beginning with Padmā.
Om! I pay homage to the guardians of the directions, beginning with Indra.
Om! I pay homage to the weapons, beginning with *dhvaja* (the staff).

Then taking two very thin-edged lengths of *kuśa* grass called *pavitra*s, each the length of a span, and placing them in the plate from which the oblation of ghee will be taken, the *purohita* divides the plate into three spaces. These spaces correspond to the three main energy channels (*nadī*) in the body cosmos. The *nadī*s do not merely exist in the physical body of the human, but in the subtle bodies (*liṅga śarīra*) as well. Furthermore, the human body is merely a microcosm within the larger cosmic body, through which the *nadī*s actually flow. The right section of the plate is *iḍā*, the left is *piṅgalā*, and the middle is *suṣumnā*. When offering oblations of ghee into the fire, the *purohita* may take ladlefuls from any of the three sections in a process that resembles the alternate breathing in *prāṇāyāma*. If he takes ghee from the right (*iḍā*), he utters

Om agnaye svāhā. Om! Svāhā to Agni.

and places it at the left of the fire. If he takes ghee from the left (*piṅgalā*), he utters

Om somāya svāhā. Om! Svāhā to Soma.

and places it to the right of the fire. If from the middle, he places it in the middle, saying:

Om agniṣomābhyām svāhā. Om! Svāhā to Agni and Soma.

The *purohita* begins by taking ghee from the right with a ladle, pouring it onto the fire and uttering:

Om agnaye svișți kṛte svāhā.

Om! Svāhā to Agni, the well-doer of sacrifices.

Mahāvyāhṛti Homa (Oblation of the Great Mystical Utterances)

The *purohita* next makes an oblation called the *mahāvyāhṛti homa*. The *mahāvyāhṛti*s are the utterances made by all *brāhmaṇa*s during their daily worship at the junctures (*sandhyā*). The utterances are "*bhūr*," "*bhuvas*," and "*svas*," and are part of the Gāyatrī Mantra.

First uttering the following:

Prajāpatir ṛṣīr gāyatrī chando agnir devatā mahāvyāhṛti home viniyogaḥ

The revealer (*ṛṣi*) is Prajāpati, the meter (*chandas*) is Gāyatrī the deity (*devatā*) is Agni, the purpose (*viniyoga*) is the Oblation of the Great Mystical Utterance

he then offers ghee, uttering the *mahāvyāhṛti*s saying:

Om bhūr svāhā/ Om bhuvaḥ svāhā/ Om svaḥ svāhā/
Om bhūr bhuvaḥ svaḥ svāhā.

He repeats the process for different meters and deities, saying:

Prajāpatir ṛṣir uṣṇik chando vāyur devatā . . .
Prajāpatir ṛṣir anuṣṭup chando sūryo devatā . . .
Prajāpatir ṛṣir vṛhatī chandaḥ prajāpatir devatā . . .

Oblations to Durgā

The *purohita* now offers twenty-five ladles of ghee oblations into the fire with the *mūlamantra* of Durgā. He uses a Vedic (rather than Tantric) form of the *mūlamantra*, using "Om" instead of other *bīja*s like "Duṃ" and "Hrīṃ."

Om durge durge rakṣaṇi svāhā.

Then the *purohita* conceives of himself as one with the fire and the Goddess Durgā, uttering:

Om vaiśvānara jātaveda ihāvaha lohitākṣa sarvakarmāṇi sādhaya svāhā.

Om! O fire, the inborn knower of everything, having red eyes, fulfill the result of every act of mine.

Figure 4.7.3 The *purohita* and patron perform the fire oblation *(homa)* on Navamī.

He offers oblations three times with that *mantra*. He then worships Durgā in this form with the *mūlamantra* offering up eleven oblations. He next offers oblations, saying:

> *Om mūlamantrasya aṅgadevatābhyaḥ svāhā*
>
> Om! I offer *svāhā* to the deity superintending over the limbs of the *mūlamantra*.
>
> *Om āvaraṇa devatābhyaḥ svāhā*
>
> Om! I utter *svāhā* unto the gods who have formed an enclosure around the main deity.

Having completed this, the *purohita* turns his attention to the *bilva* leaves, 108 of which will be offered into the *homa*. Every one should be untorn, unbroken, unmarked, and have three leaves, be washed and wiped clean of excess water. Although *bilva patra* and ghee is normally offered into the *homa* to worship Durgā, on occasion sesamum with ghee (*sājya tila*) may also be used. The patron (*yajamāna*) assists in these rites (see Figure 4.7.3).The *purohita* then makes an oath (*saṅkalpa*).

Om viṣṇurom tat sadadya āśvine māsi śuklepakṣe navamyāṃ tithau durgāpūjā karmaṇi durge durge rakṣaṇi svāhā iti mantra karaṇakaṣṭottara śata saṅkhyaka sājya bilva patra sannidbhir homāham kariṣye.

Om! . . . I will perform the fire oblation with 108 *bilva* leaves, while uttering the *mantra* "*durge durge rakṣaṇi svāhā.*"

The *mūlamantra* of the Devī is generally uttered silently (to preserve it from casual repetition by the audience who may be uninitiated), while the "*svāhā*" is always pronounced loudly. When the *bilva* leaf oblations have been given to the fire with the *mūlamantra*, the *purohita*, taking a flower, says:

Agneya tvam mṛḍanāmāsi. Agni, you are Mṛḍanāma.

Offering the flower to Agni he pays homage:

Ete gandhapuṣpe/ Om mṛḍanāmāgnāya namaḥ.
Etat havir naivedyam/ Om mṛḍanāmāgnāya namaḥ.

Pūrṇāhuti (The Final Oblation)

Taking a ladleful of ghee, the *purohita* stands up and says:

Prajāpati ṛṣir virādgāyatrī chanda indro devatā yaśas kāmasya yajanīsya prayoge viniyogaḥ.

The revealer is Prajāpati, the meter is Virādgāyatrī, the deity is Indra, and the purpose is for the person desirous of fame.

Om pūrṇa homam yaśase juhomi yo 'asmai juhoti varamasmai dadāti varam vṛṇe yaśasā bhāmi loke svāhā.

Om! I offer this final oblation for fame. Whoever makes an oblation towards god, he blesses him with a boon, therefore I pray for that kind of boon. May I remain shining in the world.

He performs a *mudrā* while pouring the oblation into the fire.

OFFERINGS TO THE *PUROHITA*

In front of the fire some unwashed rice, a fruit (e.g., banana), one betel leaf, and sometimes a ripe coconut wrapped in a red cloth is placed. This offering is symbolic of the payment to the *purohita* for his services. The *yajamāna* repeats the prayers after the *purohita*. The *purohita* purifies the offering saying:

Ete gandhapuṣpe/ om pūrṇa pātrānukalpa bhojyāya namaḥ.

Om! I pay obeisance to the food (edibles), representing the platter full to the brim.

Then while sprinkling water on the fire, he utters:

Om viṣṇurom, . . . , etat pūrṇa pātrānukalpa bhojyaṃ brahmaṇe tubhyamoham sampradade.

Om! . . . this platter [full of rice, pulses, spice, ghee, oil, and so on] representing full-food (*pūrṇa pātrānukalpa bhojya*), I offer to you, O *brāhmaṇa*.

Then he says:

Etasmai kāñcanamūlyāya namaḥ/
Etad adhipataye śrīviṣṇave namaḥ/
Etad saṃpradānāya brāhmaṇāya namaḥ

Salutations to this exact money as fees;
to the superintending lord Śrī Viṣṇu;
to the donation to the *brāhmaṇa*.

The *purohita* now utters an oath (*saṅkalpa*) of monetary offering (*dakṣina*):

Om viṣṇurom, . . . , śukle pakṣe saptamītithavārabhya mahānavamīm yāvat durgāpūjā karmaṇaḥ saṅgatārthaṃ dakṣiṇāmidam kāñcanamūlyam śrī viṣṇu daivatam, yathā saṃbhava gotranāmne brāhmaṇāya aham dadāmi.

Om! . . . for the completion of the Durgā Pūjā rituals from Saptamī to Navamī, this fee representing gold, superintended by Viṣṇu, I offer this to a person belonging to . . . lineage (*gotra*) and belonging to a *brāhmaṇa* family.

In reality, the *purohita* receives a substantial amount for his services. In 1999 at the Lahiri home the *purohita* (Pandit Nitai) received Rs. 2500 in *dakṣiṇā*. He also received about twenty *sārīs* and *dhotis*, and cooked and uncooked food offerings. In addition, he received numerous other offerings of *sārī*s, sweets, as well as cash, and anything else that was offered to the Devī by family members, friends, relatives, and visitors.[2] For his services at the Durgotsav Sammilini *pūjā*, in the same year, he received Rs. 3500–4000, 10 *dhoti*s, 12 *sārī*s, 1 *chaddar* (upper garment), 20 kg. of rice, 2 kg. of *dal* (lentils), 20 kg. of fruits, and 2 kg. of sweets. The *tantradhāraka* is entitled to 10 to 25 percent of the payment.[3] Generally, there are additional payments required for requests to recite the *Durgā Saptaśatī*, which may be read on each day during Navarātra, and to perform the *homa* (fire oblation) rite.[4]

The tradition of paying the ritual fees (*dakṣiṇā*) to the *purohita* is itself part of the ritual. This is because it is held that without the payment the merit of performing the rite would remain with the priest and not pass to the patron. It is only through the formal, ritualized payment that the transactional effect of the *pūjā* is actualized and its benefits transferred to the votary. Here again the *purohita* is the indispensable conduit of the beneficial effects of the rite.

Allayment of Errors

The *purohita* performs another *saṅkalpa*:

> *Om viṣṇurom, . . . , śukle pakṣe saptamītithavārabhya mahānavamīṃ yāvat durgāpūjāna karmaṇi yadyat vaiguṇyam jātam tad doṣa praśamanāya viṣṇu smaraṇamaham kariṣye.*
>
> Om! . . . in this Durgā worship, whatever faults have occurred, in order to allay them, I shall repeat the name of Viṣṇu several times.

He then utters "Śrī Viṣṇu" ten or more times. He finishes with:

> *Namo brahmaṇya devāya go brāhmaṇa hitāyaca jagaddhitāya kṛṣṇāya govindāya namo namaḥ.*
>
> I pay obeisance to Kṛṣṇa called Govinda, the protector of the Vedas, who is inclined to stand as a succor to cattle and *brāhmaṇa*s and the benevolent of the world.

Extinguishing the Fire

When the final oblation (*pūrṇāhuti*) has been completed, and the *dakṣiṇā* has been offered, the *purohita* sprinkles water on the fire saying:

> *Om agni tvam samudrām gaccha.* Om! O Fire, go to the ocean.

On the northeast corner of the fire, he offers some curd (*dadhi*), saying:

> *Om pṛthivītvam śītalā bhava.* Om! O Earth, be cool.

Anointing with Ashes

Taking some ashes from the northeast corner of the fire altar, the *purohita* rubs it in with ghee in his palm. Dipping his middle finger in the mixture, he places an anointing mark (*tilaka*) on his forehead, moving the finger upwards.

He then marks his throat, shoulders, and heart, and does so to worshippers present who may want these auspicious marks.The northeast corner is the traditional place of Śiva, Lord of the cremation grounds. Anointing the body with ashes forges an equation between it and the burnt offerings. The body has been symbolically cremated and offered, through the flames, to the Devī. The ashes, the debris of the fire sacrifice, are themselves a form of *prasāda*, blessed remnants from the offerings that have been consumed by the Goddess, through the tongues of flames.

He utters these *mantra*s while anointing the body parts:

Forehead:	*Om kaśyapasya tryauṣam.*
	Om! May you be blessed with three times the longevity of Kaśyapa.
Throat:	*Om yamadagnestryauṣam.*
	Om! May you be blessed with three times the longevities of Yama and Agni.
Shoulders:	*Om yaddevānām tryauṣam.*
	Om! May you be blessed with three times the longevities of these deities.
Heart:	*Om tannme astu tryausam.*
	Om! May three times these longevities be on you.

Śānti Mantra

The *purohita* now recites the Śānti Mantra, which offers peace to the worshippers. It is an important part of the *pūjā,* since it occurs at the end of Navamī, the last day of Navarātra. It serves as a benediction, conferring the grace of peace on all who have participated in honoring the Devī. He reads:

Om surāstvāmabhiṣiñcantu brahmāviṣṇumaheśvaraḥ/
vāsudevo jagannāthastathā saṅkarṣaṇo vibhuḥ/
pradyumnaścāniruddhaśca bhavantu vijayāya te/
Om ākhaṇḍalo 'gnirbhagavān yamo vai nairtistathā/
varuṇa pavanaścaiva dhanāhyakśastathā śivaḥ/
brahmaṇā sahito śeṣo dikpālāḥ pāntu te sadā.
Om kīrtirlakṣmirdhṛtirmedhā puṣṭiḥ śraddhā kṣamā matiḥ/
buddhir lajjā vapuḥ śāntistuṣṭiḥ kāntiśca mātaraḥ/
etāstvāmabhiṣiñcantu rāhu ketuśca tarpitāḥ.
Om ṛṣayo munayo gāvo devamātara eva ca/
devapatnyo dhruvā nāgā daityāścāpsarasāṃ gaṇāḥ/
astrāṇi sarvaśāstrāṇi rājāno vāhanāni ca/
auṣadhāni ca ratnāni kālasyāvayāśca ye/
Om saritaḥ sāgarāḥ sailāśtīrthāni jaladā nadāḥ/
devadānavagandharva yakṣarākṣasapannagāḥ/
ete tvāmambhiṣiñcantu dharmakāmartha siddhaye.

(For the translation, see the Saptamī ritual of the bathing of the Devī with the *bhṛṅgāra* on pg. 150).

The *purohita* may now recite the *pradakṣiṇa stotra* (details follow in the Vijayā Daśamī section). He has completed the rituals of Navamī and has finished for the day.

4.8: Vijayā Daśamī

Officially, Navarātra has come to an end but the Durgā Pūjā rites have not yet finished. This tenth day is called Vijayā Daśamī, held in honor of the Devī in the form of victory (*vijayā*). Many votaries cite this as the day on which Durgā slew Mahiṣa, the buffalo demon, but most regard it as the day Rāma slew Rāvaṇa.[1] Rāma's victory was, of course, explained as aided by the Devī's, whom he had invoked through an untimely awakening. The day is dedicated to the dismissal (*visarjana*) rituals of the Devī, which include the immersion of the clay image.[2]

The *purohita* goes to the place of worship on the morning of Daśamī, sips water three times, performing *ācamana*. He then performs *svasti vācanam*, *bhūtaśuddhi*, and makes a simple *nyāsa*. Next he performs a *dhyāna* of Durgā and worships her with a ten-part service (*daśopacāra*). He offers cooked food (*bhoga*) and other things to the Devī, including a worship with lamplight (*ārati*). On Vijayā Daśamī it is a Banārasi custom for people to offer curd, *cūra* (flat rice), and puffed rice (Hindi/Bengali: *lai*/*lāja*), as well as cooked foods. If the *pūjā* is performed at home, typical foods would be boiled rice, cooled with water, and served with bananas, coconut, and some deep-fried battered vegetables (Hindi: *vada*). Sweets (Hindi: *miṭhai*), too, are given to Durgā. The *purohita* completes the ritual quickly (perhaps within one *daṇḍa* [twenty-four minutes]).

With folded hands, he says:

Om vidhihīnaṃ kriyāhīnaṃ bhaktihīnaṃ yedarcitam
pūrṇaṃ bhavatu tat sarvam tvat prasādān maheśvari.

Om! Whatever rituals I have made that have been bereft of right method, right activity, and right devotion, all these should attain fulfillment by your grace, O consort of Śiva.

He places his hand on the main jar (*ghaṭa*) uttering:

Om hrīṃ durge devi kṣamasva

Om! Hrīṃ! O divine Goddess Durgā, I beg pardon of you.

while moving the jar slightly, dislodging it from its firm position. He also moves the platform of the Devī in the clay image cluster and the altars of the *navapatrikā* and *bilva* tree.

Then he draws a triangular *yoni* on the floor by his left side. He offers flowers into it to the goddess Nirmālyavāsinī, saying:

> *Om nirmālyavāsinyai namaḥ.*
>
> Om! Obeisance to the goddess Nirmālyavāsinī (She who Abides in Purity).

The term "*nirmālyam*" also refers to the debris which remains after ritual offerings, which although seemingly impure are, in fact, stainless. It is quite noteworthy that offerings are made to the "Goddess who Abides in the Stainless Offerings." This is an unequivocal identification of a goddess with the actual material offered in the *pūjā*. Since the Great Goddess is an amalgamation of all goddesses, it is clear that a portion of herself is present within all aspects of the material world, including the offering elements themselves, both before and after they are devotionally presented to her in the rite.

The *purohita* next brings some previously offered flowers and with the *samhāra mudrā* (arms outstretched in front, crossed, with the backs of the hands touching each other and fingers intertwined) places them in the triangle. He then worships the Devī, saying:

> *Om ucchiṣṭacāṇḍālinyai namaḥ.*
>
> Om! Obeisance to the goddess Ucchiṣṭacāṇḍālinī (She who is the Impure Outcaste).

Like *nirmālyam*, *ucchiṣṭa* carries the meaning of impure remnants from the sacrifice.[3] *Cāṇḍālinī*, picks up on common epithets of Durgā as Caṇḍā, the Fierce One, while at the same time associating her with the *caṇḍāla*, the lowest, outcaste group of Indian society. Ucchiṣṭacāṇḍālinī is, in fact, an epithet of the goddess Mātaṅgī, one of the ten Mahāvidyās. Like Mātaṅgī, with whom the Goddess is explicitly identified, Durgā is here offered previously offered flowers, which is characteristic of Mātaṅgī worship.[4] Texts also state that the worship of Mātaṅgī, whose name means "an outcaste woman," be performed by devotees whose hands and mouths are stained with leftovers (*ucchiṣṭa*).[5]

Davis (1991) considers the problem of "pure remains" (*nirmālya*) as discussed in medieval texts on *pūjā* to Śiva. After Śiva enjoys the subtle essence within offerings to him, such as food or flowers, the material remains (*ucchiṣṭa*) become pure (*nirmālya*). However, while food and water become *prasāda*, and are capable of consumption, certain Śaivite groups (e.g., Śaiva siddhāntins) claim that the *nirmālya* are so pure they cannot be used by humans at all. Thus the *nirmālya* are offered once again to Lord Caṇḍa, a fierce emanation of Paramaśiva, after whose secondary consumption, the material is still too pure for humans. "These substances are finally disposed of among those universal recipients: cows, elephants, Water, Fire, and Earth" (Davis 1991: 157). We note a parallel procedure here in the Durgā Pūjā, in which the *nirmālya*, explicitly through the use of a previously offered flower garland, are offered to Ucchiṣṭacāṇḍālinī, who could be regarded as a divine correlate of Lord Caṇḍa. Just as Lord Caṇḍa is an emanation of Śiva, so too, Ucchiṣṭacāṇḍālinī is a form of the Great Goddess. An important distinction, however, is that while the *nirmālya* in Śiva-pūjā are finally disposed off in the elements (e.g., Fire, Water), the Durgā Pūjā reveals that the *nirmālya* are, in fact, first identified with an aspect of the Devī herself (as Nirmālyavāsinī), subsequently offered to an aspect of the Devī herself (as Ucchiṣṭacāṇḍālinī), and finally disposed off (during the immersion rite) in the Devī herself (in this case, the elemental waters of the Gaṅgā).

In these acts and epithets, the crucially important symbolism of wholeness is accentuated. The Devī is the entirety of creation, from its purest, most subtle, uncreated essence, to its grossest material forms. Not only is she present in the refined and fashioned items, but in the dross and debris that accompany such creations. Her manifest presence is found in the litter, the off-scourings, and leftovers of life's activities. In a classic example of reversal, those items that are traditionally considered impure and polluting are raised to divine status. This reversal extends to the low social classes, the sweepers and cleaners, for example, whose association with polluting materials, diminish them in social status. Their role and function in society, and the materials with which they are associated, are elevated to a divine status in the person of the Devī. Alternately, one might say that the Devī's immanence is so pervasive that it extends to every iota of creation, even the material and social groups that are normally deemed the most highly polluting. A circularity is inherent in the logic of Devī worship. As the entirety of creation, the Goddess cannot but be worshipped by her own creation and with elements of herself. When her latent presence in votaries (of any gender or social position) and the offering elements (of every type) is awakened through *pūjā*, these are elevated, albeit temporarily, in purity and potency.

In a myth on the origin of Ucchiṣṭacāṇḍālinī recounted in the *Prāṇatoṣinī-tantra*, Pārvatī asked Śiva if she could go to her natal home for a visit. Reluctantly, Śiva consented. Since she failed to return after the passage of several days, Śiva, disguised as a shell-ornament maker (a low caste) paid her a visit, sold her some ornaments, and asked her if she would have sex with him. At first she was outraged, but later discerning his true identity, consented to do so at a later date. In order to play a similar trick on him, Pārvatī now disguised herself as a ravishing young *caṇḍāla* woman with large breasts, wide eyes, and a lean body. Clad in red clothes, she danced near Śiva and succeeded in seducing him. As they made love, Śiva himself was turned into a *caṇḍāla*, at which point he recognized the beautiful *caṇḍāla* woman as his own wife and granted her a boon. "Since you [Śiva] made love to me as a *caṇḍāla* woman, this form will last forever and will be known as Ucchiṣṭacāṇḍālinī," she requested. "Only after performing suitable worship to this form will you [Śiva] be worshipped and your worship be made fruitful"(cited in Kinsley 1997:213-214).

In this myth Śiva and Pārvatī's conscious transformation into low, even outcaste persons, and their willing intercourse with each other in these states, reflect facets of their identities (and origins) that lie outside of orthodox society. The worship of the Devī as an outcaste woman, often with strong libidinous energies, prefigures the raucous celebrations that were traditionally prescribed for the immersion rites to follow. These were to be performed in the tribal style of the Śabaras, which included sexual allusions and dancing. It further highlights the Tantric persona of the Goddess, whose nature and worship incorporates characteristic inversions of orthodox values and an all-embracing wholeness.

The *purohita* then says:

> *Om uttiṣṭha devi cāmuṇḍe śubhāṃ pūjāṃ pragṛhya ca/*
> *kurusva mama kalyāṇaṃ aṣṭbhiḥ śaktibhiḥ saha/*
> *gaccha gaccha paramsthānam svasthānaṃ devi caṇḍike/*
> *yat pūjitaṃ mayā devi pari pūrāṇam tadastu me/*
> *vraja tvam srotasi jale tiṣṭha gehe ca bhūtale.*

> Om! O divine goddess Cāmuṇḍā, after receiving my auspicious rituals, arise, and along with your eight *śaktis*, do good for me. Go to your highest place, O divine Caṇḍikā. Whatever rituals I have made should obtain their fulfilment. Please go to the stream. Remain in the water, in the house, and in the earth.

This piece of the litany is crucial in furthering our understanding of the nature of the Devī. The Goddess, although dismissed, is asked to remain ever-present in the home, the earth, and the water. It is from these very abodes that she will be reinvoked into the *ghaṭa* the following year.

He then recites the following small hymn of praise (*stotra*), also known as the *pradakṣiṇa* (circumambulation) *stotra*. This is traditionally performed while circumambulating the effigy in a clockwise direction, but since the *mūrti* is set against a wall, the *purohita* may pivot himself around.

> *Om janmayā upahṛtam kiṃcit vastra gandhānulepanam/*
> *tat sarvam upabhuktvā tvaṃ gaccha devi yathā sukham/*
> *rājyaṃ śūnyaṃ gṛhaṃ śūnyam sarvaśūnyam daridratā/*
> *tvāmṛte bhagavatyamba kiṃ karomi vadasva tat.*

Om! Whatever I have offered, which is very little, in the form of clothes, incense, sandalwoodpaste, and so on, after enjoying them you may retire with satisfaction. To me this kingdom of mine is nothing but a void; my house is empty; everything is nothing but a void to a person who is very poor. Without your presence, O Goddess, I do not know what I should do. Please tell me that.

Now a large vessel, into which some water is poured, is placed so that the reflection of the Devī's clay image may fall upon it. The *purohita* brings the mirror (*darpaṇa*) from the seat/platform of the image, and immersing it into the water, says:

Om minajja ambhasi sampujya patrikā varjita jale
putrāyurdhana vṛddhyartham sthāpitāsi jale mayā.

Om! After worshipping you properly, I immerse you in this water without the *navapatrikā*. I have placed you in this water for the purpose of getting increase of sons, longevity, and wealth.[6]

Then placing his hand on the Devī's clay image altar, he reads:

Om durge devi jagganamātaḥ svathānaṃ gaccha pūjyate/
prasīda bhagavatyamba trāhi mām bhava sāgarat/
yathā śaktyakṛta pūjā samaptā śaṅkarapriye/
gacchantu devatāḥ sarve dattva tu vanchitaṃ varaṃ/
kailāsa śikhare ramye saṃsthitā bhavasannidhau/
pūjitasi mayā bhaktyā navadurge surācite/
tam pragṛihya varaṃ dattva kuru kriḍam yathā sukham.

Om! O Goddess Durgā, mother of the universe, after being worshipped, go to your own place. Be satisfied, O mother goddess. Please rescue me from the sea of worldly existence. I have performed your worship, O beloved of Śaṅkara, and completed it according to my ability. Let all the deities go their respective places after giving us our desired blessings/boons. You remain at the top of Mount Kailāsa, which is very beautiful, in the company of Lord Śaṅkara. You have been worshipped by me with devotion. O Form of Nine Durgās, who is also worshipped by the gods, accepting my rituals and giving me boons, you go on sporting/playing according to your desire.

This being done, the priest places some flowers, sandalwood paste, etc. into the hands of the assembly.

Aparājitā Worship and the *Varana* Rite

The *purohita* now performs the *pūjā* of the Goddess as Aparājitā (She who is Invincible). The *pūjā* should be performed only on the *tithi* of *daśamī,* which is not associated with *ekadaśi*. Thus, if Vijayā Daśamī is in contact with the eleventh (*ekadaśi*) *tithi*, the Aparājitā *pūjā* should be performed on Navamī. Since most people do not favor doing this, during such astronomical circumstances the Aparājitā *pūjā* is abandoned.

The Devī is worshipped in the form of a floral creeper. Actually, several different plants are designated as *aparājitā*. The Lahiris used a deep indigo-flowered creeper (*Clitora ternata*), also used to bind the Navapatrikā, but some tiny white flowers with orange bases (*śephālikā*) are used in certain temple ceremonies. The *purohita* performs a *dhyāna* of Aparājitā, saying:

> *Om śuddha sphaṭika saṅkaśām candra koti suśītalām/*
> *varadābhaya hastāñca śukla vastrairlaṅkṛtām/*
> *nānā bharaṇa saṃyuktam cakravākaiśca veṣṭitām/*
> *evaṃ saṃcintayan mantri devim tām aparājitām.*
>
> Om! Her complexion is like pure crystal. She is very cool, more than millions of moons. She has the postures of giving boons and assurance. She wears white clothes and is decorated with various ornaments. She is surrounded by Cakravāka birds.[7] The person who uses her *mantra* should meditate on her thus.

He worships her with a five-, ten-, or sixteen-part service. Then a yellow string is tied to bits of divine *aparājitā* creeper, and the creeper is tied around people's wrist or arms as an symbol of blessing from the Goddess to attain victory.

Lahiri family members and friends shared certain stories with me about the power of the *aparājitā* flower, which is often placed in a small metal container and worn as an amulet. "Once a relative had epileptic fits. He placed a flower from Durgā, enclosed in a copper case, around his arm, like an amulet, and has never suffered from these problems again." "Another relative was being treated incorrectly for six years for a heart problem. The day after getting this flower amulet, his diagnosis was corrected, and he is fine. We believe that such power exists. It operates where the laws of science do not. We do believe in a power greater than science. Religion is more complete than science."[8]

Next, the time for the immersion ceremony is fixed based on astrological calculations that determine an auspicious interval. The Lahiris consult Kub Dubey's *"Panjika,"* simply known as "the Directory." Some time intervals such as the *kala bela* and *vara bela* periods in the day should be avoided. Such inauspicious periods often compromise the duration available to perform the rites on all of the other days.

At this point an exuberant rite, known in Bengali as *varana* and conducted only by the married women of the house, takes place. The women feed sweets and other delicacies to the clay images of Durgā, the lion, and the other deities (see Figure 4.8.1). Everyone, including the *vāhana*s are treated. Like the family members and guests who have enjoyed the food and hospitality of the patron during the *pūjā*, Durgā and her family are once again fed before their departure. Betel nut and leaf (*pān*) are also fed to all the images. I was initially surprised to notice that even Mahiṣa was stuffed with delicacies. The homage rendered to Mahiṣa in the entire ritual, but especially at the end affirms the importance of his role in the cosmic drama. Alf Hiltebeitel (1988) meticulously develops Madeleine Biardeau's (1984) insight that the South Indian figure of the Buffalo King (Pōttu Rāja) who serves the Devī is a transformed Buffalo demon. The attitude of devotees in the Durgā Pūjā towards Mahiṣāsura appears to support this interpretation, for he is honored at the end and encouraged to return the following year.[9]

Some devotees told me that they admired Mahiṣāsura for his courage (however misguided) to struggle against the insurmountable and unconquerable power of Durgā. One is reminded of the ubiquitous temple reliefs of the *śārdūla*, a mythical leogryph in battle with a courageous warrior. Some see it as the heroic battle of the individual against the overwhelming power of Māyā (e.g., Kramrisch 1976[1946]:334–337). The *śārdūla*, enormous and changing shape, like the Devī's lion, may represent her awesome power. The individual's battle with this power is heroic, yet futile. The iconography never shows the beast defeated by the hero, but conveys something akin to the opposite. Perhaps in this sense Mahiṣa is that hero, the individual who at first struggles to conquer the Devī, and ultimately, defeated by her formidable and invincible power, becomes her devoted worshipper. Carmel Berkson (1995) explores the heroic nature of Mahiṣa's struggle with Durgā in great detail. An important psychological dimension of the myth and ritual, she also argues, is that it reflects the perennial tension between the Hindu adolescent male and his dominating mother.

Stietencron (1983), too, examines the development of interpretations of the Devī's relationship to the demon Mahiṣa in the Purāṇic literature. Since Mahiṣa cannot enjoy the "battle of love" with the Goddess, he chooses to engage her in actual battle, claiming a union with her through death. His, too, is a sort of loving devotion (*bhakti*). However, unlike more common modes adopted by the devotee towards a deity, such as mother to child, subject to lord, or lover to lover, Mahiṣa chooses the form of an enemy or antagonist. In some versions of the myth, alluding to the perennial battle of the sexes, he is even loosely identified with Śiva, the Devī's spouse, when she is paired with one (also see Shulman 1980:176-192).

It is important to note that the delicacies used in the *varana* rite are not previously blessed *prasāda*, for it would be incongruous to offer the deities food which they themselves have previously eaten and thus consecrated. Since the deities have already been dismissed from the effigies, there is no

Figure 4.8.1 The mouths of the images have been stuffed with food in the *varana* rite, and vermillion *(sindūr)* has been applied to the foreheads of Durgā and other goddesses.

ritual impropriety incurred by direct contact between the votary and the image. Nevertheless, the rite is a significant and possibly unique example of the ritual feeding of a divine image within which the deity is no longer "present." This rite is not regarded as meaningless by votaries or priests and dramatically points to the need to reassess the nature of the divine presence within the *mūrti*. Although votaries are aware that the Devī and other deities have been ritually dismissed from the images, they still experience their presence there and engage in this unusual feeding rite. In the food offering component of traditional *pūjā*s, the food is placed before the deity and then removed. It rarely makes direct contact with the image itself. Sometimes substances such as milk or coconut water may be poured over footprints or other icons, but the deities are generally not mouth-fed, as a mother would feed her children. In the *varana* rite, the sweets are actually stuffed and smeared onto the mouths of the clay images. Quite importantly, the women stuff each other with sweets as well, at this time. The feeding of the Goddess and her female devotees is not sequential, as in the case of *upacāra* offerings, which, in turn, are consumed by votaries, as blessed food (*prasāda*). The rite resembles a group feast with the women and the Goddess all eating together, yet again evoking an identification between the Devī and the departing women of the household.

Figure 4.8.2 The hypnotic beat of the *dhāk* drummers, their faces gaily painted, adds to the exuberant mood as the images are carried to the Gaṅgā for immersion.

An explanation for the ritual is that the Devī, like Pārvatī, is returning to her husband Śiva's abode, where life with him is full of hardship. Thus she is being fattened with sweets and treated well to sustain her for her year away from home and to encourage her to return again the following season. One of Mr. Lahiri's daughters elaborated, "Durgā also symbolizes the vanity of women folk, and their tendency to tell tales. When Durgā is sent home, the last food item given is very bland, to compensate for the rich food she has been given throughout the festival. Thus when she returns to her husband, Śiva, she tells him how much she suffered, getting only this plain food throughout her stay. She is a great tale-teller."[10]

Not only are the images fed, they are garlanded and anointed. A light is waved before them, and a conch shell is blown. The rite parallels, although in abbreviated form, the *brāhmaṇa purohita*'s ministrations during the devotional service (*upacāra*) segment of the *pūjā*. However, here, devotees who were deprived of their chance to make actual physical contact with the images, finally have their opportunity. Indeed one feels that the notion of a deity consuming a food offering that has merely been placed before it, has proved too abstract. The desire to make physical contact with the divinities embodied within these images, and who have been the object of such great devotion through the course of the last few day, is irresistible. One suspects that the *varana* rite predates the male, *brāhmaṇa*-controlled forms of the Durgā Pūjā and preserves a practice in which women worshipped the Devī with offerings and in a manner that permitted or even required physical contact with the *mūrtis*.

"Women," I was informed, "feel special, since they are the ones who bring Goddess Durgā into the household. *Bodhana* welcomes her. The honey [in the *madhuparka* offering] sweetens relationships. The *dīpa* [light] enlightens relationships; the *śaṅkha* [conch shell] brings harmony. Thus women bring her in, and she is worshipped when she leaves."

> "Women exchange *sindūrs*. This is also done for the longevity of their husbands. The *sindūr* [a streak of red powdered lacquer applied to the forehead between the part in the hair] is a symbol of marriage. Thus women exchange *sindūr* with Durgā who is a happily married woman, in the hopes of remaining happily married. The eldest married woman gives *sindūr* to the Goddess."[11]

Immersion

Immersion of the clay image is the duty of the *yajamāna*. Although the Devī is no longer thought to reside in the image, it has been infused with her presence and must be treated properly. Some people gather the weapons and keep them as souvenirs. The *dhāk* drummer has a traditional right to the *navapatrikā*'s *sārī*. All other offerings go to the *purohita*.

The image is carried with much fanfare through the alleys to the river Gaṅgā, often to the rhythm of the *dhāk* drums (see Figure 4.8.2). In the Mitra family tradition, it is customary for the images to be carried on palanquins by hand and for members of the procession to walk barefoot to the Gaṅgā. Trucks often carry the larger images of the public celebrations along major arteries to Daśāśvamedha Ghat, the city's central riverbank site. At the Gaṅgā, the images are placed atop boats and carried some distance away from the bank. Then they are toppled into the water.[12] It is a time of highly mixed emotions (see Figure 4.8.3), which some votaries even regard as the climax of the *pūjā*. The *Kālikā Purāṇa* prescribes, "the *visarjana* of Devī should be made with festivals in the manner of the Śabaras, viz. people may make merry to their heart's content by throwing dust and mud, with auspicious sports and revelry, with indulgence in words and songs referring to male and female organs and with words expressive of the sexual act. The Devī becomes angry with him who does not abuse another and whom others do not abuse and pronounces on him a terrible curse" (Kane:5.177). These prescriptions of what is referred to as Śabarotsava (Festival [in the style] of the Śabara [tribes]) are no longer practiced in urban centers. They call for a temporary dissolving of caste hierarchies and resemble the fertility rites of spring festivals such as Holi.[13]

Figure 4.8.3 A sadness accompanies the mood of elation, as the Lahiri family and author (far left) gather at the banks of the Gaṅgā prior to the final immersion of the image complex.

Nevertheless, there is a mood of festive revelry at the success of the worship, mixed with sorrow at Durgā's departure. The emotional moods, easily discerned because they are highly visible at this time, are induced by a complex combination of factors, which include religio-political (i.e., Hindu) and communal (e.g., club) identity. Also present are the feelings of sadness at the end of the holidays and the parting of families that have come together. Married daughters had returned to their parent's home for the celebration and will soon be leaving. Thus mothers are often seen crying, for Durgā's departure truly marks the departure of their own daughters. The *aparājitā* creeper is also surrendered to the waters. A blossom from the creeper may be kept and sealed into a small metal (often silver) case which is worn around the neck or arm as a protective amulet. The word *aparājitā* has come to be synonymous with such a talisman.

Certain groups, such as the Mitra family, also release a *nīlakaṇṭha* bird (a blue-necked jay) as a symbol of Śiva and the Devī's upcoming reunion. Śiva saved the world from destruction by drinking a deadly poison that was unleashed when the cosmic ocean was churned. This turned his neck blue, giving him the epithet Nīlakaṇṭha (Blue Throat). The *Devī Bhāgavata Purāṇa* tells how the Devī revived Śiva by suckling him with milk from her breasts. The bird is released, I was told, so that it may fly ahead and inform Śiva of the Devī's imminent return. The Mitra family, however, includes Śiva in its image cluster, "since he accompanies Durgā on her visit to her parents' home." Nobody seemed perturbed by the apparent contradiction between Śiva's simultaneous presence both at the festival and at his abode in Mt. Kailasa.

After returning, the immersion party brings back a jar of Gaṅgā water and places it in the middle of the sitting place. The *purohita* sprinkles this sanctified water on the devotees while uttering the Śānti Mantra. The devotees arise, approach and embrace the *purohita*, and touch his feet in a gesture of reverence and thanks. He blesses them with a touch to the forehead. It is traditionally held that the last words uttered by the *purohita* in the *pūjā* are "*Bhagavatī prītaye* (May the Goddess have taken delight [in this *pūjā*])." Pandit Chakravarty explained that the spirit of this prayer is that, although votaries may have asked the Devī for all sorts of benefits throughout the course of the *pūjā*, the actual fulfilment of these wishes are ultimately offered up to the discretion and will of the Goddess.

Conclusion

The Durgā Pūjā is now officially finished. People distribute sweets (not *prasāda*) to each other. If worshippers visit the homes of relatives on Vijayā Daśamī night, it is customary to exchange sweets and embrace everyone.[14] "Sweets in square boxes are distributed during Vijayā Daśamī. Relationships must be sweet, as if dipped in honey, during Durgā Pūjā. This is the custom."[15] People send letters or greeting cards ("Bijoya" cards) to their elders which might say: "Take my respectful homage (*praṇāma*) of Vijayā, and I expect your blessings in return." Elders respond with blessings and requests for homage from youngsters. This mood of felicity and goodwill continues till Kālī Pūjā a few weeks later.

PART III

Interpretations

CHAPTER 5

The Nature of Pūjā

The term *pūjā* is most commonly applied to the rites to worship a deity already embodied in some material form. Thus, each morning when a shopkeeper waves lit sticks of incense before a framed lithograph of Durgā in his store and drapes the image with a garland of fresh flowers, he is very likely to refer to his actions as *pūjā*. The same is true for worship rites that take place at a temple, which is regarded as the abode of the deity. Votaries at temples are apt to call their visit "taking *darśana*." In fact, a former head priest (*pūjāri*) of the Durgā Kuṇḍ temple once commented, "men generally come for *darśana*, women for *pūjā*."[1] His distinction, however, should not be seen as a fundamental difference in the essential nature of the worship rite.

The majority of men and many women who visit temples arrive empty-handed and procure votive materials before entering. Although when visiting a Devī temple they are likely to purchase offerings of incense, sweets or a coconut, and a scarf from shops around the entrance, most just buy a few flowers from a vendor at the gate. They pass these to the priest who officiates at the portal of the inner sanctum, who in turn offers them to the deity. These devotees then gaze at the Devī in the sanctum and make a reverential gesture, such as an *añjali* or even a full prostration, and utter some silent prayer. Since the most prominent aspect of their worship rites is the face-to-face audience with the deity, the act is referred to as *darśana*. In contrast to this perfunctory and often spontaneous act, many women arrive at the temple armed with bags or other containers fully equipped with votive materials. They, themselves, may perform a full five-part devotional service (*pañca upacāra*), consisting of fragrant paste (*gandha*), flowers (*puṣpa*), incense (*dhūpa*), a small lamp (*dīpa*), and a food offering (*naivedya*). They perform this service while engaged in the mutual exchange of glances, commonly called *darśana*, and like other votaries offer prayers and perform gestures of reverence.

It is quite clear that the *pūjā* performed by these women is fundamentally the same type of rite as the *darśana* performed by other devotees. In the *pūjā*, votaries offer devotional service themselves while enjoying an audience with the deity, while in the so-called *darśana*, the priest plays a greater role as intermediary. The priest's role is still more prominent when he performs a formal devotional service to the deity, which in temples is often conducted at sunrise and sunset. Votaries who time their visits to the temple to coincide with these rites, may say that they are going to the temple for *ārati*. The *ārati* also refers to the flame worship (*dīpa*) segment of what may be a five-, ten, or sixteen-part devotional service (*upacāra*) to the deity. Most devotees who are within the temple in the vicinity of the sanctum gather and participate in the honorific act of the *ārati* worship by ringing bells, beating drums, or praying reverentially. Cries of salutation follow the *ārati*, and votaries then move their hands over the *ārati* flames and their own bodies, transferring some of its potency to themselves. It is quite inappropriate for devotees to try to make offerings or even conduct their own *pūjā* to the deity while the *ārati pūjā* conducted by the priest is taking place.

Clearly, both the brisk *darśana* with the offering of flowers and the longer, self-conducted *pūjā* are but abbreviations of the extended devotional service by the temple priest, which culminates in the *ārati*. All three types may be referred to by worshippers as *darśana* or *pūjā*. In all three cases, the objective is to encounter (primarily with a face-to-face audience) and render homage to the deity. Through casual conversations with devotees at the Durgā Kuṇḍ temple in Banāras, I found that most visits were explained as acts of loving devotion (*bhakti*) for a sort of general veneration of Durgā. However, extended conversations frequently revealed that spontaneous *darśana*, self-conducted devotional services, and even protracted regular temple visits for *ārati*, often had some ulterior motive. Votaries were sometimes engaged in making a request or fulfilling a promise (*manauti*) of devotional service for a request already granted by the Devī. In other cases, the temple visits formed part of a self-imposed vowed ascetic obligation (*vrata*) to enhance the votary's inner power. Evidently, there is substantial variety in the forms of worship designated as *pūjā*, as well as in the motives for its performance.

In the Durgā Pūjā, one notes all the aforementioned forms and purposes. Although the *pūjā* may be designated by the patron (*yajamāna*) as motivated by pure, selfless devotion without any specific desire (*niṣkāmya*), once the Devī is manifest in the clay image, she may be worshipped for specific objectives by votaries other than the *yajamāna*. Thus an officially designated *niṣkāmya pūjā* may very well function, in the hearts and minds of certain votaries, as a *kāmya pūjā*. A guest who drops in on the Lahiris' home *pūjā* on Aṣṭamī and participates in the flower worship (*puṣpāñjali*) is engaged in something akin to the spontaneous temple visit for *darśana*. Although the performance of private devotional services to the Devī by visitors is not encouraged/permitted at the domestic Durgā Pūjās, a number of votaries do perform such *pūjās* at the public shrines (*paṇḍal*). In both domestic and public settings the *purohita* performs numerous elaborate devotional services (*upacāra*), which culminate in *ārati* offerings in which all devotees who are present participate.

*Purohita*s explained to me that the merit of the *pūjā* goes to the *yajamāna*. However, this transfer of benefits is not always as simple as it sounds. In community *pūjā*s, an individual is chosen to function as the *yajamāna* in the rites that require his presence, but he represents the entire community. This process is mirrored in the *kumārī pūjā*, where one virgin girl may be selected as the representative of all for whom the *pūjā* is performed. Even Mr. Lahiri's domestic Durgā Pūjā was clearly not performed merely for his own benefit, but on behalf of all his family members (and friends). Besides the general purpose for the *pūjā*, articulated by the *purohita* in the oath of intent (*saṅkalpa*) on behalf of the *yajamāna*, the Durgā Pūjā does something remarkable. It makes the Devī accessible to worshippers other than the patron. She is now available to grant audience to a host of others and potentially heed their requests. A queen may make a visit to a small town in response to the specific request of a minor official, but once there, she is open to the adulation of all the townsfolk and made aware of their many needs. This dimension of divine accessibility expands our understanding of the capacity of *pūjā* as well as the nature of the Great Goddess.

Although most votaries designated Saptamī as the first day of the Durgā Pūjā, since this is the day that the Devī is fully manifest in the clay image and thus accessible to her votaries, the *pūjā* itself begins much earlier. Most worshippers regard *pūjā* to be merely what is technically designated by *purohita*s and ritual manuals (*paddhati*) as *upacāra* or devotional service. However, *upacāra* is only a portion of a potentially much lengthier series of rites that constitute *pūjā* proper. These rites include the invocation and dismissal of the deity. *Upacāra*, or devotional service, is often classified as consisting of five, ten, or sixteen parts (*pañca*, *daśa*, and *ṣodaśa upacāra*). In *pūjā*s that include Tantric stylings, such as the Durgā Pūjā, these devotional services may be offered with meditative visualizations (*mānasa upacāra*) as well as with material items. Rather than use the term *upacāra*, one often finds votaries referring to, say, a sixteen-part *pūjā*. In scholarly lists of such a *pūjā*, however, the invocation and dismissal of the deity are respectively listed as the first and sixteenth item.[2] There are, of course, numerous variations among what actually figures in the count of *upacāra* items. In the Durgā Pūjā described in Part II, there are over twenty-five items that constitute what is called a sixteen-part devotional service. However, in the Durgā Pūjā, it is clear that invocation and dismissal play no part in that *upacāra* count at all. This is because *pūjā*, as rightly acknowledged in the scholarly lists, consists of devotional service (*upacāra*) enveloped within rites of invocation and dismissal.

The equation of *upacāra* with *pūjā*, common among many votaries, is hardly unusual, since the *upacāra*s are the only aspects of *pūjā* that they generally perform. The most common settings for worship are temples or smaller shrines, abodes where the deity is thought to reside constantly. In simple *pūjās* before lithographs and such, in which a deity has not been formally installed, the images serve more as representations of the deity, unless regular, sustained devotional attention has caused the forms to become imbued with the deity's presence. In temples, elaborate installation rites were once performed to induce the deity to take up its abode in the fabricated image (*mūrti, vigraha*) placed within the sanctum, and such rites will not be performed again, unless the image is replaced. In the case of certain deities, the procedure requires the ministrations of *brāhmaṇa* priests with appropriate initiation. No invocation or installation rites are necessary, of course, at shrines and temples that have developed around natural manifestations of a deity, such as self-existent (*svayambhu*) *liṅga*s of Śiva, or certain seats of the Goddess (*yoni pīṭha*). It is little wonder that most votaries do not generally give much thought to invocation and dismissal as a part of their *pūjā* practice. In the Durgā Pūjā, however, one views the process of *pūjā* in a thoroughly expanded form, as a rite that involves the invocation, veneration, and dismissal of a deity.

Invocation rites need not be as extensive or elaborate as those in the Durgā Pūjā, and worshippers do on occasion perform them. For instance, during the spring Navarātra, most Śākta votaries will merely establish the Devī in her jar (*ghaṭa, kalaśa*) form. The entire rite may take less than an hour. It involves building a low earthen altar and placing upon it a wide-bodied, narrow-necked clay jar. Pure water is poured into the jar, whose mouth is filled with leaf-bearing twigs. This is topped with a coconut, which serves as a head, and the entire jar is then wrapped with a red cloth. A few mantras are recited and the effigy serves as the manifest form of the Devī. She will then be venerated for the entire period of Navarātra, often with a simple devotional service (*upacāra*) and recitations of the *Durgā Saptaśatī*. For many Hindus, this is also the procedure that is carried out in the autumn. The establishment of the earthen jar is a relatively simple installation and invocation rite, which, although often performed by a *brāhmaṇa* priest, I have seen performed by both men and women of all classes. It is a ritual that actualizes the presence of the Devī for her worshippers.

The Durgā Pūjā, too, commences with the installation of the jar form of the Devī. However, this rite is but the beginning of the lengthy and elaborate invocation process in which the Devī is subsequently established in the wide variety of forms including the *bilva* tree, the *navapatrikā*, and the anthropomorphic clay image. Furthermore, since she is regarded as being awakened out of her normal awakening time, the procedure is necessarily augmented, providing us with excellent data with which to examine the rites of invocation and dismissal, vital components of *pūjā*.

In the rite of dismissal, the *purohita* sends the Devī away with the request that she remain in the water, the earth, and the home (*jale tiṣṭha gehe ca bhūtale*). Thus her departure is not solely conceived of as a return to a transcendent state or abode. The Devī's abode is immanent. It is everywhere. It is the earth itself, the water, and indeed domestic life itself. When sent back to those abodes, she is merely being asked to return to a state of dormancy, where her presence and power is latent, awaiting the next invocation from her worshippers. It is precisely from these abodes that she is invoked in the rites that establish her in her jar form. From here, through the vegetative life of the *bilva* tree, where she is also thought to abide, she is progressively awakened into the *navapatrikā*, the anthropomorphic clay image, and finally even into a living virgin girl of flesh and blood. In the Durgā Pūjā, it is the very materials within which the Devī abides (earth, water, and life) that are combined to create the forms into which she will manifest.

The first rite performed on Saptamī is the *varaṇa* or selection of the *purohita*, who in the Durgā Pūjā must be a *brāhmaṇa* with appropriate initiation. This rite clearly reveals the progressive Sanskritization of Devī worship, for the Goddess, who is capable of being established in the jar or venerated in the *bilva* tree, by anyone, may only be invoked and worshipped in the other forms with the aid of an initiated *brāhmaṇa*. Invocation may be a neglected aspect of *pūjā*, precisely because there still exists a tension between the priestly classes (solely capable of making offerings to the deities in Vedic *yajña)* and *bhakti*-oriented *pūjā,* which in theory may be conducted by both genders and all classes, by themselves, without the need of the *brāhmaṇa* class. The *Durgā Saptaśatī*, which is highly influential among Śāktas, clearly portrays the king Suratha and the merchant Samādhi, members of the *kṣatriya* and *vaiśya* classes respectively, constructing images of the Devī on their own (DSS 13.7). Without the aid of a priest, they worshipped her with flowers, incense, fire, and water, while performing other austerities such as fasting and making offerings of their own blood (DSS 13.8–9). After three continuous years of such worship, they received a vision of the Goddess, who granted them their wishes.

The litany of the Durgā Pūjā itself makes reference to prince Rāma's worship of Durgā. However, Bengali votaries occasionally cite the story of how Rāma commissioned the services of Rāvaṇa, a *brāhmaṇa*, and his enemy, to perform the *pūjā*. Votaries dwell on the irony in Rāvaṇa's obligation as a *brāhmaṇa* to perform the rite for which he has been commissioned, even though it will lead to his own destruction. However, what is also implicit in this tale is that Rāma does not perform the *pūjā* himself, but requires the services of a *brāhmaṇa*. His need is so great and his options so few that he must go as far as requesting the services of his archenemy, Rāvaṇa. Rāma's worship of Durgā during the autumn Navarātra, which serves as a precedent for the Durgā Pūjā, thus reaffirms the once unnecessary place of the *brāhmaṇa* priest in rites to venerate the Devī.[3]

It is also significant that an extensive set of anointing and bathing rites of the *navapatrikā* and the clay image are performed before the *prāṇapratiṣṭha* rituals, which install life in the images. These rites are not components of the sixteen-part devotional service (*upacāra*) that will be conducted after the image is brought to life. The devotional service anointments and baths pale in comparison to the extensive rites that occur during the *adhivāsa* and *snāna* rites for the *navapatrikā* and the clay image. As the litany reveals, the baths, along with numerous anointments, will serve the purpose of removing sins or impurities (*tava lepana matreṇa sarva pāpam vinaśyati*). However, these impurities clearly cannot be attributed to the Devī. Even though the bath offered to deities as part of the devotional service is viewed as cleansing the dust accumulated from travel to the place of worship, the concept itself derives from the treatment of human guests. As Eck (1981a:37) has pointed out, deities do not accumulate spiritual much less physical pollution. Fuller's comments (1992:70) that "gods and goddesses do not actually need offerings or services, because they never are dirty, ugly, hungry, or unable to see in the dark," are also pertinent. The *Parā Pūjā*, a poem attributed to Śaṅkara, eloquently made this point by asking,

> Why summon by invocation that which fills all?
> Where is the seat for the holder of all?
> Why give water for foot washing or oblation
> to one who is transparently clear,
> and water for rinsing the mouth to one who is pure?
> Why a bath for one free of blemish,
> and a vestment for one who encompasses all?
> Why a sacred thread for one who needs no support.
> Why an ornament for one who is beautiful?[4]

Although Śaṅkara's perspective derives from his radical nondual philosophical stance, which by extrapolation dispenses with the need for external *pūjā* altogether, since a deity may be worshipped anywhere and anytime, it suggests at least a thousand years of awareness of the apparent contradiction inherent in the act of *pūjā*. The acts of devotional service are designed by human beings to demonstrate affection and honor deities, who are in little if any need of human ministrations. In what sense, then, may we regard the bathing rites, which are said to remove sins or impurities?

Besides the obvious interpretation that the anointings and bathings are honorific (in that they resemble royal consecration rituals) and express affection and care, they appear to serve other purposes as well. Through baths with waters derived from a variety of sources (e.g, dew, waterfalls) throughout the world (e.g., oceans, sacred rivers), the Devī's territorial realm is symbolically expanded. As the waters are poured on the Devī by myriad divine beings, she is progressively raised in status. It is not only humans who perform her bath, but all the heavenly rivers, the great gods and goddesses, and the full host of heavenly beings. By the completion of the bath, it is clear that the Devī's bathing has been a consecration and veneration by all beings, from heaven, earth, and the underworld, who in so doing subordinate themselves while raising her to the preeminent position in the divine hierarchy. She presides over a realm that is the cosmos itself. The deity who is being invoked in the Durgā Pūjā is not just one of heaven's many *devīs*, but the Great Goddess herself.

The anointing and bathing rites also sanctify the material substances into which the Devī will take up her abode in an awakened state. Although she resides constantly within the earth and water, these same materials, when formed and contained, need to be purified before they become suitable receptacles for her awakened embodiment. Just as it would be unthinkable to invoke a deity into a defaced or damaged icon, the same holds true for effigies whose material constituents are impure. Baths and anointments symbolically purify gross matter.

Ultimately, however, and this is a crucial observation that has mostly been overlooked, these rites enact a purification, not of the Devī, but of the votary. It is the votary's senses that are progressively cleansed and refined through the acts of *pūjā*. *Pūjā*, through its gestures of respectful honoring, whether during the invocation process or within the acts of devotional service (*upacāra*) themselves, has as its objective an encounter between deity and devotee. The meeting may take place anywhere along a path spanning the gulf between human and divine realms. At one end of the route, the encounter may occur by the deity taking on a material form that is fully apprehensible to the devotee's gross senses. At the other end, the devotee's own senses are progressively refined, purified, and elevated, so that they traverse the pathway via the gross material of the manifest effigy to a sublime encounter (even a union) with the Divine, with the deepest, most subtle part of their being. *Darśana* is the term which refers to this profoundly meaningful encounter that may occur at any point along that path, while *pūjā* is the means of achieving it.[5]

In the acts of invocation and devotional service, which constitute *pūjā*, devotees (with or without the aid of the *purohita*) actually forge a union between matter, their senses, and their highest faculties of consciousness through a series of purificatory offerings that move them towards the primordial oneness from which creation is thought to emerge. This still point is the first and most subtle manifestation of the divinely transcendent deity. Simultaneously, through the acts of *pūjā*, the deity is moved in a trajectory from transcendence to full bodily immanence. Matter, gross and subtle, is continually refined and purified in the process until the devotee's trajectory towards transcendence intersects with the deity's path of manifestation.[6]

My Sanskrit teacher Pandit Vāgīśa Śāstri's words encapsulate a sentiment I heard more than once in Banāras. "In the offerings of a *pañcopacāra pūjā* (*gandha*, *puṣpa*, *dhupa*, *dīpa*, and *naivedya*), the five gross elements of earth, water, air, fire, and space are reunited."[7] Although he did not elaborate upon what he meant, and although there is no simple one-to-one correspondence between these items and the gross elements (*mahābhūta*), there is an obvious connection. One can see in the thick sandalwood paste, formed from a powder mixed with water, in the incense smoke and other fragrances that pervade the air, in the flame that leaps from the camphor crystals to light up space, and even in the coconut water, which spills from a cracked food offering, that the gross constituent elements (*mahābhūta*) of creation are indeed present and integrated in the *pūjā* offerings.

Östör noted that "taking sight of the goddess is a reciprocal relationship: Durgā sees the devotee, and the latter receives a beneficial effect" (1980:96). Eck (1981a:5) emphasized the importance of such mutual "seeing" in the act of *darśana*. Babb (1975:57) had earlier analyzed the sharing of food between deity and devotee in the *naivedya* component of *pūjā*'s devotional service. Fuller (1992:78–79) challenged Babb's assertion that the food offerings, once consumed by the deity and returned as blessing (*prasāda*), mirror food exchanges between castes. I concur with Fuller's assertion that the relationship between the priest or lay worshipper and the deity is more akin to "institutionalized hierarchical inequality" that exists between a wife and husband, than between *brāhmaṇa*s and lower classes. These scholars do draw our attention to the sensory participation, which is evidently inherent in *pūjā*. Not only do worshippers and deities see each other and taste the same food, they interact with all their senses. In such services as anointing, bathing, dressing, and decorating, there is physical contact between the votary and the deity's manifest form. Through the fragrant aroma of sandalwood paste, flowers, incense, burning camphor, and food, they share deeply in the sense of smell. Both listen to the chanting of honorific prayers, the sounds of bells and drums, and devotional music, if those are part of the devotional service.

The integration of gross elements and the senses, which is characteristic of the devotional service offerings (*upacāra*) in *pūjā*, immediately evokes the metaphysical schemes of material manifestation found in many Hindu philosophical systems. These philosophical schools often vary in their conception of Absolute Reality, which may, for instance, be a single transcendent reality (e.g., nondualistic Vedānta's Nirguṇa Brahman), or composed of two entities, such as Sāṅkhya's Puruṣa (soul, consciousness) and Prakṛti (nature, matter). They do, however, generally concur on a progressive series of manifestations of a transcendent divine principle (e.g., Pradhāna Prakṛti, or Ādi Śakti) from the most subtle dimension within consciousness (e.g., *mahat*, *buddhi*), via the ego, mind, and senses, to the gross elements. One such scheme is ritually utilized in the *bhutā śuddhi* rite, frequently conducted by the *purohita* throughout the Durgā Pūjā and discussed in detail earlier. It involves the purification (*śuddhi*) of all the constituent elements (*bhūta*) of macrocosmic creation that are present within the microcosm of the *purohita*'s own body. The purification entails an enfolding of all the constituent elements of creation, such as the gross elements (*mahābhūta*), the five senses, as well as the most subtle elements of human consciousness, with the aid of *mantra*s and energy control (*prāṇāyāma*). As a ritual adept, the *purohita* has, in theory, mastered the process of material reintegration, which is the vector leading to the abode of divinity. It is from there that he awakens and, through the power of *mantra*s, *mudrā*s, and *nyāsa*s, via his own transformed body, leads the deity along the opposite path, into full material manifestation.

It is certain that the acts of *pūjā*, which may include honorific prayers and such gestures of reverence as prostrations, are accompanied by strong sentiments. Although they may be invisible to the observing eye, these profound feelings, sometimes evoked by cries of salutation, tears, silent entreaty, or mute stillness, stand as evidence that *pūjā* entails a total offering of the worshipper's self. Thus *pūjā*, whether or not it includes such rites as the *bhūta śuddhi* or elaborate invocations of the type found in the Durgā Pūjā, is fundamentally a process of mutual movement by the deity and the worshipper towards each other. To a worshipper with virtuoso skills, such as the *purohita*, the meeting may take place at the threshold of the deity's own abode. For others, it is the deity who journeys farthest, for *darśana* may only occur at the level of the votary's own capacity for perceiving the divine. The Durgā Pūjā offers devotees an opportunity to encounter the Goddess in a vast range of manifest forms, including a living virgin girl.

The exact nature of the encounter is also dependent upon the worshipper's predilection. For certain *bhakta*s, the most profound meeting is framed dualistically. Votary and deity never fully merge. Such worshippers frequently quip that one wants to taste sugar, not become it. However, it is equally true that for others, the most desirable encounter is the attainment of oneness with the deity. The *purohita* in the Durgā Pūjā, in the process of bringing her into manifestation, himself becomes the Devī. Young virgin girls are themselves venerated as living forms of the deity. These are but a few examples of a perspective, prevalent within Śākta Tantrism, that sees all of creation, including the votary, situated within the single reality which is the Great Goddess. The highest purpose of existence is to realize that unity with divinity. Each such sublime encounter with the Divine, albeit temporary, whether through the actions and fruits of *pūjā* or through other forms of spiritual practice (*sādhana*), augments the aspirant's capacity to achieve an abiding union with the Absolute.

CHAPTER 6

The Nature of the Great Goddess

The Great Goddess is worshipped in an astonishing assortment of names and forms during the Durgā Pūjā. Some of these, such as the jar and the polychrome clay image are readily recognizable forms of the Devī. However, there are many others forms that are far less visually obvious, even to the devotees who attend the ritual. These forms include symbolic diagrams (*yantra/ maṇḍala*), as well as less explicit forms of the Goddess, such as the constituent materials of worship. Since most votaries do not understand the Sanskrit litany, they are also often unaware of the many names by which the Devī is addressed. These names are either epithets of the Great Goddess herself or refer to minor goddesses who are regarded as aspects of her. What does the profusion of names and forms tell us about the nature of the Durgā Pūjā and the Great Goddess?

The interpretations that follow and the "meaning" they convey about the nature of the Durgā Pūjā and the Devī are those that derive implicitly from the ritual acts and symbols themselves and their traditional meanings in Hindu religious contexts. I do not wish to suggest that the entire set of interpretations that follow belongs to any particular votary, nor do I intend to provide justifications of the meanings with illustrative quotations by worshippers throughout this section. Interpretations of what particular forms of the Devī signify to worshippers themselves are not always forthcoming. Most votaries do not have a penchant for symbol analysis and experience the Durgā Pūjā as a whole, seeing it primarily as a means of connecting with the Goddess. For instance, although given to intellectual speculation, a devout Śākta, Raju Tiwari's comments are instructive. "You may interpret the jar (*kalaśa*) as the whole earth or universe, or some such thing, because it contains so many different things, water, earth, leaves, and so on, . . . , and maybe it is, but my feeling is that it is mainly a way to focus the attention. It brings our thoughts together, our concentration on the Devī."[1]

There is no simple organizational scheme with which to classify the forms assumed by the Goddess in the Durgā Pūjā comprehensively. Certain patterns, however, are evident. One significant motif is that there is a progression of embodiments that enables worshippers to encounter the Devī in the most accessible or approachable manner possible. These are divine forms that resemble a human female who may be perceived as an Earth Mother, wife, divine protectress, or chaste daughter.

Gynomorphic Forms of the Goddess

The Jar (*Ghaṭa*, *Kalaśa*)

The Devī's embodiment in the jar (*ghaṭa*) resembles a squatting or pregnant woman clad in a *sārī* (see Figure 6.1). Although it is a form of the Goddess that is recognized by most worshippers, most are not consciously aware of the goddess-based symbolism in the entire rite of establishing the *ghaṭa*. For instance, when constructing the earthen altar, the *purohita* utters verses that identify it as the Earth, the Supporter of the world, and as Aditi, the mother of the gods.[2] The altar is thus itself the Divine Feminine, the Great Mother, the foundation of the cosmos, the creatrix of all deities. The altar, sown with grain that sprouts over the course of the *pūjā*, embodies the fertile capacity of the creation to generate life. The earthen jar filled with water is composed of two natural elements with which the Goddess has long been identified in Hindu India. These are the Earth itself (deified as the goddesses Pṛthvī or Bhū Devī) and the divine waters (such as the River Gaṅgā). The jar's wide-bodied shape evokes the image of a pregnant woman or the world egg, a microcosmic representation of the universe. She is a Cosmic Mother, ready to give birth to the creation.

The leaf-bearing twigs are a symbol of the sap or essence of life that flows through nature. The coconut-head is the fruit of creation, a symbol of nourishment, and the seed of subsequent creations. Mirroring the creation, the jar form of the Goddess is adorned, as nature is itself adorned, in beauty. Her *sārī*'s colour is red, like blood, the vital force flowing through nature. It is significant that the jar form of the Goddess is composed of many of the elements normally used in devotional service (*upacāra*) to any Hindu deity. These elements include flowers (the jar is garlanded), water, earth, fruit, and fragrant paste (it is marked with an auspicious symbol). The jar form, into which the Devī is not technically invoked but merely established, reveals that the Goddess is perennially embodied in the manifold creation. Constructed of *pūjā* offerings, she will be worshipped for the remainder of the *pūjā* with the very items that are components of her own being. This motif continues to be elaborated upon more explicitly throughout the Durgā Pūjā.

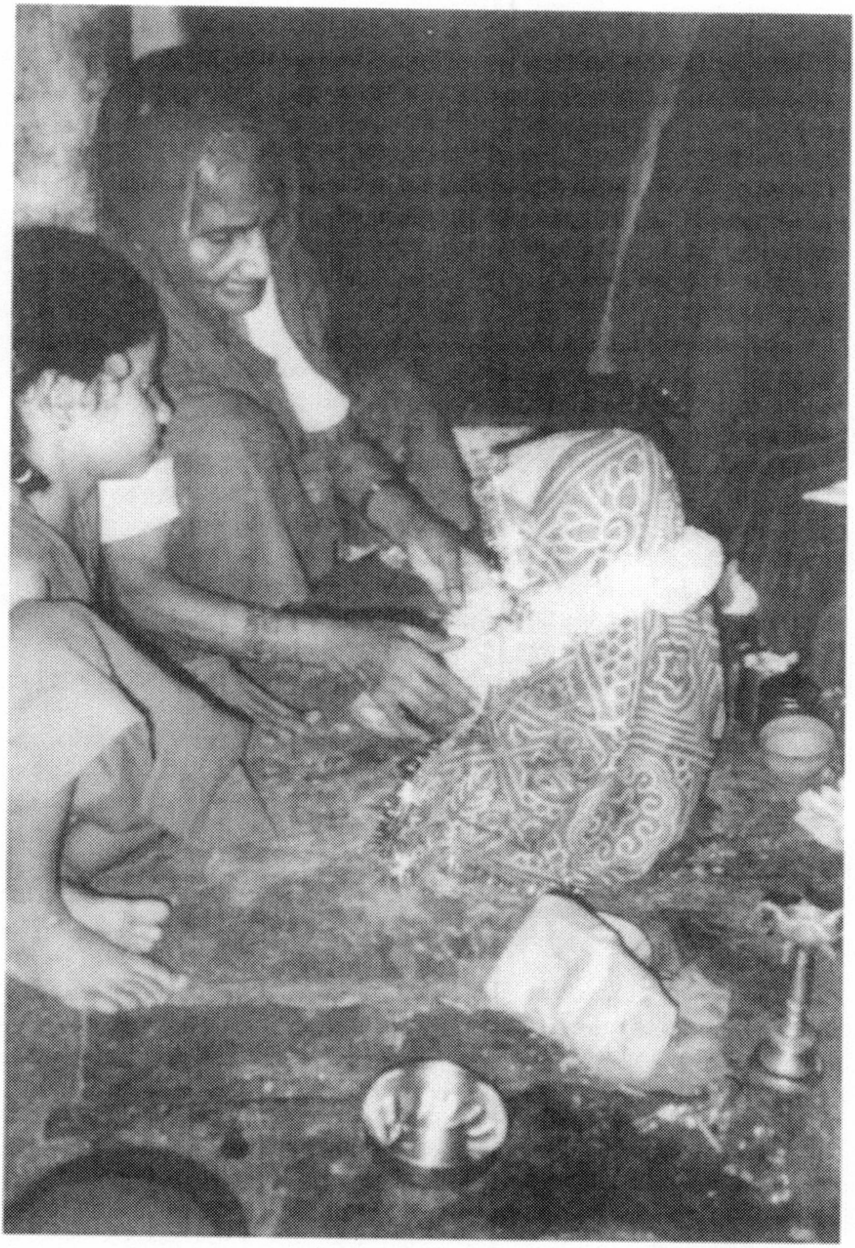

Figure 6.1. A squatting, *sārī*-draped female healer resembles the Goddess, whose jar form she is engaged in establishing.

THE CLUSTER OF NINE PLANTS (NAVAPATRIKĀ)

The jar form of the Devī is established in front of a wood-apple (*bilva*) tree, where she is thought to reside in a latent form. The *purohita* severs a branch possessing two wood-apple fruit, symbols of the breasts of the Goddess, and brings it to the place of worship (*pūjālaya*) within the house. Eight other types of vegetation are later added to the wood-apple branch to form the *navapatrikā* (Cluster of Nine Plants), another symbol of the Great Goddess. Although the wood-apple branch alone represents the Devī, when in the cluster, each of the nine plants represents a subsidiary *devī*, an aspect of the Great Goddess.

The *navapatrikā* is a choice example of how the Durgā Pūjā incorporates preexisting goddess cults and symbols. A few clay seals found in Indus Valley sites suggest a close connection between women and trees, who are often fused with each other.[3] Female tree spirits or *yakṣīs* have long been worshipped in the Hindu tradition, many eventually attaining the status of goddesses.[4] The Tulasī plant, beloved of the god Viṣṇu, and the Nīm tree, the embodiment or abode of the goddess Śītalā, are examples of trees venerated as goddesses. Although the exact manner in which the *navapatrikā* is worshipped may not resemble ancient methods of *yakṣī* worship, the *navapatrikā* itself clearly identifies the Devī with vegetation in its fertile, nourishing, and beautiful aspects. It is an icon of the Devī as *yakṣī*, a symbol of all tree goddesses. Furthermore, the *navapatrikā* incorporates the names and symbolic attributes of nine actual *devīs*, from major goddesses such as Lakṣmī to lesser-known goddesses such as Raktadantikā. The *navapatrikā* acknowledges the worship of these *devīs*, and yet subsumes them as aspects of the Great Goddess. When clad in the *sārī*, and often identified as a lithe young bride, the *navapatrikā's* feminine identity is fully evident.

THE CLAY IMAGE

The ornate, polychrome clay image is the most conspicuous and dramatic of the Devī's forms in the Durgā Pūjā. The image, constructed in accord with prescriptions for meditative visualization (*dhyāna śloka*), portray the Devī as a beautiful young woman with a serene countenance. She has three eyes, long matted hair, and a shapely body with large, well-developed breasts. She carries Śiva's trident and Viṣṇu's discus, and other weapons associated with the male gods, in her ten arms. These are symbols of her measureless powers, which are an amalgam of the powers of all the male deities. Her mount is a great tawny lion, and one of her feet crushes the dreadful male demon, Mahiṣa. Mahiṣa is portrayed in human form, emerging from the severed neck of a buffalo. The demon is snared in the Devī's snake noose, and copious amounts of blood flow from the wound where the Goddess has impaled him with her spear.

Most devotees note that the Mahādevī embodies a pure (*sattva*) and awesome power (*śakti*) that crushes unrighteousness (*adharma*), ignorance, and egotism, symbolized by the dark (*tamas*) buffalo form of the demon Mahiṣa. Durga's lion mount is also viewed as a symbol of the Devī's power (*śakti*), the active principle (*rajas*) in creation, and of royalty, since a throne is often called a lion-seat (*siṃhāsana*).[5] The demon, although slain by the Devī, is himself a symbol of certain of her own attributes. The Great Goddess is herself the power of illusion, bestowing on creation the qualities of ignorance and egotism.

Since many devotees think of the Devī as the Great Mother, whom they address simply as "Mā," they regard the attendant deities Gaṇeśa, Lakṣmī, Kārtikeya, and Sarasvatī as her children, a conception partly supported by Purāṇic myths. For instance, the Great Goddess is often identified with Pārvatī, the spouse of the Great God (*maheśvara*), Śiva. As such, the Devī is appropriately labelled the "mother" of the pot-bellied, elephant-headed Gaṇeśa and Kārtikeya, the god of war, both of whom are identified in the Purāṇas as the offspring of Śiva and Pārvatī.[6]

However, Lakṣmī and Sarasvatī are rarely, if ever, considered to be the Devī's children in Purāṇic mythology. Votaries sometimes regard these goddesses as the spouses of Gaṇeśa and Kārtikeya, with whom they are respectively paired, although such a connection is not commonly acknowledged in textual sources. Lakṣmī and Sarasvatī's presence in the clay image complex probably derives from another conceptual framework. Hindus often think of Supreme Divinity as embodying three principles. These are creation, preservation, and destruction, symbolized by the male gods Brahmā, Viṣṇu, and Śiva, respectively. Among Śāktas, who are staunch goddess worshippers, these principles are symbolized by the goddesses Sarasvatī, Lakṣmī, and Kālī, counterparts of the male gods Brahmā, Viṣṇu, and Śiva. The Great Goddess, Durgā, slayer of the Buffalo Demon, embodies the destructive nature of Śiva/Kālī, and is thus appropriately flanked by Lakṣmī and Sarasvatī. During the Sandhi Pūjā, Durgā's meditative verse is often that of Cāmuṇḍā/Kālī, whose dreadful manifestation will receive the blood sacrifice. This triad of goddesses, Lakṣmī, Sarasvatī, and Kālī, together encompass the fullness of divinity, symbolizing the inclusion of all three principles within the Great Goddess alone.

Similarly, Gaṇeśa and Kārtikeya in the clay image complex represent aspects of the Devī herself. Ancient myths link Kārtikeya/Skanda, the god of war, not Durgā, with the slaying of the Buffalo Demon (see *Mahābhārata* 3.213–221). Durgā absorbs this victory by Kārtikeya and the war god's martial nature into her own mythology. She is the supreme divine warrior, and the myths of her military exploits against various demons are widely known throughout India. Kārtikeya in the image complex is thus a symbol of the Devī's own warrior nature. The same holds true for Gaṇeśa, who is worshipped as the Lord of Obstacles, creating impediments for those who do not worship him and removing them for those who do.[7] The name Durgā itself implies that the Devī is the supreme obstacle for her opponents. Both in chastity and strength, she is likened to an impregnable fortress (*durga*). When propitiated, she offers the greatest protection to those engaged in arduous (*dur*) undertakings (*ga*).

The clay image complex thus offers a striking assembly of the Devi's many faces. Besides depicting Durgā in her most famous mythological exploit, destroying the Buffalo Demon, Mahiṣa, the complex contains myriad implicit symbols of the Devī's own attributes in the guise of her attendant deities.

The Virgin Girl (*Kumārī*)

In the person of the virgin girl, the goddess reveals herself as the living human female. The ritual actions of the *purohita* cause the young girl to become the locus for the Devī's manifestation. The Devī thus manifests, albeit temporarily, in human form, implying that any young girl, if sufficiently pure, may serve as vehicle for the embodiment of the Divine Feminine in her supreme form as the Great Goddess. In response to my questions about who the Devī in the Durgā Pūjā is, a frequent response was simply, "Our *kanyā* (daughter)."Although the Goddess is worshipped in the *kumārī pūjā* as a prepubescent girl, a state of unequivocal feminine purity in orthodox Hindu thought, the Durgā Pūjā acknowledges the Devī's presence in other stages of womanhood in more subtle ways, as we shall later see.

Appraisal of these Forms

From the foregoing examination, it becomes apparent that the Durgā Pūjā collates rites that invoke the Devī into forms that are progressively more anthropomorphically (or perhaps more correctly, gynomorphically) explicit. The jar form of the Devī, constructed of earth, water, twigs, and fruit, is clothed in a piece of cloth so that it resembles (albeit rather primevally) a pregnant woman dressed in a *sārī*. This Earth Mother form is produced during the *bodhana* rite that preceded Saptamī. The *navapatrikā*, with its two wood-apple breasts, is also draped in a *sārī* after being bathed and placed beside the clay image of Gaṇeśa. There it is often referred to as the *kala bou*, or "banana wife," since it resembles a modest, lithe, young bride, whose main shape is derived from the largest of its nine constituent plants, the plantain (*kadalī*). In the clay image complex, the Goddess takes on an even more explicitly gynomorphic shape. Although depicted with ten arms and three eyes, symbolic of her divine powers and wisdom, she is unmistakably a voluptuous and beautiful unmarried woman. Armed with weapons and portrayed in the act of slaying the buffalo demon, she appears as a regal, divine protectress. The *navapatrikā* and clay image are first worshipped on Saptamī. Finally, at the high point of the ritual, the Sandhi Pūjā, the Devī is worshipped in a form that is the culmination of her gynomorphic manifestations, that of a living human female, a virgin girl. These observations plainly illustrate that the Durgā Pūjā brings the Devī into feminine bodily manifestations, so that she may be easily approached and worshipped by her devotees.

Less obvious is that the progression of divine manifestations, from mother (the jar form), to fertile female (*navapatrikā* and clay image), to premenarche virgin girl (*kumārī*), inverts the developmental sequence of a human female's life. Here again the theme that *pūjā* is a mechanism that moves deity and devotee towards each other is reiterated. The Devī is rejuvenated. Through her awakening she is transformed from the mother of creation into the virginal female poised to engender creation. She figuratively gives birth to herself. The manifest creation that is her embodied self is thus itself reborn and renewed. In synchronous response, the *pūjā* propels the votary, and the human female in particular, in the opposite direction. It elicits the maturation of the premenarche virgin into a fertile woman, and impels the fertile woman towards marriage and motherhood.

Yantric Forms of the Devī

It is also apparent that the Durgā Pūjā has another purpose besides effecting tangible and approachable embodiments. The worship of the Goddess in the *sarvatobhadra maṇḍala* on Mahāṣṭamī, a very important day in the *pūjā*, makes us aware that the Devī's gynomorphic manifestations cannot be the *pūjā*'s sole objective.

According to Pandit Chakravarty, the Durgā Pūjā disobeys an orthodox prescription to worship a deity either within a *mūrti* or a *yantra*, but not both. The Durgā Pūjā's unorthodox stance is likely the result of its syncretic nature, for it clearly combines strands of worship rites from both orthodox (Smārta, Vedic) and heterodox (Tantric, tribal) sources. Furthermore, as Zimmer acknowledges in the quotation below, images (*mūrti/pratimā*) are themselves *yantra*s. However, if we suspend consideration of the *mūrti*s in our analysis, the pattern of *yantra/maṇḍala* use in the ritual provides us with another useful scheme to elicit insights into the nature of the Durgā Pūjā and the Great Goddess. Zimmer's penetrating analysis of the relationship between *pūjā* and *yantra*s in their diverse forms (including *mūrti*s), is pertinent here. "It is not until the spiritual activity of the devotee makes a particular *yantra* (*pratimā*, *maṇḍala*, or a *yantra* in the narrower sense) the focal point of all his powers of concentration, that the *yantra* takes on any significance. . . . This process of transformation, which human consciousness performs on the material substance of the *yantra*, occurs in the act of worship, in *pūjā*" (1984:32). In the rituals of Durgā Pūjā, we see an illustration *par excellence* of this process of transformation of human consciousness and the substance of the *yantra* that is the Devī, in which the two are fused in an encounter of sublime significance.

YANTRAS

A *maṇḍala*, or *yantra*, is a representation of a deity which through appropriate ritual construction or utilization actually comes to embody that deity. Although they are often constructed in two dimensions, *maṇḍala*s are envisioned as multidimensional. Temples, for instance, may be seen as three-dimensional *yantra*s/*maṇḍala*s. The word *yantra* appropriately translates as "tool" or "instrument," since *yantras* can be put to use. *Yantra*s are not merely representative. They actually *do* something.

The Durgā Pūjā begins with the establishment of the Devī in the clay jar in the *bodhana* rite. Aside from preparatory purifications (of himself, water, etc., where *yantra*s are also used), the *purohita's* first ritual act to establish the Goddess is the construction of a *yantra* upon which the earthen altar is erected. Although the *yantra* may be the complex *sarvatobhadra maṇḍala*, for expediency it is often a much simpler diagram. Were the *sarvatobhadra maṇḍala* used, it would dramatically illustrate the progression of its use from the *pūjā*'s inception to its central place in the veneration rites on Aṣṭamī. The simple *yantra* used on this occasion is often merely an inverted triangle, symbol of the female sexual organ (*yoni*), the orifice from which the creation emerges. Durgā's seed *mantra*, "Duṃ," may be inscribed within the triangle. Pandit Chakravarty explained that all such *yantra*s are the Devī herself. Since the altar and the jar are established upon these Devī *yantra*s, these instruments are the matrices from which her other forms emerge, implying that the Great Goddess is both the fertile mother of her own creations and the portal through which they emanate.

*Yantra*s are constructed on numerous other occasions throughout the *pūjā*. For instance, a similar *yantra* is drawn during the common (*sāmānya*) and special offerings (*viśeṣārgha*). The common offerings are executed in the *kuśī* or *kośā*, while the special offering is performed in a conch shell, which is placed upon a tripod. From their appearance and their ritual function, it is evident that the *kuśī*, *kośā*, and conch shell, like the simple inverted triangle of the most basic Devī *yantra*, also function as *yoni*s, creative orifices of the Devī, through which she manifests. If we thus extend the concept of a *yantra* to include not only sacred diagrams, but ritual implements such as the *kośā* and conch shell, one becomes aware of many other items that serve as embodiments of the Goddess or portals for her manifestation. For instance, the mirror in which she is bathed and the gleaming blade of the sacrificial sword (whose surrogate is the mirror) are obvious loci of the Devī. There are also numerous tripods and triangular structures, inscribed with yantric symbols, on which food and other offerings are placed. These tripartite structures are not peripheral to the rite, but serve symbolic and yantric functions.

In the metaphysical system of Sāṅkhya philosophy, nature or materiality (*prakṛti*) in all its manifestations is composed of three qualities or aspects (*guṇa*). These are the *guṇa*s of purity (*sattva*), passion (*rajas*), and dullness (*tamas*). Prakṛti eventually came to be identified with the feminine principle, and the scheme of the *guṇa*s to have wide-ranging commerce in Hindu thought. Also, in certain Śākta Tantric schemes, *śakti* is subdivided into three aspects. These are action (*kriyā*), knowledge (*vidyā*), and desire (*icchā*). There are numerous other trinities associated with the Devī.[8] Such tripartite symbolism, which points to the Goddess as nature, manifest reality, or the creation itself, is also evidenced in the trifoliate *bilva* leaves offered in the *homa* rite. There again, we noted that the fire pit is itself a Devī *yantra*.

The Durgā *yantra*, which is inscribed in the sand of the fire pit, illustrates how elements such as the triadic and *yoni* symbolism are fused within that yantric design (see Figure 4.7.1). The *yantra* consists of a single point over which is inscribed the seed syllable of Durgā, "Duṃ." This is surrounded by intersecting descending and ascending equilateral triangles, which produce a six-pointed star. This is circumscribed by a circle from which eight lotus petals emanate towards the cardinal and intermediate directions. This is finally bound by a square (*bhūpura*) which is pierced by gateways at the cardinal directions. Since *yantras* represent an expanding cosmic realm, they are generally interpreted from the center outward. The *bindu,* or point, symbolizes the first manifestation of the Supreme Goddess who is beyond all conceptualization or predication. The *bīja mantra* is the seed syllable from which conceptual forms or predication about the nature of the Goddess germinates. It also represents the root or primal vibration from which the particular form of the Goddess, whose *yantra* it is, begins to manifest the diverse and manifold creation. In this case it is Durgā. The descending triangle is a symbol of the female principle and generative organ, the *yoni*, the portal through which the creation will emerge. It symbolizes the triad of qualities of feminine energy that animates the creation. These are desire (*icchā*), knowledge (*jñāna*), and action (*kriyā*). The ascending triangle is sign of the male principle and generative organ (*liṅga*). It symbolizes the triad of attributes of the male principle, namely, bliss (*ānanda*), consciousness (*cit*), and existence (*sat*). The triangles also represent the triad of principles within every component of creation, namely, the three *guṇa*s. The intersection of these triangles indicates the union of male and female principles, also called Śiva and Śakti, to produce numerous other *yoni*s and *liṅga*s, symbols of the propagation of male and female principles. The circle and the lotus petals symbolize the blossoming of the manifold creation.

The symbolism of the *bhūpura* is particularly pertinent in conceptions of the goddess Durgā. The *bhūpura* serves as the foundation or support of the *yantra*. Generally depicted with entrances in the style of portals to a fortification, it is necessary to recognize that the *bhūpura* thus represents a fortified barrier enclosing a divine realm. This concept of the *bhūpura* resonates well with the Goddess's epithet, Durgā, which can be translated as "She who is Inaccessible" or "She who is Difficult to Reach." Durgā can mean a formidable fortification that is difficult to breach. Metaphysically, then, the *bhūpura* is the barrier that separates the phenomenal world from the noumenal realm. The openings into the *bhūpura* represent the routes through which the spiritual aspirant may breach the formidable enclosure that otherwise keeps the process of manifestation, namely knowledge (*vidyā*) of the Devī's true nature, mysterious. Indeed, once within, in the course of *yantra pūjā*, worship often takes place in a series of clockwise spirals from lotus petals or their interstices to the center, the nucleus of divine creation. Thus *yantra*s are two-way apertures, whose instrumental function meshes perfectly with the intended dynamic of *pūjā*. Just as *pūjā* serves as the means for divine manifestation while simultaneously moving the votary towards the deity, *yantras*, particularly Devī *yantra*s in their myriad forms, act as thresholds through which the votary's devotional self and the manifesting deity both pass.

The Sarvatobhadra Maṇḍala

The *sarvatobhadra maṇḍala* (Sphere of All-Auspiciousness) is the most complex *yantra* employed in the Durgā Pūjā. It consists of a circle in the center, surrounded by an eight-petalled lotus, and further surrounded by a network of squares (see Figure 4.5). The *sarvatobhadra maṇḍala* is a universal *yantra* that may be used in the worship of any deity. The squares that surround the circle of lotus petals are colored in such a manner that numerous "T" shapes are formed from clusters of four small squares. The fourth square sits atop a row of three squares. Pandit Nitai, who establishes a *ghaṭa* of the Devī atop this *maṇḍala* in his own home during Navarātra, explained that these clusters represent the *liṅga-yoni*, the male and female polarities, which when combined, generate the cosmos. They thus duplicate the symbolism of the intersecting triangles in the Durgā Yantra. This conjunction and balance of male and female symbolism are what also enables the *sarvatobhadra maṇḍala* to be used universally for the worship of gods or goddesses, or supreme transgendered forms of divinity.

In the ritual worship of this *maṇḍala* on Mahāṣṭamī, the *purohita* invokes various deities into particular parts of the *maṇḍala* and worships them there. He invokes Durgā's eight fierce energy manifestations (*śakti*), the sixty-four *yoginīs*, and a host of other goddesses. After an interlude to worship the Devī's weapons and ornaments, he invokes an assortment of other deities, including fierce boy forms of Śiva and the Great God himself. Only after all these deities have been invoked and worshipped, the *purohita* worships the Great Goddess as the entire sacred diagram. By implication, the Devī is supreme among these lesser attendant deities.

An alternate meaning is that the subsidiary deities are merely aspects of the Great Goddess herself. The latter notion is found in the *Durgā Saptaśatī,* in a very well-known myth of the Devī in one of her demon-slaying exploits (DSS 10.1–5). While accompanied by a large entourage of goddesses who aid her in battle, Śumbha, her demon enemy, accuses the Goddess of not fighting him alone. She replies that all the various *devīs* who are assisting her are actually her own manifestations, and to prove it she draws them back into herself. Many of the deities, such as the Mothers (*mātṛ*), which are placed and worshipped in the *sarvatobhadra maṇḍala*, are the very goddesses referred to in the influential mythic account found in the *Durgā Saptaśatī*. This mythic parallel supports the interpretation that although the deities worshipped in the *sarvatobhadra maṇḍala* appear to be different and numerous, they are actually all manifestations of the Great Goddess herself.[9]

Maṇḍalas represent spheres of power, and the *sarvatobhadra maṇḍala* in the Durgā Pūjā represents the expansive, benevolent influence of the Goddess. From the seed of her cosmic body (represented by the *ghaṭa*, which may be installed at the center of the *maṇḍala* when the Durgā Pūjā begins) the Devī germinates and sprouts (represented by the *bilva vṛkṣa* and *navapatrikā*) and then takes up her abode in the gynomorphic living earthen image (*mūrti*). From here, symbolized by the flowering of the *maṇḍala*'s lotus petals and its checkerboard matrix, Durgā expands to the farthest recesses of the cosmos.[10] The *yoginīs*, the Mothers, and every feminine conception of deity are her weapons (*āyudha*), her powers (*śakti*), while the male deities are her ornaments (*bhūṣaṇa*). Her presence is no longer localized but has grown all-pervasive.

Imagining the countless number of abodes throughout the world, where this rite is being enacted during the Sandhi Pūjā's exacting forty-eight-minute juncture of time, produces a startling vision. Evoking the imagery of the "jewelled net of Indra," in which each jewel at each interstice of the net reflects every other jewel, each with its infinitude of reflections, each of the myriad places of Goddess worship becomes a center of an all-inclusive *yantra* superimposed upon the entire cosmos and intersecting with every other center of Durgā worship. The Great Goddess has awakened, not just in a particular locale, but within the entire matrix of her cosmic manifestation.

The progression of gynomorphic forms of the Devī, together with her associated worship in abstract, yantric forms during the Durgā Pūjā, has an uncanny similarity to the development of Lajjā Gaurī icons in India. The goddess Lajjā Gaurī is often depicted as a supine nude female in the position of sexual readiness or childbirth. In her study of Lajjā Gaurī, Carol Radcliffe Bolon (1997:6) notes that the goddess is "the elemental source of all life, animal and plant, . . . and is the source of Fortune. She personifies the sap of life . . . the vivifying element embodied in water, the support of all life." Bolon also argues that the anthropomorphic forms of Lajjā Gaurī images, with legs characteristically bent and spread, and with heads of vegetative material, were elaborations upon certain aniconic forms, such as the brimming jar (*purna kumbha*) and the symbol of auspiciousness (*śrīvatsa*). Lajjā Gaurī, like the jar form of the Devī, is often referred to as Aditi, the Vedic goddess who is the mother of the gods. Lajjā Gaurī images ceased to be produced after the eleventh century, since the goddess symbolically evolved from the jar/pot to a fully anthropomorphic form and was progressively incorporated into the brāhmaṇic pantheon. As this process of Sanskritization occurred, Lajjā Gaurī soon became associated with the lion and with the male deities, Brahmā, Śiva, and Viṣṇu. Eventually, her symbolic function got replaced by abstract Tantric symbolism.

It is intriguing that in the Durgā Pūjā, one encounters examples of the ongoing worship of the Devī in almost all the iconic forms mentioned by Bolon. Durgā is worshipped on the earthen altar in a jar form marked with the *śrīvatsa* or *svāstika*. She is hailed as emanating from Viṣṇu's breast, the place of the *śrīvatsa*. As the *pūjā* progresses, she is worshipped as a tree, a cluster of plants, and a fully anthropomorphic image. She is also worshipped in Tantric symbols such as the *sarvatobhadra maṇḍala*. Since the Durgā Pūjā is clearly an amalgam of worship rituals, it conceivably incorporates the symbolic forms and the worship rites of such Sanskritized goddesses as Lajjā Gaurī. It further suggests that the evolution of iconographic images differed from ritual developments. While older iconic forms of *devī*s such as Lajjā Gaurī were supplanted by newer ones, and to such an extent that certain older images disappeared entirely, the rituals of Great Goddess worship did not discard their ancient features, but continued to add to these over time.

The Devī as Elemental Substances

While he is engaged in bringing the Devī into manifest forms that are accessible to worshippers, the *purohita* works within the framework of a Goddess-based (Śākta) metaphysics. The ritual acts and litany explicitly or suggestively identify the Devī with a number of fundamental constituent elements of the created cosmos. These offer yet another pattern of her manifest forms within the *pūjā*. In many Hindu cosmological schemes, the creation is said to be composed of five gross constituent elements (*mahābhūta*). They are earth, water, fire, air, and space/ether. The Devī in the Durgā Pūjā is quite clearly identified with most of these cosmic building blocks.

Earth

The Devī is identified with the earth element and with the planet Earth itself. At the very outset of the *pūjā*, the *purohita* begins with the construction of the earthen altar, which he identifies with the Goddess. The jar form of the Devī is generally constructed of earth (or metal, also an earth element). Earth and stone are also used in the *adhivāsa* ritual. Similarly, the central image complex in the *pūjā* is constructed of unbaked clay, which quickly dissolves when returned to the waters at the end of the *pūjā*. These earthen forms elicit certain interpretations. The Devī is always present in the earth element. Gathered at the commencement of the ritual, earth is used to fashion many of the images into which she is established, awakened, or invoked. Like the Earth, the Devī supports all life, bringing into being myriad life-forms that endure but temporarily, only to return to their source, the Earth/Goddess.

Water

The Gaṅgā is renowned as a sacred river. It is the source of life for millions who live along its banks and is considered to be a living goddess (Eck 1982b). Water is often sanctified through the utterance of sacred verses, many of which allude to the divine Gaṅgā, or by the actual addition of a small amount of Gaṅgā water. The *purohita* begins the Durgā Pūjā by purifying himself, the ritual equipment, the offering materials, and the site with such water. He fills the jar, which embodies the Goddess, with pure, sanctified water. Water is used throughout the ritual as an agent of purification and sanctification.

The most dramatic ritual use of water in the Durgā Pūjā occurs in the *snāna* rites in which both the *navapatrikā* and the Devī's clay image are bathed in an impressive assortment of waters. Although flowing water is the symbol *par excellence* of purification in Hindu religious practice and plays a significant role in the cleansing of the votary's faculties, purification is not the sole intent of the bathing rite.[11] If it were, salvific waters from the Gaṅgā or some single sacred source would be adequate. The vast array of waters used in the rite is clearly intended to symbolize every imaginable type of water, spanning every part of the Devī's earthly domain, which includes rivers, mountain waterfalls, and so on. By bathing the Goddess in these waters, regarded as auspicious, the *purohita* parallels consecration rituals routinely used for royalty. The assortment also reveals the Devī's manifest presence in all fathomable forms of water.

The final use of water occurs during the ritual of dismissal, at the end of the Durgā Pūjā, after the Goddess has been duly worshipped. The sacred waters of the Gaṅgā, into which the image complex is immersed, are thought to carry the Devī back to her heavenly abode in the mountains, where the goddess Pārvatī dwells with Śiva, or into the upper atmosphere, the celestial origin of the Gaṅgā. The act of immersion dissolves the manifest clay image of the Devī back into the undifferentiated silt of the Gaṅgā from which it originated.

Fire

A flame is one of the most commonly encountered items used in Hindu worship. It is so central to all *pūjā*s that Hindus often time their visit to a temple to coincide with *ārati*, the flame worship of a deity performed by the temple priest. Naturally, in the course of the Durgā Pūjā, the various major forms of the Goddess, such as the *navapatrikā*, the clay image, and the virgin girl are worshipped with an honorific flame. Even the jar form of the Goddess may have a flame lit before it. This flame may be kept continuously burning through the entire duration of the *pūjā*. The most sublime *ārati* is performed during the Sandhi Pūjā, in the offering of the 108 lamps. "We offer 108 lamps, because Durgā has 108 forms," one votary explained, forging a conceptual bridge between the Devī and the flame offerings.

A more explicit identification of fire with the Goddess, however, occurs on Navamī, when the central ritual is the fire oblation, or *homa*.[12] The *purohita* draws a Goddess *yantra* in the layer of sand at the bottom of the fire pit (*sthaṇḍila*), which is itself thus an instrument (*yantra*) and manifestation of the Devī, and proceeds to build the fire upon this symbol. Just before igniting the flame in the pit, the *purohita* utters a verse of meditative visualization (*dhyāna śloka*) of the goddess of speech, Vāgiśvarī. In it he imagines the goddess, who has just completed her postmenstruation purificatory bath (*ṛtusnātām*), entering into playful union with the god of speech. He kindles the tinder after uttering homage to the god of speech united with the goddess of speech. Thus fire is conceived of as the union or sexual dalliance of god and goddess.[13] The goddess of speech, Vāc, is generally identified with Sarasvatī, who is also present in the clay image array.[14] Sarasvatī is an attendant or aspect of the Great Goddess herself. It is also worth noting that in the earliest text to mention Durgā, the *Taittirīya Āraṇyaka* 10.1, she is identified with the fire of asceticism (*tapas*) and thus an aid to devotees who undergo the ordeal of asceticism. There, too, she is invoked as the wife or daughter of Agni, the god of fire.[15]

Space

In Hindu metaphysics space (*ākāśa*) is generally regarded as the substratum of sound (*śabda*), since sound fills space with its creative vibrations. It would be difficult to overestimate the importance of sound in the Durgā Pūjā.[16] The *purohita* chants prayers and sacred utterances (*mantra*) to accompany his ritual acts almost constantly throughout the procedure. He utters meditative visualization verses (*dhyāna śloka*) before every ritual act of worship. This is because he first brings the Devī into manifestation in his mind, where he renders her mental devotional service (*mānasa upacāra*). He then proceeds to transfer her to various abodes, such as the *navapatrikā* or the clay image complex, where he worships her with actual materials. Bells, symbols of creative sound, are rung at key points in the ritual, such as during the flame worship. The Goddess herself is often portrayed as adorned with, or carrying a bell.[17] Female devotees may utter a high-pitched, blood-curdling call, known as the *ululu*, during the flame worship. These further testify to the connection between sound and the Devī.

A very important procedure that precedes every meditative visualization is ritual imprintment or *nyāsa*. Through a long series of *nyāsa*s, the *purohita* imprints the consonants, vowels, and certain seed syllables of the Sanskrit language onto his body. By so doing, he transforms his body into a vibrational body of sound. This vibrational body becomes an abode of the Devī and will serve as the aperture through which the Goddess will manifest in other forms (e.g., the conch shell and the clay image complex) during the ritual. The *purohita* embodies the Goddess, and his vibrational body of sound is identified with the Goddess. Sound is both the symbol and a gross form of the subtle vibrations through which creation manifests.[18] The goddess Sarasvatī testifies to the close symbolic relationship between sound and creation. Sarasvatī, the goddess of creation, is identified with Vāc, the goddess of speech or sound.

Air

Of the five gross elements, air is the one for which there is no explicit substantial identification with the Goddess. Air does convey scent, and every item in the standard five-part *pūjā* is strongly associated with scent. Fragrant sandalwood paste, fresh flowers, incense, burning camphor, and the aroma of food are all indicative of the air element. However, in classical Hindu metaphysics, the air element is associated with the sense of touch, not scent, which is associated with the earth element. If we associate the air element with the sense of touch, we find ample examples in the plethora of anointings and bathings, where the sense of touch is engaged in the worship of the Devī. Even so, these acts do not forge an explicit connection between the air element and the Devī. However, the lack of obvious affinities between all the five gross elements, their corresponding senses, and the Goddess, does not imply that the scheme is capricious. The *Śaktisaṅgama-tantra* 4.2.89–91, for instance, links the ten Mahāvidyās with the five senses and elements, while the *Śrī Durgā Kalpataru* 41–42, a popular compendium of lore on the Great Goddess, forges such a connection with the cluster of goddesses known as the Nine Durgās.[19] Furthermore, the air element (*vāyri*) is intimately connected with the life-force or life-breath (one of which is *prāṇa*), and the Devī is intrinsically identified with numerous life-forms.

The Devī as Life Forms

It is crucial to remember that the creation in Hindu thought is imbued with life. The Great Goddess is not an embodiment of a lifeless universe, but is the source and essence of its vitality. It is she who animates the cosmos and energizes it with her presence. In the Durgā Pūjā, as Cosmic Mother, the Goddess is therefore awakened, invoked, and worshipped in a variety of living forms.

Flowers, Fruit, and Plants

The Devī is identified both explicitly and implicitly with flowers, fruit, and plants in the course of the Durgā Pūjā. She, in turn, is worshipped with these very materials. We have already noted the array of vegetative materials present in the installation of the jar form of the Goddess, where leaf-bearing twigs line the mouth of the jar, which is then topped with a coconut fruit. The earthen altar upon which the jar sits is seeded with grain, obvious symbols of fertility. The seeds sprout through the course of the ritual and may then be examined to prophesy the results of the upcoming planting season. The jar, when fully established, resembles a pregnant woman, a gynomorphic symbol of fecundity and life.

The plant symbolism of the Devī is also apparent in her manifestation as the wood-apple tree and in the *navapatrikā*. The wood-apple branch should possess two fruit, which serve as her nurturing breasts in the *navapatrikā*. Flower and fruit offerings are made to Durgā throughout the *pūjā*. A fruit, such as a melon, may be used as a substitute for the blood sacrifice performed during the Sandhi Pūjā. During the fire oblation ritual, wood-apple leaves are offered into the sacred fire. The *puṣpāñjali* is an important part of the Durgā Pūjā for devotees. It means "offerings with flowers," and it allows devotees the opportunity to recite a few prayers and make flower offerings to the Devī. On Vijayā Daśamī, the Goddess is worshipped as the embodiment of Victory (Vijayā) in the actual form of an Aparājitā flower or creeper.[20]

The aforementioned plant forms of the Devī are explicit symbols of life, as are her gynomorphic forms as the jar, the clay image, and the virgin girl. However, the Devī is also present in other life forms, which are not always obvious to all votaries. These forms include the person of the *purohita*, the animal sacrifice, and other states of womanhood.

The *Purohita*

The *purohita* is not normally perceived by devotees as a form of the Devī, but he is indeed a frequent locus for her manifestation in the course of the Durgā Pūjā. In order to invoke the Goddess into various forms, the *purohita* regularly performs the *bhūta śuddhi* ritual of purification, which involves the awakening of dormant psychic energy. This energy, which is known as the goddess Kuṇḍalinī, is visualized as rising through his body, dissolving its material elements into each other until they reach a state of undifferentiated integrity and purity. Using the appropriate rituals of imprintment (*nyāsa*), the *purohita* then charges this purified body with the vibrational components of creation, such as the seed syllables (*bīja mantra*) of the Goddess. His body, a matrix of creative vibration, thus becomes an abode of the goddess of creation. It has also become the portal through which the Goddess will manifest in the locations where he chooses to invoke her. As the vibratory manifestation of the goddess of creation (and speech), the *purohita* utilizes the vibratory sounds of the meditative verse to enable the Goddess Durgā to manifest first within himself and then transfers her to the new abodes.

The *purohita*, therefore, serves a vitally important function in the Durgā Pūjā. It is through his ritual manipulations that the Devī is embodied in forms that facilitate his patron's worship of the Goddess. However, he also performs another crucial function in the course of the ritual, namely, the regeneration of the body of the Goddess herself. This dimension may be examined through the symbolism of the sacrificial animal.

The Sacrificial Animal

Although the blood sacrifice is disappearing in practice in many Durgā Pūjā celebrations in India, it symbolically commands an important place in the ritual. Together with the worship of the Goddess in the form of a living virgin girl, and the 108-lamp offering, the blood sacrifice is one of the main rituals prescribed for Sandhi, the climax of the Durgā Pūjā. Even a surrogate offering, such as a melon, is inscribed with an effigy and smeared with vermilion paste, in clear testimony that it actually represents a blood sacrifice. Virtually all votaries with whom I conversed pointed out that the animal sacrifice is itself a symbolic surrogate. However there were varieties of interpretations on the symbolic meaning of the blood-bearing animal.

For instance, many responded that the sacrificial animal represented the buffalo demon Mahiṣa, slain in the Devī's most renowned martial exploit. Others went on to provide interpretations of the symbolic meaning of the demon, who is also depicted in the clay image complex. Even if a blood sacrifice is not actually offered, the most visually arresting image that seizes and holds the eye throughout the Durgā Pūjā is the graphically sanguine portrayal of the Devī beheading the buffalo demon. Thus, even in the home of the Lahiris, who claim to have never included either an animal or a surrogate sacrifice in their *pūjā*, family members were obliged to confront the Devī's bloody destruction of the demon.[21] In response to my queries, Mr. Lahiri responded, "Mahiṣa? Pure evil. Evil is that which performs evil deeds. The demon is also part of god. The demon knows when to attack. Our interpretation is to worship Durgā, to remove our difficulties."[22] Mrs. Lahiri's response was typical of responses by many others. "The demon represents the evil forces within us."[23] The sacrificial animal may thus represent the demon Mahiṣa, who in turn, may represent brutish, ignorant, arrogant, or other negative qualities within devotees themselves.[24]

It is also true that the blood sacrifice represents the ultimate food offering made to the Goddess. In rituals as complex as the Durgā Pūjā, where the devotional service is greatly expanded and offerings quite embellished, the ritual logic would dictate that the food offerings should be as elaborate as the devotees can possibly afford. The *Kālikā Purāṇa* states that "men and blood drawn from the offerer's own body, are looked upon as proper oblations to the goddess Chaṇḍikā."[25] What, however, is the ultimate food offering that can be made to the Goddess? Clearly, the most expensive and most elaborately prepared dishes should be offered, and these are indeed part of the ritual. The paramount offering is not the most succulent fruit, or even the head of the finest animal, but the devotee's own head. This is the most sublime "fruit" that can be presented to the Goddess, since there is no higher food offering the devotee may make.[26] It is the loftiest gift, representing the preeminent act of sacrifice. Of course, references to such acts of actual self-sacrifice are rare.[27] Devotees often do not deem themselves pure enough to be worthy of self-sacrifice. The sacrifice of a fine animal, a buffalo, or a goat, is thus often a symbolic substitute for themselves. In many instances, devotees may offer an animal sacrifice in fulfilment of a promise to the Goddess to spare their own lives in a difficult undertaking. On other occasions, the animal may represent the devotee's enemy symbolically offered to the Devī to enlist her help against this adversary. The *Kālikā Purāṇa*, for instance, notes, "A prince may sacrifice his enemy, having first invoked the axe by holy texts, by substituting a buffalo or goat, calling the victim by the name of the enemy, throughout the whole ceremony, . . . infusing by holy texts the soul of the enemy into the body of the victim, which will, when immolated, deprive the foe of his life also" (cited in Payne 1997 [1933]:10). In all of these cases the animal sacrifice is a symbol of life, especially human life.

An unusual interpretation evoked by the animal sacrifice is that it is a symbol of the Devī herself. No votary offered such an explanation, for it may certainly appear counterintuitive to suppose that the animal being beheaded is the beautiful and regal Goddess who is the object of adoration. Nevertheless, this interpretive line should not be automatically nullified, for such a symbolic identification is implicitly suggested by the rite. When we examine the constituent substances in which the Devī manifests herself through the Durgā Pūjā ritual, such as earth, water, fire, sound, vegetation, and human life, we note that these are the very materials with which she is worshipped. We are also compelled to recognize that the Goddess is present in such a plethora of forms that this very profusion evokes the variety and fullness of the created world. The constituent substances of the cosmos are identified with the Goddess, and these same materials are used to shape her many images. The Great Goddess is therefore not just the jar, but the earthen clay from which all jars are shaped. She is not just the wood-apple tree, but the seed, sap, leaves, and fruit of all vegetation. She is not merely the virgin girl, but the pure, potential mother of all life. The *sarvatobhadra maṇḍala* is a symbolic diagram of the entire manifest cosmos, full of various forms, human and divine, and it is with this that the Great Goddess is fundamentally identified.

Not only is the Goddess identified with the manifest cosmos and all its forms, but she is worshipped with the very constituents of the creation. Manifest in earth, the Goddess is worshipped with earth through the construction of the earthen altar, her earthen jar body and her clay image. Manifest in water, she is worshipped with water in her jar body and in her great bath. Manifest in space and sound, she is worshipped with the sounds of bell-ringing and utterances of adoration (*praṇāma*). Manifest in vegetation, she is worshipped with flowers (*puṣpa*) and fruit (*phala*). Manifest in animal and human life, she is worshipped with the sacrificial offering of life. Animal and human life are thus manifestations of the Devī's own body and therefore through the blood sacrifice, the Great Goddess is worshipped with her own flesh and blood. The *Kālikā Purāṇa* supports this interpretation when it claims, "Let the sacrificer worship the victim. . . . When this is done, O my children! The victim is even as myself, . . . then Brahmā and all the other deities assemble in the victim, . . . and he gains the love of Mahādevī, . . . who is the goddess of the whole universe, the very universe itself" (cited in Payne 1997 [1933]:10).

The symbolic identification of the Devī with a dismembered sacrifice is found in such well-known myth cycles as the death of the goddess Satī. Satī, identified with Pārvatī, and thus Durgā, threw herself on the flames of her father Dakṣa Prajāpatī's *yajña*. Her corpse, carried by her mourning spouse Śiva, was then systematically dismembered. Her body parts fell to the Earth, whose physical geography becomes symbolically identified with the body of the Goddess.

In other striking icons, such as that of the goddess Chinnamastā, the *devī* is shown decapitating her own head. Streams of blood flow from her severed neck into the mouths of her female attendants, as well as into the mouth of her own severed head. The goddess sits atop the copulating forms of Kāma and Ratī, suggesting a connection between sexuality, blood, self-sacrifice, and nourishment of oneself and others. Chinnamastā, often connected with the group of ten goddesses known as the Mahāvidyās, is indeed connected to Durgā. The Mahāvidyās are frequently portrayed on the semicircular painted *cāl citra* that graces the top of the Bengali Durgā Pūjā clay image complex. Votaries cannot help but see this arresting goddess image during the ritual. Chinnamastā is not merely one of the many deities in attendance. Although all goddesses are regarded as aspects or manifestations of the Great Goddess, Durgā is explicitly identified with the Mahāvidyās in such devotional hymns as the *Durgā Cālisā (Forty [Verses] to Durgā)*. Oral tradition has the Mahāvidyās emanate from Durgā in her mythic battle with the demons Śumbha and Niśumbha, recounted in the *Durgā Saptaśatī*, and other Purāṇas, although no such explicit reference to the Mahāvidyās is found in the texts themselves.[28] Durgā is, however, frequently depicted surrounded by the Mahāvidyās in popular lithographs. The only Chinnamastā temple in Banāras, to my knowledge, is found on the precincts of the Durgā temple at Ramnagar. It forges yet another connection between the self-decapitating form of the Devī, whose flowing blood nourishes herself and her votaries, and the Great Goddess.

My excursus into this line of interpretation was not to exaggerate the symbolic identification of the sacrificial animal with the Devī, but to direct attention to the symbolism of the flow of blood, which is particularly significant when examining the Devī's embodiment as living human females.

WOMEN

During the Durgā Pūjā, the premenarche virgin is explicitly identified with the Goddess during the ritual of virgin worship (*kumārī pūjā*). However, other stages of womanhood are also conferred a special status through direct or indirect identification with the Devī. Married women, for instance, who often return to their parents' home for the celebrations, are identified with the Goddess (see Figure 6.2). This is done through a cycle of myths that tell of the goddess Pārvatī's return to her parents' home in the Himālayas.[29] Himavat and Menā are thrilled at their daughter's visit. They feed her and treat her well, knowing that she has to endure many hardships as the wife of the ascetic god Śiva. In a similar manner, married women are treated distinctively during the Durgā Pūjā. Durgā is frequently addressed as "Mā," since she is most often regarded as a protective and nurturing cosmic mother. This maternal identification is reinforced in the clay image complex, where the companion deities, Gaṇeśa and Kārtikeya, and to a lesser extent, Lakṣmī and Sarasvatī, are regarded by votaries as her children. The Durgā Pūjā thus elevates both the premenarche virgin girl and the mother.

Having read much about the inferior status of widows in the Hindu tradition, I was curious about their role in the Durgā Pūjā. Pandit Chakravarty commented that due to the loss of their husbands, widows are only regarded as inauspicious and restricted from being present at wedding ceremonies. Indeed, after Mr. Lahiri's death, Anjali Lahiri has continued to conduct the Durgā Pūjā in the family home in Banāras. When asked about what role she played in the *pūjā*, now that she was a widow, she replied, "after the death of a husband, the son becomes the *yajman*, but in my case I have no son, so I am the *yajman*."[30] Due to Mrs. Lahiri's age, she is less active in actual food preparations and no longer carries the *bhog* from the third-floor kitchen to the *pūjālaya* on the ground floor. However, other women, mostly specially initiated widows, assist in the cooking, and in fact, have always been significantly active in food preparations during the Durgā Pūjā.

Anjana Moitra, the eldest of the Mr. Lahiri's married daughters, helped to clarify matters concerning restrictions on women during food preparations.[31] She explained,

- Girls who are younger than twelve can go everywhere, and they can touch the food. They can participate in cutting the vegetables for the uncooked

Figure 6.2. The strong presence of the family's women, reunited in the patron's home during the Durgā Pūjā, is most evident when they gather to worship the Goddess.

naivedya offerings, but since they have not taken the *mantra* from a guru, they cannot touch the food used for *bhog*.

- Girls older than twelve, but who are unmarried, cannot cook or touch any of the food.
- Married women can touch and prepare the uncooked food, but cannot prepare the cooked food for Durgā unless they have taken the *mantra*. I can cook the *bhog* for Sarasvatī Pūjā, and we can give Nārāyaṇa and Gopala *bhog*.
- Our Durgā Pūjā is Tantric.

Her son interrupts: No, it is Vedic.

Anjana continues: There is a *yantra* in the middle and *bel* leaves are offered. These are Tantric.

- Widows cannot touch any of the food.
- A woman after menopause can touch the food, but for Durgā and Kālī Pūjā only women with the *mantra* can prepare the *bhog*.

Anjana's son's interjection (based on his father's influence) in this excerpt highlights differences between the Lahiris and the Moitras in perspectives about the nature of the *pūjā* (Tantric vs. Vedic). Anjana felt that the Tantric nature of the Durgā Pūjā was a positive feature, while her son seemed uncomfortable with that designation, preferring to view the *pūjā* as Vedic. However, Anjana was also pointing to the distinctive nature of the Durgā and Kālī *pūjā*s, whose food preparations require a Śākta Tantric initiation. Her other comments are even more germane to the current discussion. Food, the preparation of which is an important occupation and traditional role of women in the household, is not simply an important celebratory dimension of the *pūjā*. Food offerings, in which cooked ranks higher than uncooked food, appears to stand as a symbolic parallel of womanhood. There is an unmistakable parallel between premenarche girls (*kumārī*) and uncooked foods. Uncooked food (fruit, nuts, leaves) is often regarded as very pure, the nourishment of renouncers and forest-dwelling ascetics. Indeed, one of the characteristics of renunciation (*saṃnyāsa*) is the relinquishment of the cooking fire. Like uncooked *naivedya* offerings, these *kumārī*s have not yet undergone the sort of major transformation that is induced in food by the application of the cooking fire. Cooking transforms certain inedible foods (e.g., rice) into flavorful and nutritious substance. Marriage (and by implication, motherhood) thus parallels the cooking fire, transforming daughter into mother, a woman capable of producing and nourishing life. Just as heat ripens fruit, so too does the virgin girl ripen into a woman.

Charting the relationship between females and the preparation of food offerings, we have:

Premenarche girls (i.e., *kumārī*)	• May prepare Uncooked Food offerings to Durgā and Kālī. • Although pure, they are uninitiated. • May not prepare the Cooked Food (*bhog*) offerings.
Postmenarche, unmarried girls/ women	• May **not** touch or prepare any food offerings.
Married women	• May prepare Uncooked Food offerings to Durgā and Kālī. • May prepare Cooked Food offerings to other deities.
Widows	• May **not** touch or prepare any food offerings.

Postmenopausal women	• May prepare Uncooked Food offerings to Durgā and Kālī. • May prepare Cooked Food offerings to other deities.
Initiated women (married or widowed)	• May prepare Cooked Food offerings to Durgā and Kālī.

The table unequivocally reveals that postmenarche women without husbands are restricted from all food preparations. Girls prior to the onset of their menstrual cycle, married women, and postmenopausal women enjoy a much higher status than pubescent girls, unmarried women, and widows. Premenarche girls may handle and prepare the uncooked food offerings, but only married women may prepare cooked offerings. Higher on the hierarchy of purity are postmenopausal women, who are no longer associated with reproductive blood flow. No woman during her menstrual period may cook or even handle cooked food that is to be offered to deities.[32] Higher still in status are women (married or widowed) who have received the appropriate initiation (*dīkṣā*). The highest status belongs to postmenopausal initiated women, since they are never subject to the periodic impurity brought about by menstruation, and it is precisely these who are generally commissioned to prepare the cooked food offerings for the Goddess. Thus, although they may not be explicitly identified with the Goddess, these women too enjoy an elevated status during the *pūjā*.

In response to my inquiries, Śomak Moitra, one of Mrs. Lahiri's grandchildren informed me that his grandmother (*didima*) was the only female family member who has taken the Tantric initiation, which enables her to prepare the cooked food offerings.[33] The procedure is not elaborate, I was informed, consisting primarily of receiving a special *mantra* (personal and secret) from particular *brāhmaṇa*s in such religious establishments as the Bhārat Sevāśram Saṅgha or the Rāmakṛṣṇa Mission, where Mrs. Lahiri received hers. However, only certain teachers (*guru*) there, referred to as initiation (*dīkṣā*) *guru*s, are entitled to impart it. There are only three or four such holy men (*sadhu*) at the Rāmakṛṣṇa Mission in Banāras. Initiation may also, at times, be imparted by a family's religious mentor, as well as from one's own family members to another. Quite importantly, initiation is not imparted upon request, but is based on the *guru*'s appraisal of the aptitude of the disciple. This information supports Brooks's (1990:71) observation that "perhaps Tantrism's most distinctive feature . . . is initiation (*dīkṣā*) in which the established criteria of caste and gender are not the primary tests of qualification (*adhikāra*) for *sādhana*." Such Tantric initiation is the mark of persons who are elect, selected on account of their special propensities for restricted spiritual practices, the performance of which opens them to progressively more intimate relationships with the Divine. The utterance of the very same *mantra*s and the performance of such ritual acts as constructing *maṇḍala*s, by the uninitiated, are regarded as totally ineffective.

CHAPTER 7

Functions of the Durgā Pūjā

Although there are numerous functions (e.g., social, psychological, economic, and political) of the Durgā Pūjā, my discussion of these has been necessarily limited. I do concur with Ákos Östör (1980) and Paul Courtright (1985b) who argue that *pūjā* is a distinct symbolic unit that may be analyzed on its own terms, and I have thus focused on interpreting the function of the Durgā Pūjā as *pūjā*. Furthermore, explanations of *pūjā* merely as activities that function to consolidate social relationships and power structures ignore important religious and symbolic realities and the "elaborate and ingenious worlds of meaning" (Courtright 1985b:34), which are revealed in the ritual performance. However, my emphasis in the previous sections on the interpretation of "meaning" was more a matter of choice and expediency than an oversight concerning the *pūjā*'s many other functions. My use of the term "function" refers to ways in which the ritual affects individuals and groups. These effects, to the extent that they are comprehended, are subject to being used and manipulated by participants to suit their own needs and ends. However, I am not glibly suggesting that these functions unequivocally reveal *the* rationales behind the origin of the Durgā Pūjā.

Cosmic Rejuvenation

Despite the Devī's vast variety of images and appellations discussed in the previous chapter, my examination has not been exhaustive. In the Durgā Pūjā the Great Goddess is also worshipped in many other forms, such as in weapons and ornaments, in gestures, and even in the debris of ritual offerings. However, the Durgā Pūjā is not only a procedure for the adoration of the Great Goddess through her many epithets and images, but a dynamic process of progressive manifestation of the Divine. The Devī's latent presence in living things and in the home is awakened and invoked into a succession of forms that symbolize and embody the full and fecund orb (*maṇḍala*) of creation.[1] Through the ritual art of the *purohita*, who serves as a human conduit, the Devī is encouraged to manifest in a variety of forms that are conceptually and physically accessible to her devotees. Instead of the amorphous earth, or the diffuse energy of life, the Devī manifests in particular gynomorphic images in the very home of her devotees. She is thus made visible and approachable. From the scarf-shrouded clay jar and the *sārī*-clad *navapatrikā*, to the richly ornamented clay image, and finally to the living virgin girl, the Devī's manifest form progresses from crude gynomorphic shapes to an actual human female. This progression is also an inversion of the maturation sequence of a human female, for the Goddess moves in embodiments from an Earth Mother, to a fertile female (*navapatrikā* and clay image), and finally to a premenarche virgin girl. The sprouting seeds of the earthen altar and the budding virgin girl are symbols of the fresh and fertile potential of this reanimated creation. Through the systematic gathering and shaping of earth, water, and living constituent elements into bodily forms of the Devī and the ritual use of these very same materials in the veneration of these forms, the body cosmos of the dormant Goddess is transformed into the vital and regenerated cosmic body of the awakened Great Goddess. Any of these images allow worshippers the opportunity to see her, venerate her, thank her, entreat her for favors, and even experience her presence within themselves.

The yantric forms of the Devī reveal another dynamic besides accessible manifestation. This is the expansive manifestation of the Goddess, further evoked through the wide array of the Devī's other embodiments during the *pūjā*. There are constituent earths, waters, plants, lesser gods and goddesses, the *purohita*, and women who are worshipped as aspects or manifestations of the Devī. Many of these myriad forms are encapsulated in the symbolism of the *sarvatobhadra maṇḍala*, a diagrammatic representation of the all-encompassing cosmic body of the Goddess and an instrument for her worship. The *maṇḍala* process awakens the Great Goddess into nothing less than the entire creation, purified, ritually reconstructed, and renewed. Thus the Durgā Pūjā is a ritual of renewal and regeneration of the cosmos, of nature, materiality, and life.

Empowerment: Personal, Sovereign, Communal, Political, Economic

The most obvious function of the Durgā Pūjā is to venerate a deity who is quite centrally associated with empowerment. The dominant imagery in the Durgā Pūjā, its clay image cluster, derives from myths recounted in the *Durgā Saptaśatī*, and verses from this text are also utilized in the rite's litany. Coburn (1984:116) cites instances where the *Durgā Saptaśatī* explains who

Durgā is. She is "a vessel upon the ocean of life (that is so) hard to cross" (DSS 4.10), or she is praised as "the inaccessible further shore" (DSS 5.10). The text also states, "O Durgā, (when) called to mind (by the faithful), you take away fear (or danger) from every creature" (DSS 4.16). And elsewhere it explains, "Protect us from terrors, O Goddess; O Goddess Durgā, let there be praise to you" (DSS 11.23). On the basis of these citations, Coburn concludes that from the text's perspective, "Durgā is thus the great protectress from worldly adversity (*durga*), and is at the same time herself inassailable and hard-to-approach (*durgā*)." For this reason, I opt to translate Durgā as "She who is Formidable." The English word "formidable" well captures the diverse nature of the obstacles, ordeals, and dangers faced by votaries, and which the Goddess's power can overcome. It simultaneously evokes the Devī's unassailable, inaccessible, and mysteriously impenetrable nature, as well as her persona as a dreadfully potent warrior. The worship of Durgā offers votaries an opportunity to ally themselves personally with a power more formidable than any adversity they are likely to encounter.

Among the ritual's many functions one also notes the martial aspect of the Durgā Pūjā. This dimension is dramatically evoked by the form assumed by the Devī in the clay image complex. There, as Mahiṣāsuramardinī, Durgā is depicted slaying the buffalo demon, Mahiṣa. What does this bloody victory symbolize? In response to such questioning, many devotees merely cited that the imagery depicted Mahiṣa's destruction at the hands of the Devī, an "actual" event which is described in the *Durgā Saptaśatī*. However, for others, the demon was regarded as symbolic of all sorts of enemies. Some explained that Mahiṣa represented the internal enemy of their spiritually undesirable states, such as egotism and pride.[2] By propitiating the Devī through the Durgā Pūjā a devotee might acquire a boon of power (*śakti*) to overcome spiritual defilements. Mr. Lahiri explained, "In our mind all deities are the same, worshipped with the same devotion. . . . Durgā was built with the power to destroy demons. Durgā is Power. Pure Power."[3] Resonating with interpretations of Mahiṣa as a hero, one of the grandchildren explained, "Mahiṣāsura is a great personality. I like him a lot. He knows he will be defeated by Durgā, but still he stands up and allows himself to be killed."[4] Other siblings disagreed, saying, "No, he is terrible; he is a Hitler." All agreed that "it reminds us of the sure triumph of good over evil."[5] For other worshippers, the battle signifies strife in social arenas. The demon symbolizes adversaries at work, in rival religions, and even political opponents.[6]

Since Bengal is an Indian state in which Marxist political ideas are prominent, in my study of the Bengali style of Durgā Pūjā I naturally encountered interpretations framed in the language of Marxist political philosophy. Social progress, I was told, can only occur through a tension between opposing forces. It was only through the struggle between such dialectical forces that a new synthesis could emerge. Without this struggle, society would stagnate. Wealth would remain in the hands of the rich, and the poor would suffer. There would be no change in the status quo. Mahiṣa and the Devī represent the timeless cosmic duel through which creation occurs. Prior to hearing this, the majority of opinions that I had heard had led me unconsciously to associate the Devī/demon conflict as symbolizing the struggle to maintain upper-class social purity against the impurity resulting from mixed marriages with the lower classes, or as the tension of Hindu religious and cultural values against Islamic or other antithetical doctrines. However, in the Marxist interpretation the Devī represents the economically and socially disenfranchised. Mahiṣa is a symbol of the arrogance of corrupt power and ill-gotten wealth. This interpretation adds an important dimension towards understanding the appeal that conceptions of Durgā hold for subaltern classes and their vision of empowerment by the Goddess.

Sovereignty was clearly the central purport of the Navarātra celebrations for the rulers of the last great Hindu empire, which flourished from the fourteenth to seventeenth centuries at Vijayanagara in south India.[7] Mahānavamī was their term for the Navarātra, and during this time the emperor identified himself not only with the Goddess, but with the god-king Rāma. War was the obligatory duty (*dharma*) of monarchs, to be conducted during the first half of the year following the southwest monsoon rains, and the emperors of Vijayanagara worshipped Durgā on Mahānavamī before commencing their martial activities.[8] Stein (1980:384–92) describes the lavish style and scale of these celebrations that were continued, under the name of Dasarā, by the kings of Mysore, the dynasty that succeeded Vijayanagar. The Dasarā (or Daśaharā) celebrations were also associated primarily with royal military rites and coincided with the autumn Navarātra. The all-important tenth day followed immediately after the Devī's "nine night" festival. The Navarātra and Dasarā (i.e., Vijayā Daśamī) naturally came to be regarded as a continuous celebration (Kinsley 1986:111).[9]

The month of Aśvina occurs towards the end of the rainy season, a period that still inhibits movement and effective military campaigns. One can imagine monarchs of the past using the season to build their stockpiles of weapons and engage in other preparatory activities in anticipation of the arrival of the season of warfare at the end of the rains. The *āyudha-pūjā*, a rite of worship of weapons conducted in Devī temples by rulers and soldiers (as part of the Dasarā festivals), marked the beginning of military campaigns at the end of the monsoons. More particularly, it was connected with the opening of the royal armory (Richards 1910:30).[10] In the Durgā Pūjā ritual, Vijayā Daśamī (Tenth for Victory) is the day on which the Devī is dismissed from her various abodes (such as the clay images). However, in obvious continuity with the Durgā Pūjā rites, she is also worshipped as Aparājitā (She who is Invincible) on this day, clearly associating, if not invoking, Durgā's unconquerable power with the hopes of military success. The *pūjā* of Durgā's (and other) weapons takes place on Mahāṣṭamī.[11]

Biardeau (1984:10) cites V. A. Smith in W. H. Sleeman (1915, I:213), who notes that the *śamī* tree is invoked under the name of Aparājitā. This would suggest that the Aparājitā rites of the Durgā Pūjā symbolically include those of the *śamīpūjā*. The *śamīpūjā* figures in royal and military rites and has mythic connections with events recounted in the *Mahābhārata*. In that epic, the heroic Pāṇḍava warrior brothers hide their weapons deep within the thickest part of a *śamī* tree, while they themselves prepare to go into hiding for a year. They suspend a decaying corpse in the tree, so that its odor will dissuade people from approaching and finding the weapons. Yudhiṣṭhira, the eldest, introduces a hymn of praise to the Devī, addressed as Durgā and Kālī, and also identified as a virgin, who slays the buffalo-demon, and who loves alcohol, flesh, and animal sacrifices. She delivers people from the death and dangers that may await them in wild places.[12] In response, the Goddess appears to them and promises them victory. At the end of their year of concealment, Arjuna, the greatest warrior among the Pāṇḍavas, returns to the *śamī* tree. He performs a circumambulation (*pradakṣiṇā*) worship rite around the tree before retrieving his own weapon. It marks the imminent onset of events leading to the great war between the Pāṇḍavas and their enemies, the Kauravas. Thus the *śamī pūjā* resonates with this mythic event of incipient warfare. Later in the epic, the Pāṇḍava warrior, Arjuna, on the advice of Kṛṣṇa, addresses another hymn to the Goddess on the eve of the great battle. As in the previous hymn, she is addressed as Kālī, Durgā, Jayā and Vijayā (the latter two epithets both meaning "victory"). The Devī appears and promises him the boon of victory.[13]

Biardeau also points out the synonymous relationship between the words Aparājitā (invincible) and Vijayā (victory). Indeed, the "tenth day" terminology of the royal and military Dasarā rites come to be progressively identified with the "Tenth for Victory" (*vijayā daśamī*), in which "victory" is not merely the hopeful outcome for the upcoming season of warfare, but a personification of the Goddess (Vijayā). Biardeau (1984) elaborates upon the symbolic connection between the *śamī* tree, whose wood was used in kindling the Vedic sacrificial fire, with which it is also symbolically equated, and the weapons of battle, which are identified with the sacrificial fire itself. We have already noted the explicit identification of certain weapons (such as the sacrificial sword) with the Devī, herself. The entire sequence of events, from the awakening of the Devī, her subsequent worship (with the *āyudha pūjā*) in the Durgā Pūjā, culminating with the Aparājitā/*śamī pūjā* on Vijayā Daśamī, could thus be seen as a prelude to the greater sacrificial rite that would soon take place. That sacrifice is what Hiltebeitel (1976) has called "the ritual of battle," wherein human beings (warriors and/or their enemies), through the fire of weapons, are immolated as offerings to the Devī.

Émile Durkheim (1965 [1915]), the father of modern sociology, went so far as to imply that the deity that societies worship is an emblematic form of themselves. Community solidarity, often the source of powerful emotions, particularly in public gatherings, is the greatest source of strength, offering the best defence against enemies and the surest weapon against fear. This internally felt force, or collective effervescence, is each individual's experience of the deity, which in fact is an energy generated by the group itself. In support of Durkheim's analysis, the rather militant Bhārat Sevāśram Saṅgha, an influential religious organization in Banāras, made these very points in one of its locally printed (and distributed) pamphlets (in 1991). "What is the real form of the Goddess?" asks the brochure. It replies, "The real form of the Goddess is Hindu society. Millions of Hindus will wake up and unify—that is the symbol of the waking up (*bodhana*) of the Goddess." Elsewhere it states that the "main aim of [Durgā] worship is to get victory and kill enemies. . . . Hindus must remember that worship is not only giving incense, flowers, *bilva* leaves, or crying in front of her."

This function of community organization and empowerment is also evident when one examines the evolution of public Durgā Pūjās in Banāras in the last half century. According to the main image makers, such as Vanshicharan (Bangshi) Pal, who live and work in the Bengali Tola quarter, at the time of Indian independence in 1947, there were only about thirty *mūrti*s being fashioned in Banāras.[14] There was a marked increase in the number of community groups forming clubs to celebrate Durgā Pūjā after independence, and there may have been as many as seventy or eighty *mūrti*s by the mid-1970s. In 1978 a violent incident took place in Pandey Haveli, site of the Durgostava Sammilini community Durgā Pūjā. During the immersion (*visarjana*) procession, while passing through a Muslim quarter (*muhalla*), communal friction sparked violence, which resulted in city-wide rioting and deaths. Instead of quelling the growth of the public celebrations, this event led to the further mushrooming of community *pūjā*s. These Durgā Pūjās are undoubtedly an affirmation of Hindu identity, a source of community pride, and a visible form of organization and solidarity, which offers community members a feeling of security. Estimates of the number of public Durgā Pūjās now celebrated in the larger city vary from 150 to 200.[15] It is not simply a coincidence that Durgā Pūjā is the venue of expression of Hindu unity, for Durgā is, at present, one of the most potent symbols of the divine energy that destroys all fears.

The clay image cluster is often cited as representing Durgā's embodiment as the nation and its class/caste (*varna*) system.[16] Sarasvatī, the goddess of learning, is said to represent the *brāhmaṇas*. Kārtikeya, the god of war, represents the *kṣatriyas*. Lakṣmī, the goddess of wealth and good fortune, represents the *vaiśya* class. And Gaṇeśa, as the Lord of Obstacles who is propitiated before laborious undertakings, represents the *śūdras*. Durgā integrates all these *varnas*, providing a balanced and harmonious image of nationhood. This vision of Durgā as Mother India, powerful and independent, was voiced in Bankim Chandra Chatterjee's *Bande Mātaram* (Mother, I bow to Thee), a highly influential, inspirational anthem during India's struggle for independence.[17] Among its lyrics the song exclaims,

> Who hath said, thou art weak in thy lands,
> When the swords flash out in seventy million hands
> And seventy million voices roar
> Thy dreadful name from shore to shore?
> . . .
> Thine the strength that nerves the arm,
> Thine the beauty, thine the charm.
> . . .
> Thou art Durgā, Lady and Queen
> With her hands that strike and her swords of sheen.[18]

There is convincing evidence that the autumn Durgā Pūjā was revived only a few centuries ago by wealthy Hindu landlords (*zamīndārs*). The *pūjās* were expressions of their burgeoning power in the wake of the diminishing power of their Mughal overlords. Royal families implicitly competed with each other through the pomp and grandeur of the celebrations. Rachel Fell McDermott (1995), in her study of the history of the Durgā Pūjā in Bengal, submits that patronage of Durgā served as an important economic and political indicator of the complex shifting relationships between *zamīndārs*, Mughal overlords (*nawab*s), and British power in the form of the East India Company. She also affirms that, "the Pujas have always been a means of demonstrating wealth and prestige, and the worship of Durga has long been associated with sovereignty, useful in the context of eighteenth century Bengal for bolstering the rajas' claim to identity and power. In other words, the rise of the Pujas . . . signals an important transformation in the self-perceptions of the Hindu elite."[19]

As costs escalated and the economic power of the landed gentry declined, the grand-scale domestic *pūjā*s began to yield to group celebrations. The first of these was the so-called Barowari Pūjā, named after the group of twelve friends who first celebrated it in 1790. The public (*sārvajanīna*) celebrations arranged by community clubs, which developed from this process of democratization, are still referred to by Bengalis as Barowari Pūjās. Here, too, the spirit of competition and ostentatious display endures. Groups commission the construction of huge, and at times, multistoried, temporary shrines in which are installed larger-than-life clay images of Durgā and her attendant deities. As one votary commented, the operating logic often is simply "mine is bigger than yours." The mood of the competition is generally one of friendly rivalry between Hindu communities. However, in Banāras, the exuberant energy generated by the throngs celebrating the *pūjā*, emits an unequivocal signal of Hindu religious strength and unity to non-Hindu groups. The Muslim population's passionate public celebrations in Banāras during Muharram, for instance, seem to be a clear response to the Hindu show of strength during the Durgā Pūjā.

The members of the organizing "*pūjā* clubs" are generally young men in the community, many of whom are not gainfully employed. Criticisms abound that they do not always spend the community's funds solely on the *pūjā*, but siphon off portions for club revelry. Nevertheless, the clubs play significant roles in developing organizational and executive skills while forging friendships among members. As the same pamphlet of the Bhārat Sevāśram Saṅgha, mentioned earlier, states: "to nurture the growth of Hinduism within people—this is true Durgā worship. As Hindus meet each other and become brothers, this is the fruit of this worship. The establishment of a Hindu religious society—that is the great slogan (*mahāmantra*) of this *pūjā*." Thus the Durgā Pūjā, even with its ongoing transformations from sovereign rite to public function, continues to empower individuals and social groups by creating solidarity within Hindu communities.

It is possible to distinguish at least four types of public Durgā Pūjās in Banāras, according to their various emphases. The first type, such as the Durgotsava Sammilini, emphasizes the community's culture (in this example, Bengali culture) against the backdrop of the Devī's presence and worship. It is characterized by social gatherings around organized cultural activities and performances by or for community members. The second type of public Durgā Pūjā, often staged by such religious organizations as the Rāmakṛṣṇa Mission, Ānandamayī Mā Āśrama, and Bhārat Sevāśram Saṅgha, emphasizes the dimension of worship, although religious cultural performances by organization members or lay patrons (e.g., singing devotional songs and reciting the *Durgā Saptaśatī*) are an essential component of the celebrations. The Bengali religious and cultural influence is still great among the groups I have mentioned, since their founders were from Bengal. These religious organizations also utilize the traditional Bengali style of image cluster in which Durgā and all her attending deities are connected together in a single unit called the *pratimā* or *kaṭhamo*.

The third group, exemplified by the enormous *paṇḍal* at Hathivar Market in Lahurabir and the Durgā Pūjās of the Eagle Club or the Student's Club, are characterized by having originated with distinctly non-Bengali club members and thus include non-Bengali modes of worship. These *pūjā*s, too, which are sponsored by wealthy and well-organized associations, have a long history in Banāras. The *pūjā*s combine some performative elements, such as the presence of *dhāk* drummers or *dhūṇuci* dancing (dancing with aromatic smoke containers in the hands) with elaborate images, backdrops, and structures. The most visible dimension of these *pūjā*s is the throngs of people from all over the city who flock "to take *darśana,*" not only of the large ornate images of the Devī and other figures, but also look at the enormous temporary shrines.

The fourth group is made up primarily of Hindu neighborhood clubs that developed in the aftermath of, and perhaps directly in response to, the inter-religious riots of 1978. They include organizations such as the Durgā Sporting Club situated near the Durgā Kuṇḍ temple and demonstrate little in the way of cultural performance, perhaps because the neighborhood is composed of Hindus from diverse cultural regions of India. Community members come to take *darśana* of the glittering, decorated images, watch the *purohita* perform the worship, and may socialize around the *paṇḍal* while taped music, mainly soundtracks from popular Hindi films, blares from loudspeakers. Much of the energy and activity appears to center on the club members (generally young men from the community) who, through the process of organizing the *pūjā*, have solicited funds, organized themselves hierarchically, defined and displayed their capabilities, enjoyed themselves with surplus funds, and indirectly competed with other communities.

It is very common to hear criticisms from members of the more established community *pūjā*s about the lack of religious sentiment or culture in these newer celebrations. In contrast to these opinions, a young Bengali woman summed up the prevailing attitude of the younger generation:

> It is true that these celebrations are mainly the activity of young men, but women participate peripherally by preparing food and so on. In certain housing cooperatives in Bengal, where they feel safer, women take a more active role. I think it is a good thing for these young men, many of whom are students or unemployed. It channels their energy, and gives them something to do. Sure, sometimes they coerce people for money, and they keep aside some money to booze and so on. But this is not a problem for me. The mood of the festival is one of celebration. The old *zamīndār*s did the same in a bigger way. They had big boozing parties, with dancing girls, and so on during Durgā Pūjā. The women had to watch from the balconies. Now at least, the celebrations are public. Everyone can enjoy them.[20]

The surging masses of people that move from one temporary temple to another on Saptamī, Aṣṭamī, and Navamī have created new "pilgrimage circuits" in the city. The swell of people making their way to some of the huge temporary *paṇḍal*s is greater than the crowds that visit any of the permanent Durgā temples during Navarātra. The main roads in downtown Banāras are closed to vehicular traffic. These roads are a solid mass of excited "pilgrims." People seem to enjoy the "crush" of human bodies pressed against each other, as they move together for *darśana*. Although vendors set up some stalls in the environs of these public *paṇḍal*s, the crowds are so large that they inhibit effective commerce. Curiosity and community celebration, more than reverence, are the marked motivational factors in this pilgrimage. "Have you seen the *paṇḍal* at Lahurabir? It is huge. The images are very beautiful." Such comments are typical. When one considers the number of visitors to these *paṇḍal*s, relatively few offerings are made. The dynamic is conducive to a hasty glimpse of magnificence and beauty, which leaves visitors with a feeling of awe, discerned both by the looks on their faces and their comments. Here *darśana* is primarily visual contact, overriding the notion of *darśana* as part of a larger set of devotional actions.

However, I do suggest that the *darśana* of Durgā that is actually taking place in these "pilgrimages" is more than merely the perceptual contact offered by glimpsing the *paṇḍals* and *mūrti*s. It is a vision of the capacity of the Hindu community to unite in vast numbers, to erect, almost miraculously, pavilions of extraordinary dimensions and visual impact virtually overnight, and to display within these structures, in the manifest forms of the deities, the community's noblest values of beauty, power, and affection. There is a passage in the *Mahābhārata*, in which the eldest of the five Pāṇḍava heroes, Yudhiṣṭhira, while being instructed in the arts of successful kingship, is taught the nature of the six kinds of fortresses. The term for a fortress or citadel is *durga*, the Sanskritic masculine for the name of the Devī. Yudhiṣṭhira is told, "among the six kinds of citadels indicated in the scriptures, indeed among every kind of citadel, that which consists of (the ready service and love of the) subjects is the most impregnable."[21] It is precisely such a vision of formidable strength, which derives from the uniting of the people, that is a vital constituent of this *darśana* of Durgā. Durgā is the monarch for whom the people have gathered in a display of service, loyalty, and devotion. In their numbers, and in their visible and verbalized sentiments of revelry and unity, they have a vision (*darśana*) of their own power, and with it, the certitude of being victorious in any undertaking. This vision of the victorious power (*vijayā śakti*) that permeates the community of worshippers, binding them in a union characterized by joy and fearlessness, is implicitly a view of the manifest form of the Goddess.[22]

Controlled Fertility

Three important rites are prescribed for Sandhi, the climax of the Durgā Pūjā. These are the blood sacrifice, the offering of 108 lamps, and the *kumārī pūjā*. I have already explored the significance of the lamp offering. As a paramount *ārati*, it is synecdochical for the entire process of *pūjā* and its central objective of *darśana*, which I have also discussed at length. Although many Durgā Pūjās omit the blood sacrifice and *kumārī pūjās* entirely, their prescribed performance in conjunction with each other is at first sight perplexing and certainly in need of examination. An animal is beheaded, and its blood induced to flow, almost simultaneously as a prepubescent girl is being venerated. Certainly, the 108-lamp offering takes place during Sandhi precisely because this is when the Devī is thought to be most accessible to her worshippers. The "inner light may be received," explained Pandit Chakravarty. However, during this very period she manifests as a virgin girl of flesh and blood and is rendered the ultimate food offering, a creature of flesh and blood. Furthermore, this sacrifice may represent inimical forces, the votaries, or even the Devī herself. Sudarshan Chowdhury suggested that "Sandhi means 'joining together,' and [so] both [rites] may be [performed in conjunction] to get some synergistic effect."[23] It is precisely this synergistic relationship that deserves examination.

I, too, feel compelled to see the blood sacrifice and virgin worship as intimately connected and not the result of distinct, unrelated strands of the ritual merely ending up woven together. In the myths of the *Durgā Saptaśatī*, for instance, the Devī is a beautiful maiden who bloodily dispatches a number of demons. However, I find that the flowing blood of the sacrifice in the *pūjā* carries connotations that are strongly related to fertility and womanhood, and not merely to the destruction of enemies. It is important to recognize at the outset that the Durgā Pūjā is designated as the time when married daughters return to their parental home. They inevitably bring with them their children, among whom may be daughters who will be worshipped as *kumārī*s. During the *pūjā*, the married daughters are reunited with their mother, their married and unmarried sisters, as well as aunts and the other older women who are involved in the *pūjā*'s food preparations. In this festive gathering of women of all ages and in all stages in their lives, the hierarchy of preferred states of womanhood becomes immediately obvious and is reinforced throughout the days of the *pūjā* (see Figure 6.2).

The premenarche girls enjoy immense freedom during this time. They play freely and may enter the kitchen to help with the uncooked food preparations. During the *kumārī pūjā*, they will be regarded as embodiments of the Goddess, venerated, and treated with money and delicacies. The married daughters, too, enjoy special treatment. The *pūjā* is a time for them to relax from household chores for which they are constantly responsible in their husbands' homes. Thus, although (if initiated) they may participate in the food preparations, this task is relegated to their mother (if she is initiated) or other older (often postmenopausal), initiated women. The young wives and mothers enjoy delicious homemade meals and the companionship of the other women in the house. During the *varana* rite, conducted immediately before the image complex is carried to the waters for immersion, the married women of the household gather and feed the images and each other sweets. They apply *sindūr*, a symbol of marriage, to each other and to the Goddess herself. This is one of the explicit rites in which married daughters manifest their identification with the goddess Pārvatī who, like them, has returned to her parents', Himāvat and Mena's, home during the Durgā Pūjā.

One can only imagine the feelings that accompany the dramatic shift in status and treatment that *kumārī*s undergo the moment they begin to menstruate, as well as the sentiments of married women who may have been recently widowed.[24] From embodiments of the Goddess they have been suddenly thrust into a state so inauspicious that they may play no part in the domestic food preparation rites. They are excluded from the kitchen, an important arena for contact with other women. While I had no opportunity to talk to young widows, some former *kumārī*s who were as yet unmarried, were painfully aware of their ambiguous status. They were "betwixt and between" regulated states of womanhood, the actualization of which is a significant function of the domestic Durgā Pūjā. For instance, Pallavi, an attractive and articulate unmarried niece of Tarun Kanti Basu, in the Mitra family, offered these comments in response to my inquiries about attitudes to women during Navarātra.

> These times create illusions for us, but don't change any of the social situations. Bengalis, after the Mughal period, were responsible for the worst abuses on women—two million *sati*s, and child marriages, to name some of the abuses . . . Any woman of my generation will tell you that these festivals only create an illusion and are designed to fool women into thinking their place is special. . . . I don't feel special and am not treated specially at this time of year (i.e., Navarātra). I've never heard anyone feel or talk this way. I suppose married women get special treatment in their paternal home. But to unmarried women, no special things happen. No privileges. Very young girls are made to feel special during virgin worship (*kumārī pūjā*) (October 15, 1991).

The Durgā Pūjā not only functions as a rite to effect the awakening of the Goddess and thus revivify and rejuvenate the entire creation, but in the domestic sphere serves a parallel function among human females. The *pūjā* orchestrates the life cycle of women.[25] In the conjunction of the blood sacrifice and the *kumārī pūjā*, one can see a symbolic inducement of the flow of blood. To rejuvenate the dormant creation, blood, the sap of life, must be made to flow within it. Although the *kumārī* embodies an untainted potential, her capacity to create will remain latent unless it is ripened. The spilt blood of the sacrificial offering symbolically provokes the *kumārī*'s menarche.

Although in the Bengali style of *kumārī pūjā*, the *purohita* performs the worship, in many other homes in Banāras the ritual is performed by women, for women, although "men can cooperate." The women in a *brāhmaṇa* family perform the *pūjā* in the following manner.[26] A minimum of nine girls who are not members of the immediate family, preferably *brāhmaṇa*s under the age of twelve, are invited from the neighborhood. "Nine is Durgā's form. We also say there are nine forms of Durgā." "A few parents object to send their children," I was told, "because they are concerned about what they might be fed, but generally most families like to send their daughters." The girls' feet are washed and decorated with red lacquer (*alta*). "Everything is done with a religious feeling. Washing the feet means that we are worshipping Durgā. We give water for washing the feet to any god we worship." The maidens are given a seat (*āsana*). Their hair is rubbed with oil, and they are given a decorative forehead dot (*bindi*). "This is a symbol of adoring Durgā with make-up or decorating her. . . . We decorate our Durgā." The *kumārī*s are fed a sweet (*halvā*) made from coarsely ground flour (*sūjī*), sugar, ghee, and dried fruits. A former *kumārī* provided this answer about her feelings during the ritual. "My older two sisters, my younger sister, and I, and our friends would often be chosen as *kumārī*s. We would enjoy going in a group. We would get some money (*dakṣina*) and sometimes maybe a scarf (*chunni/dupaṭṭa*). We would enjoy ourselves."

In the tradition of the women who were describing the *pūjā*, the virgins are then fed cooked food such as deep fried bread (*pūri*) and curried vegetables (*sabji*). These cooked foods are first offered to Durgā, then to the *kumārī*s, and finally eaten by the women as *prasāda*. The women who perform the rite for the *kumārī*s have been observing a restricted diet (of uncooked or unrefined food) during the nine days of Navarātra.[27] "We think that Durgā is also fasting like us," I was told. *Kumārī pūjā,* which for them takes place on Navamī, brings an end to their Navarātra celebrations. It also brings an end to their diet of unrefined/uncooked foods and climaxes in the collective consumption of cooked food with the premenarche *kumārī*s.

In this *kumārī pūjā* we again notice the structural relationship between uncooked and cooked food.[28] The immature, unripe, or uncooked food, which is consumed by the fertile women during Navarātra, is "the food par excellence of the ascetic" and stands in marked contrast to food that has been cultivated with the plough (Parry 1985:613). It is also plainly associated with the virginal Durgā and the powerful but contained creative potential of the *kumārī*. The mature, ripened, or cooked food (e.g., wheat, rice, lentils), derived through cultivation, by contrast, has obvious associations with fertility (e.g., of the earth). In the *kumārī pūjā*, the collective energy of the fertile females is harnessed through their fast. Not only does their consumption of unrefined/uncooked food enhance their power (*śakti*), it also aligns them with their own premenarche state and the *kumārīs*. The *kumārīs*, who may be restricted from cooked food preparations, are symbolically connected with the unrefined/uncooked food. The fertile females' worship of these virgins encourages or elicits a maturation in them, a movement towards fertility. In the feeding of the *kumārīs* with cooked food, the pool of energy accrued by the fertile females is symbolically transferred to the prepubescent maidens of the community. The fertile women then break their fast and consume the cooked food together with the *kumārīs*, forging an identification with them. It is noteworthy that it is not only the *kumārī*s who are identified with Durgā, but that the women, too, identify themselves in their fast with the Goddess.

However, the onset of female fertility is not the only dimension of this functional purpose of the Durgā Pūjā, for although the condition is highly desirable, it is also regarded as potentially dangerous. Fertile, unmarried females incarnate a creative power that is progressively less easily governed.[29] The controlling influence of their parents, particularly their fathers, recedes as they mature.[30] One peril that females in this transitional state embody, especially for families with strict caste restrictions on marriage, is that they may attract the attention of undesirable suitors. The *Durgā Saptaśatī*, 5.42–65, for instance, relates the myth of how the demons Śumbha and Niśumbha are intent on possessing the Goddess Durgā because of her great beauty. Although she is often regarded by votaries as a *kumārī*, the full-breasted Devī of the *Durgā Saptaśatī*, is no premenarche girl. She is a voluptuous, young, unattached woman who most closely resembles the unmarried young women of the household. The Devī's active resistance and destruction of her demonic suitors undoubtedly serves as a model of virtue and restraint for these dangerously fertile females.[31]

Thrust out of their once-favored status as *kumārī*s into a liminal state of inauspiciousness, they are offered, albeit indirectly, the option of marriage and motherhood. Since the *pūjā* serves as a reunion for married sisters, it is an occasion for these women to exchange disclosures about men and their marital lives, including its joys and tribulations. It is also an opportunity to transmit attitudes and values concerning marriage through several generations of family members. Observations and mythic stories with marital elements abound during *pūjā* days. Two such stories that I encountered convey some of these themes.

1. Goddess Durgā has a broken back. Śiva's character is somewhat unreliable, since he tends to marry a different woman every other day. One day, the goddess Mānasā, who is one of Śiva's daughters, came home with him. Durgā thought this was one of his wives and decided to kill her. A great fight broke out. Durgā injured one of Mānasā's eyes with her triśula [trident], while Mānasā took her club and broke

Durgā's back. This shows the strength of women, despite any physical problems they may have.

2. Kalkeyi, a young enchanted god born as a woodcutter, found a golden lizard, which he decided to eat. [When he took it home] his wife, Fuliro, complained that this is all he brought back. He went to get salt from the market. But the lizard changed into a beautiful woman, who said to Fuliro that she was brought back home by Kalkeyi and was going to stay. When [Kalkeyi] returned, he told her [the beautiful lizard woman] to leave, since he could not feed her. At this point she turned into the Goddess Durgā who gave Kalkeyi seven pots of gold and told him to set up a city and spread her fame. From then, Durgā's fame was spread.[32]

These myths also address such themes as tensions between deities (i.e., Mānasā and Durgā), between mother and daughter, the male penchant for other wives, female propensities towards jealousy and mistrust, a wife's necessary resilience despite adversity, and the need for a wife's tolerance of and trust in her husband's actions.

Most votaries regard Durgā in the clay image complex as a mother with her daughters, Lakṣmī and Sarasvatī, and sons, Gaṇeśa and Kārtikeya. Kārtikeya is called Kumāra, the young prince, and portrayed as a handsome and eligible husband. One of the teenage girls commented, "Gaṇesh is the sweetest. We all like him. He is cute, as is his rat. I think Kārtik is too much of a dandy. He shouldn't indulge in fashion. Men shouldn't indulge in fashion."[33] The *navapatrikā*, clothed in a *sārī*, placed next to Gaṇeśa and referred to as the "banana wife," also elicits comments. In explanation for why Gaṇeśa has a banana tree as his wife, another teenager explained, "Once Gaṇesh came home, and he saw his mother eating with all her ten hands. He asked her why she wasn't eating with just one, or at most two hands. She said, 'What am I to do? When you marry, your wife will be such a woman who will send me away or not give me very much to eat. So I might as well eat now, filling myself while I can in preparation for the lean years ahead.' Hearing this Gaṇesh promised he would marry a woman who would not be a burden to his mother. Thus he married the *kala bou* [banana wife]." Among the elements in this story, one notes maternal apprehensions about the nature of future daughters-in-law. It conveys to unmarried sons the value of choosing a wife who will not be a burden to their mothers and to unmarried daughters the concerns of prospective mothers-in-law.

Such maternal and marital motifs are further reinforced by the special status that is enjoyed by the married women in the assembled family. Marriage to the appropriate suitor and motherhood will not only restore the young, unmarried women to auspiciousness, it will enhance their spiritual status.[34] Marriage confers onto women capacities to worship deities in distinct and enhanced ways (e.g., cooked food offerings, the *varana* rite). The *varana* rite, especially with the application of *sindūr,* explicitly emphasizes the theme of marriage. Mr. Lahiri's married daughters all expressed contentment about their status during the Durgā Pūjā, which they felt made women feel special. Matrimony, it must be noted, harnesses a woman's fertility by once again placing it within the sphere of influence of her husband and extended family. Motherhood channels her creative energies in specific directions (such as the nurturance of her children).

While older widows may be under the control of their adult children, young, childless widows whose fertility is unchecked, embody the same dangerous potential as unmarried women.[35] Like the latter, young widows, as well as their older counterparts, poignantly experience the sudden drop in auspiciousness caused by the presence of menstrual blood and the absence of a husband. Since widows' remarriage is still rarely an option among orthodox upper-caste Hindu families, the alternative placed before widows in the assembly of women gathered at the Durgā Pūjā was a life of chastity, renunciation, and worship. Although many such orthodox attitudes are questioned and challenged as India modernizes, the structural thrust of the ritual's functional values remains unchanged.[36] The Durgā Pūjā, said to reenact Rāma's worship of the Devī in order to destroy Rāvaṇa, also carries with it an implicit reminder of Sītā's fidelity. Sītā was abducted by the demon Rāvaṇa precisely because he lusted after her and longed to make her his wife. She did not know if her husband, Rāma, was still alive. Yet she clung to hope and preserved her chastity until her rescue. Sītā stands as the definitive model of virtue both for married women and widows.

Menopause immediately brings a natural elevation in spiritual status to all women. They are no longer subject to the periodic ritual pollution caused by menstruation. Neither are they capable of engendering life. Their fertility has ended, as has the danger that accompanies it. Their sexual energy no longer needs to be placed under any controlling influences. For those who choose to take initiation (an enviable option for widows, in particular), the spiritual gain is greater still, for they alone are entitled to prepare the *bhog* offerings to the Devī. Their auspiciousness is reappropriated, and they are elevated to the highest spiritual status among female votaries of the Great Goddess.

From the foregoing analysis it is evident that the Durgā Pūjā is not merely a rite to worship the Great Goddess as the embodiment of the creative principle of nature, materiality, and life itself. Quite importantly, it is an attempt to control these life processes, which it does through the ritual manipulation of the feminine, both human and Divine.[37] The locus of the Devī's embodiments is from mother to wife (*kala bou*), to fertile female, to premenarche virgin, which results in a rejuvenation of the manifest cosmos. Simultaneously, the *pūjā* orchestrates the human female's maturation at each stage of her life through a progression that inverts the Devī's journey.

Religious Ritual as Illustrated by the Durgā Pūjā

The final function of the Durgā Pūjā that I wish to address is its role not specifically as a *pūjā*, but as ritual. It is important to state at the outset, however, that "ritual" is a relatively new, scholarly, conceptual construct (see Bell 1997:267). It has proved to be an effective means of circumscribing some portions of human endeavor and has rendered valuable insights into who we are. And yet, during the course of my inquiry, despite the many discerning interpretations that were offered by votaries (some of which I include below), their experience of "Pūjā," as they refer to the Durgā Pūjā, is not primarily as a "ritual" in which they periodically participate. There appears to be a relatively seamless ebb and flow to the annual rhythms of their life, in which "Pūjā" wells up as one of the most anticipated and memorable. My presence as an observer and my inquiries about "meanings" and so on heightened, if not triggered, what one might designate the "scholarly response" in the participants. It caused them to disengage from a primarily subjective experience and to reflect upon the "ritual" for my benefit. I am not suggesting that the participants had never reflected on "Pūjā" as "ritual" prior to my inquiries, since their education had already exposed most of them to such categories. However, my presence and study heightened their awareness of the "phenomenon" and their predisposition to regard it as "ritual."

In fact, then, few participants and scholars would actually contest that the Durgā Pūjā is a ritual *par excellence*. And so, despite the theoretical shortcomings alluded to above in any such scholarly enterprise, the Durgā Pūjā can serve as a choice example with which to comment on the nature and function of "religious ritual." The commentary that follows, however, is necessarily brief and is not intended to be a thorough treatment of the subject. It serves mainly as an adjunct to this study. I nevertheless hope that it provides useful tracks into the continuing scholarly exploration of the conceptual category of "ritual," via the example of the Durgā Pūjā.

Attempts to define or explain the nature of ritual are both copious and ongoing.[38] Rather than select a preexisting definition, I offer my own, since each attempt offers distinctive insights into this pervasive human practice. By demonstrating how the Durgā Pūjā illustrates it, I intend to clarify the definition as well as provide a final and general commentary on the rite itself.[39] *Religious ritual is purposeful, symbolic action, culturally deemed consequential, and intended to evoke profound psycho-physical states in its participants. Its full significance is necessarily and intentionally enigmatic since each religious ritual incorporates only portions of that culture's specific means of engagement with fundamental and enduring mysteries of existence.*

This definition is hinged on the observation that ritual is grounded in action, although the degree to which participants act may vary dramatically.[40] In the domestic celebrations of the Durgā Pūjā, the *purohita's* activity is many orders of magnitude greater than that of most votaries, some of whom primarily observe, utter a few prayers, and make occasional offerings of flowers. The actions of patrons (*yajamāna*) are more extensive than those of most votaries, since they participate in numerous formal rites such as commissioning the priest, providing him with *dakṣiṇā*, and making offerings into the *homa* fire. Initiated women who prepare food offerings engage in involved activity that cannot be excluded from consideration as ritual action. In the behaviors of all these participants we note the primacy of action in ritual. Moreover, crucial ritual acts must be performed in deliberate manners, that are traditionally transmitted, and to which any innovations are readily scrutinized and evaluated by participants in the culture. The patron and other votaries sometimes closely watch and judge the *purohita*'s performance. He, too, is vigilant that their actions comply with traditional prescriptions.

Furthermore, the ritual is not accidental, habitual, or unconscious. A priest may utter a verse or perform a gesture by habit and be unconscious of the fact that he has done so, but the ritual itself and the intent to perform it is a conscious choice and a purposeful act on the part of patrons and priests. Regardless of the Durgā Pūjā's classification as regular (*nitya*), obligatory (*nitya*), intentional (*kāmya*), or free from personal desires (*niṣkāmya*), the ritual is not undertaken unconsciously.[41] Although Staal (1989) has theorized on the origins of the ritual impulse in human beings as akin to such instincts as mating dances in animals, one cannot attribute a purely unconscious, instinctive motivation to what is clearly a conscious intent to perform a ritual such as the Durgā Pūjā.

Ritual is symbolic in that the actions performed often signify something other than what may overtly appear to be occurring.[42] The *purohita*'s *mudrās* and *nyāsas*, the use of elaborate *yantras*, and even the items offered in devotional service (*upacāra*) do, in part, symbolize purification, the Devī, and reverence, respectively. In the Durgā Pūjā, for instance, the Devī is certainly not generally regarded as in actual need of the devotional offerings rendered to her. Thus even the acts of food preparation and decoration performed by lay worshippers point to (i.e., symbolize) something else, such as loving devotion. The *purohita*'s scattering of mustard seed cannot be perceived empirically as actually driving away inimical spirits and is only understood as such when one is informed of its symbolic intent. What is distinctive about many religious ritual acts, and aptly demonstrated in Hindu *pūjā*, however, is that the actions are not merely symbolic. *Mudrā*s and *nyāsa*s do not merely signify sealing, or invoking, or imprinting; they actually induce the desired effect.[43] This, however, does not invalidate the symbolic nature of ritual action, which, despite its capacity truly to do something, does so through litany, movements, and the manipulation of items that allude to its overall intent.[44] Symbolism is not only restricted to actions, but to empirical (e.g., visual, auditory) elements utilized in the rite.[45] Here, too, the *yantra* and *mūrti* are not just emblems that point to the Devī, they actually embody her. Food offerings are not merely symbolic, but are thought to undergo a substantive transformation by being consumed by the Goddess.

Unlike a gambler's systematic pattern of shaking and blowing on a pair of dice, the actions of religious ritual are not personal and idiosyncratic, but traditionally prescribed, and are held to carry a certain weight by the cultural groups that adhere to them (i.e., the wider, socially informed body). Religious ritual practice is deeply ingrained in Hindu culture despite its varied theological and philosophical stances. Indeed a traditional classification of what constitutes legitimate (*āstika*) Hinduism is: that religio-philosophical perspective (*darśana*) that does not reject the class (*varna*) system or the status of the Vedas as divinely revealed (*śruti*). To acknowledge the *śruti* literature is tantamount to accepting the central place of ritual, for major portions of the Vedas (e.g., the Brāhmaṇas) deal with the performance of sacrificial rites (*yajña*). Similarly, acknowledgement of the *varna* system affirms the position and role of the *brāhmaṇa* priest, the often indispensable ritual officiant. From this standpoint, to be Hindu is to accept and practice its rituals.

The formality inherent in the acts of religious ritual is another method through which their importance and specialness is established. There are also, of course, historical and sociopolitical motives for introducing and enacting rituals.[46] In this sense, too, they are held to be important by the factions whose agendas they support.[47] Turner (1982) notes that ritual can be used to avoid conflict and remind people that it is advantageous to stick to their places within the social system. The domestic Durgā Pūjā demonstrates this dimension in its intention to orchestrate the lifestyle choices of women so that they comply with orthodox values. I am not suggesting that ritual is always conducive to social cohesion, or that the social values or structures it promotes are shared by all participants. Pallavi Basu, of the Mitra family, for instance, saw in the Durgā Pūjā a range of purposes that she held to be "eye wash," intended to dupe women and keep them in their traditional places. Nevertheless, she gladly participated in the *pūjā* for reasons she found deeply meaningful. Bell (1992) observes that ritual does not resolve social tension and conflict, but presents a scheme that suggests a resolution and thereby defers the resolution in favor of a temporary solution.

In any performance of the Durgā Pūjā, there is scarcely a participant who does not have a criticism of some aspect of the rite. The paucity of religious sentiment in the public celebrations is a concern voiced by virtually everyone, including the very club members who are deemed responsible for organizing the affair. Participants at one community celebration even quipped that their measure of a *pūjā's* success was noting if the *purohita* departed without grumbling and promised to conduct the rite the following year. All such bickering and criticism by participants (organizer, votaries, and the priest), while revealing a wide range of perspectives (some even in direct opposition to each other) on the forms, functions, and execution of the rite, should not be construed as indications of the ritual's unimportance in their eyes. For the most part, participants in the *pūjā* do not question the importance of the ritual, but only the particular forms it has taken and the ends to which it is put.

Votaries do not take religious rituals lightly, nor conduct them frivolously, for they are generally deemed to have consequences of import. Mr. Lahiri feared the resulting consequences from ending a family tradition that spanned over two hundred years. Although the Durgā Pūjā need not be performed, the *Devī Purāṇa* strongly encourages its execution (Kane:5.156). And even though votaries may not perform the *pūjā* for any reason other than to please the Devī, once undertaken, the rite ought to be performed to the best of one's abilities. The very performance of the ritual and the integrity with which it is performed reveals the sincerity of the worshipper's sentiments towards the Goddess. Although Anjali Lahiri said she began her preparations for the annual Durgā Pūjā a month before the actual celebration, her eldest daughter observed: "My mother prepares for Durgā Pūjā for the whole year. She shops for wheat, *dāl* (lentils), grains, and so on all year long. We store these grains in that room in the house. She then washes everything to clean it. It must be purified. She removes the stones and little sticks and so on which are in these grains. You must not touch them with night clothes or with clothes you have worn when going to the toilet."[48]

On several occasions I encountered oral versions of the story of Rāma's worship of Durgā, the human precedent for the autumn Durgā Pūjā, which recounts a mythic precedent for an act of great sincerity. At the high point of the ritual, Rāma was to perform an offering of 108 lotus flowers.[49] The 108-lamp offering on Sandhi is said to be a reenactment of Rāma's devotional rite. To his dismay, in the midst of the ceremony Rāma discovered that he was one lotus short of the requisite number. His devotion was so great that rather than displease the Devī, he immediately reached up and plucked out one of his own eyes as a substitute.[50] Pleased with his sincerity, the Devī appeared, granted him his boon to destroy Rāvaṇa, and restored his eyesight. In certain versions, the Devī stays his hand before he actually plucks out his eye, or it is she who stole the flower to test his sincerity. Such myths reinforce the powerful consequences of religious rituals, both in process and outcome.

In a similar vein, Mr. Lahiri related an incident in which a young family member once purchased a special *sārī* to make as an offering to the Devī. Upon examination, just before the *pūjā*, the family noticed a flaw, a small hole in the fabric. They advised her against offering the blemished cloth, but since there was no time to furnish an alternate, she decided to go ahead with the slightly defective gift. At the high point of the *pūjā*, during the *ārati*, a spark somehow jumped from the lamp to the fabric, which immediately burst into flames. Mr. Lahiri took this to be a sign from the Goddess, and since that day the family has not faltered in its meticulous attention to the completeness and quality of their offerings. Ritual can dramatically induce attitudes and values which, in turn, govern actions.

The gravity inherent in religious ritual promotes its intention to evoke profound psychological states in participants. These may include feelings of awe, fear, or empowerment. In the Durgā Pūjā, the priest is undoubtedly instrumental in bringing about such states, whose manifestations often serve as gauges of the success of a ritual. For example, when asked about the role of the *purohita*, Pallavi Basu, commented: "[The *purohita*] must pay attention—have a visible effect on the people. His performance can make a dead ritual into something living. It can transport and change our attitude and feelings. My attention would have wandered and I would have begun to question the usefulness of the ritual if the *purohita*'s performance had been poor."[51] Pallavi's comments confirm that a successful ritual subverts the capacity of a devotee to remain as an emotionally detached observer. By directing attention and orchestrating emotions successfully, the *purohita* disengages the rational, objective, analytic mental faculties of the observers, drawing them into deeper, subjective, intuitive participation in the ritual. Since votaries are already predisposed for such participation, the likelihood of them experiencing profound sentiments is greatly amplified when these propensities are brought into conjunction with the *purohita*'s expertise in ritual art. In such states of direct, intuitive perception, each participant experiences the "meaning" of ritual rather than questioning it.[52]

There is undoubtedly a wide range of moods and sentiments evoked by the Durgā Pūjā. Anjali Lahiri expressed her feelings as "joy and happiness." One of her sons-in-law offered these thoughts. "I feel good when I participate in the *pūjā*. A feeling of elation. . . . One fellow may be enjoying a good meal of meat, while someone else looks and says this is very bad. There are things which are relative, good and bad, based on your perspective. But if some chap is playing music and I am enjoying it, and he is enjoying playing it, then there is less of an opposite to that feeling. The elation I feel when participating in Durgā Pūjā is *ānanda*, bliss. It does not have an opposite. It covers everything."[53]

In community celebrations, I frequently observed feelings of pride and success. In the words of an organizer, "The club *pūjā*s are a sort of exhibitionism for us all. We celebrate it not totally to satisfy our religious mind, but more to celebrate our merry making purposes. . . ."[54] Other responses concerning feelings included, "festive spirits" and "feels good to be part of a large group." S. K. Rai Choudary's comments typify the feelings of empowerment experienced by many. "Śakti is a symbol of power, and it is this power which destroyed the demon. The power is a feeling which wells up and coalesces in a sense in which one overcomes the forces which cause fear and insecurity. During the *sandhi pūjā*, the *śloka*s which are recited tell of the Goddess in terrifying aspect, changing shapes from Devī to demoness (*rakṣasī*)."[55]

Thus feelings run the gamut from festive pleasure to joy, bliss, and empowerment and are as varied as the participants in the *pūjā*.[56] For some, the *pūjā* is an opportunity to attain an encounter with the Devī. This encounter may not merely be a general sense of personal empowerment, but may be actually experienced as an empirical perception of the Goddess.[57] For others it may even be a sense of identification with the Devī herself.[58] Some revealed that they "saw" Durgā in the clay image smiling upon arrival, but sorrowful upon departure. Such fortuitous experiences would undoubtedly be accompanied with profound feelings such as awe, joy, and gratitude. Whatever the feelings be that worshippers experience, it is certain that the memory of such past moods, sentiments, and perceptions, together with anticipation of the same or other states plays a pivotal role in motivating most votaries to participate in each subsequent Durgā Pūjā. The Durgā Pūjā is particularly successful in its intent to evoke deeply felt psychophysical states, and this achievement is unquestionably at the root of its widespread popularity.

Nobody with whom I conversed, not even the pandits who actually perform the ritual and know the entire liturgy of the Durgā Pūjā, including the meanings of its Sanskrit litany, would admit to knowing *the* "meaning" of the ritual. Most votaries felt they understood as much as they cared to for their own purposes and generally deferred to more knowledgeable scholars or ritualists if pressed for detailed descriptions or meanings. Among these scholars and ritualists, I found a personal sense of meaning attributed to particular symbols and ritual acts, but there was never a sense that they had plumbed "the" meaning of the ritual. Votaries recognized that there would inevitably be many differences in what individuals extracted from any religious rite. As Satyabrata Moitra, one of Mr. Lahiri's sons-in-law, put it: "Do you know about differential equations, . . . in calculus? Some series equations have a particular solution. Some have general solutions. Some have no solutions. *Pūjā* is like a series differential equation with many particular solutions. Each person participates in the ritual in their own way, and gets their own meaning from it."[59] Mr. Moitra's imagery reflects his education and occupation as an engineer, but nonetheless provides a thoughtful analogy from a earnest participant in the Durgā Pūjā. Scholars are not the only persons who reflect on the nature of ritual. In Mr. Moitra's analogy, religious rituals, in spite of their seemingly mechanical and repetitive nature, are akin to complex mathematical formulas. These are composed of constants, mathematical functions and operators, and variables, all placed in an exact order. In any particular performance of the Durgā Pūjā, the particular assortment of votaries in attendance (and the *purohita* who is chosen to conduct the rite) are like particular values entered for the various variables within the formula. Although each such variable entry generates a different solution, each of these solutions is correct and meaningful.

Mr. Moitra did hold that there were deeper truths that could be derived from the *pūjā* experience than are generally gleaned by most participants. "You ask me what the meaning of *pūjā* is, and I say that it means different things to different people. Many people see it again and again and nothing special registers. It is like Newton and the apple. Many people see an apple fall, but only the Newtons understand or grasp a deeper principle which is there."[60] But here too, his comments suggest the discovery of one or many profound truths amid a larger universe of possibilities. The meaning of ritual cannot be fully known, nor, I suggest, is it intended to be understood fully.[61]

Religious ritual, in particular, is in design and intent enigmatic. This is because religion addresses the fundamental mysteries of existence. Clifford Geertz (1973a), for instance, in his influential definition of religion, argued that religion offers a symbol system that enables human beings to confront life in arenas beyond their limits of physical endurance, moral certitude, and rational knowledge. The set of symbols that constitutes a particular culture's religious system is that cultural group's means of establishing a worldview and ethos, which circumscribe a reality that is much larger than what would be regarded as the natural world in, say, commonsensical or scientific cultural systems. Religion deals with supranatural realities, whose full compass is beyond the ken of most human beings. Knowledge of those truths is thus the purview of deities, seers, prophets, realized beings, saints, and other such spiritually elect individuals. It is they who have glimpsed the larger (what Geertz calls the "really real") reality, often in states referred to as revelation or realization. These beings, who by virtue of their insights are often regarded as possessed of divinity, are the initiators or communicators of religious truths and prescribed actions. Religious rituals are believed to have developed from such transmissions. In ritual, the mundane world of everyday experience is meshed with the broader reality of supernormal truths, which are generally only accepted on faith or imagined (vividly or not) by most worshippers.

Religious rituals offer members of a particular culture specific means of engaging with and perhaps encountering those mysterious truths for themselves.[62]

In order to achieve this fusion between ordinary and nonordinary realities, religious rituals involve the manipulation of symbols and the execution of actions that are both familiar and foreign. They serve as a bridge between this reality and another, both of which are experienced and imagined in ways that are culture specific. Religious ritual is impossible without the implicit existence, either through its presence or sanction, of what Otto (1929) called the *ganz andere* ("wholly other"), the unknowable and sacred factor that is at the hub of the rite. For no matter how well a particular culture delineates its picture of supernatural reality, it is still mostly regarded as utterly mysterious. The sage may come to realize Truth, but knows it as the mystery of mysteries. Religious truths, when communicated, are said to become "falsehood."[63] The bridge, or portal of ritual, perforce, leads from the known to the unknown, and this alone endorses its enigmatic character. It cannot achieve its purpose if it "makes sense," for this would point or lead the participant from the known to the known. In religious ritual the pointing is to another reality whose configuration, however well described by any particular culture, is at best a rough sketch. Religious ritual utilizes elements of that description, the culture's specific vocabulary and imagery, such as myths and icons, to amalgamate the two realities into one.[64] If successful, participants leave the rite transformed, their understanding of the world and their place in it expanded, and their confidence in the procedure and its conceptual framework enhanced. Ritual may thus reconstruct and reinforce a devotee's worldview and ethos.

The Durgā Pūjā is said to have originated in the worship performed by King Suratha and the merchant Samādhi as recounted in the *Durgā Saptaśatī* (13.5–17). As a result of their worship, Suratha eventually reincarnated as a Manu, and Samādhi gained liberation. Their worship, however, had divine precedents. Mythic accounts tell how the great demon Rāvaṇa reinitiated the worship of the Devī in the spring. Rāma, the warrior incarnation of Viṣṇu, initiated the autumn worship of Durgā by invoking her aid in the slaying of Rāvaṇa.[65] The *Devī Bhāgavata Purāṇa* (III.30.23–26) tells us that these godlike human worshippers, on the advice of the sage Medhas, were reenacting a ritual that had been performed earlier still by the seers (*ṛṣi*), Bhṛgu, Vaśiṣṭha, Kāśyapa, and Viśvāmitra, and the deities Indra, Nārāyaṇa (Viṣṇu), and Śiva in an earlier cycle of creation. In these myths, *ṛṣi*s and deities set ritual precedents for incarnate hero-deities and demon devotees. These celestials, in turn, through engaging in Durgā worship, set precedents for mythic human heroes. Purāṇic tales relate how the kings Subāhu and Sudarśana, of Banāras and Ayodhyā, eventually reestablished the worship of the Devī in their respective cities (see Rodrigues 1993a).

Eliade (1959a) has extensively explored the cyclical nature of creation myths, and the Durgā Pūjā complies well with this pattern of divine precedents. Antiquity and tradition are frequently invoked in the construction of ritual and offered as explanations of their inexplicability. The form of the ritual as it is received by us today has been derived from antecedents that go back to the actions of the gods themselves. We may not fully know what every detail in the rite signifies, but surely they must have. The *ṛṣi*s who authored the Purāṇas provided further details on the method of the ritual's celebration. In the *Durgā Saptaśatī*, it is the Devī herself who tells her worshippers how she ought to be worshipped. However, her instructions are recounted by the sage Medhas to King Suratha and the merchant Samādhi. Furthermore, the story of their conversation is being retold by the sage Mārkaṇḍeya to his disciple, Krauṣṭuki. Thus the purpose of the ritual, and the manner in which it should be conducted, ultimately emanate from a source of indisputable truth, the Goddess to whom the ritual is directed, through a chain of authoritative spokespersons.[66]

Despite its potential ritual complexity, Hindu *pūjā* does permit abbreviations, which do not diminish the effectiveness of the rite. Although certain elements are regarded as inviolable (e.g., the timing and duration of the Sandhi Pūjā), the Durgā Pūjā does offer ample evidence of transformations within aspects of the rite over time. Tantric liturgical variants may be substituted for lengthier Vedic ones. Surrogate offerings may be made in lieu of the blood sacrifice. Certain features (e.g., *kumārī pūjā*) may be omitted altogether, or performed on alternate days (e.g., on Navamī instead of during the Sandhī Pūjā). The domestically based celebrations, have yielded to public community celebrations where the shrines and clay images are undergoing creative transformations every year. Devotional worship (*pūjā*, *upacāra*) by individual votaries may occur at these shrines. The Durgā Pūjā thus demonstrates that ritual is somewhat malleable and capable of adaptive changes in response to the needs (e.g., moral, aesthetic, devotional) and capacities (e.g., time-constrained, economic) of the social group.

In whatever form it takes, the Durgā Pūjā seeks to bring the Devī into an awakened manifestation, which is experienced at the psychological or sensorial level by devotees. Although the Goddess may be conceived of as a mother, daughter, or protecting power, her true nature, conveyed in the ritual's own litany, as well as in scriptural and oral myths, is profoundly enigmatic. When reading the most influential text for Śākta Hindus, the *Durgā Saptaśatī*, one is often drawn to a number of its dramatic episodes, such as the Devī's creation and her many demon-slaying exploits. It is easy to lose sight of a crucial dimension of the frame story, which serves as the springboard for the tales of the Goddess's birth and deeds. In the frame story, King Suratha, who lost his kingdom, and the *vaiśya* Samādhi, deprived of his wealth, approach the sage Medhas for advice. Suratha is still preoccupied with his loss, while Samādhi continues to be affectionately disposed toward his family although they banished him. "How is it that there is delusion, even for men of knowledge?" they ask. Medhas notes that all creatures in creation are in the grip of the goddess Mahāmāyā (Great Illusion). It is she who deludes the world, and it is she who is the supreme knowledge that leads to liberation. "Who is this Goddess, whom you call Mahāmāyā?" asks Suratha. And it is in response to this question that Medhas recounts the main narratives that follow. He begins by saying, "Eternal she is, with the world as her form. All these worlds are her manifestations" (DSS 1.47). The frame story resumes near the very end of the scripture, with Medhas explaining that the Devī's great power supports the universe. "The entire universe is deluded by her; she produces everything" (DSS 12.34). The *Durgā Saptaśatī* refers to itself as the Glorification of the Goddess (*Devī Māhātmya*), a title by which it is also well known. It is essential to recognize that the although the Devī is praised for many reasons, her most glorious characteristic is her inordinate power of illusion.

The Great Goddess is thus not only nature (*prakṛti*), or the underlying cosmic power (*śakti*), but quite crucially, she is the supreme mystery (*mahāmāyā*), the power of illusion.[67] To know her, is to know her as ineffable, a formidable power that cannot be overcome, a mystery that cannot be penetrated. Parallelling the myths that portray her as an irresistibly attractive woman whose chastity cannot be breached, the Great Goddess is perennially alluring. She draws her votaries repeatedly to perform the Durgā Pūjā, the rite through which they may perhaps be graced with yet one more partial glimpse of her self. And still, even if such an encounter should occur, her real form, like a fortress (*durga*) is impenetrable; her true nature, utterly inconceivable.

Notes

Chapter 1: Introduction

1. Kinsley (1986:219) concludes "on the basis of the great number of female images found that goddesses were known and probably widely worshipped or exalted in this culture." Coburn (1991:14) more cautiously asserts that "there seems to be acknowledgment of the mystery of fertility, especially as it appears in women, and a sense that this power provides a linkage between human, natural, and animal realms." See also, Hiltebeitel and Hopkins (1986).

2. Lunar months consist of a bright or waxing fortnight leading to a full moon and a dark or waning fortnight that leads to a new moon. Āśvina falls during the months of September and October.

3. I conducted field research for this project in 1990–91 during an eighteen month stay in Banāras, India, and on subsequent short visits in 1996, 1997, 1998, and 1999. Funding was generously provided by the Social Sciences and Humanities Research Council of Canada, the School of Graduate Studies at McMaster University, and a University of Lethbridge Research Grant.

4. For studies of Banāras and its religious life, see Eck (1982), Sukul (1974), R. Singh (1986), Chandra (1962), Sherring (1868), Saraswati (1975), Havell (1905), Vidyarthi et al. (1979). For studies on the Durgā temple in Banāras, see Rodrigues (1993a) and (1993b).

5. My colleagues and friends, Christopher Justice and Patricia Seymour, while observing Durgā images under construction in one of the Bengali quarters of Banāras, met with a Lahiri family member who invited them to witness the *pūjā*. After I accompanied them on a visit to the Lahiri home, Mr. Lahiri, noting my deep interest in Durgā, welcomed me to observe and study the *pūjā* in detail. Other members of the Lahiri family soon opened up to me, and I have maintained my friendship and communication with them to the present day.

6. Among the well-known older studies are Burgess (1883), Stevenson (1920), Rangachari (1931), Joshi (1959), and Goudriaan (1970). The most notable recent

analytic study of *pūjā* is found in Davis (1991). Davis explores the relationship between Śaiva Siddhānta metaphysics and the soteriological intent of action within that universe. A comprehensive treatment of orthodox Vedic *pūjā* is found in Bühnemann (1988).

7. Exceptions to this are Babb (1975:31–67) and the excellent concise descriptive analysis of *pūjā* to Gaṇeśa found in Courtright (1985b).

8. See, for instance, Sanjukta Gupta, trans., *The Lakṣmī Tantra* (Leiden: E. J. Brill, 1972), and K. R. van Kooij, *Worship of the Goddess According to the Kālikāpurāṇa* (Leiden: E. J. Brill, 1972). Excellent descriptions of Tantric *pūjā* procedures are found in Gupta, Hoens, and Goudriaan's (1979) fifth chapter of Hindu Tantrism.

9. In retrospect, my early lack of understanding is less an indictment of the scholarly literature then available and more an indication of my haphazard readings in texts, which were either too advanced or insufficiently detailed. I have written this description with the reader who is a novice to Hindu *pūjā* in mind. I have also made an effort to provide such readers, in a single study, with as much detail as their curiosity elicits and render this in as engaging a format as a description of such a lengthy ritual will allow.

10. I am currently working on a monograph based on that work and subsequent research. My frequent references to details of Durgā worship derive from the eighteen months of fieldwork in Banāras in 1990–91 and other short visits in subsequent years. My work was not solely grounded in research on the Durgā Pūjā in Banāṛas.

11. Payne (1997 [1933]:8–9) notes, "As soon as the observance of the ancient sacrifices prescribed in the *Śrauta-sūtra*s began to decline, we find orthodox twice-born men, known as *Smārtas*, worshipping the five gods, *pañca deva*, Vishṇu, Śiva, Durgā, Sūrya and Gaṇeśa, in what is called *Pañchāyatana pūjā*. . . . A man may therefore worship Durgā without identifying himself with the Śākta sect."

12. General treatments of Śākta Hinduism are found in Woodroffe (1918), Payne (1997 [1933]), and Narendra Nath Bhattacharyya (1974). Brooks (1990) provides a commendable presentation of Śākta Tantrism.

13. Excellent studies of women's participation in *vrata*s are found in Pearson (1996), and McGee (1989).

14. Some detailed discussions of forms of worship during Navarātra are found in Babb (1975:128–140), Eck (1982: 258–9, 268–9), Fuller and Logan (1985), and Kinsley (1986: 106–115). A detailed historical survey of the literature and forms of Navarātra celebrations is found in Kane (5.154–87).

15. The Bengali Hindus are avid goddess worshippers, whose yearly religious festivals include *pūjā*s to the goddesses Kālī and Sarasvatī.

16. Domestic *pūjā*s in the home or in religious organizations such as the Ānandamayī Mā Āśram are performed only for the benefit of the family or *āśrama* members. The celebrations of all *pūjā*s begin with a *saṅkalpa* or vow of intent to

perform the *pūjā* appropriately. In the domestic *saṅkalpa*, the head of the family's name (*kartā*), lineage (*gotra*), deity's name, place, time, and so on are mentioned, while in the *sārvajanīna pūjā*, some individual is chosen as the representative patron/worshipper (*yajamāna*) of the group, which itself may be heterogeneously composed of people of different castes (*jāti*) and lineages (*gotra*).

17. In Banāras the clay images alone may cost between two and ten thousand rupees. Large-scale public celebrations, such as those in the Banāras communities of Lahurabir and Matsyodari may cost the organizers up to five hundred thousand rupees. Calcutta's largest celebrations, such as those at Santosh Mitra Square (Sealdah) and College Square cost from two to five million rupees. The shapes of the largest temporary shrines (*paṇḍal*, *maṇḍapa*) often resemble famous permanent temples in India, such as the temples of Mīnākṣī in Madurai or Viśvanātha in Banāras.

18. The elaborateness of this style of Durgā Pūjā is a telltale reminder of its origins in the homes of wealthy landowners (*zamīndār*). In this sense, the term "domestic" is appropriate. However, attendance at these celebrations was open to wider circles of family members and friends often in direct proportion to the *zamīndār*'s power and influence.

19. Wealthy patrons often contribute the funds for an entire day's celebration.

20. Although devotees may refer to the Great Goddess by other names such as Mahālakṣmī or Mahākālī, such epithets are far less frequently encountered than Durgā, or simply Mā (Mother). Although Coburn makes a compelling case for rendering Devī as Goddess, without the definite article, I have opted to use the more conventional translation of Devī as "the Goddess" (see Pintchman 2001).

21. I was told by some sources that a woman may never function as a priest; others (e.g., the Lahiris, Pandit Chakravarty) claimed that a properly initiated woman may, in theory, serve as the ritualist (*purohita*), although in practice it is extremely rare. I therefore use the pronoun "he" to refer to the priest throughout this book.

22. See C. M. Brown (1998:260).

Chapter 2: The Setting

1. See, for instance, the *Śrī Navarātra Kalpataru*, 15–17, where the worship of the Great Goddess as Nandā is prescribed for the Navarātra during the bright fortnight of the month of Māgha (January/February), and her worship as Destroyer of the demon Śumbha, for the Navarātra during the bright fortnight of the month of Āṣāḍha (June/July).

2. See *Devī Bhāgavata Purāṇa* III.24.21–22.

3. See Erndl (1993:50–55) for details on these goddesses and their temples.

4. According to Stein (1980:384), Purāṇic sources (which he does not cite) refer to the spring Navarātra as marking the harvest of the *sambā* or *rabi* crop and the

onset of the hot season, while the autumn Navarātra occurs after the harvest of the *kār* or *kharif* crop and marks the onset of the cold season.

Besides corresponding to the end of the cold and rainy seasons, respectively, these transition periods into the spring and autumn seasons are notorious for fluctuations in weather and are associated with the onset of disease. They are often referred to as *yama daṃṣṭrā* ("fangs of death"). Goddesses, such as Śītalā, have long been associated with the cause of disease and are propitiated to avoid or cure them. The timing of the Navarātra rituals of goddess worship could well be connected to the attainment of protection from these and other dangers, such as the ravages of warfare, which also began after the rains.

5. The *Durgā Saptaśatī* 12.11, which dates to the 6th century C.E., already refers to the great annual autumn worship of the Goddess.

6. Coburn (1984:9–19) traces the arguments of Srinivas (1965 [1952]), Marriott (1955), Staal (1963), and van Buitenen (1966) on the process of Sanskritization.

7. Kane (1930–62:5.187) refutes the argument that the Durgā Pūjā was originally a military rite that was later transformed into a religious festival.

8. Kane (1930–62:5.109) explains that since travel (and hence worship) is seriously impeded during the rainy season, it was appropriate for the period to be designated as the resting time of the gods. Indeed Eck (1982: 261) notes that the rainy season is called the period when Viṣṇu goes to sleep.

The *Kālikā Purāṇa* 60.9–20 (see C. M. Brown 1998:260) states that in former times the Great Goddess was awakened on the first day of the autumn Navarātra by Brahmā in order to slay Rāvaṇa. She incited Rāma and Rāvaṇa to do battle and caused the death of Rāvaṇa on the ninth day. It also mentions her awakening by the gods (on the seventh day of Navarātra) in order to slay the buffalo demon Mahiṣa, which she accomplishes on the ninth day. In both instances, she is dismissed on the tenth day.

9. Textual versions of Rāma's worship are not typically found in *Rāmāyaṇa* manuscripts, but are told, for instance, in the *Kālikā Purāṇa* 62.24–49, *Mahābhāgavata Purāṇa* 36–38, and *Bṛhaddharma Purāṇa* 1.18–22.

10. See Östör (1980:18). He further notes that Rāvaṇa only agreed to perform the *pūjā* rites of the seventh and eighth days of the autumn Navarātra, leaving Rāma to perform the rituals of the ninth and tenth days.

11. The universal appeal of the Durgā Pūjā is emphasized in the *Devī Purāṇa*, which states, "This is a great and holy *vrata* [a vowed ascetic practice] conferring great *siddhis* [supernormal powers], vanquishing all enemies, conferring benefits on all people, especially in great floods; this should be performed by *brāhmaṇas* for solemn sacrifices and by *kṣatriyas* for the protection of the people, by *vaiśyas* for cattle wealth, by *śūdras* desirous of sons and happiness, by women for blessed wifehood and by rich men who hanker for more wealth; this was performed by Śaṅkara and others" (Kane: 5.156). The *Bhaviṣya Purāṇa* asserts, "Durgā is worshipped by various groups of *mlecchas* [outcaste], by all *dasyus* [thievish tribes or outcaste Hindus], by people from Aṅga, Vaṅga, and Kaliṅga, by *kinnaras* [mythical beings, only part human], Barbaras [non-Aryans], and Śakas" (Kane: 5.157).

12. In Banāras, for instance, there are nine specific temples to goddesses such as Annapūrṇā and Kālarātrī. However, during the Navarātras, each of these otherwise different goddesses is regarded as the Great Goddess Durgā.

13. I use the terms Great Goddess, Goddess, Devī, and Mahādevī synonymously to refer to the supreme form of the Divine Feminine. For lesser forms, I use particular epithets, or the general terms, *devī* or goddess.

14. For more on the Great Goddess of Hinduism, see Brown (1990), Coburn (1991), Kinsley (1986), Kramrisch (1975), and Humes (1991). On the cycle of worship festivals to all deities throughout the year in Banāras, see Eck (1982:252–283, 364–367). Good treatments of the Hindu calendrical system and its relationship to festivals are also found in Babb (1975), and Freed and Freed (1964).

15. Devotees may refer to the Great Goddess by other names such as Mahālakṣmī, or Mahākālī. However, such epithets are far less frequently encountered. For a detailed study of scriptural references to the epithet Durgā that pre-date its occurrence in the *Durgā Saptaśatī* (c. 5th/6th century C.E.), where it occurs seven times, always in reference to the Devī in her supreme form, see Coburn (1984a: 115–121).

16. For information on the Goddess as Mother or as Durgā, see Bandyopadyay (1987), Bhattacharyya (1971), Brown (1974), Divakaran (1984), and Kinsley (1986).

17. Durgā is often metaphorically identified with a boat or raft that ferries people across the turbulent waters of existence to the far shore of liberation. See, for example DSS 4.11, or the *Devī Gītā* 1.45 (trans. C. M. Brown 1998: 69, 72). In the *Lakṣmī Tantra* 4.46, the Goddess states, "I am called Durgā, as I am difficult to reach, and also because I save my devotees" (trans. Gupta 1972:24).

18. Certain texts equate both Navarātras with the time for Durgā worship, referring to the periods as Durgotsava (Festival of Durgā)(Kane: 5.154). For other studies of the Durgā Pūjā ritual consult Ghosha (1871) and Östör (1980).

19. Supported by statements in the *Kālikā* and other Purāṇas, the *Tithitattva* lists alternative periods for celebrating Durgā Pūjā. These are: (1) from the 9th *tithi* of the preceding dark fortnight of Āśvina to the 9th *tithi* of the bright fortnight of Āśvina; (2) from the 1st to the 9th *tithi* of the bright fortnight of Āśvina; (3) from the 6th to the 9th; (4) from the 7th to the 9th; (5) from the Mahāṣṭamī to the 9th; (6) only on Mahāṣṭamī; (7) only on Mahānavamī (Kane: 5.154).

20. I am not including community celebrations that center on the recitation of the *Durgā Saptaśatī* by groups of *brāhmaṇas* commissioned for the purpose. These ceremonies may also be quite elaborate and span several days. They, too, take place under temporarily constructed pavilions, include the establishment of jar forms of the Devī and other deities, and generally terminate with a fire oblation (*havan*).

21. *Smārta brāhmaṇas*' ritual manuals (*prayoga*) (e.g., the 17th C.E., *Pūjāprakāśa* by Mitramiśra) often contain instructions on the worship of five deities, collectively known as the *pañcāyatana*, one of whom is Durgā/Devī. Three of the other four are Viṣṇu, Śiva, and Sūrya. The fifth may be Brahman, Brahmā, or Gaṇeśa.

22. One of the many web sites dedicated to Calcutta's Durgā Pūjās states that Raja Jagatsingh Deb, the king of Molla, began his celebrations at the Devī temple in Vishnupur in 997 C.E. (see *www.bangalinet.com*). I have used a few references to web sites on the Internet to draw attention to the growth in this phenomenon. These sites, primarily from Calcutta, provide city maps with locations and photos of most of the public *pūjās* being held in the city. They also provide information on the contents of special *pūjā* issues of magazines, with prose and poetry offerings by well-known authors. In addition, there may be information on special music and film releases for the holiday season, as well as recipes, tourism opportunities, shopping, and links to web sites around the world where the Durgā Pūjā is being celebrated in the Bengali diaspora. I have already (for a couple of years) been receiving electronic "Bijoya" cards from Calcutta.

23. R. Roy's account, written in Bengali in one of several magazines issued on the occasion of Durgā Pūjā, was translated for me by Sudarshan Chowdhary.

24. The family hailed from Halisahar in the north of the *zamīndārī* known as "Twenty-four Parganas" (S. Roy 1991:198).

25. This is supported by the historian S. Roy, who also states that Lakshmikanta Gangopadhyaya was born in 1570. Lakshmikanta founded the Sabarna Rai Choudary family, whose members were the first *zamīndārs* of the region of Calcutta (1991:198).

26. The Kālīghāṭ temple complex was built by Rāja Basanta Rai (S. Roy 1991:198).

27. This early date, however, would have Lakshmi Kant serving as the priest for Durgā Pūjā at the age of fifteen. Photographs of the Rai Choudhary family's "over four hundred year old image" of Durgā and the shrine at Āt Cala are found in Nair (1986:I).

28. S. Roy (1991:198) identifies these districts (*pargana*) as Magura, Khaspur, Kālikāta, Paikan, Anwarpur, and Hetegarh. Such amalgamations of estates actually facilitated Mughal governance of their territories.

29. S. Roy mentions that Lakshmikanta received the title "Majumdar" (1991:199), and the family came to be known as the Rai/Roy Choudurys (1991:9).

30. The Rai Choudary family still celebrates Durgā Pūjā in a new structure built beside the historic Āt Cala (see Nair 1986). This Durgā Pūjā is domestic, restricted to family members, and the disposable images are immersed in the Gaṅgā. Their celebration is characterized by the offering of thirteen goat sacrifices (*chāga bali*): one on Saptamī, three on Aṣṭamī, and nine on Navamī. A buffalo (*mahiṣa*) is also offered. Bodhana is performed nine days before Ṣaṣṭhī.

31. According to certain Beṇgali scholars in Banāras, Siraj-ud-daula is reputed to have abducted the young widowed daughter of Rānī Bhavānī, Tārā Sundarī, in an act that angered many members of the Hindu nobility. He released her due to the public outcry that ensued.

32. This defeat of Calcutta is the source of stories about the notorious "Black Hole of Calcutta," a dungeon in which 123 of the146 British soldiers reputedly confined there suffocated in the heat.

33. Apparently, Rānī Bhavānī opposed the conspiracy (S. Roy 1991:203; R. Bhattacharyya 1986:14).

34. There is evidence that the British system of taxation eventually eroded the wealth and power of the *zamīndārs*. As early as 1790, the first "communal" Durgā Pūjā was celebrated with the pooled resources of "twelve friends," *zamīndār* families who could not afford to stage a *pūjā* on their own. This Barowari Durgā Pūjā became the forerunner of the community-sponsored (*sārvajanīna*) *pūjās,* which have become the norm throughout India (See McDermott 1995).

35. In the *kāyastha* Tarun Kanti Basu's words, "Some *kāyastha*s were taken as *kṣatriya*s. *Kāyastha*s don't belong to the original *varṇa* system. Nobility, *zamīndār*s, and so on were there, and they were taken as *kṣatriyas*." Other sources claim the *kāyastha*s were descendants of the first *brāhmaṇas* in Bengal and their servants (Raychaudhuri and Raychaudhuri 1981).

36. The content of this section of my account derives from interviews with the current head of the Mitra family, Tarun Kanti Basu on October 15, 1991, and his niece, Pallavi, on that and other occasions.

37. I was assisted in my observations of the Chaukhamba Durgā Pūjā in 1991 by Ruth Rickard, who also photographed some elements of the rite.

38. According to the family members, this follows the tradition instituted by Govindaram Mitra and is unique in all of India, with the exception of one branch of the famous Tagore family, in Pathuriaghata, Calcutta.

39. Actual performance of the ritual varies according to the capacities and desires of the *purohita* and patron (*yajamāna*). At times a priest may embellish parts of the ritual common to most *pūjā*s according to his inclinations. Thus he may include the names of favored or local deities in invocations and propitiation. He may replace long rituals with condensed forms. The *yajamāna* may, during segments of the *pūjā*, request that the priest substitute a ritual or liturgical variant that are traditional to the family or group.

40. There are over two hundred public Durgā Pūjā sites authorized in Banāras. To my knowledge, Bengali-styled public Durgā Pūjās are also performed near Hariścandra Ghat (two), Daśāśvamedha Ghat (three), and within Bengali Tola (three or four).

41. Other centers are the Harasundari Dharmaśalā and Pandey Dharmaśalā.

42. Bandyopadhyay (1987:77–82) provides some information on the development of Durgā Pūjās in Delhi. He states that the first Devī image worshipped in a public Durgā Pūjā in Delhi was brought there from Banāras in 1912.

43. The actual city quarters include Bengali Tola, Pandey Haveli, Ramapura, Bhelupura, Shivala, Bhadaini, Kedar Ghat, Sonarpura, and Mishripura.

44. Banāras has long held the reputation as one of the preeminently holy cities for Hindus. Although the city's main deity is Śiva, it also contains temples to all the major and many minor gods and goddesses, making it an important pilgrimage center.

It is commonly believed that Hindus who die within the sacred perimeter of the city will attain instant spiritual liberation (*mokṣa*). Thus Banāras, which centuries ago was known as the Forest of Bliss, is frequently chosen as a site where the elderly retire in what was traditionally the forest-dweller (*vanaprastha*) stage in life.

45. Mr. Lahiri told me that although he had been initiated and was capable of performing the Durgā Pūjā himself, he preferred to have it executed by Pandit Nitai Bhattacharya, whose family had been *purohita*s for the Lahiris for several generations.

46. I cannot vouch for the factual accuracy of this information, which was gleaned from conversations. It appears to be consistent with information in some textual studies.

Ray (n.d.:133) cites a tradition that brāhmaṇism in Bengal began with the king Ādisura who reputedly invited five *brāhmaṇas* from Kanauj during his reign, which is placed sometime between 732 to 1017 C.E. Raychaudhuri (1981:4–5) confirms this tradition with additional details. Ādisura initially invited five *brāhmaṇas* to perform a rite in Bengal, but they did not take up residence there. Subsequently, in order to perform a rite for Ādisura's son, the sons of those five *brāhmaṇas* responded and were later granted five villages near the Gaṅgā, in which they settled with their families and servants. In time fifty-six sons were born, but some tensions arose, and they migrated to different locations. Some took up residence in the Varendra region of North Bengal and others in the Radha region closer to the Gaṅgā. There is some evidence, however, based on inscriptions of land grants, such as during the reign of Kumaragupta I, in 432 C.E., of *brāhmaṇa* presence in Bengal in the fifth and sixth century, and even as early as the third century C.E. (see Raychaudhuri 1981:11, 87). Certain of the so-called mixed classes, such as the Saptaśatī *brāhmaṇas* (whose designation has no apparent connection with the *Durgā Saptaśatī*, but refers to their number), may have descended from these early residents.

47. Bārendra *brāhmaṇa*s generally have surnames such as Sanyal, Lahiri, Bagchi, Moitra, and Bhaduri. Rāḍhi *brāhmaṇa*s have surnames such as Bandyopadhyaya (anglicized to Banerjee), Chattopadhyaya (anglicized to Chatterjee), or Mukhopadhyaya (anglicized to Mukerjee). I was also told that *brāhmaṇa*s who opted to perform rituals adopted the names Bhattacharya or Chakravarti. The Chakravartis normally had kings as clientele, while the Bhattacharyas served a general clientele.

48. Non-Bengali *brāhmaṇa*s (e.g., Saryupari and Maithili) also perform the Durgā Pūjā, but in a style that corresponds to their own tradition. It generally includes the installation of the jar form of the Devī, the recitation of the *Durgā Saptaśatī*, and a fire oblation (*havan*).

49. The form that the Durgā Pūjā takes, as described here, and performed at the Lahiris' home, utilizes Vedic Sanskrit verses, and as such, women would not be permitted to function as priests. One of Mr. Lahiri's daughters claimed to have witnessed a Durgā Pūjā performed by a woman *purohita*, but such a *pūjā* would either have been performed without Vedic *mantra*s (there are Tantric variants on most Vedic elements in the Durgā Pūjā) or would have been a breach in tradition.

50. Raychaudhuri (1981:87) surmises that the Paścatya Vaidika *brāhmaṇas* of the Bharadvaja *gotra* could not have come to Bengal much before Śrī Caitanya, the saint who died in 1533 C.E. and is known for his ecstatic devotion to Kṛṣṇa.

51. Tarun Kanti Basu, head of the Chaukhamba Durgā Pūjā, maintained that the Saradotsava Sabsang *pūjā*, held in Bhelupura, opposite the Vijayanagara Bhavan, was older than the Durgotsava Sammilini's *pūjā*. According to him, the first public *pūjā* in Banāras was started by Lalit Bihari Sen Roy, the financial advisor of the Maharaja of Banāras. It took place in what was then the Mint House, and what is now a Kashmiri Emporium opposite the Taj Hotel in the section of the city known as Nadesar. Organizers at the Durgotsava Sammilini told me that that was "their" *pūjā*, which moved shortly thereafter to the Pandey Haveli area of the city, closer to the large Bengali community there. Kumar (1988:218) places the origins of the Saradotsava Sabsang's *pūjā* at 1943.

52. Other Bengali *purohitas* who are commissioned to perform the Durgā Pūjā in Banāras include: Dr. Bishwanath Bhattacharya, Bishwanath Bhattacharya Sahityacharya, Anil Bhattacharya, Madhav Bhattacharya, Babu Bhattacharya, Chittaran Vedacharya, Shiva Kumar Nyayacharya, Bidhu Shastracharya, and Hemendra Nath Nyaya Tarkatirtha. Most are Vaidika or Rāḍhi *brāhmaṇas*.

53. He owned properties in Assam and Meghalaya as well.

54. This information derives from Mr. Lahiri's grandson. Mr. Lahiri himself told me that while his grandfather made frequent visits to Banāras, he and his wife finally retired in the city shortly after the Sepoy Mutiny (c. 1872). He also claimed that the Lahiri family *pūjā* was a tradition as venerable as the oldest Durgā Pūjā in Banāras, namely that of the Mitra family in Chaukhamba. Prior to their celebrations in Banāras, the Lahiri family *pūjās*, he claimed, had taken place for a century in Bengal.

55. It is widely believed that death in Banāras grants instant liberation (*mukti*). Retirement to Banāras is thus a common choice for elderly Hindus. Mr. Lahiri claimed that his wife holds such a belief, while he himself did not. Rather, he found Banāras to be "a good place to die." Excellent studies of the phenomenon of dying in Śiva's sacred city are found in Parry (1994) and Justice (1997).

56. Interview, October 1990.

57. Only a few translations of *pūjā* texts are available. These include Hélène Brunner-Lachaux (1963) and T. Goudriaan (1965).

58. The literature on the Navarātra celebrations, including Durgā Pūjā, is voluminous. Notable works are the *Durgotsavaviveka* of Sūlapāṇi, the *Durgābhakti-taraṅgiṇi* of Vidyāpati, the *Navarātra-pradīpa* of Vināyaka (alias Nanda-paṇḍita), and the *Durgotsavapaddhati* by Udayasiṃha, a fifteenth-century work (Kane:5.155).

59. The *Durgārcana-paddhati* is included in the *Durgāpūjā-prayogatattva* (Sanskrit Sāhitya Parishad, 1924) (Kane:5.155).

60. See Dorson (1965) for a discussion of this interpretive trend among early Indologists. Konow's article on a European parallel to the Durgā Pūjā is another example. Konow argues that Kālī and Kālī worship reveal traces of Indo-European goddess worship, which "is continued in an unbroken line in the Durgāpūjā of the present day" (1925:316). He cites Tacitus on the worship rites by seven Germanic tribes of the goddess Nerthus (Mother Earth), whose worship included the bathing of the goddess in a hidden lake and the sacrifice of slaves (through drowning) in the same lake. After some etymological maneuvering, he connects Nerthus to Kālī and Śiva (via the Sanskrit root *nṛt* (to dance), with which they are associated). He then equates Kālī (as a manifestation of the Earth) with Durgā in the Durgā Pūjā and notes that the singing, dancing, and sacrifices during the *pūjā* and the exuberant merriment that accompanies the Devī's immersion rites resonate strongly with the rites for Nerthus. He concludes, quite unconvincingly, that it is "necessary to infer that the worship of Nerthus on the one hand and that of Kālī on the other are derived from one and the same source, which must have taken its rise in the Indo-European period" (1925:323).

61. Sketchy treatments of the Durgā Pūjā are also found in Chaudhuri (1984), Bandyopadhyay (1987), Chaturvedi (1996), and Singh and Nath (1999), although these are primarily concerned with the goddess Durgā.

62. Personal communication (2000). This refers primarily to letters, rather than conversational information.

63. The version that follows is recounted in Chaturvedi (1996: 28–29) and, from the nature of the *mantras* provided, clearly belongs to the popular rather than the Sanskritic tradition.

Chapter 3: Overview of the Durgā Pūjā

1. Kane (2.705–40). The etymology of the word *pūjā* is unclear. Charpentier (1926) suggests a derivation from the Tamil root *pūcu*, 'to smear'. See Thieme (1939) for alternate suggestions that center on the honoring of a guest. Gonda (1980) examines early uses of the word.

2. See Macdonell (1954) for a discussion of Vedic religion, and Kane (2.983ff) for specific details on *yajña*.

3. Stein (1980:386–388) also observes that the apparent similarity between the Vedic *aśvamedha* and the Navarātra celebrations of the kings of the Vijayanagara empire of South India may seem "superficial or strained." Nevertheless, he notes some common features. The Pāṇḍava king, Yudhiṣṭhira, hero of the *Mahābhārata,* is reputed to have performed an *aśvamedha* during a Navarātra (see Roy n.d.:12.84, p.161). In one rite of the Vijayanagara Navarātra celebrations, the king's women (in one account about sixty of them between the ages of sixteen to twenty), heavily bejewelled, circumambulated the king's horses, paralleling the king's wives' circumambulation of the sacrificial horse in the *aśvamedha*. More strikingly, the king's horse received a

special consecration, in which it was apparently identified with the king himself and the state.

4. Sudarshan Chowdhury, Interview (1990).

5. Interview, Lahiri grandchildren, October 1991. In the Durgā Pūjā held in 2000, the Devī arrived on a horse, and departed on a boat. The horse is a harbinger of drought, anarchy, and destruction. The palanquin is said to represent widespread epidemic. In this symbolism, too, we note the ambivalent nature of the Goddess, who may bring with her prosperity and a good harvest (e.g., elephant) or leave disease and chaos in her wake.

6. See Silburn (1988) for an excellent treatment of Kuṇḍalinī Yoga in the philosophy of Kāśmir Śaivism.

7. Coburn (1991) translates these appendages, discusses their content, and explores commentaries on their content by such philosophers as Bhāskararāya, a Śakta Tantric, and Nāgoji Bhaṭṭa, a grammarian.

8. The goddess Gaṅgā is thought to flow through Śiva's hair and is depicted as such in numerous images (such as Chola bronzes of Śiva Naṭarāja or popular lithographs). In certain shrines, Gaṅgā water drips from an earthen pot placed above a Śiva *liṅga*, in a clear evocation of this mythic association.

9. Although Durgā is identified as the Great Goddess in the Durgā Pūjā, her name as merely one of nine constituent *devīs*, lingers in the *navapatrikā* rite. The *navapatrikā* form of the Devī probably belongs to an earlier, and once separate, strata of rites in which Durgā was the name of a minor goddess.

10. Mitra (1922) notes Durgā's association with vegetation in both practice and scripture. He sees the *navapatrikā* rite as a survival of the cult of Durgā as a vegetation-spirit or tree goddess. Such a cult is still in evidence in the districts of Mymensingh and Tippera in East Bengal, where the Devī is worshipped as Bana/Vana Durgā ("Durgā of the Forest"). Bana Durgā, whose *dhyāna* (meditative visualization) depicts her with forehead wrinkles, is worshipped in front of the *sheora* (*Streblus asper*) and other trees, where the Devī is believed to dwell. In the course of her *pūjā*, she is offered "fried paddy (*khai*), fried flattened rice (*chirey bhaja*), powdered rice, plantains with pips (*bichey kala*), [etc.]." She is also offered duck's eggs stained with vermillion. Barbers are commissioned to perform the sacrifice of pigs, whose throats are slit with their razors (1922: 232). This worship is performed with the express objective of saving the worshipper's son from danger.

A textual connection between Durgā and vegetation is found in the *Durgā Saptaśatī* 11.44–46. When the Devī is recounting her various incarnations in order to defeat demons, she states, "Then, I shall support the whole world with life-sustaining vegetables, which shall grow out of my own body, until the rains come. . . . I shall attain fame on earth as Śākaṃbharī ("She who supports with Vegetables"). Then I will slay the great *asura* named Durgama. Thus I will gain fame as Durgā."

11. According to early Hindu texts, a reflection in water or a mirror represents the soul of a person. See *Śākhāyana Āraṇyaka* 6.2, 8.7 and *Aitareya Āraṇyaka* 3.24.

On the pervasive use of the term "mirror" as a symbol of illusory reality and indirect perception, see Wayman (1974). For connections between Kāśmir Śaiva metaphysics and the Devī's mirror, see Dehejia (1997). Goldberg (2001) explores the relationship between a wider array of philosophical categories (drawn from Sāṅkhya, Yoga, Ch'an Buddhism, etc.) and the symbolism of Pārvatī's mirror.

12. A detailed study of Durgā's encounter with Mahiṣa in Purāṇic and other sources is found in Berkson (1995).

13. Berkson (1995:146) notes, "According to the texts, Devi harasses, becomes enraged, slaps, smashes, strikes, delivers blows, pounds, drags, bites, kicks, ties down with a noose, injures, maims, mutilates, stupefies, paralyzes, showers arrows on, breaks chariots, dismembers, swallows, blinds, tears and shatters bodies into a thousand pieces, severs necks, splits open Mahisa's breast and slays! But her lovely face is in no way perturbed." This serenity is indeed a pervasive feature in almost all her earthen images.

14. It would, however, be erroneous to draw too sharp a distinction between the Durgā Pūjā and the kind of intense worship with offerings of one's own blood, as performed by the mythic king Suratha and the merchant Samādhi. In the Cooch Bihar Durgā Pūjā, in Bengal, a member of the royal family is reputed to make an offering of his own blood to the Goddess during a private rite on the night of Aṣṭamī (see www.bangalinet.com).

15. Interview, October 1991.

16. An organizer at Durgotsava Sammilini, the oldest public Durgā Pūjā in Banāras. Interview (1990).

17. James Preston (1985) regards embodiments of the divine as "cosmic implosions," in which the entire cosmos is condensed into a particular image, contained both in space and time.

18. S. K. Rai Choudary, a patron and organizer of the Durgotsav Sammilini. Interview, September 27, 1990.

19. The blood offering, central to the *pūjā*, is disappearing in Banāras and other parts of India.

20. Some notes on Tantric prescriptions concerning virgin worship are found in Kaviraj (1987:277–280).

21. This is also a synonym of the goddess Mātāṅgī, one of the Ten Mahāvidyās, whose name means a female of the outcaste group. The best available study of the Māhavidyās is found in Kinsley (1997).

22. See Babb (1975: 53–61), and Fuller (1992:74–82) for an analysis of the meaning of *prasāda* in *pūjā*.

23. See Kinsley (1986:35–64) for a detailed examination of the mythology of Satī and Pārvatī.

24. The Garwahl is unusual in this regard, since the Navarātra is not well known there. The major annual goddess festival during which women return to their natal homes is in honor of Nandā Devī (Sax 1991:120–121).

25. Interview (1990).

26. I have on occasion seen soldiers and policemen bring new rifles to the Durgā Kuṇḍ temple in Banāras on Mahāṣṭamī for consecration. They told me that it was normal to have new items, including cars and appliances, consecrated and gave no explicit indication that their consecration was a form of weapon (*āyudha*) *pūjā*.

27. These limbs are the *Prādhānika*, *Vaikṛtika*, and *Mūrti Rahasyas*.

28. Sudarshan Chowdhury; Interview, Sept. 27, 1990.

Chapter 4: The Durgā Pūjā

Chapter 4.1: Preliminaries

1. Hudson (1999:76) points out that desire is a prime motivation for *pūjā*. However, unlike mundane desire, which is ego-centered, in *pūjā*, "the ego's desiring consciousness is turned away from the mirror image of itself towards a god." Deities, too, are desiring beings, who may desire a relationship with us in return. A loving devotee (*bhakta*) is one who "clings in a desiring or attached manner to a specific god, [and] is the slave, servant, refugee, or lover in relation to that god."

2. In support of its simultaneously obligatory and desire-based nature, however, the *Kālikā Purāṇa* (63.12–13) states that whoever does not celebrate the great festival of Durgā, because of laziness, hypocrisy, hatred, or stupidity, has all their desires frustrated by the angry Devī.

3. On the kind of *yantra* and Durgā *bīja* used, see the lengthier discussions on *yantra*s later in the work.

4. *Vidyā* may also refer to a formula that embodies a *devī*. Its counterpart is the term *mantra*, which according to Bhāskararāya, refers to male deities (Brooks 1992:82).

5. In the *Durgā Saptaśatī* 1.58, 11.21, Durgā is referred to as Mahāvidyā, and Vidyā (1.44, 4.8).

6. The *Mahānirvāṇa Tantra* 5.90, 92 describes the procedure differently. "Join the first and second fingers of the right hand, and tap the palm of the left hand three times, each time after the first with great force, thus making a loud sound, and then snap the finger while uttering the Weapon-mantra [i.e., *Phaṭ*]" (Woodroffe's [1985:102] translation).

7. *Ātapa taṇḍula* is the type of rice normally used for *pūjā* offerings. First it is dried and then husked, but it is not cooked. *Śiddha*, popular with Bengalis, is rice that is first boiled, dried, and then husked. It is not used in rituals.

8. Pandit Chakravarty's translation. Ralph T. H. Griffith (1986:16) renders this verse:

We in King Soma place our trust, in Agni, and in Varuṇa,
The Āditya, Vishṇu, Sūrya, and the Brahman-priest Bṛihaspatī.

9. "*Amuka*" is a term equivalent to "John Doe." The *purohita* replaces it with the *yajamāna*'s lineage (*gotra*). This *gotra* is related to a Vedic *brāhmaṇa* family, such as Kaśyapa. If the *pūjā* is performed for others, the *purohita* ends with the word "*kariṣyāmi*," which in Sanskrit grammar is the *parasmaipadi*, first person future form of the verbal root "*kṛ*" (to do/perform). If he is performing the *pūjā* for himself, he will use the *ātmanepadi* form, "*kariṣye*," used for actions pertaining to the self. Both forms translate as, "I will do/perform."

10. Consult the earlier section where *kāmya* and *niṣkāmya pūjā*s are discussed.

11. Translations of all *Ṛg Veda* verses are derived from R. T. H. Griffith (1995 [1889]), unless otherwise stated.

12. As previously mentioned, the *sāmānya vidhi* described here is a modification specific to a particular group of *purohita*s prior to their performance of Durgā Pūjā. If the subsequent special (*viśeṣa*) *pūjā* to be performed is not as elaborate, the procedural order is as follows: *ācamana*, *svasti vācanam*, *saṅkalpa*, *āsana śuddhi*, *jala śuddhi*, *puṣpa śuddhi*, purification of palms and fingers of the hand (*kara śuddhi*), preparation of the vessels for *argha* (*arghapātrapratipatti*), *sāmānya argha*, offerings to *dikpāla*s, *prāṇāyāma*, *bhūta śuddhi*, *mātṛka nyāsa*, *kara nyāsa*, *aṅga nyāsa*, *antarmātṛkā nyāsa*, *vahya mātṛkā nyāsa*, *pīṭha nyāsa*, *ṛṣyadi nyāsa*, *aṅga nyāsa* (again), *kara nyāsa* (again), *cakṣur dāna*, *prāṇa pratiṣṭha*, *avāhana*, *dhyāna* of the deity, *mānasa pūjā*, preparation of the vessels for *viśeṣa argha*, *viśeṣa argha*, *dhyāna* of the deity, and detailed *pūjā* of the deity.

Since Durgā Pūjā is rather elaborate, *purohita*s modify the *sāmānya vidhi*, performing many of the procedures within the context of the *bodhana* rituals that follow. The order and content of the procedures listed above differ from Purāṇic prescriptions concerning the worship of the Goddess as described, for instance, in Van Kooij's *Worship of the Goddess according to the Kālikā Purāṇa*. It serves as an example of the differences between ritual prescriptions in Purāṇic texts and actual practice.

Chapter 4.2: Bodhana

1. Stein (1980:388) citing Kane (Vol. 2,1:395) notes that the bright half of the lunar month of Āśvina is regarded as *anadhyāya* according to the *Dharmaśāstra* of Aparaka. This means that it is designated as inappropriate for Vedic learning and other activities, such as ritual performance. Thus Rāma's mythic act reflects a breach of orthodox propriety. Nicolo Conti, traveling in the Vijayanagara kingdom in 1420 C.E. observed that although *brāhmaṇas* functioned as ritualists, they certainly did not dominate the ritual arena and were even publically reviled.

I noted an ambivalent attitude to the ritualist (*purohita*) in many conversations with patrons. Despite the enormous respect Pandit Nitai has among the Lahiri family members (e.g., he is called Uncle Nitai ("Nitai *mama*")) by those junior to him in age, Mr. Lahiri noted that he could conduct the rite on his own and only commissioned *purohitas* for their greater expertise and the convenience it afforded him. Similarly, Tarun Kanti Basu of the Mitra family, who are not *brāhmaṇas* but *kayasthas*, noted, "the *purohita* just performs a socio-religious role. He does a professional job. At that moment, he has a role to perform, a special status, and he is paid for that role. He does something we cannot do for ourselves. Nothing can be done without them. . . . The *purohita* has no role to play in our daily lives" (Interview, October 15, 1991). Such comments, from both *brāhmaṇa* and *non-brāhmaṇa* patrons reflect the continued dominance of the patron (*yajamāna*) on the ritual space, in which the *purohita* is emphatically designated as a mere functionary (albeit indispensable for patrons of *non-brāhmaṇa* castes).

2. In many temples that house Śiva *liṅga*s (phallic effigies/signs), the Goddess is recognized as the *yoni* (female reproductive organ) in which the *liṅga* stands. Often, a *ghaṭa*, a clay pot, is suspended above the *liṅga* and its sanctified water (*amṛta*) is allowed to drip slowly upon the *liṅga*. This *ghaṭa*, which often contains Gaṅgā water or its metonymic equivalent, is also the Devī, identifiable through such mythic images as the descent of the goddess Gaṅgā who flows through Śiva's matted locks.

3. Pandit Chakravarty's translation.

"O Queen, thou art patient like the earth, hence control the earth. Thou, the organizer of household affairs and the conductor of full administration art firm like the earth, hence steady the earth. Thou art unagitated like the glorious sky, hence do the earth no injury!"(Chand 1965:193).

"Thou art the earth, the ground, thou art the all-sustaining Aditi, she who supporteth all the world. Control the earth, steady the earth, do thou the earth no injury"(Griffith 1987 [1899]:127).

4. Pandit Chakravarty's translation.

5. Griffith (1987 [1899]:73).

"O exalted wife, possessing vast knowledge, eatable and drinkable articles, smell thou the jar. Mayest thou obtain thousands of juices of medicinal herbs, whereby thou mayest be free from sorrow. Fill us with prosperity. Let riches come again to me" (Chand 1965:118).

"Smell the trough: may the drops enter thee, O mighty one! Return again with sap! And milk to us a thousandfold! Broad-streamed, milk-abounding— may wealth come back to me!" (Eggeling 1978 [1882]:415).

6. Coomaraswamy (1971:61) interprets it as a symbol of plenty and welfare, and Bosch (1960:112) holds that it can fulfil its owner's desires and produce treasures.

7. Kramrisch (1956:263) connects the brimming jar to a form of Lajjā Gaurī, a nude goddess depicted on her back in a position of either giving birth or sexual readiness.

8. Griffith (1987 [1899]:34).

"O God, Thou art the director of this fine world; the Creator of objects dependable on air and the Force inherent in the sun for the motion of the waters, the stay and support of all excellent objects. O Lord, Thou makest us reach the destination of true and high knowledge" (Chand 1965:68)

"Thou art Varuna's stay. Ye two are the rest of Varuna's stay. Thou art the rightful seat (*ritasadanam*) of Varuna! Seat thee on the rightful seat of Varuna" (Eggeling 1978 [1882]:83–84).

9. A vessel full of pure water, topped with a coconut may on occasion be worshiped as Varuṇa, who is the lord of the waters (Bühnemann 1988:46).

10. Ray (n.d.:139) refers to this drawing as the *sindur puttali* and states that the *ghaṭa* is a replica of Mother Earth.

11. "Upspringing from thine every joint, upspringing from each knot of thine, Thus with a thousand, Dūrvā! with a hundred do thou stretch us out" (Griffith 1987 [1899]:128).

"O woman, just as the grass increases widely from all sides, with hundreds and thousands of joints and knots, so lengthen out our line of descendants with sons and grandsons"(Chand 1965:193).

"Growing up joint by joint, knot by knot; so do thou prolong us, O Dūrvā (plant), by a thousand, and a hundred (descendants)" (Eggeling 1978 [1882]:381).

12. "Grandeur and Fortune are Thy two wives. Thy sides are Day and Night. Constellations are Thy form: the Aswins are Thy Mouth. Imploring grant salvation unto me, grant me all sorts of knowledge and pleasures" (Chand 1965:444).

"Beauty and Fortune are thy wives: each side of thee are Day and Night. The constellations are thy form: The Aśvins are thine open jaws. Wishing, wish yonder world for me, wish that the Universe be mine" (Griffith 1987 [1899]:289).

13. Pandit Chakravarty's translation.

14. Griffith (1986:215) renders this as, "May we attain that excellent glory of Savitar the God: So may he stimulate our prayers!"

15. "Upspringing from thine every joint, upspringing from each knot of thine, Thus with a thousand, Dūrvā! with a hundred do thou stretch us out" (Griffith 1987 [1899]:128).

"O woman, just as the grass increases widely from all sides, with hundreds and thousands of joints and knots, so lengthen out our line of descendants with sons and grandsons" (Chand 1965:193).

16. Tantric seed syllables (*bīja mantra*), such as Aiṃ, Hrīṃ, Klīṃ, are powerful utterances believed to embody the vibratory manifestation (subtle and gross) of the deity itself. Sometimes certain *bīja mantra*s are associated with particular goddesses (e.g., *Duṃ* with Durgā, or *Hrīṃ* with Bhuvaneśvarī), but it is also common to see their application without reference to any particular goddess. See Kinsley (1997:122–128,131–136) for a discussion on such *mantra*s as they relate to Tripura-sundarī and Bhuvaneśvarī.

17. Scholarly discussions of this procedure are also found in Gupta, Hoens, and Goudriaan (1979:136), and van Kooij (1972:14–16).

18. The Sanskrit syllable, "*ra*" (*repha*), which is composed of the consonant, "r" + the vowel "a," as well as the seed syllable (*bīja*) "*Raṃ*," formed through the addition of the nasal ending (*anusvāra*), are associated with fire (*agni*). Thus it is appropriately used to burn the *pāpapuruṣa*. Wheelock (1989:103) emphasizes that *bīja mantras* in this and other Tantric rituals "are not meant to be mere symbols of the elements, they *are* the cosmic elements in essential form."

19. The endings *namaḥ*, *svāhā*, *vaṣat*, *huṃ*, *vauṣat*, and *phaṭ* are called the *jāti* and are used in *kara nyāsa* and *aṅga nyāsa*.

The *purohita* has placed the consonants and vowels of the Sanskrit language into his hands after suffixing the nasal ending (*anusvāra*) to them. In his two thumbs (*aṅguṣṭha*) he places the aspirated and nonaspirated guttural consonants and corresponding nasal, sandwiched between the vowel "a" and its increased (*vṛddhi*) form, "long a" (i.e., *ā*). This envelopment (*sampuṭa*) of consonants by vowels unifies and empowers them. A similar procedure is used in certain forms of recitation (*sampuṭa pāṭha*) of the *Durgā Saptaśatī*. In the index fingers (*tarjanī*), he places the palatal consonants and corresponding nasal, between "i" and "long i." The retroflex (hard palate) consonants and nasal are placed between "u" and "long u" in the middle fingers (*madhyama*). The dental consonants and nasal, boxed between "e" and its *vṛddhi* "ai" are imprinted on the unnamed or ring fingers (*anāmika*). On the little fingers (*kaniṣṭha*) he places the labials and corresponding nasal, enclosed by the vowel "o" and its *vṛddhi* form "au." Finally in the backs (*pṛṣṭha*) and palms of his hand (*karatala*), he places the semivowels, sibilants, and conjunct consonant, "kṣa" contained between the nasal (*anusvāra*) and aspirated endings (*visarga*).

20. The body is here referred to as an armour (*kavaca*). This is because it has already been transformed (through *bhūtaśuddhi*) into adamantine substance. An important quality of this bodily material, conveyed through the term, *kavaca*, is its impenetrable, impregnable, and protective nature.

21. My comments on *mānasa pūjā* derive from Bühnemann (1988:54, 88–93), whose information derives from Tantric and Purāṇic texts.

22. The *praṇava* or *omkāra*, "Aum" or "Om" is composed of the letters "A," "U," and "M," corresponding to the sun, the moon, and fire respectively. The essence of the *praṇava* is the Devī. The *argha* is often connected with sun worship, but here the sun, moon, and fire are linked, along with their constituent parts, and identified with the Devī.

23. See the previous discussion of *sāmānya agrha* for the translation and interpretation of this activity.

24. D. C. Sircar (1973) speculates on the etymology of the term "*bhāgavatī*," which means one who possesses the female reproductive organ (*bhaga*), suggesting that it might predate the masculine form "*bhagavan*" which is now synonymous with "Blessed One" or "God."

25. Although the term *svāhā* is used as an utterance at the end of *mantras*, particularly in the fire oblation rituals (*homa*), it is also an epithet of the Devī (e.g., *Durgā Saptaśatī* 4.7).

26. What exactly constitutes the sixteen parts of this worship varies somewhat since certain parts (e.g., the food offerings, *naivedya*) may be subdivided and included in the count. The extended description of this part of the ritual will occur later in the study.

27. These may be fruit (*phala*), homemade food or *racanā* (*lai/taja*; H/Skt), *ladū* and other sweets (*miṭhai*), betel nut (*tambula*), *pānarthodaka*, and so on.

28. Pandit Chakravarty explained that one may also understand these prayers to mean that the gross and subtle senses (*bhūta*) should not behave inappropriately during this ritual.

29. Siddhidātrī is the ninth in the well-known list of "The Nine Durgās" contained in the *Devī Kavaca*, an appendage of the *Durgā Saptaśatī*.

30. In Koṭālīpādā, in the district of Faridpur, Bengal, the Bāro-Bhāiyā (Twelve Brothers) cult offers evidence of Durgā worship in association with demons. The cult centers on the worship of twelve deities who are regarded as brothers. They are described as demons (*daitya*) and worshipped with their mother, Vanadurgā (Durgā of the Forest), who is described as *dānava-mātā* (Mother of Demons). Some of these demons' names, such as *gābhūra-dalana* (Oppressor of the Young), *mocrā-siṃha* (Great One who Strangles to Death), and *niśā-nātha* (Lord of the Night), reflect their pernicious and frightening natures.

31. See the interpretation in the previous section on *kāṇḍā ropaṇam*. I am inclined to interpret the process as a planting ritual, not of grain, but of orchards. There appear to be motifs of pruning, grafting, transplanting, and protecting the trees in this ritual.

32. This verse serves as a good example of my deference to Pandit Chakravarty's translations over my own. My translation would have run:

Om! You, the auspiciousness in all things auspicious, O Śivā (auspicious one), granter of every aim,

O three-eyed protectress Gaurī, O Nārāyaṇī, praise be to you.

Chapter 4.3: Adhivāsa

1. Pandit Chakravarty's translation.

2. Pandit Chakravarty's translation.

"That which, divine, mounts far when man is waking, that which returns to him when he is sleeping. The lights' one light that goeth to a distance, may that, my mind, be moved by auspicious resolve" (Chand 1965:469).

"That which, divine, mounts far when man is waking, that which returns to him when he is sleeping.

The lights' one light that goeth to a distance, may that, my mind, be moved by right intention" (Griffith 1987 [1899]:307).

3. Pandit Chakravarty's translation.

4. Pandit Chakravarty's translation.

5. Pandit Chakravarty's translation.

6. Pandit Chakravarty's translation.

7. Just as portions of the *maṇḍala* serve as seats of deities, ritual texts note that lotus blossoms may also serve as *maṇḍalas* or seats, because deities may be invoked into portions of the lotus (e.g., petals, pericarp) (see Bühnemann 1987:63). The lotus is often depicted as the throne of a deity (e.g., Brahmā, Viṣṇu, Lakṣmī), and is itself a symbol of the universe. The *sarvatobhadra maṇḍala* actually contains an eight-petalled lotus in its center.

8. Each of the faces of the Mitra family images is cast from a mold, so that they retain their features every year. Members of the Pal caste would come to the Chaukhamba house and fashion the images in a room beside the *pūjālaya*. However, this practice is no longer followed (probably due to the increasing demands for images by community groups), and the images are fabricated in Pandey Haveli.

9. According to Chaturvedi (1996:6), in the fabrication of Bengali Durgā Pūjā clay images, great care is taken to incorporate some soil from all the regions of a locality, especially the red-light region. This, he suggests, signifies that the Devī encompasses all types of beings, of all moral natures. She is also intended to be a representation of the entire universe. The practice has a clear Tantric resonance, which aims at the transcendence of all dualities. In a further inversion of what one might commonly think, the earth on a prostitute's doormat is sometimes regarded as highly auspicious, rather than inauspicious, since patrons, upon entering her house, are said to leave behind their merit at the doorstep.

10. The origin of this current, popular combination of deities is unclear. According to Ray (n.d.), a seventh century C.E. image in Bengal depicts an eight-armed goddess standing atop Mahiṣa spearing him to death. Durgā images with ten arms, many wielding weapons, atop her lion mount and accompanied by Gaṇeśa or Kārtikeya are in evidence in Bengal by the ninth/tenth century C.E. Vidyāpati's (14/15th century) *Durgābhakti-taraṅgiṇi* is the first to refer to this current style of image in which the Devī is accompanied by her children.

11. Interview, October 1991.

Chapter 4.4: Saptamī

1. Compare this Durgā Gāyatrī cited by C. M. Brown (1998:74), (quoted from I. K. Taimni, *Gāyatrī: The Daily Religious Practice of the Hindus*, p. 61): *mahādevyai ca vidmahe durgādevyai ca dhīmahī tanno devī pracodayāt.*

2. The *purohita* appears to be identified with the Sun through this *argha* offering. The Sun, as previously noted, is the formless Brahman.

3. The *tantradhāraka* aids the *purohita* in the ritual by holding together the various strands of ritual activity. If the *purohita* is still learning, he may enlist the aid of a senior *brāhmaṇa* (perhaps his mentor) to serve in the role. If he is relatively

confident to see his way through the ritual, he may use a novice, for whom the role serves as training.

4. See the relevant *mantra* under the *sāmānya vidhi* section in the "Offerings to *Brāhmaṇa* Attendants" previously discussed.

5. Sir William Jones rendered it as follows:

Let us adore the supremacy of that divine sun, the godhead, who illuminates all, who recreates all, from whom all proceed, to whom all must return, whom we invoke to direct our understandings aright in our progress towards his holy seat (Quoted in Griffith 1986:215).

6. Also called *kacvi* (*Arum colocasia*), the plant is cultivated for its fleshy, edible root.

7. In his discussion of the Gingee Fort buffalo sacrifice, Hiltebeitel observes that a group of goddesses known as the Seven Virgins, who have temples within the fort, are said to guard it. The main goddess of the fort, Kamalakanniyamman, he notes, "is a form of Durgā, the goddess of forts (*durkai*, Sanskrit *durgā*, means "the inaccessible," and is a term for "fort.")" (1988:62).

8. Śiva is also known as *vyomakeśa* (He whose Hair is the Void/Sky).

9. The Maruts are wind gods mentioned in the Vedas who are generally associated with Rudra.

10. Prayāga is a city at the confluence (*saṅgam*) of three holy rivers, the Gaṅgā, the Yamunā, and the Sarasvatī, each of which is a goddess. Mundane geography reveals that only the first two rivers meet at this place, but the Sarasvatī is a divine river believed to flow underground. Since there are three holy rivers, this may provide the reasoning behind their choice as the third group to bathe the Devī.

11. The Vidyādharas are celestial beings who are possessors and revealers of knowledge (*vidyā*). They are shown subordinate to the Devī, one of whose epithets is Mahāvidyā.

12. Serpents are associated with the number five in the festival of Nāg Pañcamī, hence a possible reason for them being chosen as the fifth group of bathers. Similarly, there are six major mountains, seven sages, and eight Vasus, which are respectively selected as the sixth, seventh, and eighth groups to bathe the Devī.

13. The Vasus are "souls of the universe." They sometimes refer to the constellations.

The use of eight waters also parallels the notion of the eight lucky items (*aṣṭamaṅgala*), which are mentioned at the final bathing. These items (when associated with great occasions like coronations) are listed as a lion, a bull, an elephant, a water jar, a fan, a flag, a trumpet, and a lamp. Other listings have them as a *brāhmaṇa*, a cow, fire, gold, ghee, the sun, water, and a king.

14. Mitra (1925) discusses folk traditions in Eastern Bengal in which trees such as the *sheora* (*Streblus asper*), *uduma* (*Ficus glomerata*?) and *kamini* (*Murraya axotica*)

are believed to be embodiments, manifestations, or dwelling places of the goddess Bana Durgā (Durgā of the Forest), also known as Burha Thakurani (the Old Dame). In one cult found in the Pabna and Nadiya districts of East Bengal, unmarried girls alone may worship the deity Itokumara, believed to be present in the jujube tree (*Zizyphus jujuba*). They do so in the hopes of acquiring a husband. It is worth noting that Kārtikeya, who is present in the Durgā Pūjā's clay image complex, is known as *kumāra* and regarded as a handsome, eligible, and desirable husband.

15. Cohen (1991:124) notes that for most votaries, the new *sārī* in which the *navapatrikā* is clothed indicates her role as a new bride.

16. Cohen (1991:125) makes the identical observation. He notes how knowledgeable devotees are hard-pressed to explain the conflict inherent in the "marriage" of Gaṇeśa to the *kalā bou*, which is unequivocally, the Great Goddess, Durgā, "his mother."

17. A detailed study of Gaṇeśa's marital status (single, or paired with a wide variety of wives) is found in Cohen (1991). He cites numerous examples of Gaṇeśa associated with the goddess Lakṣmī as his sister, or more frequently, as his wife. In the Durgā Pūjā clay image grouping, he is generally placed beside Lakṣmī. Since one of the plants (i.e., Dhānya/paddy) in the *navapatrikā* is identified with Lakṣmī, it provides another rationale for its placement beside him.

18. Durgā is associated with *buddhi* (intellect) four times (1.60, 4.4, 5.14, 11.7) in the *Durgā Saptaśatī*. In the *Brahma-vaivarta-purāṇa* (Gaṇeśa-khaṇḍa 45.4, Kṛṣṇajanma-khaṇḍa 41.78, 86.97) she is called Buddhirūpā (She Whose Form is Intellect).

19. Another perspective among Bengalis is that Gaṇeśa, due to his appearance and nature, is virtually incapable of finding a wife. He is thus married to the "mute and uncomplaining banana bride," as a last hope (Cohen 1991:125). Gaṇeśa is also well-known for his love of bananas (another reason to pair him with the *kalā bou*).

20. Gaṇeśa is often found associated with the *saptamātṛkās* (Seven Mothers) after the fifth century (Cohen 1991:118), and Getty (1936:36) wonders if this leads to his later association with groups of eight goddesses (i.e., the Aṣṭa Siddhi). This association, too, might be at the basis of his placement with the *navapatrikā* (Nine Plants) form of Durgā. Such an association may well have derived from an initial equation of the Aṣṭa Siddhis with the eight *śaktis* of Durgā, worshipped during the *sarvatobhadra maṇḍala* rite.

21. Vāsudeva, Saṅkarṣana, Pradyumna, and Aniruddha, are four generations of deities related to Viṣṇu and Kṛṣṇa. In Pañcarātra philosophy they are the four arrays (*vyūha*) of consciousness.

22. Griffith (1986). Pandit Chakravarty rendered this verse as follows:
Om! Come Agni, lauded, to the feast. Come to the offering of the gifts.
As Priest be seated on the grass.

23. Griffith (1986).

24. This is the root (*mūla*) *mantra* of Durgā.

25. Chand (1965:25). "Thee for food. Thee for vigor. Ye are breezes" (Griffith 1987 [1899]:1).

26. Griffith (1986).

27. This was provided by Pandit Chakravarty as the first verse of the *Atharva Veda*, but Bloomfield's concordance lists it as AV.1.6.

28. This could be "Hrīṃ," the seed syllable of the Goddess, or it may be the specific seed syllable of Durgā, "Duṃ."

29. Bühnemann (1988:45), citing Mitramiśra's comments in the *Pūjāprakāśa*, an elaborate seventeenth-century treatise on *pūjā*, notes that all gods may be invoked into the brimming jar (*pūrṇakalaśa*), which is imagined to be the seat of the universe.

30. The *atasī* is the hemp or flax plant. Flax, itself, has a straw-like color that could parallel the molten gold (*tapta kāñcana*) color of the Goddess cited in certain variants. This yellowish hue has sometimes been identified with the color of matured rice paddy or wheat, suggesting Durgā's identification with vegetation and the harvest (Chaturvedi 1996:39). Yellow may also evoke the color of the menstrual fluid of women (Bandyopadhyay 1987:14). However, the *dhyāna* refers to the color of the *atasī* flower, not the plant, and flax flowers are blue. Pandit Chakravarty referred to the *atasī* as the hemp plant, citing that its flowers were dark (ruddy green?) in color. This color could suggest an arboreal (rather than an agricultural) image of the Devī. Alternately, it could represent a dark complexion, suggestive of the origins of this worship rite among dark-skinned votaries of the Devī. As such it would contrast with the light-skinned variant evoked by the molten gold color. The dark color also evokes a connection with dark-skinned deities such as Kālī, who is conspicuously absent from the clay image array. Durgā appears to replace Mahākālī in the renowned triad formed with Mahālakṣmī and Mahāsarasvatī.

In travels in the Himalayan foothills I encountered some Śaivite *sadhus* (holy men) who identified the Devī with the hemp/cannabis leaves and flowers they were smoking. They noted that Śiva was extremely fond of hemp and that Durgā's epithet, Śailaputrī (Daughter of the Mountain), actually referred to the hemp plant that grows on mountainsides. One elaborated that the hemp leaf was shaped like Śiva's trident. The hemp plant, he explained, may cause delusion but can also provide insight into delusion, both qualities of the Devī as Mahāmāyā. The Devi's identification with the flowers of the hemp plant (indeed with all power plants used for medicinal and consciousness-altering purposes) is certainly in need of further investigation.

31. Such uses of *kuśa* grass in this procedure and as the *purohita*'s seat (*āsana*) of worship, identify it as a "conductor" *par excellence* of divine energy.

32. Pandit Chakravarty has provided the following version:
Om! By reason of his heroic power, like a dread beast that wanders at will, that haunts the mountains, Viṣṇu is praised aloud for that, he in whose three wide strides all beings dwell.

33. Pandit Chakravarty's version runs as follows:
Om! Viṣṇu may shape the womb; let Tvaṣṭā beautify you with nice forms;
Let Prajāpati pour the semen; let Dhātā give you the embryo (the germ of life).

34. Pandit Chakravarty's translation.

"May his mind delight in the gushing (of the) butter! May Brihaspati spread (carry through) this sacrifice! May he restore the sacrifice uninjured! May all the gods rejoice here!" (Eggeling 1978 [1882]:215).

35. The exact nature of the seat of the Devī is ambiguous in this ritual sequence. The altar on which the clay image sits and the *purohita*'s own seat are two possible candidates. Since the superintending deity (*adhipati*), Viṣṇu, is then worshipped with the *kośā* which is later called the seat, one can infer that Viṣṇu himself serves as the seat of the Devī.

36. I have numbered the parts of the devotional service to illustrate that it consists of far more than sixteen parts. The alphabetic subdivisions (e.g., 7 and 7a) do not indicate less significant offerings. They are so designated since they are connected to the previous devotional offering, and because they do not possess their own *mantra*.

Ghosha:xxxi notes that *upacāra*s may consist of sixty parts. These are a mat, perfumed oil, a bath, a seat in the bathroom, pure water, ointment, warm water, water of holy places in a gold vessel, a white napkin, a red garment, a red wrapper, a painted hall, a painted seat, pomades, an ointment made of sandalwood and other fragrances, flower garlands, ornaments, a jewelled seat, a gemmed crown, canopy, vermillion, *tilaka*, collyrium, earrings, nose-rings, rouge for the lips (*misi*), necklace, gold sabbots, silver sandals, pearl-necklaces, a single necklace, a breastplate, four bracelets, wrist-rings, finger rings, gold-zones, a girdle, *śobhā* (lustrous ornament), anklets, *nūpura*s (foot ornaments), toe-rings, a noose, a goad, a bow, an arrow, a crystal footstool, a lion seat, a bedstead, a spoon, water for washing the face, camphor pills, joyous smiles, lustrations, a white umbrella, a yak-tail fan, a mirror, perfumes, flowers, incenses, lamps, eatables, water for washing and for ablution, betel leaves, and prayers.

37. The four types of food referred to are those that can be chewed (*carvya*), sucked (*cusya*), licked (*lehya*), and drunk (*peya*).

38. In her chapter in a volume on Hinduism and ecology, Madhu Khanna suggests that these identifications between Durgā and natural plants reveal that the roots of the Durgā Pūjā lie in the village-based, agricultural communities of India, whose lives are intimately linked to the crop and seasonal cycles. The veneration of such plants as rice and barley, which form the central nutrients for an agriculturally based people, as well as of forest shrubs and fruit trees, spices and roots which are used in the daily diet, reveals an ecological sensibility among these peoples. The *navapatrikā* rites reflect an orally transmitted set of cultural beliefs and values that were interwoven with the scriptural and Śāstric tradition to constitute the Durgā Pūjā. These natural vegetative personifications of the Devī also represent the fertile and fecund power of the earth, with which Durgā is clearly identified (see Chapple and Tucker 2000).

39. S. C. Mitra (1922:231) identifies the plant as *Musa paradisica* and *Musa sapientum*.

40. Mitra (1922:231) identifies Jayantī as barley (*Hordeum hexastichum*).

41. Mitra (1922:230) notes that scholars have conjectured that Śumbha and Niśumbha represent demons of drought.

42. In the *Durgā Saptaśatī* 11.39–41, when the Devī is recounting her demon-destroying incarnations, she states, "And again, having descended to earth in a very dreadful form, I shall slay the demons called Vaipracitta. Devouring those great awful demons, my teeth will become red like pomegranate flowers. Then the deities in heaven, and people in the mortal world, always praising me, will call me Raktadantikā." The litany suggests a familiarity with the *Durgā Saptaśati*, but identifies the demon whose blood reddens the Devī's teeth as Raktabīja.

43. The Devī is identified with Indra's consort Śacī as well as Cāmuṇḍā.

44. A *vanamālā* is a long garland made of forest flowers, which stretches from the neck to the knees.

45. In the Bāro Bhāiyā (Twelve Brothers) folk cult of Bengal, Vana-durgā (Durgā of the Forest) is worshipped as the mother of twelve demon (*daitya*) brothers, and a demoness sister, Raṇa-yakṣiṇī (Yakṣiṇī of the Battlefield) (See Chakravarti [1930] for details). One of the sons, Niśā-nātha (Lord of the Night), after whom the cult is also named, is described as wielding the Śakti weapon. Many of the demon sons of Vana-durgā (herself fierce) have fierce names and descriptions, such as Hari-pāgala (Hari the Mad). However, there are three demon sons named Kṛṣṇa-kumāra (Dark Youth), Puṣpa-kumāra (Flower Youth), and Rūpa-kumāra (Beautiful Youth), and a fourth named, Rūpa-mālin (the Beautiful). The meditative descriptions (*dhyāna*) of these deities reveal that Rūpa-kumāra and Rūpa-mālin are handsome, without any negative characteristics. It is conceivable that Kārtikeya's presence (as Kumāra, the son of Durgā) in the clay image complex derived from such folk cult associations. Kārtikeya is associated with the Śakti weapon.

This cult clearly demonstrates Durgā's folk identification as the mother to several sons and a daughter who are not part of the orthodox pantheon. In fact, they are dangerous and destructive entities, clearly identified as *yakṣīs* or demons, but propitiated and venerated as "deities." But it is difficult to ascertain if this is evidence of original forms of Durgā worship, or if it illustrates the permeation of Sanskritic Durgā worship into a folk cult. The current array of clay images (as well as those painted by folk artists on the *cāl-citra*) in the Durgā Pūjā are derived primarily from the orthodox (i.e., *purāṇic*) pantheon. Indeed the Bengali Durgā Pūjā ritual, as constructed by Tantric *brāhmaṇa* ritualists, utilizes an array of orthodox imagery broad enough to encompass the symbolic needs of devotees to a large assortment of regional goddess cults. Perhaps this is why certain votaries regard Sarasvatī and Lakṣmī as Durgā's daughters and sisters to Gaṇeśa and Kārtikeya.

46. Cohen (1991) offers an assortment of evidence in which Lakṣmī is paired with Gaṇeśa as his sister, his *śakti*, or more frequently, as his wife. In the Dasboddhi Gaṇeśa temple in Mathurā, for example, Gaṇeśa as Mahāgaṇapati, holds his *śakti*, Mahālakṣmī (regarded as Gaṇeśa's wife by the temple priest), upon his knee. During the Divālī festival they may also be paired and worshipped together due to their joint association with the removal of misfortune.

47. In his study of the South Indian cult of the goddess Draupadī, Hiltebeitel (1988) notes that she is identified as both the lion mount and the rider of the lion.

Although in that regional setting the lion is the vehicle of such village goddesses as Māriyamman, such folk beliefs evoke an equation between the Devī and her lion, both symbols of regal power.

48. The verse derives from the *Durgā Saptaśatī* 11.9. The epithet Tryambakā is ambiguous. It may refer to the triple form of the Devī as Mahālakṣmī, Mahāsarasvatī, and Mahākālī, or to the Devī as mother of the trinity, Brahmā, Viṣṇu, and Śiva. It may also be rendered as "O Three-eyed Goddess."

Chapter 4.5: Mahāṣṭamī

1. Its name may derive from its symmetry, since it is regarded as auspicious (*bhadra*) from all (*sarvato*) sides (Bühnemann 1987:62). However, it is also deemed as a sort of generic or universal *maṇḍala*, usable for all deities and ritual purposes, a capacity that provides another rationale for its name.

2. The reference is to the Devī's destruction of the demon generals Caṇḍa and Muṇḍa, in the battle with Śumbha and Niśumbha (see *Durgā Saptaśatī* 6.17–7.23). In the *Durgā Saptaśatī* version it is Kālī who destroys them and obtains the epithet, Cāmuṇḍā. The word "*caṇḍa*" means fierce and its more common feminine form, "*caṇḍī*," is associated with Durgā. Here, the less-common feminine form "*caṇḍā*" is attributed to the *śakti* who destroyed Caṇḍa.

3. The list possesses sixty-five names, although Viṣṇumāyā is repeated twice. This list seems more appropriate than the one found in the *Purohita Darpaṇa*, which follows. The *Purohita Darpaṇa* lists sixty-six *yoginī*s, but Caṇḍikā is listed three times and Kātyāyanī twice. It includes some of the *śakti*s previously invoked in the petals, suggesting its unsuitability. The *yoginī*s are: Brahmāṇī, Caṇḍikā(1), Raudrī, Gaurī, Indrāṇī, Kaumārī, Bhairavī, Durgā, Nārasiṃhī, Caṇḍikā(2), Cāmuṇḍā, Śivadūtī, Vārāhī, Kauśikī, Maheśvarī, Śaṅkarī, Jayantī, Sarvamaṅgalā, Kālī, Karālinī, Medhā, Śivā, Śākambharī, Bhimā, Śāntā, Bhrāmarī, Rudrāṇī, Ambikā, Syāmā, Dhatrī, Kātyāyanī(1), Svāhā, Svadhā, Pūrṇā, Mahodarī, Ghorarūpā, Mahākālī, Bhadrakālī, Kapālinī, Kṣemaṅkarī, Ugracaṇḍā, Caṇḍogrā, Caṇḍanāyikā, Caṇḍā, Caṇḍavatī, Caṇḍī, Kālarātrī (1), Mahāmohā, Priyaṅkarī, Balavṛddhikarā, Balapramathinī, Manonomanī, Sarvabhūtadamanī, Umā, Tārā, Mahānidrā, Vijayā, Jayā, Śailaputrī, Caṇḍikā(3), Caṇḍaghaṇṭā, Kuṣmāṇḍā, Skandamātā, Kātyāyanī(2), Kālaratrī (2), and Mahāgaurī.

4. Pandit Chakravarty explained that here he is invoking not just the group of sixty-four, but the full collection of *yoginī*s, said to number in the crores (i.e., ten millions) (*koṭi*).

5. Notice the use of *klīṃ* instead of *śrīṃ* for the Mātṛs related to forms of Viṣṇu.

6. In the not-too-distant past, warrior patrons had their special new weapons consecrated at this time. This rite thus evokes the myth, recounted in the *Mahābhārata* (*Virāṭa-parva* 6), in which the Pāṇḍava princes conceal their weapons in a *śamī* tree, prior to going into hiding for the last year of their thirteen-year exile. Yudhiṣṭhira, the

eldest prince, prays to Durgā (and Kālī) to help them from being discovered (if found, they will have to repeat the terms of exile) and for success against their enemies. The Devī appears and grants his wishes. The weapons are later retrieved and used in the great war in which they are victorious.

7. This refers to the myth of the creation of Devī, which is recounted in the *Durgā Saptaśatī* 2.19, where Śiva arms her with a trident produced from his own.

8. There is a pun here. The weapon (and the Devī) is the *śakti* (power) of all the gods, especially Kārtikeya, who traditionally wields the *śakti* weapon.

9. The staff is generally associated with Yama, Śiva, and Kālī. It is more commonly called the *khaṭvaṅga*. The club (*gadā*) is associated with Viṣṇu.

10. There are certain noteworthy differences between the ritual use of the *sarvatobhadra maṇḍala* in the Durgā Pūjā and the way it is employed in Smārta rituals, as described by Bühnemann (1987). Flowers are used to invoke and worship the deities in the Durgā Pūjā, while Smārta rites utilize areca nuts. While Durgā is relegated to a peripheral place and Brahman is invoked into the center of the pericarp in Smārta *maṇḍala* practice, here it is Caṇḍikā as the Nine Durgās, who commands the central position, clearly indicating her preeminence and suggesting her identity with Absolute Reality. A number of other goddesses, such as the *yoginīs,* are also invoked into the center, forging identifications between the host of subsidiary *devīs* and the Great Goddess. The guardians of the field (*kṣetrapāla*) are invoked into places generally held by the *dikpālas* (guardians of the directions) in Smārta rituals. In Smārta rites, the weapons of the *dikpālas* are worshipped outside the *maṇḍala*, in the white circumference. In the Durgā Pūjā, it is the Devī's weapons that are worshipped, not in the *maṇḍala* at all, but in her clay image, and the *purohita* completes these rites by worshipping the Devī as the Bearer of All Weapons (*sarvāyudhadhāriṇī*). He then worships the Devī's ornaments in the clay image. By returning to the *maṇḍala* after these rites, he illustrates a typical Tantric inversion of Smārta tradition in a number of ways. First, *maṇḍala* and *mūrti* are not worshipped in the same ritual according to orthodox convention. In this rite, that convention is explicitly broached as *maṇḍala* and *mūrti* are fused together. The *purohita* also worships the *mātṛkās* (Mothers), within the *maṇḍala*, while in Smārta rites they are worshipped outside the *maṇḍala* in the black circumference (with slight variations in names and directional placements). The Baṭukas and Bhairavas, who are invoked into the *maṇḍala* during the Durgā Pūjā, have no place in the Smārta *sarvatobhadra maṇḍala*. Although the Bhairavas do figure in Smārta *liṅgatobhadra maṇḍala* rites, they still occupy marginal positions in the white circumference outside the *maṇḍala*.

Chapter 4.6: Sandhi Pūjā

1. In the village of Lavapur, in Birbhum, Bengal, known for its community of magicians, the Durgā Pūjā takes place at the local Devī temple. An area of the floor is sprinkled with vermilion and covered with a cloth. Only when the Devī's footprint appears on the cloth does the Sandhi Pūjā commence (see *www.bangalinet.com*).

2. Prescriptions concerning blood offerings vary widely in the literature. The *Kālikā Purāṇa* lists the following animals as fit for sacrifice to Durgā: birds, tortoises, crocodiles, fish, nine kinds of deer, buffalo, the *gavaya* (the Indian Gayal), bulls, goats, mongoose, boars, the rhinoceros, black antelope, the *śarabha* (a mythic animal), the lion, the tiger, a human being, and blood from one's own body. If females of the species were offered, the sacrificer would go to hell. While Durgā is only satisfied for one month by offerings of fish, a human sacrifice or blood from the worshipper's own body satisfies her for a thousand years (Kane:5.165–167).

3. This is different from the Sanskrit *devanāgarī*, or the Bengali script.

4. Kinsley (1986:110) describes the legends of a sword belonging to the fourteenth-century Paṇḍyan prince Kumāra Kampaṇa and a sacred sword of the Rajput kingdom of Mewar. As an interesting aside, the clay images in certain public Durgā Pūjās were/are occasionally equipped not just with the assortment of conventional weapons, but with missiles and atom bombs (see Chaturvedi 1996:42). India's actual acquisition of such weapons cannot but be placed in the context of the perceived beneficence of the Devī towards her devotees.

5. Pandit Chakravarty's translation.

"O seeker after knowledge, in this world, fire is a thing of beauty. Just as learned persons perform yajnas with it, so shouldst thou do. Just as a learned person masters this beautiful place of sacrifice, so shouldst thou do. If thou wilt properly manage the place of yajna, fire will manifest itself as a thing worth seeing. Drink thou the waters purified by the yajna" (Chand 1965:358).

"Agni was the victim. With him they sacrificed. He won this world in which Agni is. This shall become thy world. This shalt thou win. Drink these waters" (Griffith 1987 [1899]:231).

"Agni was an animal; they sacrificed him, and he gained that world wherein Agni (ruleth): that shall be thy world, that thou shalt gain, drink thou this water!" (Eggeling 1978 [1882]:319).

6. Generally, three levels of reality are referred to in Śākta metaphysics. These are *para*, *parāpara*, and *apara*. *Apara* is the nontranscendent, *para* is the transcendent, and *parāpara* is the connection between these two realms. *Parameṣṭhi* is regarded as the supreme or fourth level.

7. Preston (1980:64–67) describes the autumnal rites of Durgā/Caṇḍī worship in Cuttack, Orissa, which occur over sixteen days. The ritual climaxes on the last three days, on the first of which the Devī is worshipped as Sarasvatī, then as Kālī (where she is offered blood sacrifices), and finally as Caṇḍī.

8. Personal communication (2000)

9. Personal communication (2000).

10. Evans-Pritchard (1974 [1956]) also notes the use of a cucumber as a substitute for an ox sacrifice among the Nuer, a sub-Saharan people. Kondos (1986) cites the use of duck eggs as surrogates in offerings to Durgā in Nepal.

11. Kondos (1986:185) notes an interesting variant on the drawing of this effigy. Among the Newar Buddhists of Nepal, who participate in the Navarātra/Dasain rites, a pumpkin is used as a surrogate offering. However, since the traditional enemies of the Newars are the Parbatya twice-born, the effigy on their sacrificial offering sports a topknot, symbolic of the twice-born.

12. Personal communication (2000).

13. Personal communication (2000).

14. Interview, October 1991.

15. Östör (1980:56) mentions that rice and lentils mixed together are substitutes for the animal sacrifice in the king's Durgā Pūjā in Vishnupur, Bengal. It is noteworthy that this mixture, when cooked, constitutes *kichiṛi*, which is the central *bhog* offering in most locales (e.g., the Lahiri home, Durgostav Sammilini) that claim not to include blood sacrifice at all.

16. The Kumārī cult is referred to in manuscripts as early as the thirteenth century (Allen 1975).

17. Personal communication (2000).

Chapter 4.7: Mahanavamī

1. The eight forms (*aṣṭamūrti*) of Śiva are: the five elements (earth, water, fire, air, and ether), the Sun, the Moon, and the *purohita*.

2. Personal communication from the Lahiri family (2000).

3. Personal communication from Sudarshan Chowdhury (2000).

4. Personal communication from Pandit Chakravarty (2000). On the various modes of recitation of the *Durgā Saptaśatī* as performed by pandits at the temple of Vidhyavāsinī, see Humes (1991).

Chapter 4.8: Vijayā Daśamī

1. The *Kālikā Purāṇā* 60:9–20, places both slayings on the ninth day of Navarātra. Among votaries who cited the Rāma-Rāvaṇa myth cycle, one explained that as a result of Rāma's worship, the Devī first appeared to him as a young girl (*kumārī*), and only after further worship, revealed her true form. On Saptamī, she entered his bow; on Aṣṭamī, the final battle occurred, and he slew Rāvaṇa during the Sandhi period. He finally retrieved Sītā on Vijayā Daśamī.

2. Certain authors (e.g., Chaturvedi 1996:39) suggest that the duration of the Durgā Pūjā symbolically reflects the formalized three-day menstrual period of women, which terminates on the fourth day with a purifying bath. The immersion ceremony

is interpreted as the postmenstrual bath of the Devī. *Kumārī* (premenarche virgin girl) worship on the first three days also serves the purpose of inducing fertility in the young women and the creation.

3. Kramrisch (1981:66) cites the *Atharva Veda* 11.7.1–3, 16 in which the residue of sacrificial offerings (*ucchiṣṭa*) is said to contain cosmic creative force.

4. See the *dhyāna mantra* of Ucchiṣṭa-mātaṅginī (e.g., *Bṛhat Tantrasāra*, p. 449), which states that the goddess should be offered leftovers (*ucchiṣṭa*).

5. Kinsley (1997:215). In villages in Andhra Pradesh and Karnataka, the Mātaṅgī, a virgin girl from an untouchable caste, plays an important role in goddess festivals by serving as a manifestation of the goddess. She is selected from a group of prepubescent, untouchable girls, initially on her capacity to be possessed by the goddess and later undergoes further tests and initiation (Brubaker 1978:267–268).

6. The *aparājitā* creeper used to bind the *navapatrikā* will be worshipped later. Mitra (1925) mentions that the Bengali goddess Manasā, who presides over snakes and cholera, is also worshipped in the form of a *siju* or spurge-wart (*Euphorbia neriifolia*) tree. A branch of this tree is planted in the house on the tenth of Jyaiṣṭha (May/June) and worshipped by *brāhmaṇas* daily, and by *śūdras* on the fifth day of successive bright and dark fortnights. On Vijayā Daśamī day in Āśvina both the *navapatrikā* and this plant are immersed.

7. These birds (*Anas casarca*) are known for their mournful cries, as they call from opposites sides of river banks for their mates.

8. Interview, October 1991.

9. Bāṇa's literary work, the *Caṇḍīśataka*, dedicates a hundred verses in praise of the Devī's foot, which presses down upon Mahiṣa, crushing him, and yet while so doing, compassionately saves him. The implication is that in being slain by the Devī, the demon is expiated of his evil and himself becomes worthy of veneration.

10. Interview, October 1991.

11. Interview, October 1991. The rite is also popularly known as *sindūr khelna* (play).

12. Ray (n.d.:137–8) speculates that the tradition of creating clay images and disposing of them after four days may have derived in response to Muslim intolerance. Ray notes that on the first day of the Bengali New Year in a village in the Burdwan district, a stone image of Durgā Mahiṣamardinī is brought out of water, worshipped, and immersed in water again after the rite. Stone images were routinely hidden in wells and other bodies of water to save them from desecration.

Since the Durgā Pūjā images are fabricated of unbaked clay, they rapidly dissolve back into the silt of the Gaṅgā. Within days after the immersion rites, entrepreneurial young men dive to the river bottom to salvage the wood and straw "skeletons" of the images, which are then sold back to the image makers for their materials.

13. See Anderson (1993), for a study of ancient Indian spring festivals as described in Sanskrit sources.

14. Gifts of new clothes to as many people as one can is a traditional part of Durgā Pūjā. These gifts are normally given before the *pūjā* begins, so that worshippers may wear the clothes during the festival days.

15. Interview, October 1991.

Chapter 5: The Nature of Pūjā

1. Interview with Śītalā Prasād Chaubey (1990).

2. See, for instance, Fuller (1992:56), following Gonda (1970:186).

3. On the nature of the *purohita*'s actions, Hudson (1999:80) comments, "He has turned her symbolic form (*mūrti*) into her icon (*archa*). In Hindu terms, an icon is a descent (*avatāra*) of the Goddess into a body, one version of the familiar idea of a god's avatar or incarnation. But her descent requires priestly rites and her presence requires carefully prescribed behavior on the part of those who serve her as priests and those who visit her as worshipers."

4. Translation by Gussner (1973:202–204) quoted in Bühnemann (1988:92).

5. In reference to *darśana,* Dehejia (1999) comments, "Such seeing does not merely mean using one's eyes, but is a dynamic act of awareness; it is this type of 'seeing' that lies behind the choice of the word 'seer' to designate a holy prophet or sage."

6. See Logan (1980:123), who regards *pūjā* as a process "embodying the diety and disembodying man."

7. Personal conversation, 1990.

Chapter 6: The Nature of the Great Goddess

1. A pseudonym. Interview (1990).

2. *Om bhūrasi bhūmirasi aditirasi viśvadhāya viśvasya bhuvanasya dhartrī pṛthivī yaccha pṛthivīṃ dṛṇha pṛthivīm mān himsī.*

3. See, for example, Marshall (1931), plate nos. 12, 17, and 18.

4. As early as the *Ṛg-veda* 10.146, a forest goddess, Araṇyānī, resembles the *yakṣī*s of Indian tradition.

5. Singh and Nath (1999:53) see the lion's association with passion for food, as symbolic of lust, and greed for all forms of enjoyment. Durgā's presence atop the lion teaches the need for control of such base animal instincts in human beings. They also identify the lion with "the golden rayed sun, the lord of the Day, whose appearance kills the God of the night." In contrast, Chaudhuri (1984:34) identifies Mahiṣa with the sun or fire.

6. See for example the *Śiva-Purāṇa*, Rudra-saṃhitā 4.2.9–70 for a discussion on Pārvatī's relationship with Kārtikeya, and 4.13–18, which discusses her relationship with Gaṇeśa.

7. On the mythology of Gaṇeśa, see Courtright (1985a).

8. See, for instance, Brooks (1990), who explores the triadic symbolism in Śrī Vidyā Tantrism.

9. Kurtz (1992) speculates that it is the joint family system in Indian society that facilitates such a conception. Children are raised not solely by their biological mother, but may be attended to by aunts, cousins, and a host of other female relations, all of whom are regarded as "mothers" (i.e., nurturers, protectors) of a sort. Since they are thus accustomed to a system of multiple earthly mothers, the belief in numerous divine mothers is not unusual. When asked about the relationship between any two goddesses, or between a particular goddess and the Great Goddess, it is quite common for votaries to respond with the phrase, "*ek hi hai*" (They're one and the same!). In the formulation of the *sarvatobhadra maṇḍala*, however, the Devī is venerated not only as all goddesses, but as all deities.

10. Ray (n.d.:139) interprets the *sarvatobhadra maṇḍala's* eight-petalled lotus as "symbolising the female genital organ."

11. See Eck (1982b, 1981b), for a discussion of the salvific powers of flowing waters and the Gaṅgā in particular.

12. Cynthia Humes, in a personal communication (1996) with C. Mackenzie Brown offered that the Goddess herself is often represented by a flame, for instance during the *homa* rite, as well as during ritual recitation (*pāṭha*) of the *Durgā Saptaśatī* (see C. M. Brown 1998:306).

13. *Om vāgīśvarīṃ ṛtusnātāṃ nīlendī vara locanām/*
vāgiśvareṇa saṃyuktām krīḍa bhāva.

14. For more information on Vāc, see Padoux (1990). In *Ṛg Veda* 10.125, Vāc describes herself saying, "My *yoni* is within the waters, in the ocean." (Quoted in Pintchman 1994:38). This and numerous other connections between the waters and her creative capacities mesh well with her subsequent identification with the river goddess, Sarasvatī. The waters are placed in a maternal role in such verses as *Ṛg Veda* 1.95–4–5, 1.143.1, 2.35.2–13, 7.9.3, 10.8.5, 1.22.6, and 6.50.13, which imply that Agni/Savitṛ is the "son of the waters."

15. "That goddess who is the color of fire, who blazes forth with her *tapas*, who is the wife (or daughter) of Virocana (Agni), who delights in granting the fruits of one's actions, that goddess Durgā I seek as my refuge. Hail to you who know how to cross safely, you will make us cross (*sutarasi tarase namaḥ*)" (cited in Divakaran 1984:272).

16. A good introduction to the use of sound and litany in Hindu worship traditions is found in Coward and Goa (1991). A more advanced study of sound in the Hindu tradition is found in Beck (1993). *Ākāśa* may also be associated with the heart/mind, *manas*. There are numerous such associations with *manas* discernable in the

Durgā Pūjā. Most notably, the Devī is repeatedly first "embodied" as a mental image through the creative meditative visualizations of the *purohita* and then rendered a mental devotional worship (*mānasa upacāra*).

17. In the *Devī Kavaca*, an appendage of the *Durgā Saptaśatī*, the Goddess is praised as Candraghaṇṭā (Bell of the Moon) or Citraghaṇṭā (Wonderful Bell). The Devī is well known under this name in Banāras and is worshipped by tens of thousands in the annual pilgrimage to the temples of the Nine Durgās.

18. In his examination of the term *vidyā*, as a mantric formulation, Kinsley (1997:59) notes, "[it] is also significant that the goddess—who is the mantra—appears or exists only when the mantra is invoked. She remains in latent form until a particular adept invokes her through the mantra that is her animating essence. It is in this sense, perhaps, that the emphasis upon the adept and the goddess being one may be understood in the tantric context. One cannot exist without the other."

19. This is the well-known cluster of Nine Durgās named in the *Devī Kavaca (The Armour of the Goddess)*, a hymn that forms one of the appendages (*aṅga*) of the *Durgā Saptaśatī*.

20. As the *Kālikā Purāṇa* 69.106–107 states, "Flowers delight the gods. The gods reside in flowers. . . . The supreme light manifests in flowers and is delighted by flowers." (See C. M. Brown 1998: 300–310).

21. I have noted earlier that in the male rite of cutting and eating the *kumru* squash/pumpkin, as well as in the rice and lentil *bhog* offering, homes such as the Lahiris may well be engaging in a surrogate sacrificial offering, without consciously knowing it.

22. Interview, March 1991. Samanta (1994) forwards the argument that the sacrifice represents the votaries' own self, whose baser qualities are progressively consumed and digested by the Devī with each sacrificial offering. In this manner, the devotee becomes liberated from the material bonds (*pāśa*) that bind the "self-animal" (*paśu*), by degrees, until final union with the Devī is achieved.

23. Personal communication, 2000. Her comments resonate with Östör's observations that "the meaning of sacrifice is the casting away of one's sins and faults. By sacrificing their sins, making them into demonic beings through mantras, men not only please the gods but recognize what is divine in themselves" (1980:57).

24. Two of the Lahiri grandchildren commenting in tandem said, "I think if all this blood and killing wasn't there, Durgā Pūjā would be nicer. The tiger is okay. It's kind of gory. I like the lion. This buffalo being killed is bad" (Interview, October 1991).

25. Payne (1997 [1933]:10).

26. Although one might suggest that the sacrifice of one's offspring ("the fruit of one's loins") is a higher offering, the thrust of the interpretation is unaltered. Whether it be devotee or child, the human sacrifice of self or loved one is

perceived as sublime. Shulman (1993) discusses Hindu myths of sacrifice of one's own child.

27. A study of ancient iconographic representations of head-offerings to the Goddess, such as the striking depictions in the Pallava sculptures at Mahabalipuram, is found in Vogel (1930–32), who concludes that the motif of self-sacrifice was well known. He also cites Lal (1927:144) who refers to sects who cut off their heads and tongues in a pavilion specially constructed for the purpose. Kinsley (1997:151–152) explores some of the literary accounts of head offerings in such works as the *Kalingattuparaṇi* (eleventh century, Tamil) and the *Śilappadikāram*.

The Durgā Pūjā of the Raikanth family of Jalpaiguri, in Bengal, is reputed to have performed human sacrifices to the Devī in antiquity. Currently, a human doll made of flour is sacrificed before their fifteen-foot high image (see *www.bangalinet.com*).

28. Kinsley (1997:30–35) discusses the Mahāvidyās as forms of Durgā, who on occasion is herself included in the group. (See also, S. C. Banerji 1986:30). There is a visual resonance between the image array in the Durgā Pūjā and the representations of the goddess Chinnamastā. Like Chinnamastā, Durgā is flanked by two female attendants, Lakṣmī and Sarasvatī. While Chinnamastā is atop a copulating couple, Durgā is placed atop the bloody, decapitated form of Mahiṣa, himself a symbol of lust. The Goddess and certain attendants are offered the blood of the sacrifice, just as Chinnamastā and her attendants drink of the blood from her own severed head. Votaries later consume the blood sacrifice as *prasāda* and are nourished by it. It reiterates themes of the Devī nourishing the world with material from her own body.

29. Kinsley (1986:114) discusses the Bengali songs of welcome and farewell to the Goddess who is identified with the daughter who returns home for the Durgā Pūjā.

30. Personal correspondence (2000).

31. Interview (1991).

32. See Frederick M. Smith's (1991:17–45) "Indra's Curse, Varuṇa's Noose, and the Suppression of the Woman in the Vedic Śrauta Ritual," for a discussion of the mythological basis of this attitude to menstruation.

33. Personal communication (2000).

Chapter 7: Functions of the Durgā Pūjā

1. In support of the cosmic symbolism, Ray (n.d.:138) comments, "the complete iconography . . . —comprising the ten-armed goddess and her children along with the accessory figures, standing close to each other and in repose, held in tight composition by a *cālcitra* painted with the scenes of the Devī's exploits where Śiva happens to be the central deity, and a *pūrna kumbha* placed just in front on the ground—seems to demonstrate the entire universe held in one place."

2. For example, ". . . at the subjective level, Mahisāsur stands for ignorance and stubborn egoism. Its subjugation and conquest are possible only when the Sādhaka (spiritual aspirant) pools all his energies together and fights it with tenacious will" (Singh and Nath 1999:42). The same authors also cite K. Narayan Iyer, who in his *The Permanent History of Bharatvarsha* notes that the Devī's slaying of Mahiṣa "merely represent[s] the conquest of ignorance and discordant variety by wisdom and unity" (1999:42).

3. Interview, March 1991.

4. See Berkson (1995) who develops the theme of Mahiṣa as "hero."

5. Interview, October 1991.

6. The *paṇḍal* at Muhammad Ali Park in Calcutta in 1997 had Durgā slaying images of corrupt politicians who were the "demons" (see *www.allindia.com*).

7. The festival has been compared to the Vedic *rājasūya* in its themes of reintegration. The festival of the Goddess, worshipped under her regional epithet, Pampā, served as the occasion for officials to pay tribute to the king. "All the tributary chiefs and provincial governors, revenue collectors, foreign ambassadors, eminent merchants and bankers of the capital—in brief, everyone of any importance—were to attend the durbars on that occasion" (Gupta and Gombrich 1986:133).

8. Dehejia (1999:24). The Durgā Pūjā occurs during the same time as the celebrated Rām Līlās in Banāras. Those month-long ritualized dramatizations of Rāma's adventures contribute to the martial atmosphere of the period. Since the mythology of Rāma's battle with Rāvaṇa intersects with Durgā's worship, the mood of the two festivals reinforce each other. Vijayā Daśamī is often regareded by votaries as the day on which Rāma slew Rāvaṇa, and Durgā slew Mahiṣa. For more on the Rām Līlā celebrations, see Lutgendorf (1989 and 1991).

9. The king of Banāras is a major patron of the Rām Līlā celebrations at Ramnagar, which overlap the autumn Navarātra. He holds his own worship rites to the Devī during Navarātra and includes a visit to the Durgā Kuṇḍ and other important Devī temples in the city during the festival. Both festivals are thought to end on the tenth day, when large effigies of Rāvaṇa are shot with flaming arrows and burned. Similarly, in Nepal, the only extant Hindu kingdom, the king's celebration centers on Durgā Taleju, his tutelary deity.

10. Biardeau (1984:6) notes that in Jaipur, Rajasthan, a story circulates that Rāma's weapons rusted during the rainy season. A special rite, which involves the worship of a *śamī* tree, is celebrated after the cleaning of rusty weapons, purifying them and restoring their fire. This rite restored to Rāma's weapons the fire that the monsoon waters had taken away. She suggests that the *śamīpūjā* is a *saṃskāra* (rite of passage) for weapons.

11. Biardeau (1984:7) notes that the Candravaṃsī kings of Rajasthan conduct their weapon *pūjā* on the eighth day of Navarātra. This is also the case in Mysore, where kings would consecrate their own weapons and those of their warriors at the

altar of the Goddess. On the morning of the tenth day (Dasarā), the king, mounted on an elephant, would then head a grand procession of the court and the army, and the consecrated arms would be displayed (Gupta and Gombrich 1986:133).

12. For a translation of this hymn, known as the *Durgā Stava,* see Coburn (1984:267–271).

13. A translation of that hymn, known as the *Durgā Stotra* is found in Coburn (1984:272–275). Both the *Durgā Stava* and the *Durgā Stotra* are obvious interpolations in the *Mahābhārata,* since the Devī's role in the epic appears minimal. However, Biardeau (1984) argues that through the female characters of the narrative, such as Draupadī, the Goddess's presence is constantly implicit. Hiltebeitel's studies (1991, 1988) of the Draupadī cult in South India amply substantiate this observation.

14. "Until the middle of this century, Durgā Pūjā is not even mentioned as a festival or *mela* worthy of note among the thirty plus *mela*s of Banāras" (Kumar 1988:218).

15. Conversations with image makers. See also Kumar (1988:219). In 1991 the city of Banāras had placed a cap of two hundred permits for public Durgā Pūjās, although I was aware of at least two that were operating without permits.

16. I have heard this in casual conversation with numerous devotees, but it is also mentioned in Chaudhuri (1984). Stein (1980) notes the central place of the capital city of Vijayanagara in the total moral order of the empire of the kings of that South Indian dynasty. The city "never stands for anything specific; it is never less than the whole world, and its parts are the parts of the world" (Stein 1980:391, quoting Hocart 1970:250). Quite importantly, the city of Vijayanagara and its establishment was persistently linked to the Goddess Durgā, as Bhuvaneśvarī (Mistress of the World). The city may well have derived its name, "The City of Victory," from the Goddess herself (as Victory [*vijayā*]), since the preceptor of the city's founders was Vidyaranya or Madhvacharya, renowned for his worship of the Devī.

17. In 1903 Sarala Devi, Rabindranath Tagore's niece, who had organized a group of young Bengali men willing to be martyred for the cause of Indian independence, instituted an annual festival of heroes on the second day (i.e., Aṣṭamī) of the Durgā Pūjā. On the third such celebration, there was a dramatic performance of Bankim Chandra Chatterji's *Ānandamaṭh* (*Monastery of Bliss*), an anti-British novel that contains *Bande Mātaram* (see Ghose 1940). This event launched the song and its title into use as the nationalists' call to duty, inspiring both Gandhian pacifists and more militant revolutionaries. See McKean (1996) for details and a discussion of how these events are woven into the development of the cult of the goddess Bhārat Mātā (Mother India).

Also see Paola Bacchetta's (1993) case study of Kamalabehn, a member of the militant Hindu nationalist organization, the Rashtra Sevika Samiti, which is the women's wing of the Rashtriya Swayamsevak Sangh (RSS). Bacchetta discusses both the Sangh and the Samiti's use of the goddess Bhārat Mātā as a symbol of the territory of the Hindu nation. The Sangh has "historically attempted to curb powerful symbolic femininity by depicting Bharatmata as benevolent and violated by the enemies of the

Hindu nation" (1993:41). In contrast, the Samiti accentuates the powerful traits of the goddess, referring to her as Durgā, and linking her character to the Devī of the *Durgā Saptaśatī*.

In addition, the Samiti has created a goddess named Ashta Bhuja (Eight Armed), whose icon is installed at Wardha, their earliest headquarters. Ashta Bhuja is referred to as a combination of Mahākālī, Mahāsarasvatī, and Mahālakṣmī. She wields a lotus, the *Bhagavad Gītā,* a bell, fire, a *mālā,* a sword, and a saffron flag, symbol of the Hindu nation, in seven of her eight hands. The eighth is in a gesture of blessing. The Samiti's literature explicitly identifies her with Durgā in her enemy-destroying persona. Ashta Bhuja is worshipped in the home as the personal diety of many members of the Samiti (see Bacchetta 1993). Thus, not only is the Devī a symbol of the nation, or of Hinduism, but, in Geertz's (1965) terminology, as a *model of* the powerful divine feminine, she serves as a *model for* the actual empowerment of individual women, such as Kamalabehn.

18. Aurobindo Ghose's translation (Bandyopadhyay 1987:63–64).

19. *Http://www.lib.uchicago.edu/e/su/southasia/Rachel.1.html.* Page 5.

20. Interview, October 1991.

21. Translation from Pratap Chandra Roy's *The Mahabharata of Krishna Dwaipayana Vyasa* (n.d.:Vol. VIII). The six types are the fortresses formed by a desert (*marudurgam*), by water (*jaladurgam*), by earth (*pṛthvīdurgam*), by a forest (*vanadurgam*), by a mountain (*parvatadurgam*), and by human beings (*manuṣyadurgam*). See *Mahābhārata,* Śānti Parva, Chapter 56.35. Quoted in Mani 1975:254.

22. In this interpretation I am not advocating a Durkheimian reductionism, which would imply that the force and majesty felt by Hindu society in the Durgā Pūjā gatherings is the entire substance of their conception of the divine that is Durgā. I have already shown how Durgā is conceptualized in complex ways such as through a sophisticated metaphysics that includes a "science" of nature with numerous variant forms. Durkheim's analysis does not adequately account for the existence of variations in the construction of religious symbols. Nevertheless, the felt force of the collective consciousness to which Durkheim alludes in his seminal work, *The Elementary Forms of Religious Life,* does, in my opinion, play a role in shaping the conceptual image of Durgā and in devotees' experience of her. See Durkheim (1965[1915]).

23. Personal communication, 2000.

24. The drop in status with the onset of menstruation is most poignant in the case of Nepal's Kumārīs, who cease to be worshipped as living goddesses. See Allen (1975).

25. Certain elements in this feature of the Durgā Pūjā synchronize with Lincoln's (1991) analysis of women's initiation rituals. Unlike typical male rites of passage, the female is isolated yet kept in close proximity to her family. The process of her transformation is less akin to the victorious survival of an ordeal, as in male initiations, but more like a butterfly's emergence from a chrysalis. The girl undergoes a metamorphosis from a cocooned state into a glorious, but culturally normative image

of womanhood. Through the course of the Durgā Pūja, one might thus argue that the premenarche virgin girl, the wife and mother, and the postmenopausal initiated woman are affirmed as the butterflies, while the unmarried postmenarche woman and premenopausal widow are affirmed as cocooned states.

26. The following description and comments derive from an interview (1991) with the wife of *brāhmaṇa* Sanskrit teacher Vagish Shastri and his married daughter.

27. This is a type of vowed ascetic observances (*vrata*) commonly practiced by Hindu women to enhance their personal power (*śakti*). This power is routinely understood as being transferred to others (e.g., husbands, sons) for their well-being (see McGee 1989, and Pearson 1996). Pearson points out that *vratas* are not performed exclusively for the well-being of others, but may satisfy women's own needs and desires. *Vratas* are also used to enhance a woman's feminine potential (*saubhagya*), which is conventionally realized in her being a desirable and fertile wife.

28. On the analysis of such classic polar structures, see Lévi-Strauss (1955 and 1963).

29. On the dangerous power of sexually fertile women, see Wadley (1975), O'Flaherty (1980), and Shulman (1980).

30. S. Wadley (Jacobson and Wadley 1986:125), cites the *Manusmṛti's* injunction that daughters be under the protection of their fathers, wives their husbands, and widows their sons, emphasizing the long-held tradition that men must control the energy of women.

31. Yalman (1967) forwards evidence on the importance of maintaining rigid control over women's sexuality and reproductive powers in order to avoid the contamination of the lineage through the entry of low-status blood. Sax (1991:138) and Beck (1981:124–125) offer examples from anthropological studies in North and South India, respectively, of the symbolic equation drawn between the demon's advances on the Devī and the suit of a high-caste woman by a lower caste male. Kondos (1986) emphasizes that kinsmen (father, brothers, or close male relatives) are also unsuitable suitors.

32. Mrs. Lahiri's stories, conveyed by her granddaughter. October (1991).

33. Interview, October 1991.

34. Attitudes about women find a symbolic parallel in goddesses who are dangerous and wild when single, and auspicious when controlled and married. See, for instance, Jacobson and Wadley (1986), Leslie (1991a), Shulman (1980), and Harman (1989).

35. The hazard posed by the perceived threat (from the male perspective) of the sexual power of widows is evidenced in one of Banāras's many popular sayings. "Widows, bulls, stairs, and *saṃnyāsins*: if you can save yourself from these, for you awaits the liberation of Kashi." Each of these, which is found in abundance in the city, poses its own unique dangers to the unwary seeker of *mokṣa*.

36. A wide variety of sociocultural processes in flux in modern India are examined in Singer (1972). Since the gathering of women during the Durgā Pūjā is an important venue for the transmission of cultural values by women to other women, the rite holds enormous potential for the dissemination of changing values among Hindu women.

37. Berreman (1993) discusses how aspects of the process of Sanskritization function to perpetuate female oppression in India. The Durgā Pūjā, an example of Sanskritization in operation, could be seen to concur with his analysis. The personas of the Devī, as she was envisioned and worshipped in a plethora of rites belonging to the "little traditions" of India, have progressively been amalgamated and shaped into a more unified vision of the Goddess in the Durgā Pūjā. This vision complies with upper-class *brāhmaṇa* notions of feminine divinity and womanhood, and thus pressures women of all classes who participate in the Durgā Pūjā, to conform to these ideals. While there appeared to be less resistance to these *brāhmaṇa* values expressed by the married daughters in the Lahiri family, who are themselves upper-class *brāhmaṇas*, the comments of the young unmarried *kayastha* woman, Pallavi Basu, cited above, revealed an unequivocal recognition of the oppressive dimensions of the Durgā Pūjā's "great tradition" values on both her and her friends. However, as the Durgā Pūjā undergoes modernization and greater democratization, with the rise of community celebrations, many such domestic social dimensions are vanishing. Different dynamics have emerged. In community Durgā Pūjās, it is still young men who are primarily members of the organizing clubs, and the presence of women is negligible. It is worth noting, incidentally, that the Durgā Pūjā does not only reveal Sanskritization at work, but "Prakritization" as well, in its community manifestations. Prakritization is exactly the inverse of Sanskritization. It is the process in which the masses, who are composed primarily from the non-brāhmaṇic classes, and who are purveyors of the vernacular languages and popular traditions, adopt Sanskritic texts and traditions and progressively adapt these to suit broader audiences.

38. See, for instance, Radcliffe-Brown (1952:139), Turner (1967:19), Geertz (1973a, 1973b), Ortner (1978), Staal (1989), Bell (1992), Bloch (1992), Humphrey and Laidlaw (1994), and Rappaport (1999). Such theorizing on ritual often reveals as much about the intellectual orientations of the proponents as it does about this form of human activity.

39. Humphrey and Laidlaw (1994) offer an entire monograph towards a theory of ritual (in general) based on Jain *pūjā*. Brooks (1992), invoking Durkheim's principle that "generalization cannot come from the study of things-in-general and requires at least one thoroughly considered example," also serves as inspiration. He dedicates half a monograph towards a theory of Tantric ritual based on a close study of Śrīvidyā rites, particularly the Śrīcakra *pūjā*.

40. This emphasis on action runs somewhat contrary to theories that give primacy to the communicative function of ritual (e.g. Douglas [1973], Leach [1976], Geertz [1973a]). It is aligned with such theoreticians as Staal (1989), although only to a degree, Bell (1992), and Humphrey and Laidlaw (1994). Gerholm (1988), too, designates ritual as "formal, rigidly prescribed action." I do not deny ritual's capacity

to communicate, but these messages are not precisely embedded within the component ritual acts and are not unequivocally received by participants. Furthermore, if the *pūjā* was performed by a *purohita* alone, by himself, its communicative nature would have to be interpreted (perhaps more tenuously) as self-referential or directed towards a greater power, while the nature of the rite as action is unchanged.

41. There undoubtedly are multifarious unconscious values and motives at the basis of the decision to perform the *pūjā*, but this is quite likely true for any and all conscious decisions.

42. Fernandez (1977) has suggested the notion of metaphor rather than symbol. Metaphor is ambiguous and permits a range of interpretations for the symbols involved in ritual.

43. Tambiah (1985), for instance, terms particular forms of language or action as illocutionary or performative, for they do not merely communicate intent, but actually enact the intention. The performative nature of ritual, as action that both shapes and manipulates conceptions of reality, is currently at the heart of most theories of ritual.

44. Rappaport (1975:42) articulates the intimate relationship between liturgical words and acts, thus: "By drawing himself into a posture to which canonical words give symbolic value the performer incarnates a symbol. He gives substance to the symbol as that symbol gives him form."

45. I am including here the large assortment of distinctions offered by semiotic theorists such as Pierce (1960), Leach (1976), and Rappaport (1999). These encompass such terms as "sign," "symbol," "index," "icon," and "signal," and the relationships they assert (e.g., metaphoric, metonymic).

46. Social functionalist analyses, developing upon the ideas of Durkheim (1965 [1915]), Radcliffe-Brown (1952), and Malinowski (1974 [1925]) demonstrate that rituals are mechanisms that play a vital part in regulating the intrinsic and desired structures within a social group. Gluckman (1962), for instance, proposes that ritual provides a cathartic venue through which tensions, which are rampant in any social group, may be ameliorated. This might be accomplished by a temporary inversion of a normative (and perhaps protested) social structure, providing a contained release of rebellious feelings, combined with a reinforcement of that very structure when the rite terminates. In the case of the Durgā Pūjā, Gluckman's approach would suggest that the elevation of women to the status of divinity and their veneration during the festival are atypical and quite the inverse of common attitudes towards women in Hinduism. The temporary shift in status acts as a safety valve to release women's pent up dissatisfaction with their position in the generally oppressive social structure.

47. Bourdieu's (1977) notion of structuring practices (i.e., ritual) being derived from structured and determined attitudes is applicable. Bell (1992, 1997), too, has proposed and developed in far greater detail an approach to ritual as practice. Rather than seeing ritual as "the vehicle for the *expression* of authority, practice theorists tend to explore how ritual is a vehicle for the *construction* of relationships of authority and

submission" (1997:82). Diverse social groups (e.g., priests, wealthy classes, artisans, merchants) have differing, yet vested interests in the annual performance of the Durgā Pūjā. Their dispositions towards the ritual are structured by values that are held, often subconsciously, and that manifest in practices (i.e., the Durgā Pūjā) that transmit and reinforce similarly structured attitudes. The Durgā Pūjā serves as a vehicle through which their social position (e.g., indispensable, powerful, invaluable) is actually established, or their needs (e.g., monetary) served. Recognition of the rite's capacity to fulfil these functions buttresses social disposition towards its purposeful future performance.

48. Interview, October 1991.

49. Chaturvedi (1996:29–30) adds that the rite was performed by Rāma especailly for the destruction of Rāvaṇa, whose head, when decapitated, instantly grew back due to a special boon granted to him. In his version, a thousand flowers were offered. In other versions, the number is one thousand and eight. Biardeau (1982:6) also discussed the myth, indicating that "Durgā grants [Rāma] the favour of killing Rāvaṇa precisely on the day of Durgāṣṭamī . . ."

50. He does so because he is known as the "lotus-eyed one."

51. Pallavi was, in effect, evaluting the *purohita's* performance. See Grimes (1990) for a discussion of "ritual criticism," and the scholar's place in evaluating, with ritualists, the quality and success of a ritual performance.

52. I am not implying that this "meaning" is singular, or even that some shared "meaning" is obtained by every participant. Neither am I suggesting that every participant actually experiences powerful emotional responses. Evans-Pritchard's (1974[1956]:207–208) astute observations of Nuer sacrificial ritual, where there is no discernable collective emotional state, for some people do not even pay attention to the rite, is applicable to the Durgā Pūjā. "What is important in sacrifice is not how people feel, or even how they behaved," he stated. "What is important is that the essential acts of sacrifice be carried out." However, I contend that ritual carries the intention of eliciting profound sentiments in its participants, even though there is no guarantee that it will be successful. Such lack of success, however, does not negate the efficacy of the rite.

53. Interview, October 1991.

54. Interview, November 1990.

55. Interview, September 1990. Turner (1977, etc.), has aptly noted that ritual is often invoked when there is a threat to human community during times of social conflict. It is put into play to rejuvenate community and in response to threats to community. The revival of the autumn Durgā Pūjā celebrations in Bengal supports his observation. They emerged with the rise of a socially and economically burgeoning Hindu society in need of consolidation in the wake of Mughal rule.

56. One might here see confirmation of Girard's proposal that ritual is fundamentally a projection of a culture's feelings of desire and violence. In the figure of the buffalo demon Mahiṣa, whose bloody demise is graphically depicted in the central

clay image, and who is often regarded as symbolically slain in the blood sacrifice, one may intuit what Girard (1986) denotes as the scapegoat. Social solidarity arises through characterizing an entity as an "other" (e.g., the demon), whose subsequent sacrifice, a central feature of ritual, becomes an outlet (i.e., a scapegoat) for a culture's repressed feelings of violence. In the 2001 Durgā Pūjā celebrations, held after the destruction of the twin towers of World Trade Center (WTC) in New York on September 11, anti-Islamic sentiments felt by many Hindus found expression. Some *paṇḍals*, as the backdrop to the Devī's destruction of Mahiṣa, depicted with multicolored electric bulbs the terrorist attacks and the ensuing war in Afghanistan, complete with airplanes flying towards the WTC towers, or with U.S. president George W. Bush, and Saudi-born terrorist, Usama Bin Laden, crossing swords. Calcutta police had to intervene to stop certain *pūjā* groups from replacing the buffalo demon's head with that of Usama Bin Laden, for fear of repercussions against the Hindu community from his Muslim supporters. (See *http://news.bbc.co.uk/hi/english/world/south asia/newsid 1617000/ 1617885.stm*). Although Girard's thesis may be regarded as reductive, since the Durgā Pūjā exhibits a wider array of feelings by participants than projected violence (or desire), it confirms the presence of powerful emotional states evoked by the rite.

57. Östör notes that Sandhi is the moment of the Goddess's appearance. Favored devotees are believed to see the Devī taking form in the image, "the image beginning to move, nodding her head, and giving blessings" (1980:83). In certain places, he mentions, the Goddess is said to leave her footprints in a plate of vermillion dust at this time.

58. Erndl (1997), for instance, provides a case study of female empowerment through possession by the Goddess, whose grace and healing powers flow through the Rajput leader Tara Devi. Navarātra (if not the Durgā Pūjā) is typically an important period for such empowerments.

It is certain that the Durgā Pūjā has played a very important role in the shaping of Bengali female ecstatics and saints, such as Ānandamayī Mā. Hallstrom (1999:28) recounts an episode that occurred during the Durgā Pūjā celebrations, when Ānandamayī Mā was a child. Nirmala, as she was then known, fell into a trance and began to recite certain *mantras* during the *pūjā,* which was held at her maternal uncle's home. Later, during the Kumārī Pūjā, her uncle, recognizing her supernatural behavior, served the blessed food to her first. Ānandamayī Mā has subsequently come to be worshipped by some of her devotees, not merely as a saint, or even an *avatāra* (descent/incarnation), but as an *avatārin.* This designation, as developed by her renowned scholar-devotee, Gopinath Kaviraj, refers to Godhead itself. While *avatāras* are divine emanations which may be forgetful of their divinity, *avatārins* are the source of *avatāras* and possess an uninterrupted consciousness of their nature (see Hallstrom 1999:171–178). Such perceptions by devotees equate Ānandamayī Mā with the Divine Feminine in an identity that even transcends Durgā (who is regarded as a *saguṇa* form of the Goddess). Nevertheless, the effect of (or response to) the Durgā Pūjā on the young Nirmala, is evident. Incidentally, the Ānandamayī Mā Ashram in Banāras is perhaps the only location in the city where an autumn-styled Durgā Pūjā, complete with the clay image complex, is also celebrated during the spring Navarātra.

59. Interview, October 1991.

60. Interview, October 1991.

61. I am aligned with Lévi-Strauss (1963), who asserted that people impose order (typically bipolar, structural categories) onto what is otherwise chaotic human experience.

Fernandez (1977) points out that ritual shares a commonality of symbolic action, which can simultaneously be open to an array of meanings. The common actions forge unity, while leaving individuals open to a diversity of cultural meanings, and it is this capacity that enables social solidarity.

62. Campbell (1972), too, proposes that one of ritual's important functions is to produce a profound sense of awe and reverence in participants. The implication is that ritual is potentially capable of inducing an encounter with what Otto (1929) labelled the *mysterium tremendum,* the awesome and fascinating mystery that is the basis of all religious experience.

Many of the apparent shortcomings in Geertz's approach to ritual, raised by Asad (1983), such as the role of authority and history in the fabrication of symbolic action, are accounted for in this brief definition under the notions of "purposeful," "culturally deemed consequential," and "portions of that culture's specific means of engagement with . . ."

63. This is not to say that scripture, for instance, cannot be regarded as containing truth. However, it is generally held that the "whole truth" cannot be communicated, and in that sense, it is an incomplete presentation of Absolute Reality. The Qur'an is not Allah and all his works.

64. Munn's (1973) observation that the symbols used in ritual utilize items derived from a lexicon of categories that are part of a particular society's cultural code is pertinent here. These categories (e.g., human/divine, male/female), which convey values (e.g., the dangerous power of the divine), are objectified in symbols. Ritual selects from the large, symbolic, culture-specific code at its disposal and presents these in ways that are cognitively palatable, in order to inculcate normative values that are "felt" by its participants.

I am not implying that culture itself is monolithic. The "portions" of the cultural lexicon that are selectively utilized in any given rite derive from a complex array of select societal and cultural sources, which exercise influence in the construction of the ritual.

65. This episode is not typically found in *Rāmāyaṇa* manuscripts, but is told, for instance, in the *Kālikā Purāṇa* 62.24–49; the *Mahābhāgavata Purāṇa* 36–38; and the *Bṛhaddharma Purāṇa* 1.18–22.

66. The Purāṇic claim that the Durgā Pūjā was performed in antiquity by various divine beings draws our attention to the question of precedence. To Eliade, myths recount a cosmogonic narrative, which rituals reenact. The Purāṇic stories, however, tell us through myth of the primacy of the ritual. Clearly, myth and ritual are closely interconnected. In the case of the Durgā Pūjā, as it is currently and actually per-

formed, the clay images and certain liturgical prayers reveal an evident utilization of symbols derived from myth. One simultaneously notes that the rite may not have been performed in the manner indicated were it not for prescriptions found in the *Durgā Saptaśatī* or other mythic compendiums.

67. On the identification of these three aspects (*prakṛti, śakti,* and *māyā*) with feminine forms of divinity and their consequent fusion into the persona of a Great Goddess, see Pintchman (1994).

Glossary

ācamana	Ritual sipping of water.
adhivāsanam	Anointing ritual performed during Durgā Pūjā. Also *adhivāsa.*
akāla bodhana	Untimely awakening. Rāma's invocation of Durgā in the autumn.
alaṅkāra	Ornament. Ritual of ornamenting a deity.
aṅga nyāsa	Yogic imprintment (of vibrations, etc.) on the limbs of the body.
añjali	Gesture of reverence made by placing one's hollowed palms together.
anna	Food.
antarmātṛkā nyāsa	Ritual of inner imprintment.
aparājitā	Unconquerable
ārati	Honorific passing of a flame before a deity. Also designates the entire process of devotional service and offerings to a deity.
argha	Valuable offering. Also *arghya.*
artha	Aim, purpose, objective, or wealth.
Aṣṭamī	Eighth day of Navarātra. Also called Mahāṣṭamī (Great Eighth).
Āśvina	Autumn month (September/October) in which an annual nine-night (*navarātra*) festival of the Goddess is celebrated.
avatāra	An incarnation. One of Viṣṇu's incarnations.
āyudha	Weapon.
bahya mātṛkā nyāsa	A type of external yogic imprintment ritual.
bali	Sacrificial offering.
Banāras	Indian city on the river Gaṅgā renowned as a religious center. Also called Kāśī or Vārāṇasī.
baṭuka	Young lad. A fierce boy-form of Śiva.
Bhairava	Fierce form of Śiva.
bhakti	Devotion.
bhoga	Cooked food.
bhṛṅgāra	Spouted vessel used in royal consecration.
bhūpura	The outer enclosure of a *yantra*, usually pierced by four gateways.

bhūta	An elemental spirit.
bīja	A seed. A germinal cause.
bilva	Wood-apple tree. Also called the *bel* tree. Sacred to Śiva.
bilva patra	A *bilva* leaf.
bindu	A drop. A point. Zero.
bodhana	Ritual of awakening the goddess Durgā.
Brahmā	Creator god.
brāhmaṇa	Brahmin. Member of the priestly class in Hindu society.
buddhi	Discriminative intellect. A constituent element of consciousness.
cakṣur dāna	Ritual of giving eyesight to a divine image.
Cāmuṇḍā	Name of a terrifying goddess often equated with Kālī.
Caṇḍī	She who is Fierce. Name of a goddess. Epithet of Durgā.
Caṇḍikā	Little Fierce One. Epithet of Durgā.
Chinnamastā	Tantric goddess portrayed in an act of self-decapitation.
dakṣiṇā	Monetary payment to a priest.
darpaṇa	Mirror.
darśana	Intimate perceptual contact with a deity. Temple worship.
Daśa Mahāvidyā	Ten Great Knowledges. A cluster of goddesses.
Daśamī	"Tenth." The day after the autumn Navarātra. Also called Vijayā Daśamī (Tenth for Victory), or Dasarā.
daṣopacāra	Ten-fold devotional service to a deity.
Devī	Goddess.
dhāk	A kind of drum played during Durgā Pūjā.
dharma	Orthodox prescribed social and religious duty.
dhūpa	Incense.
dhyāna śloka	Verses describing a deity which are to be used for meditative visualization.
dikpāla	Guardians of the Directions.
dīkṣa	Initiation.
dīpa	Lamplight.
Durgā	Formidable. Difficult to overcome. Inaccessible. Name of the Great Goddess whose ambivalent nature encompasses nurturing and protecting maternal qualities as well as fierce, destructive powers.
Durgā Kuṇḍ	Sacred pond in Banāras. Site of a renowned temple to Durgā.
Durgā Saptaśatī	Seven Hundred [Verses] to Durgā. Scripture glorifying the Great Goddess and containing myths of her origin and demon-slaying exploits. Also known as the *Devī-Mahātmyā* and the *Caṇḍī*.
dūrvā	A resilient grass used in worship.
dvija	Twice-born. The upper three classes (*brāhmaṇa, kṣatriya,* and *vaiśya*) in the orthodox Hindu hierarchy.
gandha	Fragrant ointments such as sandalwood paste.
Gaṇeśa	Elephant-headed god often considered to be the son of Durgā.
Gaṅgā	Name of a sacred river that is considered to be a goddess.
Gaurī	She who is White. Goddess who is the spouse of Śiva.
Gāyātrī	Name of a goddess. *Mantra* uttered by *brāhmaṇas*.

ghaṭa	A jar or pitcher (*kalaśa*) in which a deity is ritually embodied.
ghaṭasthāpana	Ritual of establishing a jar that embodies a deity.
gotra	Family or lineage.
homa	Ritual oblations into the sacrificial fire.
icchā	Will or desire. One of the three qualities of power (*śakti*).
kalaśa	Jar; Pitcher (*ghaṭa*) in which a deity is ritually installed.
Kālī	Name of a dark goddess with a dreadful appearance.
kāma	Wish, desire, or love.
kāṇḍa ropanam	Ritual of erecting staffs around a consecrated image.
kanyā	A virgin; an unmarried daughter.
kara nyāsa	Ritual imprintment of the hand.
Kārtikeya	God of War. Son of Śiva. Also called Skanda.
Kāśī	Ancient and sacred name for the city of Banāras.
kavaca	Armor. A type of hymn or formula recited for protection.
khaḍga	Sword.
kośa	A sheath. A large vessel used in worship rituals.
kriyā	Action. One of the three qualities of power (*śakti*).
kṣatriya	Member of the warrior class.
kṣetrapāla	Guardian of the Field. One of a cluster of divine beings. 'Field' refers to both a physical space and plane of reality.
Kuṇḍalinī	Name of a goddess identified with a serpentine energy in the body.
kūśa	A sacred grass with widespread use in ritual ceremonies.
liṅga	Sign. The phallic symbol of Śiva.
lokapāla	Guardian of the Worlds/People. One of a cluster of divine beings.
Mā	Mother. Epithet of Durgā.
madhuparka	A honeyed mixture offered in *pūjā*.
mahābali	A great sacrifice. An animal or human sacrifice.
mahābhūta	One of the five gross elements (*tattva*).
Mahādevī	The Great Goddess. Epithet of Durgā.
mahāsiṃha	The Great Lion mount of Durgā.
mahāsnāna	Great Bathing ritual.
mahāsurī	Great Demoness. An epithet of Durgā.
māhātmya	Greatness of Essence. A hymn of glorification.
mahāvidyā	Great Knowledge. Supreme Science. One of a cluster of goddesses. An epithet of Durgā.
mahāvyāhṛti	Great Utterance.
Mahiṣāsura	Buffalo Demon slain by Durgā.
Mahiṣāsuramardinī	Crusher of the Buffalo Demon. Epithet of Durgā.
maṇḍala	A sphere of influence; a sacred diagram.
mantra	Sacred utterance or formula.
māśa bhaktabali	Offering of a portion of pulse [legumes].
mātṛkā nyāsa	Ritual of imprintment with syllables.
mokṣa	Liberation. Release. Ultimate goal in orthodox Hindu tradition.
mūlamantra	Root or primary sacred formulaic utterance.
mūrti	Image. Generally refers to the image of a deity.

naivedya	Offerings of morsels of food to a deity.
namaskāra	Respectful salutation.
Navamī	Ninth day of Navarātra. Also called Mahānavamī (Great Ninth).
navapatrikā	"Cluster of Nine Plants" worshipped as a form of Durgā.
Navarātra	"Nine-night" festivals to the Great Goddess mainly held in spring and autumn.
nityā pūjā	Obligatory rituals of worship.
nyāsa	A ritual of yogic imprintment on the body.
om-kāra	The sacred syllable "Om."
pādya	Offering of water for washing the feet.
pañca upacāra	Five-part devotional service.
paṇḍal	Temporary shrine established for Durgā Pūjā.
paramānna	Supreme food.
paramaśiva	The Supreme Śiva.
phala	Fruit.
pīṭha	A seat or abode of the goddess.
pitṛ	Paternal ancestor. One of a class of divine beings.
prakṛti	Nature. Material existence.
prāṇa	Vital air. Breath. Vital energy.
praṇāma	A salutation.
prāṇa pratiṣṭha	Installation of vital energy into an image of a deity.
prāṇāyāma	Control of the vital airs.
prasāda	Blessing. Sanctified offerings.
pratimā	An image. The clay image cluster worshipped in Durgā Pūjā.
pūjā	Devotional worship rituals.
pūjālaya	Place of worship.
pūjāri	Priest.
Purāṇa	Genre of sacred texts containing mythic history.
purohita	A priest. Ritual practitioner.
puruṣa	Person. Pure spirit. Consciousness.
puṣpa	Flower.
puṣpāñjali	Veneration with flower offerings.
rajas guṇa	The quality of passion or activity. Symbolized by blood.
ṛṣyādi nyāsa	A ritual imprintment with a sage and other entities.
ṛtusnātam	Postmenstrual bath.
rūpa	Form.
śabda	Sound. Vibration.
sahasrāra padma	Thousand-petalled lotus; psychic center at the top of the head.
Śākta	Goddess-worshipping sect in the Hindu tradition.
Śakti	Power. Energy. Principle animating the cosmos. The goddess.
śakti pīṭha	A seat or place of power.
Samādhi	State of deep contemplative union with the object in consciousness. Name of a mythical merchant who worshipped Durgā.
saṅkalpa	Oath.
Sāṅkhya	Indian philosophical school often paired with Yoga.

Saptamī	Seventh day of Navarātra. Also called Mahāsaptamī (Great Seventh).
śāradīya	Autumnal.
Sarasvatī	She who is Full of Juice. Goddess of creativity and the arts.
sārī	Long, single piece of cloth worn by Indian women.
sārvajanīna	Relating to everyone. Communal.
Ṣaṣṭhī	Sixth day of Navarātra.
sattva guṇa	Quality of purity, stasis. Equated with spirit as opposed to matter.
siddhi	Spiritual or other attainments.
Śiva	Auspicious. Great God of Hinduism.
Skanda	War god. Son of Śiva and Durgā. Also called Kārtikeya.
ṣoḍaśopacāra	A devotional service consisting of sixteen parts.
Śrī	Auspiciousness. Goddess of good fortune. Epithet of Lakṣmī.
sthaṇḍila	Fire altar.
sthāpana	Installation ritual.
sthirī karaṇa	Ritual of confirming the installation of a deity.
śuddhi	Purification.
śūdra	Laborer class ranked lowest in the orthodox Hindu hierarchy.
sūkta	Hymn of praise.
Suratha	Name of a mythical king who performed the Durgā Pujā.
suṣumnā	The central channel of the psychic body.
svāstika	Sign of auspiciousness and well-being.
tamas guṇa	The quality of inertia, dullness, and disintegration.
Tantra	A genre of text and a religious philosophy.
tantradhāraka	Supporter of the procedure. The *purohita*'s helper during the rite.
tithi	A lunar day.
triśūla	Trident. Weapon of Śiva. Symbol of the goddess.
ucchiṣṭa	The remnants. Refuse. Impure leftovers from a sacrifice.
vāhana	A mount. Vehicle.
vaiśya	Merchant class.
vastra	Clothing. Cloth.
Vidyā	She who is Knowledge. Epithet of the goddess.
Vijayā	Victory personified as a goddess.
Vindhyavāsinī	She who Dwells in the Vindhya Mountains. Epithet of Durgā.
visarjana	Dismissal. Ritual of sending away a deity.
viśeṣa argha	Special offering.
Viṣṇu	Great deity in Hinduism. Preserver of the cosmic order.
vṛkṣa	Tree.
yajamāna	The patron or offerer of a sacrifice.
yajña	Sacrificial rite.
yakṣa/ī	Demigods associated with nature.
yantra	Multidimensional mystical diagram embodying a deity.
yoni	Female generative organ. Symbol of the goddess.
zamīndār	Proprietor of a landed estate. A landlord.

Bibliography

Aiteraya Āraṇyaka. 1995. Translated by Arthur Berridale Keith. Delhi: Eastern Book Linkers.

Atharva Veda

Hymns of the Atharva-Veda. 1969 [1897]. Translated by Maurice Bloomfield. New York: Greenwood Press.

Brahma-vaivarta-purāṇa. 1935. Poona: Ānandāśrama Sanskrit Series.

Brahma-Vaivarta Puranam. 1920, 1922. Translated by Rajendra Nath Sen. 2 parts. Allahabad: Sudhindra Nath Vasu.

Bṛhaddharma Purāṇa. 1897. Banāras: Chaukhamba Amarabharati Prakashan.

Bṛhat Tantrasāra. 1984. Kṛṣṇānanda Āgamavāgiśa. Calcutta: Navabharat Publishers.

Devī-bhāgavata-purāṇa. 1969. Banāras. Paṇḍita Pustakālaya.

[Devī-bhāgavata-purāṇa]. 1921–23. *The Sri Mad Devi Bhagavatam*. Translated by Swami Vijnanananda. Allahabad: Sudhindra Nath Vasu.

Durgā-Saptaśatī. (Devī-Māhātmya). Mārkaṇḍeya Purāṇa.

1. *Devī-māhātmya: The Glorification of the Great Goddess*. 1963. [Text with English translation and annotations] by Vasudeva S. Agrawala. Varanasi: All-India Kashiraj Trust.

2. *The Devī-Māhātmyam or Śrī Durgā-Saptaśatī*. 1969. 3rd ed. [Text and translation by] Swami Jagadīśvarānanda. Madras: Sri Ramakrishna Math.

3. *Durgā-saptaśatī saptaṭīkā-samvalitā*. 1984 [1916]. The Durgā-Saptaśatī with seven commentaries, by Bhāskararāya, Caturdharī, Śantanu, Nāgojibhaṭṭa (Nāgeśa), Jagaccandracandrikā, Daṃśoddhāra, and Durgā-pradīpa. Edited by Harikṛṣṇaśarma. Bombay: Venkateśvara Press, 1916; reprint, Delhi and Baroda: Buṭālā and Company, 1984.

4. *Glory of the Divine Mother (Devīmāhātmyam).* 1968. [Text with English translation and notes by] S. Shankaranarayanan. Pondicherry: Dipti Publications.

5. *Śrī-durgā-saptaśatī.* n.d. Gorakhpur: Gītā Press.

6. *Śrī Śrī Chaṇḍī* n.d. Translated by Swami Tattwananda. Calcutta: Nirmalendu Bikash Press.

Kālikā Purāṇa

Kālikā Purāṇa. Bombay: 1891. Venkateśvara Press.

Worship of the Goddess according to the Kālikā Purāṇa. 1972. Trans. K. R. van Kooij. Leiden: E. J. Brill.

Kāśī Khaṇḍa (Skanda Purāṇa). 1961. Gurumaṇḍala Granthamālāyā No. XX, Vol. IV. Calcutta: Manshukaraja Mora.

Kulārṇavatantra. 1956. Edited by T. Vidyāratna. Madras: Ganesh and Company.

Kūrma Purāṇa. 1972. Edited by Anand Swarup Gupta. Translated by Ahibhushan Bhattacharya and others. Banaras: All-India Kashiraj Trust.

Lakṣmī Tantra, a Pāñcarātra Text. 1972. Translated by Sanjukta Gupta. Leiden: E. J. Brill.

[Lalitā-sahasranāma]. Sri Lalita Sahasranaman. 1962. Translated by Chaganty Suryanarayanamurthy. Madras: Ganesh.

Lalitā-sahasranāmam with Bhāskararāya's Commentary. 1951. Translated by R. Ananthakrishna Sastry. Madras: Theosophical Publishing House.

The Laws of Manu. 1975. Translated by G. Buhler. Delhi: Motilal Banarsidass.

Mahābhāgavata Purāṇa. 1913. Bombay: Manilal Itcharam Desai.

Mahābhārata.

1. *Mahābhārata.* 1933–59. Edited by Vishnu S. Sukthankar (and others). 19 vols. Poona: Bhandarkar Oriental Research Institute.

2. *The Mahābhārata.* 1973–78. Translated and edited by J. A. B. Van Buitenen. 3 vols. completed. Chicago: University of Chicago Press.

3. *The Mahabharata of Krishna Dwaipayana Vyasa.* n.d. 12 vols. Translated by Pratap Chandra Roy. Calcutta: Oriental Publishing Company.

Mārkaṇḍeya Purāṇa

1. *The Mārkaṇḍeya Purāṇa.* 1904. Translated with notes by F. Eden Pargiter. Calcutta: The Asiatic Society.

2. *Śrīmanmārkaṇḍeyapurāṇam.* 1910. Bombay: Venkateśvara Press.

Padma Purāṇa. n.d. Edited by Khemaraj Srikrishnadas. Bombay: Venkatesvara Press.

Prāṇatosinī-tantra. 1928. Calcutta: Basumati Sahitya Mandir.

Purohita darpaṇa. 1973–74. Bhattacharya, Surendramohana, ed. 37th ed. Revised by Yogendracandra Vyā karaṇatīrtha Vidyāratha. Calcutta: Satyanārāyaṇa Library.

Ṛg Veda.

1. *The Hymns of the Ṛg Veda*. 1995 [1889]. Translated by Ralph T. H. Griffith. New Delhi: Motilal Banarsidass.

2. *The Ṛg Veda: An Anthology*. 1981. Translated by Wendy Doniger O'Flaherty. London: Penguin Books.

The Śākta Upaniṣads. 1967. Translated by A. G. Krisna Warrier. Madras: Adyar Library and Research Center.

Śaktisaṅgama-tantra. 1978. Edited by B. Bhattacharyya and Vrajavallabha Dvivedi. Baroda: Oriental Institute of Baroda.

Sāma Veda

Hymns of the Sāmaveda. 1895–96. Reprint, 1986. Translated by Ralph T. H. Griffith. New Delhi: Munshiram Mahoharlal Publishers Pvt. Ltd.

Śāṅkhāyana Āraṇyaka

The Śāṅkhāyana Āraṇyaka: with an Appendix on the Mahāvrata. 1975. Translated by Arthur Berridale Keith. New Delhi: Oriental Books Reprint Corporation.

Śatapatha Brāhmaṇa

The Śatapatha-Brāhmaṇa: According to the text of the Mādhyandina School. 1978 [1882]. Translated by Julius Eggeling. 5 vols. New Delhi: Motilal Banarsidass.

Saundaryalaharī or *Flood of Beauty*. 1958. Edited and translated by W. Norman Brown. Cambridge, Mass.: Harvard University Press.

Śiva Purāṇa. 1970. Translated by a Board of Scholars. 4 vols. Delhi: Motilal Banarsidass.

Skanda-purāṇa. 1959–62. 5 vols. Calcutta: Mansukharaja Mora.

Taittirīya Āraṇyaka. 1967–69. 3rd ed. 2 vols. Poona: Ānandāśrama Sanskrit Series.

Tantrasāra, by Abhinava Guptācārya. 1986. Hindi translation and annotation by Pandit Shree Hemendra Nath Chakravarty. Varanasi: Varanaseya Sanskrit Sansthan.

Tīrthavivecana Kāṇḍam, by Lakṣmīdhara. 1942. *Kṛtyakalpataru* (Vol. III). Edited by K. V. Rangaswami Aiyangar. Gaekwad's Oriental Series, Volume XCVIII. Baroda: Oriental Institute.

Vājasaneyi Saṃhitā. 1912. Bombay: V. L. Panikhar.

Vāmana Purāṇa with English Translation. 1968. Critical editor, Anand Swarup Gupta. Trans. Satyamsu Mohan Mukhopadhyaya, et. al. Varanasi: All India Kashiraj Trust.

Yajur Veda

1. *The Texts of the White Yajurveda.* 1987 [1899]. Translated by Ralph T. H. Griffith. New Delhi: Munshiram Manoharlal Publishers Pvt. Ltd.

2. [The] *Yajur Veda.* 1965. Translated by Devi Chand. New Delhi: S. Paul & Co.

Hindi Texts and Translations

Chandra, Moti. 1962. *Kāśīkā Ithihās.* Bombay: Hindi Granth-Ratnākar Private Limited.

Śrī Durgā Kalpataru. 1984. Edited by 'Kulabhūṣaṇa' Paṇḍita Ramādatta Śukla and Ṛtaśīla Śarma. Prayaga: Śākta Sādhanā Pīṭha, Kalyāṇa Mandira Prakāśana.

Śrī Navarātra Kalpataru. 1984. Edited by 'Kulabhūṣaṇa' Paṇḍita Ramādatta Śukla and Ṛtaśīla Śarma. Prayaga: Śākta Sādhanā Pīṭha, Kalyāṇa Mandira Prakāśana.

Sources in English and Other Languages

Agrawala, Prithvi Kumar. 1967. *Skanda-Kārttikeya: A Study in the Origin and Development.* Vārāṇasī: Banāras Hindu University.

Allen, Michael. 1975. *The Cult of Kumari: Virgin Worship in Nepal.* Kathmandu: Tribhuban University.

Alper, Harvey P., editor 1989. *Mantra.* Albany: State University of New York Press.

Altekar, A. S. 1973 [1938]. *The Position of Women in Hindu Civilization, from Prehistoric Times to the Present Day.* Delhi: Motilal Banarsidass.

———. 1937. *History of Banaras (From Earliest times down to 1937).* Banaras: The Culture Publication House, Banaras Hindu University.

Anderson, Leona. 1993. *Vasantotsava: The Spring Festivals of India: Texts and Traditions.* New Delhi: D. K. Printworld (P) Ltd.

Apte, Usha M. 1978. *The Sacrament of Marriage in Hindu Society: From Vedic Period to Dharmaśāstras.* Delhi: Ajanta Publications.

Apte, Vaman Shivaram. 1986 [1957]. *The Practical Sanskrit-English Dictionary.* Kyoto: Rinsen Book Company.

Aranya, Swami Hariharananda. 1983. *Yoga Philosophy of Patañjali.* Translated by P. N. Mukerji. Albany: State University of New York Press.

Asad, Talal. 1983. "Anthropological conceptions of religion: reflections on Geertz." *Man* 18:237–59.

Babb, Lawrence A. 1996. *Absent Lord: Ascetics and Kings in a Jain Ritual Culture*. Berkeley and Los Angeles: University of California Press.

———. 1975. *The Divine Hierarchy: Popular Hinduism in Central India*. New York: Columbia University Press.

Bacchetta, Paola. 1993. "All Our Goddesses Are Armed: Religion, Resistance, and Revenge in the Life of a Militant Hindu Nationalist Woman." *Bulletin of Concerned Asian Scholars*. Vol. 25. No. 4:38–51.

Bandyopadyay, Pranab. 1987. *Mother Goddess Durga*. Calcutta: Image India.

Banerjea, J. N. 1974 [1956]. *The Development of Hindu Iconography*. New Delhi: Munshiram Manoharlal.

Banerji, S. C. 1986. *A Brief History of Tantric Literature*. Calcutta: Naya Prokash.

Beck, Brenda E. F. 1981. "The Goddess and the Demon: A Local South Indian Festival and Its Wider Context." *Puruṣārtha* 5:83–136.

Beck, Guy. 1993. *Sonic Theology: Hinduism and Sacred Sound*. Columbia, S.C.: University of South Carolina Press.

Bell, Catherine. 1997. *Ritual: Perspectives and Dimensions*. New York: Oxford University Press.

———. 1992. *Ritual Theory, Ritual Practice*. New York: Oxford University Press.

Bennett, Lynn. 1983. *Dangerous Wives and Sacred Sisters: Social and Symbolic Roles of High-caste Women in Nepal*. New York: Columbia University Press.

Berkson, Carmel. 1995. *The Divine and the Demoniac: Mahisa's Heroic Struggle with Durga*. Delhi: Oxford University Press.

Berreman, Gerald D. 1993. "Sanskritization as Female Oppression in India." In Barbara Diane Miller, ed. *Sex and Gender Hierarchies*. pp. 366–392. Cambridge: Cambridge University Press.

Bharati, Agehananda. 1965. *The Tantric Tradition*. London: Rider.

Bhattacharya, Surendramohana, ed. 1973–74. *Purohita-darpaṇa*. 37th ed. Revised by Yogendracandra Vyākaraṇatīrtha Vidyāratha. Calcutta: Satyanārāyaṇa Library.

Bhattacharyya, Narenda Nath. 1974. *History of the Śākta Religion*. New Delhi: Munshiram Manoharlal Publishers.

———. 1971. *Indian Mother Goddess*. Calcutta: Indian Studies Past and Present.

Bhattacharyya, Raghunath. 1986. "Lokamata Maharani Bhavani." Translated by Anima Das. In *Bengal and Varanasi: A Study of Cultural Synthesis and National Integration (Bengal's Contribution to Varanasi)*. Edited by Ram Dular Singh. Calcutta: Biographical Society of India.

Biardeau, Madeleine. 1989a. *Hinduism: The Anthropology of a Civilization.* Delhi: Oxford University Press.

———. 1989b. "Brahmans and Meat-Eating Gods." In Alf Hiltebeitel, ed. *Criminal Gods and Demon Devotees: Essays on the Guardians of Popular Hinduism.* Albany: State University of New York Press.

———. 1984. "The *śami* tree and the sacrificial buffalo." *Contributions to Indian Sociology* 18 (1):1–23.

Bloch, Maurice. 1992. *Prey into Hunter: The Politics of Religious Experience.* Cambridge: Cambridge University Press.

Bloomfield, Maurice. 1981 [1906]. *A Vedic Concordance.* Reprint of Harvard Oriental Series edition. New Delhi: Motilal Banarsidass Publishers.

Bolon, Carol Radcliffe. 1997. *Forms of the Goddess Lajjā Gaurī in Indian Art.* Delhi: Motilal Banarsidass Publishers.

Bosch, F. D. K. 1960. *The Golden Germ.* 's-Gravenhage, The Netherlands: Mouton.

Bourdieu, Pierre. 1977. *Outline of a Theory of Practice.* Translated by Richard Nice. Cambridge: Cambridge University Press.

Brooks, Douglas Renfrew. 1992. *Auspicious Wisdom: The Texts and Traditions of Śrīvidya Śākta Tantrism in South India.* Albany: State University of New York Press.

———. 1990. *The Secret of the Three Cities: An Introduction to Hindu Śākta Tantrism.* Chicago: University of Chicago Press.

Brown, Cheever Mackenzie. 1998. *The Devī Gītā: The Song of the Goddess: A Translation, Annotation, and Commentary.* Albany: State University of New York Press.

———. 1990. *The Triumph of the Goddess: The Canonical Models and Theological Visions of the* Devī Bhāgavata Purāṇa. Albany: State University of New York Press.

———. 1986. "Purāṇa as Scripture: From Sound to Image of the Holy Word in the Hindu Tradition." *History of Religions* 26 #1 (August):68–86.

———. 1974. *God as Mother: A Feminine Theology in India.* Hartford, Vt.: Claude Stark.

Brown, Robert L., ed. 1991. *Ganesh: Studies of an Asian God.* Albany: State University of New York Press.

Brubaker, Richard L. 1978. "The Ambivalent Mistress: A Study of South Indian Village Goddesses and Their Religious Meaning." Ph.D. diss., University of Chicago.

Brunner-Lachaux, Hélène. 1963. *Somaśambhupaddhati, première partie.* Pondichéry: Institut Français d'Indologie.

Bühnemann, Gudrun. 1988. *Pūjā: A Study in Smārta Ritual*. Vienna: Institut für Indologie der Universität Wien.

———. 1987. "Bhadramaṇḍalas in the Ritual Practice." *Wiener Zeitschrift für die Kunde Sudasiens* 31:43–73.

Burgess, James. 1883. "The Ritual of Ramesvaram." *Indian Antiquary* 12:315–26.

Caldwell, Sarah. 1999. *Oh Terrifying Mother: Sexuality, Violence, and Worship of the Goddess Kālī*. New York: Oxford University Press.

Campbell, Joseph. 1972. *Myths to Live By*. New York: Viking.

Chakravarti, Chintaharan. 1930. "The Cult of Bāro Bhāiyā of Eastern Bengal." *Journal of the Royal Asiatic Society of Bengal*. XXXVI:379–88.

Chand, Devi. 1965. See *Yajur Veda* ([The] *Yajur Veda*).

Chapple, Christopher Key, and Mary Evelyn Tucker, eds. 2000. *Hinduism and Ecology: the Intersection of Earth, Sky, and Water*. Cambridge, Mass.: Harvard University Press.

Charpentier, J. 1926. "Über den Begriff und die Etymologie von Pūjā." *Beiträge zur Literaturwissenschaft und Geistesgeschichte Indiens*. Festgabe Hermann Jacobi zum 75. Geburstag. Ed. W. Kirfel. Bonn. 279–297.

Chatterji, Bankim Chandra. 1992. *Anandamath*. Translated by Basanta Koomar Roy. New Delhi: Vision Books.

Chaturvedi, B. K. 1996. *Durga* (Gods and Goddesses of India: 7). Delhi: Books For all.

Chaudhuri, Dulal. 1984. *Goddess Durgā: The Great Mother*. Calcutta: Mrimol Publishers.

Clifford, James. 1988 [1983]. *The Predicament of Culture: Twentieth Century Ethnography, Literature, and Art*. Cambridge, Mass.: Harvard University Press.

Clifford, James, and George Marcus, eds. 1986. *Writing Culture: The Poetics and Politics of Ethnography*. Berkeley and Los Angeles: University of California Press.

Clothey, Fred W. 1978. *The Many Faces of Murukan: The History and Meaning of a South Indian God*. The Hague: Mouton.

Coburn, Thomas B. 1991. *Encountering the Goddess: A Translation of the* Devī-Māhātmya *and a Study of Its Interpretation*. Albany: State University of New York Press.

———. 1984a. *Devī-Māhātmya: The Crystallization of the Goddess Tradition*. Delhi and Columbia, Mo.: Motilal Banarsidass and South Asia Books.

———. 1984b. " 'Scripture' in India: Towards a Typology of the Word in Hindu Life." *JAAR* 52, no. 3:435–459.

———. 1982. "Consort of None, *Śakti* of All: The Vision of the *Devī-Māhātmya*." In John Stratton Hawley and Donna Marie Wulff, eds. *The Divine Consort:*

Rādhā and the Goddesses of India, pp. 153–165. Berkeley, Calif.: Berkeley Religious Studies Series.

Cohen, Lawrence. 1991. "The Wives of Gaṇeśa." In Robert L. Brown, ed. *Ganesh: Studies of an Asian God*. Albany: State University of New York Press.

Coomaraswamy, A. K. 1971. *Yakṣas*. 2 Vols. Delhi: Munshiram Manoharlal.

Courtright, Paul B. 1985a. *Gaṇeśa: Lord of Obstacles, Lord of Beginnings*. New York: Oxford University Press.

———. 1985b. "On This Holy Day in My Humble Way: Aspects of Pūjā." In *Gods of Flesh/Gods of Stone: The Embodiment of Divinity in India*, edited by Joanne Punzo Waghorne and Norman Cutler. Chambersburg, Penn.: Anima Publications.

Coward, Harold, and David Goa. 1991. *Mantra: Hearing the Divine in India*. Chambersburg, Penn.: Anima Books.

Craven, Roy C. 1976. *Indian Art: A Concise History*. London: Thames & Hudson.

Dange, S. S., ed. 1987. *Sacrifice in India: Concept and Evolution*. Aligarh: Viveka Publications.

Das, Sudhendukumar. 1934. *Sakti or Divine Power*. Calcutta: University of Calcutta.

Davis, Richard H. 1991. *Ritual in an Oscillating Universe*. Princeton, N.J.: Princeton University Press.

Dehejia, Vidya. 1999. *Devi: The Great Goddess: Female Divinity in South Asian Art*. Washington, D.C.: Arthur M. Sackler Gallery, Smithsonian Institution.

———. 1997. *Pārvatīdarpaṇa: An exposition of Kāśmir Śaivism through the images of Śiva and Pārvatī*. New Delhi: Motilal Banarsidass.

Dhal, Upendra Nath. 1978. *Goddess Laksmi: Origin and Development*. New Delhi: Oriental Publishers.

Divakaran, Odile. 1984. "Durgā the Great Goddess: Meanings and Forms in the Early Period." In Michael W. Meister, ed. *Discourses on Śiva: Proceedings of a Symposium on the Nature of Religious Imagery*, pp. 271–288. Philadelphia: University of Pennsylvania Press.

Dorson, Richard M. 1965. "The Eclipse of Solar Mythology." In Alan Dundes, ed. *The Study of Folklore*. Englewood Cliffs, N.J.: Prentice Hall, Inc.

Douglas, Mary. 1973. *Natural Symbols: Explorations in Cosmology*. London: Barrie & Jenkins.

Dumont, Louis. 1970a [1966]. *Home Hierarchicus: The Caste System and Its Implications*. London: Weidenfeld and Nicholson.

———. 1970b. *Religion, Politics and History in India*. Paris: Mouton.

Durkheim, Émile. 1965 [1915]. *The Elementary Forms of Religious Life*. Translated by J. W. Swain. New York: Free Press.

Eck, Diana L. 1982a. *Banaras, City of Light*. New York: Alfred A. Knopf.

———. 1982b. "Gaṅgā: The Goddess in Hindu Sacred Geography." In John Stratton Hawley and Donna Marie Wulff, eds., *The Divine Consort: Rādhā and the Goddesses of India*, pp. 166–183. Berkeley, Calif.: Berkeley Religious Studies Series.

———. 1981a. *Darśan: Seeing the Divine Image in India*. Chambersburg, Penn.: Anima Books.

———. 1981b. "India's *Tīrthas:* Crossings in Sacred Geography." *History of Religions* 20, no. 4 (May):323–344.

———. 1980. "Sanskrit Sources for the Study of Varanasi" *Purana* XXII, No. 1.

Eggeling, Julius. 1978 [1882]. See *Śatapatha Brāhmaṇa*.

Eliade, Mircea. 1991. *Images and Symbols: Studies in Religious Symbolism*. Translated by Philip Mairet. Princeton, N.J.: Princeton University Press.

———. 1969 [1958]. *Yoga: Immortality and Freedom*. Translated by Willard R. Trask. Princeton, N.J.: Princeton University Press.

———. 1963a. *Myth and Reality*. Translated by Willard R. Trask. New York: Harper and Row.

———. 1963b. *Patterns in Comparative Religion*. Cleveland: World Publishing Co.

———. 1959a [1949]. *Cosmos and History: The Myth of the Eternal Return*. Translated by W. R. Trask. New York: Harper and Row.

———. 1959b [1957]. *The Sacred and the Profane*. Translated by W. R. Trask. New York: Harcourt, Brace and World.

———. 1958. *Patterns in Comparative Religion*. Translated by Rosemary Sheed. New York: New American Library.

Erndl, Kathleen M. 1997. "The Goddess and Women's Power: A Hindu Case Study." In *Women and Goddess Traditions: In Antiquity and Today*. Edited by Karen L. King. Minneapolis: Fortress Press.

———. 1996. "Śerāṅvālī: The Mother Who Possesses." In *Devī: Goddesses of India*. Edited by John S. Hawley and Donna M. Wulff. Berkeley and Los Angeles: University of California Press.

———. 1993. *Victory to the Mother: The Hindu Goddess of Northwest India in Myth, Ritual, and Symbol*. New York: Oxford University Press.

Evans-Pritchard, E. E. 1974 [1956]. *Nuer Religion*. New York: Oxford University Press.

Fernandez, James W. 1977. "The Performance of Ritual Metaphors." *The Social Use of Metaphor: Essays on the Anthropology of Rhetoric.* J. David Sapir and J. Christopher Crocker, editors. Philadelphia: University of Pennsylvania Press.

Freed, Ruth S., and Stanley A. Freed. 1964. "Calendars, Ceremonies, and Festivals in a North Indian Village: Necessary Calendric Information for Fieldwork." *Southwestern Journal of Anthropology* 20:67–90.

Fruzetti, Lina. 1982. *The Gift of a Virgin: Women, Marriage, and Ritual in a Bengali Society.* New Brunswick, N.J.: Rutgers University Press.

Fuller, C. J. 1992. *The Camphor Flame: Popular Hinduism and Society in India.* Princeton, N.J.: Princeton University Press.

———. 1984. *Servants of the Goddess: The Priests of a South Indian Temple.* Cambridge: Cambridge University Press.

Fuller, C. J., and Penny Logan. 1985. "The Navarātri Festival at Madurai." *Bulletin of the School of Oriental and African Studies* 48:79–105.

Gatwood, Lynn E. 1985. *Devi and the Spouse Goddess: Women, Sexuality and Marriage in India.* Delhi: Manohar.

Geertz, Clifford. 1988. *Works and Lives: The Anthropologist as Author.* Stanford, Calif.: Stanford University Press.

———. 1973a. "Religion as a Cultural System." In *The Interpretation of Cultures.* New York: Basic Books Inc.

———. 1973b. "Ethos, World View, and the Analysis of Sacred Symbols." In *The Interpretation of Cultures.* New York: Basic Books Inc.

———. 1965. "Religion as a Cultural System." In *Reader in Comparative Religion,* ed. William A. Lessa and Evon Z. Vogt, 204–216. New York: Harper and Row.

Gerholm, Tomas. 1988. "On Ritual: A Postmodernist View." *Ethnos* 53:190–203.

Getty, Alice. 1936. *Gaṇeśa: A Monograph on the Elephant-faced God.* Oxford University Press.

Ghose, Aurobindo. 1940. *Bankim - Tilak - Dayananda.* Calcutta: Arya Publishing House.

Ghosh, Kashyacharya Tapan Kumar. 1986. "Bengal's Contribution to Varanasi." In *Bengal and Varanasi: A Study of Cultural Synthesis and National Integration (Bengal's Contribution to Varanasi).* Edited by Dr. Ram Dular Singh. Calcutta: Bibliographical Society of India.

Ghosha, Pratāpachandra. 1871. *Durgā Pūjā: With Notes and Illustrations.* Calcutta: "Hindoo Patriot" Press.

Gimbutas, Marija. 1989. *The Language of the Goddess.* San Francisco: Harper & Row, Publishers.

Girard, René. 1986. *The Scapegoat.* Trans. Yvonne Freccero. Baltimore, Md.: Johns Hopkins University Press.

Gluckman, Max. 1962. *Essays on the Ritual of Social Relations.* Manchester: Manchester University Press.

Goldberg, Ellen. 2001. "Pārvatī through the Looking Glass." *Acta Orientalia,* Vol. 62. In Press.

Gonda, Jan. 1980. *Vedic Ritual, The Non-Solemn Rites.* Leiden, The Netherlands: E. J. Brill.

———. 1970. *Viṣṇuism and Śivaism: A Comparison.* Leiden, The Netherlands: Athlone.

———. 1969. *Ancient Indian Kingship from the Religious Point of View.* Leiden, The Netherlands: E. J. Brill.

———. 1963. "The Indian Mantra." *Oriens* 16:244–97.

Goudriaan, Teun. 1970. "Vaikhanasa Daily Worship according to the Handbooks of Atri Ahrgu, Kasyapa and Marici." *Indo-Iranian Journal* 12:161–215.

———. 1965. *Kasyapa's Book of Wisdom.* The Hague: Mouton.

Goudriaan, Teun, and Sanjukta Gupta. 1981. *Hindu Tantric and Śākta Literature.* Wiesbaden, Germany: Otto Harrassowitz.

Griffith, Ralph T. 1995 [1889]. See *Ṛg Veda (the Hymns of the Ṛg Veda).*

———. 1987 [1899]. See *Yajur Veda (The Text of the White Yajur Veda).*

———. 1986. See *Sāma Veda (Hymns of the Sāmaveda).*

Grimes, Ronald. 1990. *Ritual Criticism: Case Studies in Its Practice, Essays on Its Theory.* Columbia, S.C.: University of South Carolina Press.

Gupta, Chitrarekha. 1983. *The Brahmanas of India: A Study Based on Inscriptions.* Delhi: Sundeep Prakashan.

Gupta, Sanjukta. 1988. "The Maṇḍala as an Image of Man." In *Oxford University Papers on India, Vol. 2, Part 1. Indian Ritual and its Exegesis,* pp. 32–41. Edited by Richard F. Gombrich. Delhi: Oxford University Press.

Gupta, Sanjukta, Dirk Jan Hoens, and Teun Goudriaan. 1979. *Hindu Tantrism.* Leiden, The Netherlands: E. J. Brill.

Gupta, S., and R. Gombrich. 1986. "Kings, Power and the Goddess." *South Asia Research* 6:2:123–138.

Gussner, R. E. 1973. "Hymns of Praise: A Textual-critical Analysis of Selected Vedantic Stotras attributed to Sankara with Reference to the Question of Authenticity." Dissertation: Harvard University, Cambridge, Massachusetts.

Hallstrom, Lisa Lassell. 1999. *Mother of Bliss: Ānandamayī Mā (1896–1982).* New York: Oxford University Press.

Harman, William P. 1989. *The Sacred Marriage of a Hindu Goddess.* Bloomington, Ind.: Indiana University Press.

Havell, E. B. 1905. *Benares, the Sacred City.* London: Blackie and Son Limited.

Hawley, John Stratton, and Donna Marie Wulff, editors. 1985. *The Divine Consort: Rādhā and the Goddesses of India.* Berkeley, Calif.: Berkeley Religious Studies Series.

———. 1996. *Devī: Goddesses of India.* Berkeley and Los Angeles: University of California Press.

Hazra, R. C. 1963. *Studies in the Upapurāṇas, Vol. 2: Sakta and Non-Sectarian Upapurāṇas.* Calcutta: Sanskrit College.

———. 1942. "The Devī-Purāṇa." *New Indian Antiquary* 5 (April):2–20.

Heesterman, Johannes C. 1957. *The Ancient Royal Indian Consecration.* 's-Gravenhage, The Netherlands: Mouton.

Hiltebeitel, Alf. 1991. *The Cult of Draupadī 2: On Hindu Ritual and the Goddess.* Chicago: The University of Chicago Press.

———. 1988. *The Cult of Draupadī 1: Mythologies: From Gingee to Kurukṣetra.* Chicago: The University of Chicago Press.

———. 1985. "On the Handling of the Meat, and Related Matters, in Two South Indian Buffalo Sacrifices." *L'Uomo* 9 (2):171–99.

———. 1980a. "Rama and Gilgamesh: The Sacrifices of the Water Buffalo and the Bull of Heaven." *History of Religions* 19 (3):16–44.

———. 1980b. "Śiva, the Goddess and the Disguises of the Pāṇḍavas and Draupadī." *History of Religions* 20:147–174.

———. 1976. *The Ritual of Battle: Krishna in the Mahābhārata.* Ithaca, N.Y.: Cornell University Press.

Hiltebeitel, Alf, and Thomas J. Hopkins. 1986. "Indus Valley Religion." In Mircea Eliade, ed. *The Encyclopedia of Religion.* New York: Macmillan. Vol. 7:215–223.

Hocart, A. M. 1970. *Kings and Councillors: An Essay in the Comparative Anatomy of Human Society.* Edited by R. Needham. Chicago: University of Chicago Press.

Hubert, Henri, and Marcel Mauss. 1964. *Sacrifice: Its Nature and Function.* Translated by W. D. Halls. Chicago: University of Chicago Press.

Hudson, Dennis. 1999. "The Ritual Worship of Devi." In Vidya Dehejia, *Devi: The Great Goddess: Female Divinity in South Asian Art.* Washington, D.C.: Arthur M. Sackler Gallery, Smithsonian Institution.

Humes, Cynthia Ann. 1997. "Glorifying the Great Goddess or Great Woman?" In *Women and Goddess Traditions: In Antiquity and Today.* Edited by Karen L. King. Minneapolis: Fortress Press.

———. 1996. "Vindhyavāsinī: Local Goddess yet Great Goddess." In *Devī: Goddesses on India*. Edited by John S. Hawley and Donna M. Wulff. Berkeley and Los Angeles: University of California Press.

———. 1991. "The Text and the Temple of the Great Goddess." Ph.D. dissertation. University of Iowa.

Humphrey, Caroline, and James Laidlaw. 1994. *The Archetypal Actions of Ritual: A Theory of Ritual Illustrated by the Jain Rite of Worship*. New York: Oxford University Press.

Jacobson, Doranne. 1978. "The Chaste Wife." In *American Studies in the Anthropology of India*, 95–138. Edited by Sylvia Vatuk. New Delhi: Manohar.

Jacobson, Doranne, and Susan S. Wadley. 1986 [1977]. *Women in India: Two Perspectives*. New Delhi: Manohar Publications.

Joshi, R. V. 1959. *Le ritual de la devotion Krsnaite*. Pondichéry: Institut Français d'Indologie.

Justice, Christopher. 1997. *Dying the Good Death: The Pilgrimage to Die in India's Holy City*. Albany: State University of New York Press.

Kandiah, M. 1990. *Sri Durga Devi Temple of Tellippalai*. Studies on Sri Lanka Series No. 14 Delhi: Sri Satguru Publications.

Kane, Pandurang Vaman. 1930–62. *History of Dharmaśātra (Ancient and Medieval Religious and Civil Law)*. 5 vols. Poona: Bhandarkar Oriental Research Institute.

———. 1953. *Kinship Organization in India*. Poona: Deccan College Press.

Kaviraj, Gopinath M. M. 1990. *Selected Writings of M. M. Gopinath Kaviraj*. Varanasi: M. M. Gopinath Kaviraj Centenary Celebrations Committee.

———. 1987. *Navonmesa: Mahamahopadhyaya Gopinath Kaviraj Commemoration Volume*. Edited by Jaideva Singh, Govindagopal Mukhopadhyaya, and Hemendra Nath Chakravarty. Varanasi: M. M. Gopinath Kaviraj Centenary Celebration Committee.

———. 1986. *Gopinath Kaviraj: Notes on Religion and Philosophy*. The Princess of Wales. Sarasvati Bhavana Studies. Edited by Gaurinath Sastri. Varanasi: Laksmi Narayan Tiwari, Librarian, Sampurnanand Sanskirt Vishvavidyala.

Kinsley, David R. 1997. *Tantric Visions of the Divine Feminine: The Ten Mahāvidyās*. Berkeley and Los Angeles: University of California Press.

———. 1986. *Hindu Goddesses: Visions of the Divine Feminine in the Hindu Religious Tradition*. Berkeley and Los Angeles: University of California Press.

———. 1982a. "Blood and Death Out of Place: Reflections on the Goddess Kālī." In John Stratton Hawley and Donna Marie Wulff, eds., *The Divine Consort: Rādhā and Goddesses of India*, pp. 144–152. Berkeley and Los Angeles: Berkeley Religious Studies Series.

———. 1982b. *Hinduism: A Cultural Perspective*. Englewood Cliffs, N.J.: Prentice-Hall.

———. 1979. *The Divine Player—A Study of Kṛṣṇa Līlā*. Delhi: Motilal Banarsidass.

———. 1978. "The Portrait of the Goddess in the *Devī-māhātmya*." *Journal of the American Academy of Religion* 46, no. 4(December):489–506.

———. 1975. *The Sword and the Flute: Kālī and Kṛṣṇa, Dark Visions of the Terrible and the Sublime in the Hindu Religious Tradition*. Berkeley and Los Angeles: University of California Press.

Klostermaier, Klaus. 1989. *A Survey of Hinduism*. Albany: State University of New York Press.

Kondos, Vivienne. 1986. "Images of the Fierce Goddess and Portrayals of Hindu Women." *Contributions to Indian Sociology* (n.s.) 20, 2:173–197.

Konow, Sten. 1925. "A European Parallel to the Durgāpūjā." *Asiatic Society of Bengal, Calcutta: Journal and Proceedings*. No. 21:315–324.

Kramrisch, Stella. 1981. *The Presence of Śiva*. Princeton, N.J.: Princeton University Press.

———. 1976 [1946]. *The Hindu Temple*. 2 vols. Delhi: Motilal Banarsidass.

———. 1975. "The Indian Great Goddess." *History of Religions* 14, no. 4 (May):235–265.

———. 1956. "An Image of Aditi-Uttānapad." *Artibus Asiae* 19, nos. 3–4:259–70.

Kumar, Nita. 1988. *The Artisans of Banaras: Popular Culture and Identity, 1880–1986*. Princeton, N.J.: Princeton University Press.

Kumar, Pushpendra. 1974. *Śakti Cult in Ancient India*. Banaras: Bhartiya Publishing House.

Kurtz, Stanley. 1992. *All the Mothers are One: Hindu India and the Cultural Reshaping of Psychoanalysis*. New York: Columbia University Press.

Lal, Rai Bahadur Hira. 1927. "The Golaki Matha." *Journal of the Bihār and Orissa Research Society*. Vol. XIII.

Larson, Gerald J. 1969. *Classical Sāṃkhya: An Interpretation of Its History and Meaning*. Delhi: Motilal Banarsidass.

Leach, Edmund. 1976. *Culture and Communication: The Logic by which Symbols are Connected*. Cambridge: Cambridge University Press.

Leslie, Julia. 1991b. "Suttee or Satī." In *Roles and Rituals for Hindu Women*, 175–191. Edited by Julia Leslie. Rutherford, N.J.: Fairleigh Dickinson University Press.

———. 1991a. "Śrī and Jyeṣṭhā." In *Roles and Rituals for Hindu Women*, pp. 107–129. Edited by Julia Leslie. Rutherford, N.J.: Fairleigh Dickinson University Press.

———. 1989. *The Perfect Wife: The Orthodox Hindu Women according to the Strīdharmapaddhati of Tryambakayajvan.* Oxford University South Asian Series. Delhi: Oxford University Press.

Lévi-Strauss, Claude. 1963. *Structural Anthropology.* Trans. Claire Jacobson and Brooke Grundfest Schoppf. New York: Basic Books.

———. 1955. "The Structural Study of Myth." *Journal of American Folklore* 67:428–444. Reprinted in *Reader in Comparative Religion: An Anthropological Approach.* 2nd ed. Edited by William A. Lessa and Evon Z. Vogt, 562–574. New York: Harper and Row, 1965.

Lewis, Oscar. 1958. *Village Life in Northern India: Studies in a Delhi Village.* Urbana: University of Illinois Press.

Lincoln, Bruce, 1991. *Emerging from the Chrysalis: Rituals of Women's Initiation.* New York: Oxford University Press.

Logan, Penelope. 1980. "Domestic Worship and the Festival Cycle in the South Indian City of Madurai." Ph.D. thesis. University of Manchester.

Lutgendorf, Philip. 1991. *The Life of a Text: Performing the Rāmcaritmānas of Tulsidas.* Berkeley and Los Angeles: University of California Press.

———. 1989. "Rām's Story in Shiva's City: Public Arenas and Private Patronage." In Sandria B. Freitag, ed., *Culture and Power in Banaras: Community, Performance, and Environment, 1800–1980.* Berkeley and Los Angeles: University of California Press.

Macdonell, A. A. 1954. "Vedic Religion." *Encyclopedia of Religion and Ethics.* E. Hastings, ed. 12:601–18.

Madan, T. N. ed. 1991. *Religion in India.* Delhi: Oxford University Press.

Maity, Pradyot Kumar. 1966. *Historical Studies in the Cult of the Goddess Manasā.* Calcutta: Punthi Pustak.

Majumdar, R. C., H. C. Rachaudhuri, and Kalikinkar Datta. 1967. *An Advanced History of India.* New York: St. Martin's Press.

Majumdar, R. C., ed. 1943. *History of Bengal.* 2 vols. Dacca, Bangladesh: Dacca University.

Malinowski, Bronislaw. 1974 [1925]. *Magic, Science and Religion and Other Essays.* Glencoe, Ill.: Free Press.

Mandelbaum, David G. 1970. *Society in India.* Berkeley and Los Angeles: University of California Press.

Mani, Vettam. 1975. *Purāṇic Encyclopedia.* Delhi: Motilal Banarsidass.

Marcus, George, and M. Fisher. 1986. "Ethnography and Interpretive Anthropology." In *Anthropology as Cultural Critique.* Chicago: University of Chicago Press.

Marriott, McKim. 1966. "The Feast of Love." In *Krishna: Myths, Rites, and Attitudes,* 200–212. Honolulu: East-West Center Press.

———. 1955. "Little Communities in an Indigenous Civilization." In *Village India: Studies in the Little Community.* Edited by McKim Marriott. The American Anthropological Association, Vol. 57. No. 3. Part 2: 171–222.

Marshall, Sir John, ed. 1931. *Mohenjo-daro and the Indus Civilization.* 3 vols. London: Arthur Probshtan.

McDermott, Rachel Fell. 1995. *Unanswered Questions on the Relationship between Politics, Economics, and Religion: The Case of Durga Puja in Late Eighteenth-Century Bengal.* Bengali Studies Conference, April 28–30. Georgetown. On *http://www.lib.uchicago.edu/e/su/southasia/Rachel.1.hmtl.*

McGee, Mary. 1991. "Desired Fruits." In *Roles and Rituals for Hindu Women,* 71–88. Edited by Julia Leslie Rutherford, N.J.: Fairleigh Dickinson University Press.

———. 1989. *Feasting and Fasting: The Vrata Tradition and its Significance for Hindu Women.* (Th.D. dissertation, Harvard University, 1987). Ann Arbor, Mich.: University Microfilms.

McKean, Lise. 1996. "Bhārat Mātā: Mother India and Her Militant Matriots." In *Devī: Goddesses of India.* Edited by John S. Hawley and Donna M. Wulff. Berkeley and Los Angeles: University of California Press.

Meyer, Eveline. 1986. *Aṅkāḷaparamēcuvari: A Goddess of Tamilnadu, Her Myths and Cult.* Wiesbaden: Franz Steiner Verlag.

Mitra, Sarat Chandra. 1925. "On the Cult of the Jujube-Tree." *Man in India.* Vol. V:98–110.

———. 1922. "On the Cult of the Tree-Goddess in Eastern Bengal. *Man in India.* Vol. II:227–239.

Monier-Williams, Sir Monier. 1986 [1899]. *A Sanskrit-English Dictionary.* Oxford: Clarendon Press.

Munn, Nancy D. 1973. "Symbolism in a Ritual Context." In John J. Honigmann, ed. *Handbook of Social and Cultural Anthropology,* 579–612. Chicago: Rand McNally.

Nair, P. Thankappan. 1986. *Calcutta in the 17th Century.* Calcutta: Firma KLM Private Limited.

Narayanan, Vasudha. 1982. "The Goddess Śrī: The Blossoming Lotus and Breast Jewel of Viṣṇu." In John Stratton Hawley and Donna Marie Wulff, eds., *The Divine Consort: Rādhā and the Goddesses of India,* 224–237. Berkeley, Calif.: Berkeley Religious Studies Series.

O'Flaherty, Wendy Doniger. 1984. *Dreams, Illusion and Other Realities.* Chicago: University of Chicago Press.

———. 1981. *Śiva, the Erotic Ascetic.* New York: Oxford University Press. Reprint of *Asceticism and Eroticism in the Mythology of Śiva.* London: Oxford University Press, 1973.

———. 1980. *Women, Androgynes, and Other Mythical Beasts.* Chicago: University of Chicago Press.

———. 1977. *The Origins of Evil in Hindu Mythology.* Berkeley and Los Angeles: University of California Press.

———. 1975. *Hindu Myths.* Baltimore, Md.: Penguin Books.

Ortner, S. 1978. *Sherpas through their Rituals.* Cambridge: Cambridge University Press.

———. 1975. "God's Bodies, God's Foods." In *The Interpretation of Symbolism.* Edited by Roy Willis. New York: John Wiley and Sons.

———. 1973. "On Key Symbols." In *American Anthropologist* 75:1338–1346.

Östör, Ákos. 1991. "Cyclical Time: Durgāpūjā in Bengal: Concepts, Actions, Objects." In *Religion in India.* Edited by T. N. Madan. Delhi: Oxford University Press, pp. 176–193.

———. 1980. *The Play of the Gods: Locality, Ideology, Structure, and Time in the Festivals of a Bengali Town.* Chicago: University of Chicago Press.

Ostroff, Pearl. 1978. "The Demon-slaying Devī: A Study of Her Purāṇic Myths." M.A. thesis, McMaster University.

Otto, Rudolph. 1929. *The Idea of the Holy.* Translated by John W. Harvey. New York: Oxford University Press.

Padoux, André. 1990. *Vāc: The Concept of the Word in Selected Hindu Tantras.* Translated by Jacques Gontier. Albany: State University of New York Press.

———. "Mantras—What are They?" 1989. In *Mantra.* Albany: State University of New York Press.

Parry, Jonathan P. 1994. *Death in Banaras.* Cambridge: Cambridge University Press.

———. 1985. "Death and Digestion: The Symbolism of Food and Eating in North Indian Mortuary Rites." *Man* 20, no. 4 (December).

Paul, Harendra Chandra. 1966. "Mystic Significances of the Madhu-Kaiṭava Myth." *Aryan Path* 37:210–215.

Payne, Ernest Alexander. 1997 [1933]. *The Śāktas.* New Delhi: Munshiram Mahoharlal Publishers Pvt. Ltd.

Pearson, Anne. 1996. *Because It Gives Me Peace of Mind: Ritual Fasts in the Religious Lives of Hindu Women.* Albany: State University of New York Press.

Pierce, Charles S. 1960. The Collected Papers of Charles Sanders Pierce. C. Hartshorne and P. Weiss, editors. Cambridge, Mass.: Cambridge University Press.

Pintchman, Tracy. 2001. *Seeking Mahādevī.* Albany: State University of New York Press.

———. 1994. *The Rise of the Goddess in the Hindu Tradition.* Albany: State University of New York Press.

Preston, James J. 1985. "Creation of the Sacred Image: Apotheosis and Destruction in Hinduism." In *Gods of Flesh/Gods of Stone: The Embodiment of Divinity in India,* edited by Joanne Punzo Waghorne and Norman Cutler. Chambersburg, Penn.: Anima Publications.

———. 1980. *Cult of the Goddess: Social and Religious Change in a Hindu Temple.* New Delhi: Vikas.

Radcliffe-Brown, A. R. 1952. *Structure and Function in Primitive Society.* London: Routledge & Kegan Paul.

Rangachari, K. 1931. *The Sri Vaisnava Brahmans.* Madras: Government Press.

Rao, T. A. Gopinatha. 1968. *Elements of Hindu Iconography.* 2nd ed. 2 vols. New York: Paragon.

Rappaport, Roy A. 1999. *Ritual and Religion in the Making of Humanity.* New York: Cambridge University Press.

———. 1975. "Obvious Aspects of Ritual." *Cambridge Anthropology,* 2:3–69.

Ray, Amita. "The Cult and Ritual of Durgā Pūjā in Bengal." In *Shastric Tradition in Indian Art.* Vol. I. Heidelberg: The University of Heidelberg Press.

Raychaudhri, Tarak, and Bikash Raychaudhuri. 1981. *The Brahmans of Bengal: A Textual Study of Social History.* Calcutta: The Anthropological Survey of India.

Richards, F. J. 1910. "Fire-walking Ceremony at the Dharmaraja Festival." *Quarterly Journal of the Mythic Society* 2, 1:29–32.

Rocher, Ludo. 1986. *The Purāṇas.* Wiesbaden: Otto Harrassowitz.

Rodrigues, Hillary. Forthcoming. "Women in the Worship of the Great Goddess." In Arvind Sharma, ed. *Women in Indian Religions.* Leiden: E. J. Brill.

———. 1993a. "Some Puranic Myths of the Durgākuṇḍa Mandir in Vārāṇasī." *Purāṇa* XXXV (2) (July): 185–201.

———. 1993b. "Textual Genres and the Hindu Temple in Durgā Worship." In Elliot Tepper and John R. Wood, eds., *Enriched by South Asia,* Vol. I (Montreal: South Asia Council, Canadian Asian Studies Association), 385–399.

Roy, Atul Chandra. 1986. *History of Bengal: Turko-Afghan Period.* New Delhi: Kalyani Publishers.

———. 1968. *History of Bengal: Mughal Period (1526–1765 a.d.).* Calcutta: Nababharat Publishers.

Roy, Raga Rammohan. 1990. "Bangla Practintomo Durgā Pūjā." *Navakalola*. Calcutta: 31st year, Pūjā Issue.

Roy, Samaren. 1991. *Calcutta: Society and Change 1690–1990*. Calcutta: Rupa and Company.

Samanta, Suchitra. 1994. "The 'Self-Animal' and Divine Digestion: Goat Sacrifice to the Goddess Kālī in Bengal." *The Journal of Asian Studies* 53. No. 3. August:779–803.

Saraswati, Baidyanath. 1975. *Kashi: Myth and Reality of a Classical Cultural Tradition*. Simla: Indian Institute of Advanced Study.

[Śarma], Pushpendra Kumar. 1974. *Śakti Cult in Ancient India*. Varanasi: Bhartyiya Publishing House.

Sax, William S. 1991. *Mountain Goddess: Gender and Politics in a Himalayan Pilgrimage*. New York: Oxford University Press.

Sherring, M. A. 1868. *The Sacred City of the Hindus: An Account of Benares in Ancient and Modern Times*. London: Trubner and Co.

Shulman, David D. 1993. *The Hungry God: Tales of Filicide and Devotion*. Chicago: The University of Chicago Press.

———. 1980. *Tamil Temple Myths: Sacrifice and Divine Marriage in the South Indian Śaiva Tradition*. Princeton, N.J.: Princeton University Press.

Silburn, Lilian. 1988. *Kuṇḍalinī: Energy of the Depths*. Albany: State University of New York Press.

Singer, Milton. 1972. *When a Great Tradition Modernizes*. London: Pall Mall.

———, ed. 1959. *Traditional India: Structure and Change*. Philadelphia: The American Folklore Society.

Singh, Chitralekha, and Prrem Nath. 1999. *Durgā (Parmā Śakti Maheśwari, Mahādevi)*. New Delhi: Crest Publishing House.

Singh, Rana P. B. 1986. "Siva's Universe in Varanasi." In *Varanasi Through the Ages*. Varanasai: Bharatiya Itihas Sankalan Samiti, U.P.

Sircar, D. C., ed. 1973. *The Śākta Pīthas*. Delhi: Motilal Banarsidass.

Sivaramamurti, C. 1976. *Gaṅgā*. New Delhi: Orient Longman.

Sleeman, Sir W. H. 1915. *Rambles and Recollections of an Indian Official*. Edited, with annotations, by Vincent A. Smith. London: Humphrey Milford/Oxford University Press.

Smith, Brian K. 1989. *Reflections on Resemblance, Ritual and Religion*. New York: Oxford University Press.

Smith, Frederick M. 1991. "Indra's Curse, Varuṇa's Noose, and the Suppression of Women in the Vedic Śrauta Ritual." In *Roles and Rituals for Hindu Women,* 17–45. Edited by Julia Leslie. Rutherford, N.J.: Fairleigh Dickinson University Press.

Smith, Wilfred Cantwell. 1975. "Methodology and the Study of Religion: Some Misgivings." In *Methodological Issues in Religious Studies.* Edited by Robert D. Baird. Chico, Calif.: New Horizons Press.

———. 1962. *The Meaning and End of Religion.* San Francisco: Harper & Row.

Spear, Percival. 1978. *A History of India. Volume Two.* London: Penguin Books.

Srinivas, M. N. 1976. *The Remembered Village.* Delhi: Oxford University Press.

———. 1965 [1952]. *Religion and Society among the Coorgs of South India.* Bombay: Asia.

Staal, Frits. 1989. *Rules without Meaning.* New York: Peter Lang Publishing, Inc.

———. 1983. *AGNI: The Vedic Ritual of the Fire Altar.* 2 vols. Berkeley and Los Angeles: University of California Press.

———. 1979. "The Meaninglessness of Ritual." *Numen. International Journal of the History of Religions* 26:2–22.

———. 1963. "Sanskrit and Sanskritization." *Journal of Asian Studies.* Vol. 22. No. 3:361–375.

Stein, Burton. 1980. *Peasant State and Society in Medieval South India.* Delhi: Oxford University Press.

Stevenson, S. 1920. *The Rites of the Twice-Born.* London: Oxford University Press.

Stietencron, Heinrich von. 1983. "Die Göttin Durgā Mahiṣāsuramardinī: Mythos, Darstellung und Geschichtliche Rolle bei der Hinduisierung Indiens." In *Visible Religion: Annual for Religious Iconography,* 118–166. Volume II: Representation of Gods. Leiden: E. J. Brill.

Sukul, Kuber Nath. 1974. *Varanasi Down the Ages.* Vārāṇasī: Bhargava Bhushan Press.

Tambiah, Stanley. 1985. "Form and Meaning of Magical Acts." Reprinted in *Culture, Though, and Social Action: An Anthropological Perspective.* Cambridge, Mass.: Harvard University Press.

Thieme, P. 1939. Indische Wörter und Sitten. 1. Pūjā. *Zeitschrift der Deutschen Morgenländischen Gesellschaft.* Weisbaden: Harrassowitz Verlag. 93:105–123.

Tiwari, J. N. 1985. *Goddess Cults in Ancient India.* Delhi: Sundeep Prakashan.

Turner, Victor. 1982. *From Ritual to Theatre and Back: The Human Seriousness of Play.* New York: PAJ Publications.

———. 1977 [1966]. *The Ritual Process: Structure and Anti-structure*. Ithaca, N.Y.: Cornell University Press.

———. 1974. *Dramas, Fields, and Metaphors: Symbolic Action in Human Society*. Ithaca, N.Y.: Cornell University Press.

———. 1973. "The Center Out There: Pilgrim's Goal." *History of Religions* 12:191–230.

———. 1967. *The Forest of Symbols: Aspects of Ndembu Ritual*. Ithaca, N.Y.: Cornell University Press.

Turner, Victor, and Edward Bruner, eds. 1986. *The Anthropology of Experience*. Urbana: University of Illinois Press.

Tyler, Steven A. 1986. "Post-Modern Ethnography: From Document of the Occult to Occult Document." In *Writing Culture: The Poetics and Politics of Ethnography*. J. Clifford and G. Marcus, eds. Berkeley and Los Angeles: University of California Press.

van Buitenen, J. A. B. 1966. "On the Archaism of the Bhāgavata Purāṇa." In *Krishna: Myths, Rites, and Attitudes*. 23–40. Edited by Milton Singer. Honolulu: East-West Center Press.

van Kooij, Karel R. 1983. "Protective Covering (*Kavaca*)." In *Selected Studies on Ritual in Indian Religions*. 118–129. Edited by Ria Kloppenborg. Leiden: E. J. Brill.

van Kooij, K. R., trans. 1972. See *Kālikā Purāṇa*.

Vaudeville, Charlotte. 1982. "Krishna Gopāla, Rādhā, and the Great Goddess." In *The Divine Consort: Rādhā and the Goddesses of India*. 1–12. Edited by John Stratton Hawley and Donna Marie Wulff. Berkeley: Berkeley Religious Studies Series.

Vidyarthi, L. P., M. Jha, and B. N. Saraswati. 1979. *The Sacred Complex of Kāshī (A Microcosm of Indian Civilization)*. Delhi: Concept Publishing Company.

Vogel, J. P. 1930–32. "The Head-offering to the Goddess in Pallava Sculpture." *Bulletin of the School of Oriental Studies* (London) 6:539–543.

Wadley, Susan S. 1975. *Shakti: Power in the Conceptual Structure of Karimpur Religion*. Chicago: Department of Anthropology, The University of Chicago.

Waghorne, Joanne Punzo and Norman Cutler, eds. 1985. *Gods of Flesh/Gods of Stone: The Embodiment of Divinity in India*. Chambersburg, Penn.: Anima Books.

Wayman, Alex. 1974. "The Mirror as a Pan-Buddhist Metaphor Simile." In *History of Religions* 13:251–269.

Weber, Max. 1967 [1917]. *The Religion of India: The Sociology of Hinduism and Buddhism*. New York: Free Press.

Wheelock, Wade T. 1989. "The Mantra in Vedic and Tantric Ritual." In *Mantra.* Albany: State University of New York Press.

Woodroffe, John (Arthur Avalon). 1985. *The Great Liberation (Mahānirvāna Tantra).* 6th Ed. Madras: Ganesh and Company.

———. 1966. *The World as Power.* Madras: Ganesh and Company.

———. 1918. *Śakti and Śākta: Essays and Addresses.* Madras: Ganesh and Company.

———, ed. 1982. *Hymns to the Goddess and Hymn to Kali.* 3rd ed. Madras: Ganesh and Company.

Woods, James Haughton. 1966 [1914]. *The Yoga System of Patañjali.* Delhi: Motilal Banarasidass.

www. bangalinet.com. Durgā Pūjā pages.

Yalman, Nur. 1967. "On the Purity of Women in the Castes of Ceylon and Malabar." *The Journal of the Royal Anthropological Institute of Great Britain and Ireland.* 93 (1):25–28.

Zimmer, Heinrich. 1984. *Artistic Form and Yoga in the Sacred Images of India.* Translated by Gerald Chapple and James B. Lawson. Princeton, N.J.: Princeton University Press.

———. 1976. "The Indian World Mother." In *The Mystic Vision.* Joseph Campbell, ed. Princeton, N.J.: Princeton University Press.

———. 1962. *Myths and Symbols of Indian Art and Civilization.* Edited by Joseph Campbell. New York: Harper and Row.

Index

Breinigsville, PA USA
22 December 2010
251991BV00001B/124/A

9 780791 454008